NO LONGER PROP
GLENDALE LIBRARY,
ARTS & CULTURE DEPT.

D0149424

ROGUES

ALSO BY PATRICK RADDEN KEEFE

Empire of Pain

Say Nothing

The Snakehead

Chatter

ROGUES

TRUE STORIES OF GRIFTERS, KILLERS, REBELS AND CROOKS

PATRICK RADDEN KEEFE

DOUBLEDAY | NEW YORK

Copyright © 2022 by Patrick Radden Keefe

All rights reserved. Published in the United States by Doubleday,
a division of Penguin Random House LLC, New York.

www.doubleday.com

DOUBLEDAY and the portrayal of an anchor with a dolphin are
registered trademarks of Penguin Random House LLC.

The pieces in this work originally appeared in a
slightly different form in *The New Yorker*.

Front-of-jacket image © Memory Stockphoto / Shutterstock
Jacket design by Emily Mahon
Book design by Michael Collica

LCCN 2021047117

ISBN: 9780385548519 (hardcover)
ISBN: 9780385548526 (ebook)

MANUFACTURED IN THE UNITED STATES OF AMERICA

1 3 5 7 9 10 8 6 4 2

First Edition

To Justyna

CONTENTS

PREFACE

ONE OF THE STRANGER moments in my career as a magazine journalist was a phone call in May 2014. I had just published "The Hunt for El Chapo," an article in *The New Yorker* about the criminal career, and eventual capture, of the fugitive Mexican drug baron Joaquín Guzmán Loera, and I got a voicemail in the office from an attorney who said that he represented the Guzmán family. This was, to put it mildly, alarming. I had developed a minor specialty, over the years, in what editors call "the writearound": an article about a subject who declines to grant an interview. Some journalists hate writearounds, but I've always enjoyed the challenge they pose. It takes a lot of creative reporting to produce a vivid portrait of someone without ever getting to speak to them, but these pieces are often more revealing than the scripted encounters you end up with when the politician or the CEO actually cooperates. When I wrote about the reality TV producer Mark Burnett, he wouldn't talk to me—but he had two ex-wives who did, and in the end, I think I learned more about Burnett from speaking to them than I would have from Burnett himself.

In the case of El Chapo, the drug lord was locked up in a Mexican prison by the time I started my piece, and not giving interviews, so I had taken it for granted that he wouldn't be sitting down with me. Nor did I ever entertain the notion that when the article came out, he might read it. Despite running a multibillion-dollar narco-conglomerate, he was said to be practically illiterate. Even if he *could* read, he did not strike me as a *New Yorker* subscriber. But when my article was published, it contained a series of revelations that were subsequently picked up in the Mexican press. So somehow, it must have come to his attention.

I waited a while before calling the lawyer back. I figured that he would probably raise objections to some detail or other in the piece (and worried that it might be the passage in which I revealed that El Chapo was a prodigious consumer of Viagra). I spoke to a source of mine who made some discreet inquiries and was able to confirm that this attorney really did work for the Guzmán family. "Just call him up, I'm sure it's no big deal," my source said. Then he added, "But use your work phone, and never, under any circumstances, give them your home address."

Summoning my nerve, I called the lawyer back. He spoke with an accent, in a starchy, formal idiom, and when I told him, as casually as possible, that it was Patrick Keefe from *The New Yorker,* he announced, with an almost theatrical seriousness, "We have read your article."

"Oh," I said, bracing.

"It was"—dramatic pause—"very *interesting.*"

"Oh!" I blurted. "Thank you." I'll take "interesting." Could be worse.

"El Señor . . . ," he began, before lapsing into another pregnant pause. "Is ready . . ." Seconds ticking by. I clutched the phone, my heart hammering. "To write his memoirs."

In advance of the phone call, I had gamed out the conversation like a high school debater: If he says this, I'll say that. I had prepared for every contingency, every direction the discussion might take. But not this one.

"Well," I stammered, floundering for something remotely coherent to say. "That's a book I would love to read."

"But sir," the lawyer interjected. "Is it a book you would like to write?"

I confess that when the opportunity to ghostwrite El Chapo's memoir was first presented, I did give it a moment of serious consideration. During his years on the run, he had become an almost mythical figure, and, as a journalist, the idea that I might get to hear his story in his own words was genuinely tantalizing. But before getting off the phone that day I had already declined the offer. Guzmán was responsible, directly and indirectly, for thousands of murders, maybe tens of thousands. There would be no way to accurately write his story that did not explore that side of things—and the lives of his many victims—in great detail. But it seemed unlikely that this was the sort of book

El Señor was envisioning. The whole scenario felt a bit like Act I of a thriller in which the hapless magazine writer, blinded by his desire for a scoop, does not necessarily survive Act III.

"Even under the best of circumstances," I pointed out to the lawyer, trying to be as tactful as possible, "the relationship between ghost writer and subject can occasionally . . . *fray.*"

The lawyer was very courteous about the whole thing. After another brief phone call a week later (in which he said, "As you continue to consider our offer . . . ," and I said, "No, I've considered! I've considered!") I never heard from him again. What had started as a genuinely frightening experience became an amusing dinner party anecdote. But the encounter also seemed emblematic of the adventure of magazine writing: the uncanny intimacy that a reporter can feel with a subject he has never met, the strangeness of putting a story out into the world for anyone to read and watching it assume a life of its own.

● ● ●

I was in junior high school when I first fell for magazines. This was the late 1980s, and magazines—the physical thing, these bright bundles of stapled paper—were ubiquitous and felt as if they would be around forever. In our school library there was a "periodicals room," where one wall was festooned with the latest issues of *Time, Rolling Stone, Spin, U.S. News & World Report.* And, of course, *The New Yorker.*

Nobody used the adjective "long-form" back then; that would come later, to distinguish the sprawling stories more typical of magazines from snappier pieces on the web. But even as a student I came to think that at least where nonfiction was concerned, a big magazine article might be the most glorious form. Substantial enough to completely immerse yourself in but short enough to finish in a sitting, these features had their own fine-hewn structure. There was an economy in the storytelling that felt, in contrast to the nonfiction books I was reading, both attentive to the reader's attention and respectful of her time.

So I grew up reading *The New Yorker* and nurturing a secret fantasy that I might someday write for the magazine myself. For a long time this was *just* a fantasy; it took many years of false starts and strange detours (law school is not a route I would recommend to aspiring journalists) before the magazine published my first freelance piece in 2006.

The paradox of magazines is that they're both perishable and permanent. Printed on flimsy paper, they're eminently disposable, like a Dixie cup, *designed* to be discarded. Yet at the same time, people hold on to them. I used to love, as a child, arriving at the house of some family friend to discover a shelf of *National Geographic*s, those resplendent yellow squared-off spines all lined up in a row.

In the conventional narrative, the internet killed magazines. And in many ways, it did. It upended not just the economic conditions that allowed magazines to flourish but also a whole culture of metabolizing the printed word: when you hurried home to snatch the latest issue from your mailbox, or stood for an hour at a newsstand to flip through the offerings, or toted around an old issue as it gradually tattered in your backpack. In another sense, though, the web *saved* the magazine story, retrieving it from the recycling bin and giving it permanent life. A big magazine feature used to be as evanescent as the cherry blossoms: here today, gone next week. Now it's just a click away, forever.

And this only accentuates a deeper paradox in the form itself. If I'm going to devote the better part of a year to researching and writing an article, and you're going to devote the better part of an hour to reading it, I'd like to try to tell the complete and definitive version of the tale. I want to capture the reality of a story, in all its vivid, dynamic glory, and pin it down, like a lepidopterist with a butterfly, arranging it under glass, just so.

But of course, life doesn't stop when you publish. The story keeps moving, unfolding, fluttering its wings. Your characters continue to act, often in confounding ways. After all, they're real people. They break out of prison again, like Chapo Guzmán. Or they see a legal defeat turn into a victory, like the undefeated death-penalty lawyer Judy Clarke. Or they suddenly kill themselves, like Anthony Bourdain.

These stories were written over a dozen years, and they reflect some of my abiding preoccupations: crime and corruption, secrets and lies, the permeable membrane separating licit and illicit worlds, the bonds of family, the power of denial. I've never had a particular beat (a great luxury of magazine writing), and instead I tend to pursue stories that pull me in for one reason or another, because of the complexity of the characters or the intrigue of events. But certain themes keep recurring, and these pieces are connected by other small coincidences. El Chapo ends up residing in the same bleak supermax prison as Judy Clarke's client Dzhokhar Tsarnaev. The arms trafficker known as the Prince of Marbella is erroneously accused of involvement in the bombing of Pan Am Flight 103, a crime that Ken Dornstein, whose older brother was on the plane, spends a quarter of a century trying to solve.

Reporting a story can be a wonderfully consuming project, so consuming that when the undertow takes hold, I sometimes feel as if I could happily float away, following the research wherever it takes me. But I always remind myself that I have to come back and tell the story, and hopefully capture, in the telling, some of what made it feel so captivating to me in the first place. These are wild tales, but they're all true, each scrupulously fact-checked by my brilliant colleagues at *The New Yorker.* Together, I hope that they illuminate something about crime and punishment, the slipperiness of situational ethics, the choices we make as we move through this world, and the stories we tell ourselves and others about those choices.

ROGUES

THE JEFFERSON BOTTLES

How could one collector find so much rare fine wine? (2007)

THE MOST EXPENSIVE BOTTLE of wine ever sold at auction was offered at Christie's in London on December 5, 1985. The bottle was made of handblown dark-green glass and capped with a nubby seal of thick black wax. It had no label, but etched into the glass in a spindly hand was the year 1787, the word "Lafitte," and the letters "Th.J."

The bottle came from a collection of wine that had reportedly been discovered behind a bricked-up cellar wall in an old building in Paris. The wines bore the names of top vineyards—along with Lafitte (which is now spelled "Lafite"), there were bottles from Châteaux d'Yquem, Mouton, and Margaux—and those initials, "Th.J." According to the catalog, evidence suggested that the wine had belonged to Thomas Jefferson and that the bottle at auction could "rightly be considered one of the world's greatest rarities." The level of the wine was "exceptionally high" for such an old bottle—just half an inch below the cork—and the color "remarkably deep for its age." The wine's value was listed as "inestimable."

Before auctioning the wine, Michael Broadbent, the head of Christie's wine department, consulted with the auction house's glass experts, who confirmed that both the bottle and the engraving were in the eighteenth-century French style. Jefferson had served as America's minister to France between 1785 and the outbreak of the French Revolution and had developed a fascination with French wine. Upon his return to America, he continued to order large quantities of Bordeaux for himself and for George Washington and stipulated in one 1790 letter that their respective shipments should be marked with their initials. During his first term as president, Jefferson spent $7,500—roughly $120,000 in today's currency—on wine, and he is generally regarded as America's first great wine connoisseur. (He might also have been America's first great wine bore. "There was, as usual, a dissertation upon wines," John Quincy Adams noted in his diary after dining with Jefferson in 1807. "Not very edifying.")

In addition to surveying the relevant historical material, Broadbent had sampled two other bottles from the collection. Some nineteenth-century vintages still taste delicious, provided they have been properly stored. But eighteenth-century wine is extremely rare, and it was not clear whether the Th.J. bottles would hold up. Broadbent is a "master of wine," a professional certification for wine writers, dealers, and sommeliers that connotes extensive experience with fine wine and discriminating judgment. He pronounced a 1784 Th.J. Yquem "perfect in every sense: colour, bouquet, taste."

At two thirty that December afternoon, Broadbent opened the bidding, at £10,000. Less than two minutes later, his gavel fell. The winning bidder was Christopher Forbes, the son of Malcolm Forbes and a vice president of the magazine *Forbes*. The final price was £105,000—about $157,000. "It's more fun than the opera glasses Lincoln was holding when he was shot," Forbes declared, adding, "And we have those, too."

After the auction, other serious collectors sought out Jefferson bottles. The publisher of *Wine Spectator* bought a bottle through Christie's. A mysterious Middle Eastern businessman bought another. And in late 1988 an American tycoon named Bill Koch purchased four bottles. The son of Fred Koch, who founded Koch Industries, he lived in Dover, Massachusetts, and ran his own highly profitable energy company, the Oxbow Corporation. (His brothers Charles and David would become well-known for their sponsorship of conservative political candidates and causes.) Bill Koch purchased a 1787 Branne Mouton from the Chicago Wine Company in November 1988. The next month, he bought a 1784 Branne Mouton, a 1784 Lafitte, and a 1787 Lafitte from Farr Vintners, a British retailer. Altogether, Koch spent half a million dollars on the bottles. He installed them in his capacious, climate-controlled wine cellar and took them out occasionally over the next fifteen years to show them off to friends.

Koch's collection of art and antiques is valued at several hundred million dollars, and in 2005 the Boston Museum of Fine Arts prepared an exhibition of many of his possessions. Koch's staff began tracking down the provenance of the four Jefferson bottles and found that apart from Broadbent's authentication of the Forbes bottle they had nothing on file. Seeking historical corroboration, they approached the Thomas Jefferson Foundation at Monticello in Charlottesville, Virginia. Several days later, Monticello's curator, Susan Stein, telephoned. "We don't believe those bottles ever belonged to Thomas Jefferson," she said.

• • •

Koch lives with his third wife, Bridget Rooney, and six children, from this and previous marriages, in a thirty-five-thousand-square-foot Anglo-Caribbean-style house in Palm Beach. When I visited him there not long ago, the front lawn had been excavated to extend the house's basement. Koch explained that he needs more storage space. "I'm a bit of a compulsive collector," he said. We strolled past Modigliani's 1917 *Reclining Nude* and Picasso's blue-period *Nightclub Singer*, a Renoir, a Rodin, and works by Degas, Chagall, Cézanne, Monet, Miró, Dalí, Léger, and Botero. Surveillance cameras, encased in little bulbs of black glass, protruded from the ceiling. "My father was a collector of sorts," Koch said. "I guess I got it from him. He had a small collection of impressionist art. He collected shotguns. Then he collected ranches."

We sat down in Koch's "cowboy room," surrounded by Charles Marion Russell paintings, Frederic Remington bronzes of men on horseback, antique cowboy hats, bowie knives, and dozens of guns, displayed in glass-topped cases: Jesse James's gun, Jesse James's killer's gun, Sitting Bull's pistol, General Custer's rifle. Koch, who is sixty-seven, is rangy and tall, with tousled white hair, round spectacles, and a boyish, high-pitched laugh. At MIT, where he received his undergraduate degree and a PhD in chemical engineering, he contracted hepatitis and could no longer stomach hard alcohol. But he could drink wine. At restaurants, he started ordering the most expensive wines on the list and, using this method, discovered some that he liked. Eventually, he began purchasing wine at auction: first-growth Bordeaux, like Lafite and Latour, and the famous Burgundies of Romanée-Conti.

"When I went crazy is when I sold my stock in Koch Industries," Koch said. That was 1983; he made a reported $550 million on the sale.

At that point, he decided he would build a world-class wine collection. When I asked why, he looked at me as if I had failed to grasp the obvious. "Because it's the best-tasting form of alcohol in the world," he said. "That's why."

Koch may be as compulsive about filing lawsuits as he is about collecting. He waged a twenty-year legal battle against his own brothers relating to the family business. (The matter was settled in 2001.) He sued the State of Massachusetts over an improperly taxed stock transaction and won a $46 million abatement. When a former girlfriend whom he had installed at a condo in Boston's Four Seasons hotel refused to leave, Koch took her to housing court and had her evicted. He talks about "dropping a subpoena" on people as if he were lobbing a grenade. Fine-wine fraud was almost unheard of when Koch bought his four bottles of Th.J. Bordeaux, and the only assurance he demanded was that they came from the same collection that Michael Broadbent had authenticated. He was angry to find out that Monticello believed his bottles were fake. "I've bought so much art, so many guns, so many other things, that if somebody's out to cheat me, I want the son of a bitch to pay for it," he told me, his color rising. "Also," he said, relaxing a bit and breaking into a smile, "it's a fun detective story."

• • •

The extraordinary inflation of rare-wine prices, of which the Jefferson bottles are the most conspicuous example, has led in recent years to an explosion of counterfeits in the wine trade. In 2000, Italian authorities confiscated twenty thousand bottles of phony Sassicaia, a sought-after Tuscan red. Chinese counterfeiters have begun peddling fake Lafite. So-called trophy wines—best-of-the-century vintages of old Bordeaux—that were difficult to find at auction in the 1970s and 1980s have reemerged on the market in great numbers. Serena Sutcliffe, the head of Sotheby's international wine department, jokes that more 1945 Mouton was consumed on the fiftieth anniversary of the vintage, in 1995, than was ever produced to begin with. The problem is especially acute in the United States and Asia, Sutcliffe told me, where wealthy enthusiasts build large collections very quickly. "You can go into important cellars and see a million dollars' worth of fakes among $5 or $6 million worth of nice stuff," she said.

Since much of the fine-wine business is conducted in off-the-books "gray market" exchanges between buyers and resellers with no direct link to the château, ascertaining who actually put a particular bottle of wine into circulation can be difficult. But Koch sent emissaries to the Chicago Wine Company and to Farr Vintners and learned that all four bottles originally came from the person who had supplied the bottle auctioned at Christie's, a flamboyant German wine collector named Hardy Rodenstock. Rodenstock was a former music publisher who managed German pop acts in the 1970s. He maintained residences in Munich, Bordeaux, and Monte Carlo and was rumored to be part of the wealthy Rodenstock family, which manufactured high-end eyeglasses. He told people that he had started out as a professor and intimated that he had made a fortune on the stock market.

Rodenstock became interested in wine in the 1970s and developed a passion for the sweet white wines of Château d'Yquem. He especially loved wines that predated the phylloxera epidemic of the late nineteenth century, when a grapevine pest decimated Europe's vineyards, forcing growers to replant with phylloxera-resistant rootstocks from North America. "In the pre-phylloxera wines of Yquem, you find more flavors, more caramel, more singularity, more power, more class," he once told an interviewer. He boasted to *Wine Spectator* that he had tasted more vintages of old Yquem than the owner of the château had—and the château owner agreed.

Starting in 1980, Rodenstock began holding lavish annual wine tastings, weekend-long affairs attended by wine critics, retailers, and various German dignitaries and celebrities. He opened scores of old and rare wines, all provided at his own expense and served in custom-made "Rodenstock" glasses that were supplied by his friend the glassmaker Georg Riedel. Impeccably dressed, wearing stylish Rodenstock eyeglasses and shirts with stiff white collars, he bantered with guests, exclaiming, over an especially fine bottle, "*Ja, unglaublich!* One hundred points!" He was punctilious about being on time, barring latecomers, and when serving older wines, he banned spitting, which prompted some guests, alarmed at the number of bottles they would be sampling, to hide spittoons in their laps. "You don't spit away history," Rodenstock admonished them. "You drink it."

Rodenstock made no secret of having discovered the Jefferson bottles; on the contrary, the record sale to Forbes had made him a celebrity in the wine world. In the spring of 1985, he would later explain, he received a phone call about an interesting discovery in Paris, where someone had stumbled upon some dusty old bottles, each inscribed with the letters "Th.J." Rodenstock refused to reveal who had sold him the bottles, but apparently the seller did not realize the significance of the initials. "It was like the lottery," Rodenstock said of the experience. "It was simply good luck." He would not say how many bottles there were; in some accounts, it was "a dozen or so," in others, as many as thirty. Nor would he disclose the address in Paris where they were discovered. The Jefferson bottles were the first in a series of astonishing finds. Rodenstock became known as an intrepid hunter of the rarest wines. One collector, who was a friend of Rodenstock's in the 1980s and 1990s, told me that in 1989 he had arranged a "horizontal" tasting of bottles of 1929 wines from many different châteaux. The one bottle he had been unable to find was a 1929 Château Ausone. Several days before the tasting, he received a telephone call from Rodenstock. "I'm in Scotland," Rodenstock announced. "I found a bottle of Ausone '29!" Rodenstock traveled to Venezuela, where, according to press reports, he found a hundred cases of Bordeaux; in Russia, he uncovered "the tsar's lost cache" of nineteenth-century wine. At Munich's Hotel Königshof in 1998, he held a "vertical" tasting of 125 different years of Yquem, including two bottles from the Jefferson collection. "Amazingly, they didn't taste over the hill or oxidized," *Wine Spectator*'s correspondent remarked. "The 1784 tasted as if it were decades younger."

Some members of the wine press avoided the events. The critic Robert Parker attended only one tasting; he told me that the extravagance of the affairs kept him away. Rating the selections would be of little use to most of his readers, he said, because they could hardly find, much less afford, such wines. And the policy against spitting, combined with Rodenstock's tendency to withhold the most exciting offerings until the end of a tasting, could seriously impair any objective assessment of the wine. "He always seemed to serve the great stuff after you were primed pretty good," Parker said of the one event he did attend, a 1995 tasting in Munich. "People were getting shit-faced."

Even so, Parker was amazed at some of Rodenstock's wines. "Out of this universe!" he wrote of a large-format magnum of Pétrus from 1921 that Rodenstock served. "This huge, unbelievably concentrated wine could have been mistaken for the 1950 or 1947." In his journal, the *Wine Advocate*, Parker deemed the three-day tasting "the wine event of my lifetime." "I quickly learned," he wrote, "that when Hardy Rodenstock referred to a '59 or a '47, I needed to verify whether he was talking about the nineteenth or the twentieth century!"

Michael Broadbent regularly attended Rodenstock events. In his book *Vintage Wine: Fifty Years of Tasting Three Centuries of Wines*, Broadbent acknowledges that it was through Rodenstock's "immense generosity" that he was able to taste many of the rarest entries. Much of his section on eighteenth-century wines consists of notes from Rodenstock tastings. Bill Koch was never invited to one of these tastings, but he had heard of Rodenstock, and the two had met on one occasion, in 2000, when Christie's held a tasting of Latour in its offices in New York. According to Koch, Rodenstock arrived late, and Koch approached him. "Hi, I'm Bill Koch," he said. "I bought some wine from you." Rodenstock shook Koch's hand. He looked uncomfortable, Koch thought.

"So you're the famous collector," Rodenstock said, before hastily walking away.

• • •

In legal disputes, Koch has occasionally relied on the services of a retired FBI agent named Jim Elroy. During his law-enforcement career, Elroy worked on fraud investigations, and when questions about the Jefferson bottles arose, he told Koch, "If you want your money back, I'll get it." But that wasn't enough for Koch. "I want to lock him up," he told Elroy. "Saddle up." (Koch's enthusiasm for cowboy culture has rubbed off on Elroy. He describes his boss as "the new sheriff in town." His cell-phone ringtone is the whistled theme from *The Good, the Bad, and the Ugly*.)

Elroy is in his sixties and has a weathered, tanned face and a conspiratorial smile. He's a bit of a raconteur, and when we met for lunch recently, he related the details of his investigation in the studied cadences of someone who had told the story before. "Cases either get better or they get worse," he told me. "This one just kept getting better." From the beginning, Koch was interested in suing Rodenstock, Elroy explained, but he also wanted to privately finance the preparation of a criminal case that could ultimately be handed to federal authorities. Elroy was invigorated by Koch's ambitions. "This investigation has all the earmarks of an FBI investigation," he told me. "Only with the best people in the world available instantly. And with none of the bureaucracy." He estimated that since 2005 Koch has spent more than $1 million on the Rodenstock case: twice what he paid for the wine.

As Elroy and his team—a former Scotland Yard inspector in England, a former MI5 agent in Germany, and several wine experts in Europe and the United States—began their investigation in 2005, they learned from the staff at Monticello that doubts about the authenticity of the Jefferson wines date back to the auction of the original bottle. Broadbent had approached Monticello in the fall of 1985 to inquire about references to wine in some of Jefferson's letters. A researcher named Cinder Goodwin, who had spent fifteen years studying Jefferson's voluminous papers, responded to Broadbent that November, expressing skepticism. "Jefferson's daily account book, virtually all of his letters, his banker's statements, and miscellaneous internal French customs forms survive for this period and mention no 1787 vintages," she wrote. When a reporter from *The New York Times* reached Goodwin, before the auction, to ask about the connection, she noted that whereas the initials on Rodenstock's bottles were written "Th.J.," in his correspondence Jefferson tended to use a colon—"Th:J." Broadbent did not mention these doubts in the catalog, and the *Times* story did not dissuade the bidders. (In an article published in *The New Yorker* at the time, Broadbent told a reporter that he found "no proof" but plenty of circumstantial evidence—"masses of it"—that Jefferson had owned the bottle.)

Shortly after the auction, Cinder Goodwin prepared a research report on the bottles in which she concluded that although they could very well be authentically eighteenth century, the specific connection with Jefferson was not borne out by the historical record. She was at pains to insist that she was not questioning the good faith of Rodenstock or Broadbent, but she wondered, "Were there not Thomases, Theodores, or Theophiles, and Jacksons, Joneses, and Juliens who also had a taste for fine Bordeaux wine, and who would have been resident in Paris?" She pointed out that historical records document the inhabitants at various addresses in Paris. If Rodenstock would reveal the address where he discovered the wine, "a proper connection might be made."

Soon a flurry of letters from Rodenstock began arriving at Monticello. Though he speaks passable English, the letters were in German; a Monticello tour guide translated them. On December 28, 1985, Rodenstock wrote, referring to Goodwin, that "one should courteously keep back one's dubious and unfounded remarks and one shouldn't make oneself important in front of the press." Dan Jordan, Monticello's executive director, wrote back, protesting that Goodwin was a highly regarded Jefferson scholar and that, unlike Rodenstock or Christie's, she had no financial interest in the determination of authenticity.

"Can you study 'Jefferson' at university?" Rodenstock replied. "She doesn't know anything about wine in connection with Jefferson, doesn't know what bottles from the time frame 1780–1800 look like, doesn't know how they taste." Broadbent wrote letters to Monticello as well, standing by Rodenstock and the bottles. Some unbridgeable philosophical gap seemed to separate the historians in Virginia and the connoisseurs in Europe. Broadbent, like Rodenstock, expressed confidence that the sensory experience of consuming a bottle of wine trumped historical evidence. In June 1986, he noted that he had just tasted a bottle of Rodenstock's 1787 Th.J. Branne Mouton. The wine was "sensationally good," Broadbent wrote. "If anyone had any lingering doubts about the authenticity of this extraordinary old wine, they were completely removed . . . Admittedly, there is no written evidence that these particular bottles had been in the possession of Jefferson, but I am now firmly convinced that this indeed was the wine that Jefferson ordered."

It wasn't only the researchers at Monticello who raised doubts about the wine. Before Christie's auctioned the bottle to Forbes, Rodenstock had offered a bottle of the Th.J. Lafitte to a German collector named Hans-Peter Frericks, for around 10,000 deutsche marks. After Forbes spent forty times that sum, Frericks decided to auction his own bottle and approached Broadbent. But Rodenstock intervened, saying that he had sold the bottle to Frericks on the condition that Frericks not resell it. (Frericks denies that such a condition existed.) Frericks turned to Sotheby's, but after examining the evidence, the auction house declined, citing the bottle's uncertain provenance. Rodenstock's efforts to stop the sale, along with Sotheby's doubts about the bottle, made Frericks suspicious, and in 1991 he sent the bottle to a Munich lab to have its contents carbon-dated.

All organic material contains the radioactive isotope carbon 14, which exhibits a predictable rate of decay; scientists can thus analyze the amount of the isotope in a bottle of wine in order to approximate its age. Carbon 14 has a long half-life, and carbon dating is a relatively imprecise method when it comes to evaluating objects that are several centuries old. But nuclear atmospheric tests in the 1950s and 1960s offer a benchmark of sorts, since levels of carbon 14 rise sharply during that period. In this case, the amounts of carbon 14 and of another isotope, tritium, were much higher than one would expect for two-hundred-year-old wine, and the scientists concluded that the bottle contained a mixture of wines, nearly half of which dated to 1962 or later.

Frericks sued Rodenstock, and in December 1992 a German court found in his favor, holding that Rodenstock "adulterated the wine or knowingly offered adulterated wine." (Rodenstock appealed and sued Frericks for defamation. The matter was ultimately settled out of court.) In addition to the former MI5 agent, the indefatigable Elroy employed two private investigators in Germany, who discovered that Hardy Rodenstock was a fictitious name. The investigators visited Rodenstock's hometown, Marienwerder, in what is now Poland. They reported to Koch that Rodenstock had started out as Meinhard Goerke, the son of a local railroad official. They interviewed Rodenstock's mother and visited his elementary school. The investigators told Koch that Rodenstock had trained as an engineer and taken a job with the German Federal Railway; they could find no evidence to support his claims of being a professor. They also interviewed Tina

York, a German pop singer with whom Rodenstock was romantically involved in the 1970s and 1980s. York told them that during her decade-long relationship with Rodenstock he hid the fact that he had two sons from an earlier marriage. "He always talked about two nephews," she said.

Rodenstock had adopted his new identity at about the time he met York, the investigators said, and told her that he was part of the famous Rodenstock family. It was while he was with York that he first became interested in wine. She didn't share his devotion to the hobby. She remembered placing a bowl of potato salad in his air-conditioned wine cellar one day, to keep it cool. "Rodenstock just flipped out," she said. Rodenstock was known for his discerning nose and his ability to identify wines in blind tastings. Elroy wondered whether he might possess the skills of a mixer, the type of expert that vineyards employ to achieve a precise blend of grapes. There are no scientific tests that can reliably determine the grape varietals in a bottle of wine, and Elroy speculated that Rodenstock might have concocted forgeries by mixing various wines—and even a dash of port, as forgers have been known to do—in order to create a cocktail that tasted like the real thing.

Pursuing these suspicions, Elroy's team of investigators asked several people they interviewed whether they had any recollection of Rodenstock's having a laboratory where counterfeits could be made. Then, in October 2006, a German man named Andreas Klein approached Koch's team and said that Rodenstock had lived for several years in an apartment owned by his family. The two had quarreled over Klein's desire to add an apartment above Rodenstock's, and ended up in court. In 2004, after Rodenstock abandoned the apartment, Klein entered his former tenant's cellar and discovered a collection of empty bottles and a stack of apparently new wine labels.

• • •

There are two types of wine counterfeiters: those who do not tamper with what is inside the bottle and those who do. Because the price of a great vintage of fine wine often dwarfs the price of an indifferent one, many forgers will start with a genuine bottle of, say, 1980 Pétrus and simply replace the label with one from 1982. (The 1982 vintage is especially coveted and expensive.) With a good scanner and a color printer, labels are easy to replicate; one former auctioneer I spoke with called it "desktop publishing." The cork in the bottle is marked with the year, but forgers sometimes scratch away the last digit, assuming that the buyer won't notice. Moreover, because corks tend to deteriorate after decades in the bottle, some vineyards offer a recorking service, so a bottle with a newer cork might not immediately arouse suspicion. In any event, the cork is generally concealed by the foil capsule until the buyer opens the bottle.

The forger's greatest advantage is that many buyers wait years before opening their fraudulent bottles—if they open them at all. Bill Koch told me that he owns wine that he has no intention of ever drinking. He collects bottles from certain vineyards almost as if they were baseball cards, aiming to complete a set. "I just want 150 years of Lafite on the wall," he said. He would hesitate before consuming the harder-to-come-by vintages, because to do so would render the set incomplete, but also because the rarest old wines often come not from the best vintages but from the worst. Historically, when good vintages were produced, collectors would lay them down to see how they would age, Koch explained. But when renowned vineyards produced mediocre vintages, people would drink them soon after they were bottled, making the vintage scarce. When I wondered why he would buy old wines that he never intended to drink, Koch shrugged. "I'm never going to shoot Custer's rifle," he said.

The second great advantage for wine forgers is that when collectors do open fraudulent bottles, they often lack the experience and acute sense of taste to know that they have been defrauded. To begin with, even genuine old wines vary enormously from bottle to bottle. "It's a living organism," Sotheby's Serena Sutcliffe told me. "It moves, it changes, it evolves, and once you're into wines that are forty, fifty, sixty years old, even if the bottles are stored side by side in similar conditions, you will get big differences between bottles." Studies suggest that the experience of smelling and tasting wine is extremely susceptible to interference from the cognitive parts of the brain. Several years ago, Frédéric Brochet, a PhD student in oenology at the University of Bordeaux, did a study in which he served fifty-seven participants a mid-range red Bordeaux from a bottle with a label indicating that it was a modest *vin de table*. A week later, he served the same wine to the same subjects but this time poured from a bottle indicating that the wine was a grand cru. Whereas the tasters found the wine from the first bottle "simple," "unbalanced," and "weak," they found the wine from the second "complex," "balanced," and "full." Brochet argues that our "perceptive expectation" arising from the label often governs our experience of a wine, overriding our actual sensory response to whatever is in the bottle.

Thus there is a bolder kind of forger who actually substitutes one type of wine for another. He often works with genuine bottles bearing genuine labels, obtaining empties from restaurants or antiques shops, filling them with another type—or types—of wine, and replacing the cork and the capsule, assuming that the status-conscious buyer will never taste the difference. And in many cases this assumption is correct. Sutcliffe believes that the vast majority of fake wines are happily enjoyed. Rajat Parr, a prominent wine director who oversees restaurants in Las Vegas, told me that several years ago some of his customers ordered a bottle of 1982 Pétrus, which can sell in restaurants for as much as $6,000. The party finished the bottle and ordered a second. But the second bottle tasted noticeably different, so they sent it back. The staff apologetically produced a third bottle, which the diners consumed with pleasure. Parr closely examined the three bottles and discovered the problem with the second one: it was genuine.

If the Th.J. bottles were counterfeit, the question facing Jim Elroy was whether someone else's genuine eighteenth-century bottles had been passed off as Thomas Jefferson's or whether the wine itself had been adulterated. The fact that Broadbent and other connoisseurs had tasted several Jefferson bottles and declared them authentic seemed to suggest that the wine in the bottles was the real thing. Jancis Robinson, another master of wine and the wine columnist for the *Financial Times*, had attended the 1998 Yquem tasting and found the two Th.J. bottles "convincingly old," slightly moldy initially, but then, as "the miracle of great old wine began to work," opening up, with the 1784 giving off a "feminine fragrance of roses" and the 1787 "autumnal aromas of burnt sugar and undergrowth." But Brochet told me that in tastings, experts are more susceptible than average drinkers to interference from their own experience and presumptions. And these endorsements seem to be disputed by the scientific test commissioned by Hans-Peter Frericks, which found that nearly half of the wine in his 1787 Lafitte dated to some time after 1962.

Following Frericks's test, Rodenstock had commissioned a test of his own, on another bottle of 1787 Lafitte, from Dr. Georges Bonani, a Zurich scientist. Bonani carbon-dated the wine and determined that no wine in the bottle dated to 1962 or later, thus contradicting the specific finding of Frericks's study. Rodenstock frequently referred to Bonani's results as "conclusive" in their authentication of the bottle. But it seems difficult to consider any of these tests truly conclusive. For one thing, the different tests were conducted on different bottles, and it would be rash to extrapolate from the results of one bottle anything about the authenticity of the others. Further, carbon dating can't provide a reliable determination of the age of wines bottled during the eighteenth and nineteenth centuries, and an examination of Bonani's lab report reveals that his findings reflected a considerable margin of error. While the test might have ruled out the presence of late-twentieth-century wine, it did not provide absolute proof that the wine dated to 1787. "The test says only that the wine is from somewhere between 1673 and 1945," Bonani wrote in a recent email.

Skeptical of both parties' tests, Elroy sought out a French physicist named Philippe Hubert, who had devised a method of testing the age of wine without opening the bottle. Hubert uses low-frequency gamma rays to detect the presence of the radioactive isotope cesium 137. Unlike carbon 14, cesium 137 is not naturally occurring; it is a direct result of nuclear fallout. A wine bottled before the advent of atmospheric nuclear testing contains no cesium 137, so the test yields no results for older wines. But if a wine does contain cesium 137, the short half-life of the isotope—thirty years—allows Hubert to make a more precise estimate of its age. Elroy flew to France, with the Jefferson bottles packed in two bulletproof, impact-resistant cases, which he carried as hand luggage. (He had obtained a *carnet*, a sort of passport for objects, so that he would not have to pay any duties while crossing borders with half a million dollars' worth of wine. When airport security scrutinized the bottles between flights at Heathrow, Elroy deadpanned, "You just can't get a good bottle of wine on the airplane.")

The lab where Hubert and Elroy tested the wine is under a mile-high stretch of the Alps on the French-Italian border. The bottles were placed in a detector that was surrounded by ten inches of lead and were subjected to a week of tests. Elroy was confident by now that he and his investigators were closing in on Rodenstock. "With the evidence I'm seeing from Monticello, combined with what I'm seeing from Germany, I'm 99 percent sure this guy is a fraud," he recalled. When Hubert completed the tests, however, he identified no cesium 137 in the bottles. "I don't know whether it's 1783 or 1943," Hubert told Elroy. But the wine predated the atomic age.

"I can't tell you how disappointing it was," Elroy told me. "I've got the historical evidence, but if we're going to do this criminally, there's got to be more than that. I've got to have some kind of scientific or other evidence, or it's not going to be prosecutable." On the plane back to the United States, Elroy took one of the bottles down and held it in his hands. "I'm looking at the capsule and the glass itself," he said. "I run my hand over the engraving. I can feel it. And then I think, This is a tool mark. This was done with a *tool.*"

When Elroy landed, he called the FBI's laboratory in Quantico, Virginia. The lab's ballistics experts specialize in tool-mark examinations, noting the telltale impression that a gun barrel leaves on a bullet, or a screwdriver makes when it pries open a window. The lab gave Elroy the names of some recently retired specialists. He also visited the Corning Museum of Glass in upstate New York, where he was referred to an expert glass engraver named Max Erlacher, an Austrian-born craftsman who had done work for a number of American presidents. Several weeks later, Elroy hired Erlacher and a retired FBI tool expert named Bill Albrecht to examine the bottles at Bill Koch's estate in Palm Beach. Elroy wanted to know whether the writing on the bottles had been done with a copper wheel, the sort of tool used in the eighteenth century to engrave glass. In Jefferson's time, the copper wheel, usually operated by a foot pedal, spun in a stationary position, and the engraver moved the bottle around it. Erlacher and Albrecht inspected the bottles, examining the ridges of the engraving under a powerful magnifying glass. Letters engraved by a copper wheel tend to vary in thickness, like the strokes of a fountain pen. But the lettering on the bottles was strangely uniform, and it slanted in a way that a copper-wheel engraving would not. The initials could not have been made in the eighteenth century, Erlacher concluded. Instead, they looked as if they might have been done with a handheld tool like a dentist's drill or a Dremel—a tool powered by electricity. This was "a quantum leap," Elroy thought. As it happened, he had a Dremel tool at home. "I get a bottle of wine, and I screw with it," he recalled. "And in an hour I can engrave 'Th.J.'"

• • •

On August 31, 2006, Bill Koch filed a civil complaint against Hardy Rodenstock ("a.k.a. Meinhard Goerke") in New York federal court. Although it was the Chicago Wine Company and Farr Vintners that had sold Koch the wines, the complaint alleged that Rodenstock had orchestrated an "ongoing scheme" to defraud wine collectors. "Rodenstock is charming and debonair," the complaint read. "He is also a con artist." Before filing the suit, Koch's lawyers were interested to see whether Rodenstock would acknowledge a personal connection to Koch's Jefferson bottles (given that Koch had not bought them directly from him) and whether he might effectively continue the alleged fraud by still insisting that they were real. So Koch faxed Rodenstock a cordial letter, in January 2006, saying that he was trying to authenticate his Jefferson wines and asking Rodenstock to send a letter indicating that he had "every reason to believe" that the bottles "once belonged to Thomas Jefferson." Rodenstock replied on January 10, saying, "The Jefferson bottles are absolutely genuine and . . . come from a walled up cellar in Paris." He pointed out that Christie's had vouched for the bottles' authenticity, and enclosed a copy of Bonani's report. "You will surely understand that the discussions on the genuineness of the Jefferson bottles [are] herewith closed for me," he wrote.

In April, Koch wrote to Rodenstock again, asking whether the two could meet, "over a good glass of wine, at a place of your choosing," to discuss some of his concerns about the bottles. Rodenstock declined. "From a legal point of view the purchase and the sale are barred by the statute of limitations," he wrote. The person who sold him the bottles in 1985 was in his sixties at the time, he continued, and might no longer be alive. Questions about the bottles' authenticity were "grist for the mill of the yellow press." When the suit was filed, Rodenstock moved to dismiss it. Koch's lawyers flew to London in October to interview Michael Broadbent, who was by then seventy-nine years old but still active on the international wine circuit. Broadbent said he had asked Rodenstock "over and over again" to divulge the address where the bottles were found. But he continued to maintain that the Jefferson bottles were real.

In a way, Broadbent had little choice. He had based hundreds of tasting notes in his books and auction catalogs on wines supplied by Hardy Rodenstock. The notion that twentieth-century connoisseurs could testify to what an eighteenth-century wine tastes like depended on the integrity of Rodenstock, one of the primary suppliers of those wines. If Rodenstock was exposed as a fraud, the credibility of Broadbent—who had repeatedly certified Rodenstock's findings—would suffer a considerable blow. When asked why he had not done more research into the Th.J. Lafitte before the auction, he replied, "We are auctioneers; we are like journalists on deadlines. I did not have the time." The lawyers asked whether Christie's had prepared any written evidence back in 1985 to buttress the wine department's claims about the bottles. Broadbent responded that it never occurred to him to put anything in writing. "With Christie's we are all perfect gentlemen," he said.

In the fall of 2006, Richard Brierley, the head of Christie's wine sales in the United States, told *The Wall Street Journal* that while he wasn't involved in the 1985 authentication of the Jefferson bottles, "looking back, more questions could have been asked." (Christie's contends that Brierley was quoted out of context.) Hugo Morley-Fletcher, who, in 1985, was the head of Christie's ceramics department and was one of the glass experts Broadbent consulted about the authenticity of the Forbes bottle, told me, "My opinion at that time, within my experience, was that it was correct . . . The trouble is we are engaged in an activity which is not a precise science." He explained that he had judged that the bottle dated to the eighteenth century and that the engraving dated to the same period. When I asked whether there was any possibility that he could have been mistaken about the engraving, he replied, "Of course," and added, "One has to come up with an opinion." Then he said, "It is possible that one was conned."

Despite numerous attempts, I was unable to reach Michael Broad-

bent, but a Christie's spokesman told me that "Mr. Broadbent's decision to go forward with the sale represented his considered opinion
based on all of the facts available to him at that time—a decision that
we would not speculate upon twenty-two years later." Still, Christie's
fine-and-rare-wine auction in New York in December 2006 featured
a 1934 Pétrus accompanied by a description, taken from Broadbent's
book, of a 1934 Pétrus imperial that he had tasted years earlier. "Where
Hardy Rodenstock finds these wines I know not," it read. "There are
simply no records of production, of stock or sales prior to 1945. All
I can say is that the big bottle was delicious." Koch did not know
whether Rodenstock had consigned the bottle (Christie's told me he
had not). But he was angry that even in the face of the allegations in
his suit the auction house would promote wine with Broadbent notes
on Rodenstock bottles. He telephoned the auction house to complain,
but Christie's proceeded with the auction. The wine was offered at
$2,200. It went unsold.

No one knows how many bottles of wine—real or fake—Hardy
Rodenstock has sold over the years. His deals were often in cash. ("If
you pay in cash, then people don't have to declare the sale for tax purposes," he once told an interviewer. "Two hundred thousand dollars
in cash can sometimes be better than a million-dollar check.") Protective of both his suppliers and his buyers, he did not volunteer information about particular sales. Jim Elroy thinks that at $10,000 a bottle or
more, Rodenstock could have sold ten bottles a month and made more
than $1 million a year. As Koch was launching his suit against Roden-
stock, a Massachusetts software entrepreneur named Russell Frye filed
a lawsuit against the Wine Library, a distributor in Petaluma, California, alleging that it had sold him nineteenth-century Lafite and
Yquem, along with dozens of other rare old wines, that were counterfeit. Frye's complaint notes that one of the defendants in the case
"has recently informed plaintiff that many of the bottles that plaintiff
alleges are counterfeit or questionable were ultimately obtained from
Hardy Rodenstock."

Koch owns some forty thousand bottles of wine, stored in three
cellars. In May, I visited one, a refrigerated warren of dark-wood
racks underneath his house in Osterville, on Cape Cod. Jim Elroy
had sought the help of two experts, David Molyneux-Berry and Bill

Edgerton, to go through the cellar and identify suspicious bottles. Molyneux-Berry worked at Sotheby's for years before becoming a private wine consultant, and it was he who rejected Hans-Peter Frericks's bottle of Th.J. Lafitte. In Frericks's cellar, he had identified one obvious fake after another. According to the collector's detailed records, they had all come from Hardy Rodenstock. Molyneux-Berry was also suspicious of Rodenstock's many colorful discoveries. As a representative of Sotheby's, Molyneux-Berry had made frequent official trips to Russia. "I went to Kiev and saw the cellar there," he told me. "I went to Moldova and saw the cellars there. I had the highest introductions you can get. Yet Rodenstock goes to Russia and finds the tsar's cellars somewhere else. And it's the entire first growth of Bordeaux . . . And he found magnums. In volume."

From a sample of 3,000 bottles of pre-1961 vintages of often counterfeited brands, Molyneux-Berry and Edgerton identified about 130 suspicious or obviously fake bottles in Koch's collection. "You get to know what bottles look like," Molyneux-Berry told me. "Obvious fakes stand out like a sore thumb." They put a white sticker on each suspicious bottle. The next day, a professional photographer took high-resolution pictures, which, if necessary, could be introduced in court. In some cases, the bottle, the label, and the capsule all appeared genuine, but the rarity of the wine alone was ground for suspicion. Koch owns two magnums of Lafleur from 1947, for instance. "Forty-seven is the great Lafleur," Molyneux-Berry said. But, he continued, he has heard that in 1947 the vineyard bottled only five magnums. "What's the chance of him having two out of five?" he asked. Edgerton maintains an online database that tracks auction sales and prices. Nineteen magnums of 1947 Lafleur have sold at auction since 1998.

Serena Sutcliffe, of Sotheby's, told me that most wealthy collectors would rather not know about the fakes, or, if they do know, would rather not make it public. She said that on a number of occasions she has inspected a cellar that a collector was interested in auctioning and rejected it, in whole or in part, because of the preponderance of fakes, only to learn that the collector sold the phony wine through one of her competitors. The collectors "don't want to take the hit," she said.

"The case is much bigger" than Rodenstock, Koch told me. "When I get finished going through all the wine in my collection, I'm going after all the people who sold it to me," he said. "The retailers, they know they're doing it. They're complicit." One of Koch's problem bottles is a magnum of 1921 Pétrus that he bought for $33,000 at an auction organized by the New York wine retailer Zachys in 2005. Koch believes that the wine originated from Rodenstock; he mentions the bottle in his lawsuit. (Zachys says it has no evidence to indicate whether the wine originally came from Rodenstock.) It was another magnum of 1921 Pétrus that Robert Parker had awarded a hundred points and pronounced "out of this universe" at Rodenstock's Munich event in 1995. Last spring, Jim Elroy took Koch's magnum to Bordeaux to have it inspected at the winery. The Pétrus staff ultimately concluded that the cork was the wrong length and that the cap and the label appeared to be artificially aged. Pétrus confirmed that they had doubts about the authenticity of the bottle. And the cellar master, in his interview with Elroy, said that he had never heard of a magnum of 1921 Pétrus—and did not believe that any were bottled at the vineyard.

This raised an interesting question. If Pétrus made no magnums in 1921, what was Parker drinking at the Rodenstock event? Parker's nose is insured for $1 million; it seems almost pathological that Rodenstock would invite such a man to his table and serve him a fake. Elroy sees this as further proof of Rodenstock's guilt, maintaining that this kind of risk taking is not unusual in a counterfeiter. "I know a lot about fraudsters," he said. "I put a lot of them in prison. They feel, 'I'm so smart. I'm smarter than anyone in the world.' Rodenstock feels that way." If indeed Parker's hundred-point 1921 Pétrus was a fake, such hubris might not be misplaced. Could Rodenstock have become so proficient at making fake wine that his fakes tasted as good as, or even better than, the real thing? When I asked Parker about the bottle, he hastened to say that even the best wine critics are fallible. Yet he reiterated that the bottle was spectacular. "If that was a fake, he should be a mixer," Parker said. "It was wonderful."

• • •

In the summer of 2007, Hardy Rodenstock fired the Manhattan lawyers he had engaged to contest Koch's suit. In a letter to the trial judge, he objected that the court had no jurisdiction over him, as a German citizen; that Koch had bought the bottles not directly from him but from third parties; and that the case should be barred by the statute of limitations. It might be Koch's "hobby to take actions against people for years," he suggested, but he wanted no part of "such 'silly games.'" After spelling out his objections, he announced, "I get out of the procedure."

Rodenstock would not agree to be interviewed for this piece, but in a series of faxes, most of them in German, he maintained his innocence and fiercely objected to Bill Koch's portrayal of him, denouncing Koch's "concoctions and shenanigans." He acknowledged that his legal name is Meinhard Goerke but insisted that many people change their names, pointing to the CNN host Larry King (who was born Lawrence Harvey Zeiger) as an example. Rodenstock denied telling Tina York that he was a member of the Rodenstock family, and maintained that he was indeed a professor, writing, "That is a fact! Verifiable!" He disputed accounts that he found a hundred cases of Bordeaux in Venezuela, observing, "That would be 1200 bottles?!?!?!" As for Andreas Klein's allegations about finding empty bottles and labels in his basement, Rodenstock wrote that it was not uncommon for wine connoisseurs to save empties after a wine tasting. "I take the labels from old bottles to have them framed," he said. "This looks very nice!" He denied supplying any bottles to the Wine Library, or the magnum of Pétrus that Koch mentioned in the lawsuit, and insisted, "My 1921 Pétrus bottles were always absolutely genuine!!!" He cited Parker's hundred-point review, and asked, "Is there any better proof that the wine was genuine when world-renowned experts described it as superb and gave it the highest possible grade?"

Rodenstock took particular exception to Bill Koch's account of their one meeting, in 2000, at Christie's Latour tasting. "I was not late!!" he insisted. "I neither looked uncomfortable nor did I run away from him fast. My facial expression was, I am sure, full of pleasant anticipation of the wonderful Latour tasting. I was in a very good mood!!!" In Rodenstock's recollection, Koch said that he owned some Jefferson bottles, and Rodenstock replied, "Good for you, but you didn't get them from me."

When it comes to the authenticity of the Th.J. bottles, Rodenstock offers a number of sometimes contradictory defenses. "If Christie's had the slightest doubt about the authenticity, they would not have accepted the bottle of 1787 Lafitte," he wrote. "I am therefore beyond reproach!" He suggested that Koch's analysis of the initials was performed not by scientists but by "amateur engravers" who were friends of Koch's and were being paid for their conclusions. But in his letter to the court, he entertained the possibility that the initials *were* modern, hypothesizing that whoever originally sold him the wines "had some bottles re-engraved over the old engravings . . . because they were no longer clearly legible." Rodenstock also suggested that it might have been Koch himself—or one of his staff—who had the bottles reengraved, pointing out that "A great deal can have happened to the bottles in twenty years!!!" (When Hans-Peter Frericks sued over his Jefferson bottle, Rodenstock made a similar claim, suggesting that Frericks had tampered with his own bottle in order to frame Rodenstock.)

On August 14, the magistrate judge, who supervises pretrial procedural issues, recommended that the court enter a default judgment against Rodenstock because of his refusal to participate. The trial judge must now decide whether to accept Rodenstock's various procedural defenses. But even if he is handed a default judgment, Rodenstock insists that German courts will not enforce it. Meanwhile, Jim Elroy has turned over the findings of his investigation to the authorities, a grand jury has been convened to hear evidence, and the FBI has begun issuing subpoenas to wine collectors, dealers, and auction houses. "It's going to have a salutary effect on the whole industry," Koch told me. "And if the judge throws the lawsuit out for some technical reason, I've got five others I could bring."

• • •

In the back of his Palm Beach wine cellar, past rows of priceless bottles, behind elegant cast-iron grille work, is a closet in which Koch keeps his very oldest bottles, many of which he now believes are fake. I picked up a bottle of the 1787 Th.J. Lafitte. It was cold and surprisingly heavy in my hands, and I ran my fingers over the letters. Could a shared passion for the rarest old wines have blinded everyone—the collectors, the critics, the auctioneers—to the sheer improbability of those initials? Jefferson had asked in the 1790 letter that his wine and

Washington's wine be marked, but surely he was referring to the cases and not the individual bottles.

Koch uncorked a bottle of 1989 Montrachet, and we walked upstairs and settled into comfortable leather chairs in the cowboy room. The wine was crisp and minerally; to my untutored palate, it tasted pretty good. As we discussed the case, I noticed that Koch seemed anything but aggrieved. He has thrown himself into his battle against Rodenstock and phony wine with the same headlong enthusiasm that he devoted to collecting wine in the first place. "I used to brag that I got the Thomas Jefferson wines," he said. "Now I get to brag that I have the fake Thomas Jefferson wines."

Outside, the sun was beginning to set, and Koch's chef informed him that dinner would be softshell crab and venison. Koch flipped through his cellar book, a hefty binder listing his wines. Upstairs, one of the children was bouncing a basketball. Bridget Rooney walked in, with the couple's one-year-old daughter, Kaitlin, in her arms. "We're talking fake wine," Koch said. "Want to join us?" Rooney took a seat next to him. She wore a rope of enormous pearls around her neck, and didn't seem to notice that Kaitlin was chewing on them. She reached for Koch's glass and took a sip. "Mmm," she murmured. "That's not fake."

In 2018, Hardy Rodenstock died, at seventy-six, after an illness. Bill Koch eventually expanded his crusade against fine-wine fraud, targeting other fraudsters and launching new lawsuits. He continues to pursue his investigation, very happily, to this day.

CRIME FAMILY

*How a notorious Dutch gangster was
exposed by his own sister.* (2018)

ASTRID HOLLEEDER HAS ARRESTING eyes that are swimming-pool blue, but that's all I can reveal about her appearance, because she is in hiding, an exile in her own city, which is Amsterdam. For the past two years, she has lived in a series of furnished safe houses. She prefers buildings with basement parking, in order to minimize her exposure during the brief transit to a bulletproof car. She bought the car used, for €15,000. She also owns two bulletproof vests. She thinks a lot about how she might be assassinated, gaming out fatal scenarios. Whenever she stops at a red light and an unfamiliar vehicle sharks up alongside her, she clutches the wheel, her heart hammering. Then the light changes, and she exhales and keeps moving.

Amsterdam, a city of fewer than a million people, is a difficult place to stage your own disappearance, particularly if you grew up there. Fortunately for Holleeder (which is pronounced "Hol-LAY-der"), she guarded her privacy even before her life became threatened, and no photographs of her as an adult can be found on the internet. Today, she arranges furtive visits with a small circle of friends, but otherwise stays mostly at home. When she moves through Amsterdam, she does so in secret, and sometimes in disguise: she has a collection of fake noses and teeth. Holleeder typically dresses in black, but if she suspects she's being followed, she may duck into a bathroom and emerge in a wig and a red dress. Occasionally, she has posed as a man. Such subterfuge is not conducive to a social life. Certainly, it is risky for her to meet anyone she doesn't already know. Holleeder is a vibrant woman who draws energy from having people around her, but she has armored herself. She told me recently that at fifty-two she is single, and added, "Relationships are overrated."

The threat to Holleeder's life stems from a decision that she made, in 2013, to become the star witness in a Mob trial. She agreed to testify against the most notorious criminal in the Netherlands, a man known as De Neus—the Nose, a reference to his most prominent facial feature. This was a risky choice. "Everyone else who has turned on him ended up dead," she pointed out. The Nose is being held at the Netherlands' only maximum-security prison. In 2016, he allegedly asked gang leaders at the prison to enlist members on the outside to execute Holleeder, along with two other witnesses in the case against him. The plot was disrupted when one of the prisoners confessed to officials. But the threat lingers. "Of course he would do it," Holleeder said. "He would kill me." If she speaks with unusual conviction about what the Nose might do, it is in part because she used to be his legal adviser: until Holleeder went into hiding, she was a successful criminal-defense attorney. More to the point, she is his younger sister.

The Nose's name is Willem "Wim" Holleeder. He is standing trial on five counts of murder, two counts of attempted murder, and "participating in a criminal enterprise." The proceedings take place in a secure courtroom, on the industrial outskirts of Amsterdam, known as the Bunker. When Astrid testifies, she sits in an enclosure behind an opaque screen, which guarantees that nobody in the courtroom can see her face and also ensures that she cannot see Wim, who might seek to inhibit her testimony with a menacing glance or a gesture that only she could understand. As one prosecutor recently explained in court, Wim "can be extremely intimidating."

The "mega-trial," as the Dutch press calls it, has become such a spectacle that people often line up at dawn in the hope of securing a seat in the small public gallery. Part of the allure is Astrid herself. In 2016, she published a memoir, *Judas,* about growing up with Wim and about her decision to betray him. The book sold half a million copies in a country of seventeen million people. Although Astrid is now a famous author, she has met almost none of her readers. A bookstore signing is out of the question. The book's title reflects her profound ambivalence about her decision to accuse her brother of murder. But the high drama of that choice is what made the book a success and what attracts so many rubberneckers to the Bunker: the clash of the Holleeders is sibling rivalry distilled to a courtroom duel.

"This is the ultimate betrayal," Astrid told the court in March.

Through sobs, she explained that despite Wim's many crimes she still loves him. It was "crazy and horrible" to be testifying against him, she admitted. "But, if you have a very sweet dog that bites children, you have to choose the children, and put the dog down."

• • •

Wim is the oldest of four kids, Astrid the youngest. Sonja and Gerard are the middle siblings. They grew up in the Jordaan, a picturesque district of narrow homes and canals in central Amsterdam. Today, the Jordaan is full of hip cafés and expensive boutiques, but in the 1960s it was a working-class neighborhood. Astrid's father, who was also named Willem, worked at the nearby Heineken brewery. He revered Alfred "Freddy" Heineken, the potentate who ran the company. Heineken's green bottles reportedly came to account for 40 percent of the imported beer consumed in the United States, and Freddy Heineken was one of the Netherlands' richest men. When Astrid was young, the children did their homework with Heineken-logo pens and drank milk from Heineken-logo glasses. The house was "drenched in Heineken," Astrid recalled. So was her father: he was an alcoholic. He was also a tyrannical sadist who belittled and abused Astrid's mother, Stien, and their children.

When Astrid reflects on the circumscribed nature of her current existence, she sometimes recalls her childhood. "I'm used to being in prison, because home was a prison," she told me. Wim was a tall and handsome teenager, with muscular arms and a Gallic nose. Like his father, he was temperamental, and the two often clashed; Wim started going out in the evening and coming home very late. He sometimes woke Astrid on his return and whispered, "Assie, are you asleep? Has Dad gone to bed yet? Did he go crazy again?" Astrid whispered back, "He was yelling that you were late. But Mom turned back the clock so he wouldn't catch you." Stien told me that her son was sweet "until he was twelve or thirteen," adding, "I didn't know that he was hanging around with the wrong people." Then again, she pointed out, "they were all criminals in the neighborhood."

The Netherlands officially has one of the world's lowest crime rates. In recent years, some two dozen Dutch prisons have shut down, because there aren't enough convicts to fill them. Toleration of cannabis and prostitution, combined with low levels of poverty and robust social-welfare protections, has burnished the country's reputation as a peaceful, progressive utopia. But a recent confidential report by the Dutch police, which leaked to the press, suggested that official figures don't reflect the actual volume of crime in the country. The police estimated that millions of minor thefts and other violations go unreported every year, because victims conclude that crime is an inevitable nuisance or that the authorities are unlikely to apprehend the perpetrators. There is also a fair amount of serious crime. According to a Europol report, as much as half of the cocaine that enters Europe passes through the port of Rotterdam. When a jumbo shipment went missing a few years ago, a gang war erupted; more than a dozen people were murdered, and hit men sprayed bullets down Amsterdam's streets.

Wim Holleeder's early forays into the underworld were modest: he provided muscle for landlords who were looking to evict squatters, and dabbled in various fraudulent schemes. By his early twenties, he had advanced to armed robbery. He'd begun showing some of the abusive tendencies of his dad, including menacing his sisters. According to Astrid, he would tell them, "I'm the boss."

"He's a narcissist, like his father," Stien told me. He came home occasionally, to visit his siblings and their mother, and often brought along his childhood friend Cornelius van Hout, who went by Cor. Astrid liked him. "He had a joie de vivre," she told me, and he didn't take the tempestuous Wim too seriously. Sonja also found Cor charming and, to Astrid's delight, began dating him. Sonja was beautiful, blond, perfectly dressed, and subservient to men. "Sonja was like a doll," their mother told me. "Astrid was like a tank." Astrid was so fiercely independent that her siblings joked that she must have been a foundling. She took this notion half seriously, sometimes wondering when her real family would show up to retrieve her.

Astrid excelled in school and, feeling confined by the Jordaanese slang she'd grown up speaking, made a point of mastering "proper" Dutch. Wim mocked her for putting on airs. She learned English, too, and found it comforting to have access to a language that her abusive father could not comprehend. Even today, she finds that slipping into English provides an emotional refuge. As Astrid grew into adulthood, she had a tendency to think in starkly gendered terms: women were victims, and men were perpetrators. "I was like a man," she told me. "I didn't want to be a victim. I never wore a dress." She played basketball, eventually rising to a semiprofessional level. At seventeen, she left home, turning her back on her father forever. Her plan was to flee the Netherlands by winning a college scholarship abroad. "I was ready to go to the United States," she recalled. "It was only with the Heineken kidnapping that I got sucked back in."

•   •   •

On November 9, 1983, Freddy Heineken was leaving his office in Amsterdam when an orange minivan pulled up beside him. Several masked men shoved him and his chauffeur into the vehicle at gunpoint. The minivan careered along a bicycle path and headed to a warehouse on the edge of the city. Heineken and the chauffeur were thrust into a pair of soundproofed cells. That night, the Dutch police received a note demanding a colossal ransom—the equivalent of more than $30 million in today's money. "Kidnapping was the sort of thing that happened in other places, like the United States," Peter R. de Vries, a Dutch crime journalist who wrote a book about the kidnapping, told me. Freddy Heineken was a national icon, and the Dutch public was riveted by the story. By then, Sonja was living with Cor van Hout, with whom she'd recently had a daughter, Frances. One night, Astrid and Wim joined them for dinner and watched the news. "It's extremely stupid," Astrid remembers saying. "Who would kidnap Heineken? They'll be hunted the rest of their lives."

"You think so?" Wim asked.

"I'm pretty damn sure of it," she replied.

Three weeks later, the authorities had made no progress in solving the crime. The Heineken family handed a driver five sacks containing the ransom money in four currencies, as the kidnappers had specified. The driver went to Utrecht, deposited the sacks in a storm drain, and left. The hostages were not released when the money was delivered, but around this time the police received an anonymous tip that led them to the Amsterdam warehouse. Inside, they found Freddy Heineken and the chauffeur. "I was chained by my left hand, limiting my freedom of movement to almost nil," Heineken said in a statement, adding that he'd combed his hair with the tines of a plastic fork. "Trying to establish a rhythm gives you something to do," he said. The captives had been rescued, but the culprits had disappeared, apparently getting away with the crime and the ransom money. One morning, however, while Astrid was staying at Sonja's house and Cor was away, heavily armed policemen burst through the door. An anonymous informant had provided Dutch authorities with the identities of the kidnappers. The alleged ringleaders were Wim Holleeder and Cor van Hout. The police placed the sisters under arrest. Astrid was seventeen.

Early this spring, I contacted Astrid's publisher, Oscar van Gelderen. A jaunty man with an impish smile, he has experience representing a star author who is subject to death threats: he was the first foreign publisher to translate Roberto Saviano, the Italian journalist who wrote the 2006 book *Gomorrah*, about the Neapolitan Mafia, and has lived in hiding ever since. Van Gelderen connected me with Astrid, who agreed to see me—but on her terms. I could not know in advance where in Amsterdam we would meet: if Wim's associates were aware that I had a rendezvous with Astrid, they could tail me. Before I met her, van Gelderen urged me to be sensitive about the emotional toll that Astrid's precarious situation had taken on her. "She is very intellectual," he said. "But she is a raw nerve."

One evening, as dusk fell over Amsterdam, a driver picked me up and brought me to a sleek hotel, where we descended to the basement parking lot. I took an elevator to a Japanese restaurant, where I was escorted to a low table in a private room enclosed by shoji screens. Then a screen slid open and Astrid entered. For a hermit, she is impressively fit. Dressed in black, she greeted me warmly, then commenced a serious perusal of the menu. "I don't go out to eat much, only when it's a private room," she said, with undisguised exuberance, before selecting the most extravagant option, a twelve-course tasting menu, and recommending that I do the same. Then she started speaking about her brother—rapidly and assuredly, in perfect English—with the babbling-brook urgency of a shut-in who is starved for conversation. Without a doubt, she observed, there was a patricidal impulse behind Wim's decision to kidnap Freddy Heineken, the man her father revered but who also "provided the beer that he drank all day." Even so, she said, "Wim would never have consciously decided to take Freddy Heineken for that reason—he's not self-aware enough for that."

When the police arrested the Holleeder sisters, Wim and Cor fled to France. Astrid and Sonja told investigators that they'd been unaware of the plot; Wim wouldn't have confided in his sisters, and Sonja knew better than to ask Cor about his work. The women were released without charges. Six weeks later, Wim and Cor were captured in Paris, at an apartment near the Champs-Élysées; Cor had been making calls to Sonja, which the authorities had traced. The Dutch government initiated an extradition of Wim and Cor, but the process became mired in legal complications, and the men remained in French custody for nearly three years. During this period, they gave occasional interviews to the Dutch press, coming across as insolent, dashing antiheroes—working-class toughs who'd dared to kidnap a plutocrat. Though Astrid was privately appalled by their self-promotion, her feelings about them were complicated: Wim was her brother, and Cor was her sister's partner. Sonja never wavered in her support for Cor, and Stien traveled to France every week to visit Wim in prison.

Astrid's ambition to distance herself from her family was thwarted, because she now felt a sense of embattled allegiance to them—and because her last name had become infamous. While Wim and Cor were in France, Astrid fell in love with an artist named Jaap Witzenhausen, who was twenty years her senior. He was nothing like the men in her family; he had a mild temperament and was happy to subordinate himself to Astrid. "He was my housewife," she recalled fondly. "He did the household chores. He cooked very nicely. He was the total picture." When Astrid's family visited and saw Witzenhausen vacuuming, they found it hilarious. At nineteen, Astrid gave birth to a girl, Miljuschka. For several months, she told me, she tried to shield her baby from her kin, including Stien, because she was afraid that Miljuschka would be infected by "the mechanisms of my family." She began seeing a therapist. This was not something that people from her neighborhood did ("It meant you were crazy"), but she was determined not to subject her daughter to the pathologies that had warped her own childhood. Her first question to the therapist was, "What is normal? How do normal people act?"

Wim and Cor were finally extradited to the Netherlands in 1986, and sentenced to eleven years in prison. Under the country's liberal sentencing regime, they were released after only five. The Dutch public was scandalized when the kidnappers marked the occasion by throwing a decadent party at which a band performed a Heineken jingle. The men had ample reason to celebrate: as Astrid explained to me, "The authorities didn't get the money." After Heineken and the chauffeur were liberated, the Dutch police claimed to have found most of the ransom buried in a wooded area near the town of Zeist, thirty-five miles southeast of Amsterdam. But roughly a quarter of it—the equivalent, today, of $8 million—was never recovered. According to Astrid, Wim and Cor entrusted some of these funds to criminal associates, with instructions to invest in the drug trade. "So, while they were in prison, the eight million was working for them," she said. They went into prison as rich men and came out richer.

• • •

When Cor was released, he and Sonja settled into a life of gangster splendor, with ostentatious cars and holidays on the Mediterranean. They had another child, a boy, and Cor named him Richie, for its aspirational overtones. Cor and Wim were still partners, and through Cor's relationship with Sonja, the Holleeders had effectively become a crime family. Astrid's father had died while Wim was imprisoned, and Wim returned home as the paterfamilias. (Astrid's other brother, Gerard, drifted away from the family.) Peter de Vries, the crime reporter, had gotten to know Cor and Wim while they were being held in France, and in 1987 he published *Kidnapping Mr. Heineken,* which became a best seller. In the book, Cor says that he has no major regrets about his actions and celebrates his bond with Wim and the other kidnappers as a "unique, indestructible, all-encompassing, eternal comradeship." The Heineken family never attempted to recover the balance of the ransom by pursuing legal action against Cor and Wim. De Vries explained to me that Freddy Heineken was traumatized by the kidnapping and fearful that these criminal entrepreneurs might strike again. The Dutch culture of permissiveness is sometimes said to stem not merely from a liberal spirit of tolerance but also from clear-eyed pragmatism: What is the sense in prohibiting prostitution if doing so won't stop it? Heineken was a rich man who wanted to live in peace. In the early 1990s, de Vries brokered a meeting in which Wim and Cor sat down with Heineken's head of security. "They told him, 'Freddy doesn't have to be afraid,'" de Vries recalled. But this promise was given with an implicit expectation: that Heineken, in a spirit of reciprocity, wouldn't attempt to get his money back. As de Vries put it, "They would stay out of each other's way." After the kidnapping, Heineken became something of a recluse. He died in 2002. (The Heineken family did not respond to a request for comment.)

The Holleeders suspected that the authorities would begin monitoring them, so they spoke about nothing of consequence in their homes or their cars. "To protect the money, we had to keep quiet," Astrid recalled. She told me that they communicated in code— "I got you some dried pineapple" meant "Come over, because we have a problem"—and in improvised silent gestures. When Wim wanted to talk candidly with Astrid or Sonja, he ordered them to join him on a walk. ("I am an outdoorsman," he later joked in court.) Even then, Astrid covered her mouth when discussing delicate subjects, in order to stymie any police lip-readers who might be watching them with binoculars. If Wim needed to say anything potentially incriminating, he whispered it into her ear. "We got better at it, sharing the secret, letting them live off the Heineken money," Astrid told me. She recognizes now that her instinct to be loyal to her family amounted to a form of moral compromise. "That was when we all became accomplices," she said.

One sector in which Wim and Cor invested the ransom money was the sex trade. They acquired interests in several prominent establishments in Amsterdam's red-light district. Their names were not on any of the paperwork, because the investments were made through proxies. "Legally speaking, there *was* no Heineken money," Astrid said. When people asked Wim what had happened to the missing millions, he recounted a vague story about the money having been burned on a beach. "There's what everybody knows, and then there's what you can prove," Astrid said.

Wim and Cor's involvement in red-light businesses became an open secret in Amsterdam. After they invested in the Casa Rosso, a venue famed for its "erotic theater," the Heineken company reportedly informed the management that its beer could no longer be sold there. Astrid felt that Wim bullied and derided women and that he was becoming every bit as abusive as their father had been. Nevertheless, the siblings maintained a deep connection, having survived a nightmarish childhood. "Our bond is based on misery and secrets," she told me. "The closest relationships are the ones that are based on fear, threats, and violence. If you are together with someone in that situation, you have a bond for life." There was "codependency" in her family, she continued. "I learned to love people I don't like."

For a time, she worked behind the counter at one of her brother's clubs. "Maybe I wanted to belong to my family," she said. "I didn't have a problem with prostitution, because it was so close to me. It was the only way to become independent of a man if you had no brain, no ability to learn. It could have been an option for me." Instead, when Astrid was twenty-three, she went to college and studied law, drawn to its rigor and clarity. She was the only young mother in her program, but her husband accommodated her ambitions and helped care for their daughter, Miljuschka. Astrid planned to specialize in corporate law, but once she obtained her degree, she found that prospective employers were put off by her family name. Once again, she had failed to break free from the Holleeder legacy. As it happened, Wim was acquainted with some of the top criminal-defense attorneys in Amsterdam, and he arranged introductions. In these circles, Astrid discovered, her name was an *asset*. "They thought I was fantastic, because I was Wim Holleeder's sister," she said. Even in the underworld, nepotism has its benefits.

Astrid developed a real affinity for defense work. Having learned to code switch between the fusty Dutch of the courtroom and the richly accented argot of her youth, she found it effortless to connect with the hardscrabble relatives of her criminal clientele. "I knew how to talk to the families," she told me. "I knew how important hope is. It's like with my family: I don't know them as criminals; I know them as people." As she recalled her work with clients, there was a tremor in her voice, and I asked her if she missed the job. After a pause, she said yes: "You meet people in the depths of their misery, and they cling to you." Once she became a witness against Wim, doing legal work got too risky, for her and for her clients. She shook her head and said, "The truth is, I'm between four walls, just like my brother."

Astrid talks about Wim as if he were a black hole, sucking in and corrupting everything that gets caught in his orbit. Even her husband—the gentle, progressive artist—was not immune. When Miljuschka was an infant, Witzenhausen took a job as the manager of one of Wim and Cor's bordellos. "Jaap likes to rescue women," Astrid said. "Every woman in a brothel needs to be saved." At a certain point, Astrid discovered that he was skimming money from the establishment—a potentially suicidal gamble, because if Wim found out, he might kill him. "Jaap gradually went from an intellectual to a thief," Astrid recalled. In 2005, Witzenhausen was interviewed by detectives, and told them that Wim had physically abused Astrid and Sonja and that there was "enormous intimidation" in the family. Astrid antagonized Wim, Witzenhausen told the police, because she defied him. "That's why she gets a beating every time," he said.

When I mentioned this remark to Astrid, she said that she didn't have any recollection of Wim abusing her in adulthood. She didn't dispute that it happened, though, adding, "As long as it wasn't my face, I didn't see it as hitting." Wim spat at her, shoved her, and tried to break down the door of her office. "But it was normal to me," she said. Today, Astrid recognizes the contradiction: "I had two lives. I had my own life, with my friends and my work, and I had my life with my family, in which I played a certain role." In the professional realm, she had blossomed into a vigorous, well-connected attorney. Yet, as the little sister of Wim Holleeder, she was locked into the role of the victim. Eventually, she discovered that Witzenhausen was cheating on her with women from the bordello. They split, and she began raising Miljuschka alone. It was such a clean break that neither mother nor daughter knows where Witzenhausen is today. (I tried to track him down, without success.)

But Astrid was unable to show the same strength in jettisoning her family. "I should have walked away," she said. "It would have been easier for me. But I can't let them go." She has been seeing the same therapist for nearly thirty years, and I was struck, in our conversations, by the fluid candor with which she interrogates her own decisions. At one point, she said, of her inability to break free, "Is that thrill seeking? Is that empathy? I think it's maybe both. Living a dangerous life is what I'm used to."

• • •

One spring day in 1996, Cor and Sonja drove Richie home from preschool. Before going inside, they lingered in the car: a song by Andrea Bocelli was on the radio, and Richie wanted to sing along. As he did so, Sonja saw a man approaching. He pulled out a gun and started shooting. Sonja frantically clambered out of the car, opened the rear door, and pulled Richie out of the backseat. The shooter ran off. Cor had been hit in his arm and his shoulder, and a bullet had shattered his jaw, but he survived. Astrid met them at the hospital and noticed a trail of tiny feathers leaking from a hole in Sonja's down coat. She stuck her finger in and fished out a bullet. It had lodged in the fabric and somehow missed Sonja.

As soon as Cor was released from the hospital, Wim helped to shuttle him, Sonja, and the children to France, where they went into hiding. After some investigation, Wim reported that two Amsterdam gangsters, Sam Klepper and John Mieremet, had apparently authorized the hit. It seemed that Cor and Wim had become too prominent in the Dutch underworld for their own good. According to Wim, the gangsters promised to stop pursuing Cor if he paid them a million Dutch guilders. Wim urged Cor to be pragmatic: pay the money and make the problem go away. Cor indignantly refused. While he recuperated with his family, at a French farmhouse hidden in the woods, Wim returned to Amsterdam to deal with Klepper and Mieremet.

Cor had always been the dominant personality in the criminal partnership; when they were young men, Wim picked up breakfast for him each morning. But by the time of the attempt on Cor's life, their relationship had grown strained. Peter de Vries, who saw both men during this period, told me, "They were arguing quite a lot. Willem didn't want to play his role anymore." Whereas Cor was becoming more involved in the drug trade and other criminal activity, Wim maintained that he wanted to go legit. "It was my goal to launder all my money and then quit the underworld," he later testified, adding, "I am a long-term thinker."

Another source of tension was Cor's drinking. He had a garrulous, life-of-the-party persona, but Wim—mindful, perhaps, of his father's pathologies—rarely touched alcohol. Cor acknowledged that he had a problem. Sometimes he raised a beer, flashed a sardonic smile, and said, "Heineken caught me." He, too, was physically abusive and beat Sonja. Yet it never occurred to her to leave him. "Sonja had an alcoholic father and sought an alcoholic as a man," Astrid told me. In their world, this was how men treated women.

Cor, fearful that his enemies would eventually find him, started stockpiling weapons. He told Sonja that should he be killed, he wanted a funeral with a horse-drawn carriage hearse. Wim, meanwhile, continued to pressure Cor to pay the extortion that the gangsters were demanding, to the point that Cor began to question his friend's loyalty. Wim insisted that he had only Cor's interests in mind. But Cor, disgusted, denounced Wim as a Judas. In the winter of 2000, a few days before Christmas, Cor narrowly escaped a second attempt on his life. A sniper tried to gun him down as he was about to enter his house, but he wasn't hit. The family panicked. Astrid dates some of her obsessive survival instincts to this period. "We were always expecting someone to get killed," she recalled.

One day in January 2003, Cor was chatting with an associate outside a Chinese restaurant when two men drove up on a red motorcycle and opened fire. This time, they succeeded in killing him. In accordance with his request, Cor arrived at his grave in a white carriage hearse pulled by Frisian horses. Guests rode in white limousines. Some Amsterdammers were put off by the pimped-out funeral. "It shook the whole town," Astrid recalled, adding, "We were just trying to do what he wanted." She was shattered by the murder. Cor was hardly an ideal partner or father, but Sonja and the children loved him, and Astrid had long regarded him as another brother. It may be that Cor's early death allowed the Holleeder women to sentimentalize him in a way that they cannot with Wim; in any case, Astrid and Sonja speak of Cor with great tenderness and affection.

After the murder, Wim appeared to consolidate his authority in the underworld. One by one, his criminal associates were killed. He was never explicitly connected to any of these murders, but they were a bit like the Heineken money: nobody could prove anything, but everyone assumed that he was behind the crimes. Wim began spending more time with Sonja and her family. But he made no pretense of mourning Cor; indeed, he openly denigrated him. As Richie grew into a gangly adolescent, he increasingly resembled his late father, and Wim picked on the boy, telling him that Cor had been a "nobody." Meanwhile, he suggested to Sonja that all assets tied to the Heineken kidnapping should belong to him. Unlike her, he'd taken the risk of orchestrating the operation.

In 2007, Wim was convicted of blackmailing several businessmen in Amsterdam and was sent back to prison. On his release, five years later, he became more famous in the Netherlands than ever before. He took to riding a Vespa around fashionable districts of Amsterdam and recorded a hip-hop single, "Willem is terug," or "Willem Is Back," with the Dutch rapper Lange Frans. ("I was imprisoned like an animal, and released as a man.") He began writing a boastful column in the magazine *Nieuwe Revu*, name-dropping famous acquaintances and suggesting that, having become a writer, he would now be embraced by the journalists who had "always written dirt about me." He engaged a personal paparazzo to compile images of him fraternizing with celebrities. Books about his criminal exploits, with titles like *Holleeder: The Early Years,* became a cottage industry. A film was made from de Vries's book about the Heineken kidnapping, with Anthony Hopkins playing the part of Freddy. Wim even appeared on *College Tour,* a popular Dutch television show that featured interviews with such notable figures as Bill Gates and Archbishop Desmond Tutu. The press took to describing Wim as a *knuffelcrimineel,* or "huggable criminal." When young people in Amsterdam saw him out on the town, they asked him for a selfie. One local Mob boss, a Serb named Sreten Jocić, joked that Willem Holleeder was the Netherlands' best-known product since cheese.

For Astrid, the public's embrace of her brother was confounding. One explanation was nativist nostalgia. Immigrants from Morocco and the Dutch Antilles were said to have taken over the Amsterdam underworld, and Wim was often portrayed as a member of a dying breed: the homegrown criminal. With his broad accent and white skin, Wim was a crowd-pleasing anachronism, and he was celebrated in Amsterdam in the same fashion that John Gotti was once celebrated in New York. But it seemed a bit strange to herald someone as the last of the dinosaurs when there was a distinct possibility that all the other dinosaurs were dead only because he'd killed them. People around Wim Holleeder had an alarming mortality rate. When I asked de Vries to name friends of Wim's who knew him well, he thought for a moment, then said, "Most of them are dead." The 2007 case against Wim was largely drawn from a series of clandestine interviews that a onetime associate of his, Willem Endstra, had given to Dutch investigators. Endstra estimated that Wim was responsible for two dozen murders. Wim had long boasted that he maintained paid informers in the police department; if this were true, it posed a risk for anyone who might turn on him. Not long after Endstra became a witness, he was shot to death. Wim has been charged with ordering his murder.

Astrid knew that her brother was a killer. He often turned to her for legal counsel, and for each murder in Amsterdam in which Wim might potentially be implicated, she created a detailed dossier, sketching out possible witnesses and means of discrediting them. The *knuffelcrimineel* routine was, in her estimation, an elaborate diversion. "He was laundering his past," she told me. It sickened her. Wim would arrive at her house early in the morning and insist that they step outside for a walk. She began waking up very early herself so that she'd be dressed when he showed up. Sometimes, when he needed "clean cash" to cover his expenses, she supplied it. More than once, she deliberately misled investigators in order to protect her brother. When she was subsequently questioned in court about such transgressions, she replied, "If you have to choose between having justice on your neck or Wim on your neck, you choose justice."

As one confederate of Wim's after another turned up dead, Astrid nursed a dark suspicion. Although her brother had blamed the early efforts to kill Cor van Hout on the gangsters Sam Klepper and John Mieremet, he had ended up going into business with Mieremet himself. By the time Cor was killed in 2003, Klepper had been gunned down in Amsterdam. Mieremet was murdered in Pattaya, Thailand, in 2005. The more Astrid thought through the sequence of events leading to Cor's death, the more evident it became that Klepper and Mieremet had not ordered Cor's murder. Wim had.

• • •

One Sunday morning, a driver picked me up by a canal in the center of Amsterdam, and we drove to the apartment building where Sonja lives. Astrid greeted us at the door. She had arranged to have lunch with her family and had invited me to join her. Sonja presided in the kitchen. She has honey-blond hair, a deep tan, a quiet smile, and, like Astrid, a tendency to dress in black. The apartment was spotless and furnished in white; sunlight filtered through closed blinds. Astrid is surprisingly forthright about the fact that Sonja continues to live on the proceeds of the kidnapping. "The state didn't take it away from them, and Heineken didn't start a proceeding to take it back, so it was theirs," she said. On the walls, framed photographs of Cor hung alongside pictures of Sonja posing with the stars of the film *Kidnapping Mr. Heineken*. Her children, Frances and Richie, sat at the dining room table; Stien sat on a couch by herself, carefully eating from a bowl of soup. Pastries and little cubes of cheese were passed around.

"We were fighting before you came," Astrid announced, explaining that Richie may testify against his uncle in the trial, even though Sonja thinks that he shouldn't.

Richie said, "The media makes it look like we had such a great time as a crime family, but he was a terrible man for me and my sister." He looks uncannily like his father, with long limbs, close-cropped blond hair, and a small, round face. He reminded me that he was three years old—and in the car—the first time that men tried to kill his father, and nine years old when Cor was murdered. "Now I'm twenty-five," he said.

Richie could have slipped into a life of crime himself. As the nephew of Wim Holleeder and the son of Cor van Hout, he was underworld royalty. Instead, he did what Astrid had hoped to do before the Heineken kidnapping: he left for the United States on an athletic scholarship, playing tennis at the University of San Francisco. After college, he returned to Amsterdam and set up a business as a personal trainer. But he harbored deep resentment of his uncle, he told me. "I thought about killing him," he said. "He took someone that I loved. Still love."

Several months after the 1996 assassination attempt, Cor returned from hiding in France and bought a villa in the Netherlands. Wim pressed Astrid and Sonja for details on where it was, but they resisted, having promised Cor to keep his location secret. At one point, Wim brandished a gun and pointed it at Richie, hissing, "Tell me where he is!" (Wim has called this account "a nauseating lie.") Astrid told me that her brother subscribes to the logic of Greek tragedy: he was always uneasy around the children of his victims, because they might grow up to seek vengeance. Frances, a thirty-five-year-old with a warm face and green eyes, told me that Wim used to spit when he shouted at her, but she couldn't wipe the spittle off her face, for fear of offending him. "It was tough to pretend to like him," she said. She recalled that her father's casket had been open at his funeral and that Wim had instructed the funeral director to apply extra makeup to Cor's face. "He looked like a clown," Frances said, with a bitter sob.

Astrid seemed happy to be surrounded by her family, and there was a sense of collective relief at being able to speak openly about Wim's abuse, after years of fearful silence. At the same time, it was anguishing to revisit some of these memories. Sonja did not say much but hovered near the table, refilling my coffee and making sure that everyone had enough to eat. For years, she told me, Wim worried that someone might hide an incendiary device in his car. So, whenever he wanted to drive somewhere, he instructed Sonja to go out and start the engine for him. (Wim denies this.) "Now I think, 'How could I do that?'" she said. "But I did."

Both Astrid and Sonja had long suspected that Wim had orchestrated Cor's murder, but they never spoke about it, treating the subject as another family secret. Finally, in 2012, they confided in each other and devised a plan. They asked Peter de Vries, who had become a trusted friend, if they should approach the authorities as potential witnesses. He urged caution. Wim killed people who crossed him, and if they turned on him and he found out—which he probably would, given his alleged police connections—he'd have them murdered.

But Astrid would not abandon the idea. "Wim was a suspect in murders, but they never had the proof to bring him to court," she told me. She was almost uniquely positioned to supply such proof, and as an attorney she was intimately acquainted with the rules of evidence under Dutch criminal law. She worried that if she and Sonja took the risk of becoming witnesses, it would end up being their word against his. But what if they could surreptitiously record him talking in the unfiltered and brutal fashion in which he spoke to them?

Astrid started researching hidden microphones. There was a shop in Amsterdam that specialized in spy gadgets, but she dared not go herself, she told me, because Wim went there sometimes and "he might see me." Instead, she sent a friend. Initially, she hid a small, wireless, voice-activated microphone in her bra. Wim was so distrustful that he was not above searching his sisters: she had seen him rifling through her drawers and going through her mail. But she figured that he wouldn't search his sister's décolletage.

In January 2013, she began wearing the wire on their walks. The first few times, it didn't pick up Wim's whispers, so Astrid pried apart the casing of the device, to reduce its bulk, then sewed the microphone into the collar of her jacket. This worked, and she supplied Sonja with similar equipment and coached her on how to use it. The sisters were convinced that if Wim discovered their betrayal, he would fly into a rage and beat one or both of them to death. But when I asked Sonja if she was terrified, she told me that she wasn't. Astrid chuckled. "I look like the bitch, but I'm the softy of the two of us," she said. "If you want to rob a bank, she's the one to do it." Sonja just smiled.

By the time the sisters started recording Wim, he had few confidants left. In the tabloids, he continued to play the part of the raffish bad boy. But in private conversations with Astrid and Sonja he revealed that he was consumed by paranoia and hostility. He was fixated on money and, in particular, on what was left of the Heineken ransom. In January 2013, the press reported that Sonja had reached a million-euro settlement with the Dutch state, over allegations of money laundering and tax fraud connected to Cor's estate. To Wim, the settlement suggested that Sonja was sitting on a much larger sum. In conversations she recorded, he berated her, calling her, among other epithets, a *kankerhoer,* or "cancer whore." Any hint of real or perceived defiance by the sisters provoked a torrent of abuse. "I'll kick your diseased head in," he told Sonja in one recording. "I'm a Dutch celebrity. Nobody gets to bawl me out." He raged to Astrid about Sonja, saying that if she were to betray him to the authorities he'd "beat her in the bushes," or even shoot her. Wim also warned, "If I go inside for a day, her children will go first."

Not long after we sat down to eat at Sonja's, there was a knock at the door. It was Miljuschka, Astrid's daughter, who is thirty-three and beautiful, with a mane of brown hair and Astrid's blue eyes. She is divorced, with two small children. She and her mother embraced. With only nineteen years between them, they are very close, but Miljuschka told me that it was refreshing to see Astrid in person, because these days they speak mostly on FaceTime. Miljuschka is a former model who now hosts a popular Dutch cooking show. Her celebrity adds a layer of complication to Astrid's plight: because strangers recognize Miljuschka on the street, Astrid cannot spend time in public with her daughter.

When Astrid decided to turn on Wim, she discussed the possible consequences with Miljuschka. "I told her I could get killed—and *she* could get killed," Astrid said. But Miljuschka endorsed the idea. "It's about honor," she told me. "Also, you know, doing the right thing. By deciding to testify, we are ready to die. I'm a public person. He can find me if he wants to." If she were murdered, she said, "it would be tough for my kids, but they would manage." The fact that the family can finally confront Wim feels like a "revolution," Miljuschka went on. When she was growing up, she told me, "I saw my mother working her ass off. I saw this strong woman being abused by her brother. When she told me what she was doing, that she was taping him— I'd been waiting for this moment all my life."

As we were talking, I was distracted by a stranger who had suddenly appeared in the doorway: a bald man, dressed in black, with squishy facial features. I half stood, my heart racing. Then everyone burst out laughing, and I flushed with embarrassment as Astrid, striding across the room, pulled off an intricate latex mask. She tapped me playfully on the shoulder and said, "I told you, I have disguises."

· · ·

One day in the summer of 1995, a philosophy professor in upstate New York, Linda Patrik, sat down for a difficult conversation with her husband, a social worker named David Kaczynski. She asked him, gently, if it had ever occurred to him that his brother, Ted, might be the terrorist known as the Unabomber. She'd been reading about the Unabomber's manifesto, a screed on the perils of technology, and thought that it sounded a lot like her troubled brother-in-law. Initially, David was dubious. He believed that Ted was mentally ill, but to David's knowledge he had never been violent. David began to investigate, however, and came to suspect that his wife was right. He approached the authorities, and in April 1996, Ted was arrested. David attended the subsequent court hearings, in which Ted pleaded guilty to numerous killings and was given a quadruple life sentence. Throughout the proceedings, Ted refused to look at him.

David had been anguished about his decision. "It was a feeling of being trapped," he said afterward. "Trapped in this brother relationship." If he did nothing, more people might die. If he contacted the authorities, he would likely condemn his own brother to life in prison. Many people, faced with such a test, would side with family. Antigone, in the tragedy by Sophocles, argues that loyalty to her brother trumps the laws of Thebes. During the years when the Boston hood James "Whitey" Bulger was responsible for at least eleven murders, his brother Billy served as the president of the Massachusetts State Senate, but he never turned Whitey in. Cases in which a witness voluntarily reports on a sibling are rare. "I hope that Ted will someday forgive me," David Kaczynski said after his brother's sentencing. But Ted never has.

In December 2014, Wim was arrested and charged with the murder of several gangland associates. Four months later, the Dutch newspaper *NRC Handelsblad* revealed that Astrid and Sonja had been cooperating with authorities and gathering evidence against him. The headline was "My Brother Willem Holleeder Is a Psychopath." Astrid gave an interview to the paper, calling Wim a "serial killer."

Wim was stunned by the betrayal. Later, in court, he likened it to "thunder in clear skies." The police had given Astrid and Sonja emergency buttons, which they could press if they needed help. The sisters had guided Wim, on tape, into making a series of important legal admissions. But, by releasing to the press some of the recordings of their conversations with him, they also radically upended the public image of the Nose. There was nothing huggable about the thug who screamed at members of his family and threatened to murder them. The revelations electrified the Dutch press, and an author friend of Astrid's suggested that she write a book. "It's already halfway done," she told him.

Astrid had started writing not so much to publish anything as to create an honest record of her story for Miljuschka, in case something happened to her. In her efforts to shield Miljuschka from the family legacy of dysfunction and violence, she told me, "I never spoke to her about my upbringing—about my father." Her writer friend introduced her to his publisher, Oscar van Gelderen, who was interested in Astrid's project. "It wasn't about the crimes," van Gelderen told me. "It was about the family." Astrid said that she found the act of writing cathartic but unnatural: "Normally, I wouldn't write anything down, because anything that you write down can be found!" Eventually, she handed van Gelderen a memory stick with 300,000 words on it. It was just a cascade of vivid fragments; van Gelderen would have to turn it into a book. "I had to, as we say in Dutch, 'make chocolate,'" he told me.

Astrid selected *Judas* as a title because it captured both her brother's betrayal of Cor and her betrayal of her brother. "He hates that I portrayed him as the person he does not want to see," she told me. "I'm his mirror." Van Gelderen edited the book in secrecy and arranged for it to be printed outside the Netherlands, lest the manuscript leak. And, even though Astrid was preparing to testify in the mega-trial against Wim, she elected not to inform her government handlers, much less the prosecution, that she was about to release a memoir. Shortly before publication, van Gelderen said to Astrid, "Normally, we do a party. Do you want to have a party?"

"For this?" she asked. "This isn't a party. I'm doing this to another human being. It's not a comic book."

Van Gelderen threw a party anyway. He knew a hot commodity when he saw one. He mentioned to me that he'd been an early collector of the street artist Banksy, whose identity is a closely guarded secret.

Van Gelderen understands the theater of spectacle, and he has cannily capitalized on the intrigue surrounding his author. At last year's Frankfurt Book Fair, he threw an invitation-only dinner for buyers of foreign-publication rights. When everyone was seated, Astrid strode in. "People were really in shock," van Gelderen said with a grin. *Judas* was released in the Netherlands on November 5, 2016, and the first printing—eighty thousand copies—sold out that day. Not unlike the television series *The Sopranos,* the book presented a lurid crime story in the form of an intimate domestic drama. Astrid vividly recounts the sadism of her father, who, among other cruelties, demanded that his children finish every bit of food on their plates. One night, Astrid was forced to eat so much that she vomited. He then ordered her to consume her own vomit, bellowing, "Eat it, ungrateful bitch." Astrid fainted. On regaining consciousness, she writes, "I saw my father beating my mom. She'd pulled the plate from under my nose and was being beaten for it."

Elsewhere in the book, Astrid describes a drive she took with Wim in which she brought up the murder of one of his associates. "Pull over," Wim tells her. They stop the car and walk a safe distance away, in case it is bugged. "He stands in front of me, a savage look on his face. 'We killed them all, all of them.'" (Wim denies saying this.)

A stage play and a Dutch TV adaptation of *Judas* are in the works, as is an American series, to be produced by Amblin Entertainment, Steven Spielberg's company. When Wim recently complained in court that there would soon be "a television series in America," one of the judges pointed out, "It wouldn't all fit in one episode."

Van Gelderen often speaks about Astrid's life in the snappy cadences of promotional copy. "She made a decision: if he will be the best criminal, I will be the best witness," he told me at one point. "He was unrivaled—and now he's met his rival," he said at another. Astrid possesses a similar flair. Not long ago, she told a Dutch newspaper, "Wim will rest only when I am dead. And I will rest only when he is gone. Maybe a shoot-out is the best solution: us together in one room and then, afterward, you can carry the bodies out." From time to time, I wondered if Astrid's elaborate security protocols did not themselves have an element of theater. How much danger was she in, really? Over several months, I spent some twenty hours speaking with her, and there were a few small ways in which her story evolved. When we first met, she informed me that she owned not one armored car but five and launched into an amusing—and entirely convincing—riff on the challenges of purchasing a bulletproof automobile: "If you need one, it costs a lot, but if you want to get rid of one, there's nobody who wants to buy it." She then noted that on the internet, secondhand bulletproof vehicles can be had for a song. But when I pressed her on the mechanics—Why five? Where do you keep them?—she was evasive.

At our initial meeting, she told me that she split her time between two safe houses (both comprehensively bulletproofed), and in court she gave a grim account of her life in hiding, announcing, "My daughter does not know where I live." But after visiting Sonja's place, I had another meeting with the sisters, and Astrid acknowledged in passing that "at the moment" she was living with Sonja—in the very apartment where we'd had lunch. (She has since moved to yet another safe house.) In court, Wim Holleeder has insisted that Astrid is not in peril. "I have not terrorized my family," he told the judges. Wim's denials, however, are impossible to square with the many threats that Astrid and Sonja recorded him making against them.

Jan Meeus, the Dutch journalist who broke the news that Astrid was cooperating with the authorities, told me that even without an explicit command from the Nose, an aspiring gangster might try to hunt down Astrid in order to impress him. "There are people who might think that it would look good on their CV," Meeus said.

I spoke recently with Wim's lawyer Sander Janssen, who said, "It's possible that she really believes she is in danger. For my part, it is impossible to say that she is not in danger. I would have to be godlike to have that kind of certainty." He continued, "Willem says that she is not in danger, that he is not going to hurt her." Nevertheless, Janssen acknowledged, Wim is "very angry with Astrid."

In April 2016, Wim was arrested yet again, in his prison cell, for allegedly soliciting two members of a gang known as the Curaçao No Limit Soldiers to kill Astrid, Sonja, and Peter de Vries, who is also a witness in the mega-trial. Wim dismissed the charge as "nonsense," insisting that it would not be in his "interest" to kill his sisters. The gang member who informed the authorities about the plot subsequently recanted his confession, though Astrid believes that he did so only because he, too, is afraid of Wim. A representative for the prosecutors told me that it is still their position that Wim ordered Astrid's murder. I ended up concluding that Astrid was sincere in her fear that Wim wants her dead. If she was sometimes inconsistent when I inquired about the logistics of her life, it was more likely out of a cautious disinclination to give too much away than from a desire to heighten drama. By talking to a journalist about bulletproof cars, Astrid was sending Wim a message: she'd figured out how to keep herself safe, and he shouldn't even bother trying to catch her. She was terrified by the news about the Curaçao No Limit Soldiers, she told me. The notion that Wim might enlist a street gang, rather than discreet assassins, struck her as a sign of desperation—an indication that he'd do anything to kill her. She doesn't trust the Dutch authorities, whom she derides as "amateurs," to protect her. Not long after she and Sonja were given their panic buttons, the sisters discovered that the buttons didn't work. But, despite her dread about being a target, she was not entirely displeased when she was informed that Wim had made plans to assassinate her. Some people had dismissed her as a hysteric. Now, perhaps, they would believe her.

• • •

One day in March, I took a taxi to the western edge of Amsterdam and passed through a line of onlookers and a cordon of security, arriving at the press gallery of the Bunker. The proceedings of the mega-trial are spread out over many months and presided over by three judges. As the hearing commenced, one of them joked, "The courtroom is not a theater, although it sometimes looks like one."

Wim Holleeder sat at a long table facing the judges. He was dressed casually, in a dark pullover, and he fidgeted and whispered with his lawyers. Then, from behind a screen, Astrid's commanding voice filled the room. Having practiced law for so many years, she was on a first-name basis with the attorneys and the judges, and she spoke in spirited, peppery Dutch, occasionally sliding into Jordaanese vernacular when her emotions got the better of her. At one point, Sander Janssen, Wim's lawyer, interrupted her, and she snapped, "You're not letting me talk."

"But there's no *end* to it," Janssen protested. "You keep talking!"

At the outset, the prosecution had announced, "The man on trial is not a master criminal or a huggable criminal but a cold, everyday kidnapper." Whenever Astrid was giving testimony, Wim performed a symphony of passive-aggressive gestures: shifting in his chair, shaking his head, taking off his eyeglasses and twirling them like a propeller. His lawyers have asserted that he was only a minor figure on the periphery of the Amsterdam underworld who, through sheer coincidence, became acquainted with a multitude of people who happened to have met tragic ends. Janssen told me, "The prosecution's theory is 'Ultimate criminal kills everybody,' but, of course, it is not that simple. There is really not very much evidence linking him to these murders."

A major strategy of the defense was to read the transcripts of cordial conversations between Wim and his siblings that were captured by police wiretaps. When Sonja was challenged in court to account for her warm tone toward her brother, she retorted, "He killed Cor. What do you think, man, that I'm going to contradict him?" As for the many recordings in which Wim was threatening or abusive, the defense maintained that he had simply been trying to "scare" or "persuade" his sisters. He might have spouted the odd empty threat, but he never intended to batter or to kill anyone. Epithets like "cancer whore" might be inelegant, but they were part of his native idiom. "Every bird sings in the way it was raised," Wim declared in court. "I am Willem, a boy from the street."

Wim has argued that he is actually the *victim* in this family saga: a devoted, unwitting brother tricked by his conniving sisters into making verbal indiscretions. He warned the judges not to be fooled by "the games that Astrid plays" and characterized the entire proceeding— including the hundreds of hours of secretly recorded conversations— as a spectacle that she'd engineered. Her testimony was a show, he said: "the Jordaan cabaret."

Astrid told me, "If this case were decided by jury, he would probably win, because he's so charismatic." Wim is an earthy presence in court, joking with the judges, guffawing at statements he disputes, and murmuring remarks out of turn. "I do not care about money at all," he said at one point.

"That's quite a statement from someone who has kidnapped people to get millions," one of the judges replied.

Without skipping a beat, Wim said, "I had to start somewhere."

But when the subject turned to Cor, Wim had no good-guy routine; he seemed unable even to feign compassion. "That man was really impossible," he said. "If you did not quarrel with him, something was wrong with you." At one point, the defense played a recording in which Wim informed Sonja that he had no intention of killing her children.

"To him, that's empathy," Astrid told me later, with amazement. "He *wanted* his lawyer to play that tape. No lawyer in his right mind would play that tape! You're talking about *not* killing your sister's children? So the other option is . . . killing them? Is that normal? If I had done this case, I would have done it totally differently," she said, shaking her head. "Normally, he has me."

Astrid knows Wim's lawyers and thinks that they're good, leading her to suspect that he's been ignoring their advice. When I relayed this to Janssen, he called it an "insult in disguise." But he conceded that Wim is a "very strong character" who "knows what he wants." Before every court date, Astrid forms a game plan for her testimony, then thinks about how Wim might react to each move she makes. But she knows that he is probably sitting in his cell, playing a similar game of conjectural chess, trying to anticipate how *she* will react to *his* stratagems. "I can't see my brother in the courtroom, but I can hear him," she told me. "He's maybe two or three meters away from me. I can hear his laugh. I can predict everything he is going to do."

Astrid has not spoken with Wim outside the courtroom in more than three years. I asked her if she felt as though she were still communicating with him.

"I am," she said.

• • •

After Salman Rushdie published *The Satanic Verses* in 1988, the Ayatollah Khomeini of Iran declared the book blasphemous and issued a fatwa urging Muslims to murder him. Rushdie spent the next decade in hiding, under round-the-clock police protection, a life that he later described as "a fretful, scuttling existence." In 1998, the Iranian government announced that it was no longer enforcing the fatwa, and the danger to Rushdie subsided. The threat to Astrid Holleeder is

much more limited—only one person wants her dead—and I wondered about the circumstances in which she might one day be able
to emerge from hiding. If Wim's trial ends in a conviction, he will
likely be imprisoned for the rest of his life. But when I asked her if she
would be safe at that point, she said, "No. There's no happy ending. I
know him very well. As long as he has the slightest hope of freedom,
we have a chance to live. But as soon as he hears the life sentence, it
will be only revenge." In his cell, there will be nothing to focus on but
retaliation. "I will pay for what I've done," she concluded. "Even if he
kills my kid or kills Sonja, because he can't get to me." Sonja agrees:
"Even if he's convicted, he will not let us be."

Astrid speaks about this alarming prospect in her customary
straightforward manner, with no trace of indignation. "If I were in
his shoes, being betrayed like that, I would do the same," she said. "I
would kill him." While the mega-trial grinds on, Astrid is furthering
her publishing career. In October 2017, she released a second book,
Diary of a Witness, an account of her time in hiding, and she is working
on a third book, the subject of which she will not disclose. In court,
Wim has suggested that Astrid was always obsessed with money and
fame and that she is shamelessly exploiting her family's story. "Now
she has plenty of money," he said. "She will notice that it does not
make people happy." Astrid has responded, angrily, that she made a
very comfortable living as an attorney. But she freely acknowledges
that she hopes to sell as many books as possible, because the profits
might provide a means of escape. She mentioned to me several times
that she would like to move her extended family out of the Netherlands, perhaps to America.

Another potential outcome, which the Holleeder sisters are trying
not to dwell on, is an acquittal. Thus far, the mega-trial has unfolded
very much on Wim's terms. Weeks of testimony have been devoted
to analysis of the recorded conversations, and to scrutiny of his sisters, from Sonja's finances to Astrid's sex life. When Janssen alleged
that Astrid had been romantically linked to a prominent drug trafficker, she denied it with a tart riposte: "Have you seen me fucking
him?" Janssen conceded, primly, that he had not. Later, Astrid told
me, "These lawyers want to have a discussion with me, but they aren't

from the street, so I fuck with them. I can talk dirty all day. The judges are confused, because they know me as a lawyer."

Astrid might cherish the clarity and order of the law, but the trial feels like a circus. Astrid and Sonja are under oath, because they are witnesses, but Wim, as a defendant, is not, and he freely makes misleading statements and throws out red herrings. Even with three judges, the court seems incapable of constraining the hullabaloo. "You are a fabulist, a liar, and a parasite!" Wim barked at Astrid a few weeks ago. "You destroyed my life!" Astrid shouted back. "I should have shot you through the head!" Family tension was on abundant display at the trial, but I was surprised to hear relatively few details about the murders of which Wim stood accused. When I asked Astrid about this imbalance, she explained that in a Dutch criminal case, due process can be taken to extremes: "They don't want to have a European court reverse them and say that they didn't give him every opportunity to defend himself. So they give him a lot of space."

A verdict is unlikely before next year, and Astrid noted to me that one Dutch criminal trial lasted a decade. For now at least, Wim's mega-trial has been hijacked by psychodrama. When I asked Astrid about her outburst regarding shooting Wim in the head, she said that he had been provoking her with the tone of his voice, in a manner that others in the courtroom couldn't recognize. (One of the judges subsequently admonished both siblings for their theatrics.) During the lunch at Sonja's house, Astrid's niece, Frances, had mused, "It would have been nice to prosecute him in the U.S."

"It would have been nice to prosecute him in Iran," Astrid replied.

At times, Astrid seemed to be manipulating the proceedings with an aplomb to match her brother's. She made it clear to me—and to Wim, in court—that she has not supplied prosecutors with all her recordings. She'd made a habit of taping not just Wim but anyone who might later be inclined to lie about her. "The problem with criminals is that they change their stories," she told me. "They're like whores. They'll spread their legs for whoever pays." In her testimony, she has suggested that if other witnesses lie, she may unveil further recordings, in order to impeach their testimony. "Wim knows I know about other murders," she said. "This is my insurance. If anything happens to my children or my grandchildren, the tapes will come out." Once, in court, when she felt that the judges were not giving her adequate time to speak, she threatened, "If you do not let me finish, I'll put everything I cannot tell you here on YouTube, and then we will have a public resource that everyone can take notice of."

Sander Janssen suggested that part of the reason that the trial is dragging on is the weakness of the prosecution's case. "If you have a murder weapon and someone's DNA on it, you don't need all this testimony," he noted. Astrid and Sonja, he continued, were basically saying, "We know he did this, because we've lived with him all his life." But, Janssen said, it wasn't clear why anyone should trust them: "Willem says we should regard them not as normal female citizens but as fellow criminals, which they have been, from day one." I asked him what would possibly motivate the sisters to frame their brother for murder at such high personal cost. "That will be one of the most important questions for the court to answer," Janssen replied, adding, vaguely, "We are still investigating."

Astrid is confident in her trove of evidence. She has recordings of Wim obliquely acknowledging his role in the murder of Cor and in other slayings and naming one of the individuals who was directly involved in killing Cor. But in many of their exchanges Wim stopped short of an explicit confession. I wondered what would happen if, by some slim chance, Astrid's testimony and recordings are not enough. What if the risks that she and Sonja undertook do not result in a conviction, and Wim gets off?

"Then I'll have to kill him," she said. "I should have done it years ago."

Astrid's mother, Stien, is eighty-two. Two years ago, she wrote a letter to an official at the prison where Wim is being held, saying that, should she succumb to illness, "I under no circumstances want Willem Holleeder to be able to visit me at the hospital or come to say goodbye at my funeral." She continued, "The reason is that I know that my other children, grandchildren, and great-grandchildren would be in danger if he were allowed to leave prison." Nevertheless, Astrid told me, her mother hasn't entirely let go of Wim. She used to hang on to pocket money for him so that he could pay his bills, and she still keeps €1,500 of his in an envelope in a drawer. As Astrid told me this, her eyes were rimmed with tears. "Sonja says, 'Throw it out,' and my mother says, 'No, because maybe he'll need it,' and I'm like, 'He's not going to need it.'" She continued, "There is no sense of revenge. I don't even feel hate. I hated my father. I never had contact with him again. But with Wim it's different, because he's in my system."

In one of our final conversations, I asked Astrid what she would say to Wim if they could speak to each other outside the tense arena of the courtroom. "That I still love him, in spite of everything," she said. "That I wish he could be a brother to me. And, yeah, that I could take him home."

In July 2019, Wim Holleeder was convicted of five murders, including the killing of Cor van Hout. Astrid has continued to write. She still lives in hiding.

THE AVENGER

*Has the brother of a victim of the Lockerbie
bombing finally solved the case?* (2015)

WHEN KEN DORNSTEIN FIRST learned that Pan Am Flight 103
had exploded, he did not realize that his older brother, David, was
on the plane. It was December 22, 1988, and Ken, a sophomore at
Brown University, was at home in Philadelphia on winter break. Over
breakfast, he read about the disaster in the *Inquirer:* all 259 passengers
and crew were killed, along with 11 residents of Lockerbie, Scotland,
where flaming debris from the plane fell from the sky. David, who
was twenty-five, had been living in Israel and was not scheduled to fly
home until later that week, so Ken absorbed the details of the crash
with the detached sympathy that one accords a stranger's tragedy.
That evening, the airline called. David had changed his plans in order
to come home early and surprise his family.

Ken's father, Perry, took the call. A successful physician, Perry was
a stern and withdrawn parent; David had been boundlessly expres-
sive, forever writing in a notebook or a journal. Their relationship had
often been strained, and now the tensions between them could never
be resolved. Ken felt that his father's loss was "unspeakable," and so
they didn't speak about it. Ken's sister, Susan, told me that after the
funeral Perry rarely mentioned David's name again. A hundred and
eighty-nine of the victims were American, and as news outlets across
the country memorialized the dead, Ken felt that siblings "didn't rank
very highly" among surviving relatives. But he had adored David.
Their parents had divorced when Ken was a toddler, and their mother,
Judy, had struggled with mental illness and addiction. David had
become protective of Ken and had mentored him when he expressed
an interest in writing. After the crash, Ken found a box among David's
possessions labeled "The Dave Archives"; it was stuffed with journals,
stories, poetry, and plays. David had always seen himself as being on

the verge of a celebrated literary career. Not long after his death, a local paper ran an obituary suggesting that he had written a novel in Israel. To Ken's surprise, his father was quoted as saying, "He was about to submit the first part for publication." This wasn't true, and Ken was dismayed that his father had "rounded up" David's literary achievements. (Perry Dornstein died in 2010, Judy in 2013.) Ken arranged the journals chronologically and sorted the manuscripts into color-coded files. The process was eerie: David had sometimes suggested, mischievously, that he was destined to die young, and in the margins of his notebooks Ken discovered winking asides "for the biographers."

When terrorists strike today, they often claim credit on social media. But Lockerbie, Dornstein told me recently, was a "murder mystery." Flight 103 had left London for New York on December 21, with David assigned to row 40 of the economy section. After the plane ascended to thirty thousand feet, an electronic timer activated an explosive device hidden inside a Toshiba radio in the luggage hold, and a lump of Semtex detonated, shearing open the fuselage. The plane broke apart in midair, six miles above the earth. Many of the victims remained alive until the moment they hit the ground. But who built the bomb? Who placed it in the radio? Who put it on the plane?

For years, Dornstein said little to his friends or family about Lockerbie or about his brother. But he began applying the same quiet compulsiveness that he had channeled into the Dave Archives to the larger riddle of the bombing. He clipped articles, pored over archival footage, and sought out people who had known David. One day, at Penn Station in Manhattan, he spotted Kathryn Geismar, who had dated David for two years. They ended up on the same train, stayed in touch, and eventually fell in love. Initially, Ken hid the romance from his family, fearful that they might consider it an "unholy way to grieve." But the relationship didn't revolve around David; part of what comforted Ken about being with Geismar was that he didn't need to talk with her about his loss. She already knew.

After college, Dornstein moved to Los Angeles and took a job at a detective agency. His colleagues knew nothing of his brother, but he privately took solace from accumulating investigative skills. "I was interested in the tradecraft of how you *find* people," he recalled. He wondered about the shadowy culprits behind the Lockerbie bombing. "I wasn't a worldly person, I hadn't traveled," he told me. "But I kept thinking, These guys are out there."

• • •

When the FBI dispatched agents to Scotland, it was the largest terrorism investigation in U.S. history. Debris from the plane had spread so widely that the crime scene spanned nearly nine hundred square miles. Initially, suspicion fell on a Palestinian terrorist group that operated out of Syria and was backed by Iran. But when Department of Justice prosecutors announced the results of the U.S. investigation in November 1991, they indicted two intelligence operatives from Libya. Prosecutors said that the Libyans had placed the bomb in a Samsonite suitcase and routed it, as unaccompanied baggage, on a plane that went from Malta to Frankfurt. It was then flown to London, where it was transferred onto Pan Am 103.

Throughout the 1980s, Libya was a major state sponsor of terrorism. President Ronald Reagan referred to the Libyan leader, Muammar Qaddafi, as "the mad dog of the Middle East." In 1986, after Libyan terrorists detonated a bomb at a Berlin disco that was popular with American soldiers, Reagan authorized air strikes on Tripoli and Benghazi. Qaddafi narrowly survived the bombing, which killed dozens, and some observers later speculated that Lockerbie was Qaddafi's deadly riposte to this assassination attempt. But when the indictments were announced, Qaddafi denied any Libyan involvement. He refused to turn over the two Libyan defendants until 1998, when he allowed them to stand trial at a special tribunal in the Netherlands. More than two hundred people appeared on the stand, but the testimony of one of the prosecutors' key witnesses proved unreliable, and the prosecution's case against the operatives was largely circumstantial. One of the suspects, Lamin Fhimah, was acquitted. The other, a bespectacled man named Abdelbaset al-Megrahi, was sentenced to life in prison. He was the only suspect to be convicted of the bombing.

Dornstein believed that Megrahi was guilty—but that he had not acted alone. In 2003, Qaddafi released a carefully worded statement allowing that Libya might have been responsible for the blast, and he established a $2.7 billion fund to compensate the victims. But he never acknowledged authorizing Lockerbie. Brian Murtagh, the lead American prosecutor on the case, admitted to me that the plotters of the attack had eluded his grasp. "Our mandate was to try to indict everybody we could indict, not everybody we suspected," he said. Dornstein recalls asking himself, "How could such a big act of mass murder have no author?"

Dornstein married Geismar, a psychologist, in 1997, and they settled in Somerville, Massachusetts. Ken began working for the PBS show *Frontline*, producing documentaries about Afghanistan and Iran. He developed a reputation as a tirelessly analytical researcher. All the while, he kept thinking about Pan Am 103. He traveled to Scotland and spent several weeks in Lockerbie interviewing investigators and walking through the pastures where the plane had gone down. He read the transcript of the Scottish Fatal Accident Inquiry, which exceeded fifteen thousand pages, and he located the patch of grass where David's body had landed. In 2006 he published a book, *The Boy Who Fell Out of the Sky*. It was a tribute to David, drawing on his journals and other writings. "David left so many things behind, the beginnings of things," Richard Suckle, a longtime friend of the family, told me. "In writing the book, it was as if Kenny had found a way that the two of them could collaborate." The book also explores, with bracing self-awareness, Dornstein's drive to investigate: "I had found a less painful way to miss my brother, by not missing him at all, just trying to document what happened to his body."

In 2009, Abdelbaset al-Megrahi was released from a Scottish prison, after serving only eight years. He had developed prostate cancer, and over strong objections from the Obama administration the Scottish government had granted him compassionate release. He returned to Libya, where he was greeted as a hero. Dornstein couldn't suppress the feeling that Megrahi was literally getting away with murder. He suspected that other perpetrators remained at large in Libya. The lead Scottish investigator on the case, Stuart Henderson, gave him a list of eight "unindicted co-conspirators" who had never been captured. He told Dornstein that if he could get to Libya, it might be possible to track down the men who were responsible. But Qaddafi was still running a police state, and it was too risky for Dornstein to go there and ask questions about Lockerbie. Then, in 2011, revolution broke out.

That summer, as rebels gained territory, Dornstein told Geismar that he wanted to make a film in which he traveled to Libya and confronted culprits who were still alive. Dornstein was not a habitual risk taker: though he had worked with many war reporters, he didn't frequent conflict zones himself. He and Geismar had two children, and he respected her right to object. But in his marriage, he told me, there is something called "the Lockerbie dispensation."

"As a wife, I didn't want him to go," Geismar told me. "But as a friend, I knew he needed to."

• • •

One day last November, I met Dornstein at his house on a leafy street in Somerville. At forty-six, with a slight build and a boyish flush in his cheeks, he looks remarkably like the older brother whose image was trapped in time at twenty-five. Dornstein ushered me up to the third floor, where two cramped rooms were devoted to Lockerbie. In one room, shelves were lined with books about espionage, aviation, terrorism, and the Middle East. Jumbo binders housed decades of research. In the other room, Dornstein had papered the walls with mug shots of Libyan suspects. Between the two rooms was a large map of Lockerbie, with hundreds of colored pushpins indicating where the bodies had fallen. He showed me a cluster where first-class passengers landed, and another where most of the economy passengers were found. Like the coroner in a police procedural, Dornstein derives such clinical satisfaction from his work that he can narrate the grisliest findings with cheerful detachment. Motioning at a scattering of pushpins some distance from the rest, he said, "They were the youngest, smallest children. If you look at the physics of it, they were carried by the wind."

Before setting off for Libya, Dornstein sat his own children down for dinner. They had always known that they had an uncle who died, but they were unaware of the precise circumstances of his death. Now Dornstein told them the story, and explained that even though Libya was in tumult, he wanted to make a documentary there. He filmed the exchange. "Would you do it, even if it meant leaving your kids who you love so much and your wife and your life together?" he asked. His son Sam, who was eleven at the time, said, "To find the culprit? It would mean a lot to me."

When I watched the scene later, it seemed staged. But Dornstein insisted that it wasn't. "It's the producer in me," he said. "I wanted their natural reactions."

Dornstein enlisted Tim Grucza, an Australian cameraman with experience in conflict zones. By this point, Dornstein had left his job at *Frontline* and was financing the film himself. This posed a challenge: he needed to pay for everything in cash, because Libya lacked functioning banks, and the wartime rates at the Tripoli Radisson were exorbitant. But Dornstein had funds at his disposal—he could draw on the money that his family had received from the Lockerbie fund set up by Qaddafi. "Some people in Libya would try to shut down discussion about Lockerbie by saying, essentially, 'We paid the money; the file is closed,'" Dornstein said. Some relatives of Lockerbie victims refer to the payment as blood money. "The money is supposed to be the end of it for them. But for me the money was the beginning, because it enabled me to try to get what I really wanted—the story." When I asked Grucza what he thought of Dornstein's conviction that he could track down terrorists in Libya, he replied, with a chuckle, "I figured he was either completely insane or pretty much right."

In September 2011, Dornstein flew to Tunisia and paid a man to drive through the night and escort him across the Libyan border. Disconcertingly, the driver pulled one beer after another from a cooler that he kept behind the front seat. But by the morning they had arrived safely in Tripoli. Dornstein and Grucza needed a local fixer, and they connected with Suliman Ali Zway, a young man from Benghazi who had worked as a stringer for *The New York Times* and other publications. Conditions in Libya were unstable—warplanes had been bombing regime strongholds, and Qaddafi was on the run—and there had been talk of delaying the trip. But in Grucza's experience this was the moment to strike. "You go in while it's chaotic," he told me.

Ali Zway guided Dornstein and Grucza into bombed-out villas and abandoned intelligence bunkers, where they searched for clues about Lockerbie. "At first, I thought they were just another TV crew coming to do a quick story," Ali Zway told me. "I didn't understand the obsession until later." Over the course of three trips to Libya, Dornstein sought out the eight men on his list. One by one, he struck them off. Abdullah Senussi, Qaddafi's chief of intelligence and one of the likely architects of the bombing, had fled Tripoli and disappeared; Dornstein visited his villa and found a crater in the center of it, where a missile had struck. Said Rashid—a cousin of Megrahi, the convicted terrorist—had remained a central figure in the regime, but when revolution broke out, he was shot, in an execution that many suspect Qaddafi had ordered.

In October 2011, Qaddafi himself was discovered by rebels and murdered. At the time, he was hiding out with Ezzadin Hinshiri, who was also on Dornstein's list. The rebels shot Hinshiri, too.

At one point, Dornstein visited Libyan state television and found a skeleton crew still working there. In the archives, he discovered footage that had been recorded when Megrahi returned to Libya from Scotland: Megrahi slowly descends the stairs from the airplane, waving to a crowd that had turned out to greet him. When he boarded the plane in Scotland, he had been hunched over, his face wrapped in a white scarf, looking like an invalid. But when he disembarked, he was dressed in a double-breasted suit with a pink tie and a pocket square. Megrahi was expected to die soon after he was released, but he was still alive in 2011, ensconced with his family in a large villa in Tripoli. Dornstein asked several times to meet Megrahi, but was rebuffed. On one occasion, he and Grucza drove to the villa and were turned away at the front gate. When Dornstein climbed back into their van, he slammed his fist into the seat in front of him. "I've never seen Ken so upset—really physically angry," Grucza said. Then, that December, an Englishman named Jim Swire came to Tripoli.

Swire is perhaps the most famous member of the Lockerbie bereaved. His daughter, Flora, was killed, and he was so devastated that he abandoned his medical practice and devoted himself to understanding how the bombing happened. Swire helped persuade Qaddafi to allow Megrahi and Fhimah to be tried in the Netherlands, and Swire attended nearly every day of the trial. But as he watched the evidence unfold, he came to believe that Libya had not actually been responsible for the bombing—and that both defendants were innocent.

After Megrahi was imprisoned in Scotland, he and Swire developed an unlikely friendship. Like most of the American officials who investigated the case, Ken Dornstein believed in Megrahi's guilt. But he recognized a kinship in Swire's profound engagement with the intricacies of the tragedy. Swire, he learned, had come to Libya in order to pay a final visit to Megrahi, whose condition was worsening. Swire, a slim man in his late seventies, with a gently emphatic manner, allowed him to come along for the visit. Adopting the role of open-minded investigator, Dornstein asked Swire questions and remained vague about his own conclusions. "He was used to being chronicled," Dornstein said. "And I naturally like to keep myself out of things."

Cameras would not be welcome in Megrahi's villa; a CNN reporter had recently climbed the front wall. But Dornstein knew that any confrontation with Megrahi would be an important moment in his film. He was haunted by a detail in *Manhunt*, a book by Peter Bergen about the pursuit of Osama bin Laden. A Pakistani journalist, Hamid Mir, had secured an interview with bin Laden in the wake of September 11. After instructing Mir to turn off his tape recorder, bin Laden had acknowledged ordering the attack. But when Mir turned his recorder back on, bin Laden said, "I'm not responsible." What if Megrahi whispered a confession on his deathbed and Dornstein had no record of it? Before heading to the villa, he concealed a camera lens in a custom-made button on the front of a black shirt. The camera was affixed to his chest with surgical tape and connected by a thin wire to a receiver that was hidden in his boot.

A dark-eyed young man greeted Dornstein and Swire at the front entrance. It was Megrahi's son Khaled. He escorted them into an expansive compound with a swimming pool. But when they reached the main house, Khaled told Dornstein, "Only one," and made him wait on the porch while Swire went in to see Megrahi. Flustered, Dornstein asked to use the bathroom. He stepped inside and looked at himself in the mirror. Megrahi was in the next room. Dornstein could have barged in—but he didn't. When I asked Geismar why she thought that her husband had not forced a confrontation with

Megrahi, she said, "Ken has too much respect for Swire to do that." She went on, "He may disagree with Swire's conviction that Megrahi is innocent, but he respects the process that Swire had to go through to get to that conclusion, and he wasn't going to interfere with that moment." Dornstein was convinced that Jim Swire had devoted his life to a misguided effort to exonerate the man who killed his daughter. There was tragedy in that, but for Swire there was also meaning—and sustenance similar to what Dornstein had derived from his own investigations. Later, when Dornstein inquired about the meeting, Swire told him that Megrahi, as a dying wish, had asked Swire to keep fighting to clear his name. "There were tears on both sides," Swire said.

Badri Hassan, a close friend of Megrahi's, was another name on Dornstein's list. He, too, died—of a heart attack—before Dornstein could confront him. But Dornstein tracked down his widow, Suad, a middle-aged woman with nervous eyes and long black hair. Over several meetings at her family home, she told Dornstein that she had long nursed a suspicion that her husband had been involved in Lockerbie. She had asked him about it repeatedly, yet he never confessed. "But I'm absolutely sure of it," she said.

When Dornstein revealed that his brother had been on the plane, Suad was visibly moved. "Badri left behind such suffering," she murmured. Unlike the others on Dornstein's list, who were spies or government officials, Hassan had been a civilian, working for Libyan Airlines. Suad's brother, Yaseen el-Kanuni, told Dornstein that for more than a year prior to the bombing, Hassan and Megrahi had rented an office together in Switzerland. "You would get a lot of information out of a certain Swiss person," he said. "Mr. Bollier. He's located in Zurich."

• • •

After Flight 103 went down, hundreds of Scottish police constables scoured the countryside, inch by inch, collecting evidence. Miles outside Lockerbie, a fragment of the circuit board from the bomb's timing device was discovered. This plastic shard, which was smaller than a fingernail, was embedded in a shirt collar, and investigators deduced that the shirt had been wrapped around the radio containing the device. They traced the label on the shirt to a shop in Malta, and this clue led them to suspect Megrahi, who had been in Malta the day before the blast. The owner of the shop subsequently recalled Megrahi's buying the shirt.

The FBI sent photographs of the circuit-board fragment to the CIA, which often examines the components of explosive devices linked to radical groups. A technical analyst at the agency thought that the Lockerbie timer looked familiar. In Togo in 1986, after an attempted coup that Libya was accused of backing, authorities discovered an arms cache that included two custom-made timing devices. In a separate incident in early 1988, two Libyan operatives were stopped at an airport in Senegal with a time bomb. All these timers appeared to have been made by the same hand. On the circuit board of one of the timers, CIA investigators discovered a tiny brand name that had been partially scratched out: "MEBO."

MEBO is a boutique electronics company based in Zurich and operated by a man named Edwin Bollier. When FBI officials approached Bollier, they found him to be remarkably cooperative. He flew to Quantico, Virginia, in February 1991 and was debriefed by U.S. officials for five days. They showed him the fragment found in Lockerbie, and he identified it as part of a set of timers that he had sold to Libya several years earlier. When I visited Dornstein in Somerville, he showed me a declassified copy of the original FBI report; it revealed, he said, that Bollier "had even gone to Libya" to help the regime develop bomb timers. In Libya, Bollier met a colonel who instructed him on the kinds of timers that the regime required, explaining that the timers were intended for bombs. The colonel, Bollier told investigators, was "very dark-skinned." Bollier also informed the agents that two nights before the Lockerbie crash he visited the office of Megrahi—the convicted terrorist—in Tripoli and saw several Libyan "thugs" huddled in discussion. According to the FBI account, Bollier believed that this meeting "could have been part of the preparations for the Pan Am Flight 103 bombing."

Bollier then made it clear that he would be happy to serve as a witness in court, adding that he hoped the United States could pay him for his efforts. He also wondered if American intelligence agencies might have some use for his technical expertise. "Bollier had this whole notion that he was going to be the new Q for the CIA," Dornstein said. But by the time of the trial in the Netherlands, a decade later, Bollier had realized that the U.S. government had no intention of partnering with him—and he changed his story. On the stand, he recanted his original statements to the FBI, insisting that the fragment found outside Lockerbie had been doctored to frame him.

"The problem was that Bollier was treated like a witness," Dornstein said. "He should have been treated like a suspect."

In the fall of 2012, Dornstein flew to Zurich. Bollier still works out of the same building where he made the timer that was used in Lockerbie. Dornstein, relying on his charm, persuaded him to spend a few days talking on camera. But Bollier, a beady-eyed man in his seventies, was not an easy interview. He met any suggestion of a disparity between his story and the accepted facts with a cryptic smile, saying, "It's *curious*." Bollier acknowledged selling timers and other electronic equipment to the Qaddafi regime, telling Dornstein that his dealings with the Libyans made him "very, very rich." But he denied knowing that the timers were used in terrorist attacks. It was no crime to deal with Libya, he insisted: "Switzerland is neutral, and I'm neutral in this thing."

Bollier admitted knowing Megrahi and Badri Hassan and pointed to an office down the hall, which they had rented prior to the Lockerbie bombing. But when Dornstein asked if he believed that Megrahi had been involved in the bombing, Bollier shook his head dismissively. Megrahi was a "tip-top" man, he said. Bollier acknowledged that at one point in Libya he had been taken to the desert, where Qaddafi's military was testing bombs and timers. "Can you see why it's suspicious?" Dornstein said. "It looks like you are helping the Libyans make the bomb that blew up Flight 103." Bollier smiled. "I have nothing to do with Pan Am," he said.

Dornstein then pressed Bollier about his claim to the FBI that he'd met a colonel in Libya who had "very dark skin." This sounded like a man who had been a recurring, if mysterious, figure in Dornstein's research. Dornstein had discovered a declassified CIA cable that described a Libyan technical expert named Abu Agila Mas'ud who had traveled with Megrahi to Malta in December 1988. According to the cable, which was based on an interview with an informant, Mas'ud was "a tall black Libyan male who is approximately 40 to 45 years of age." Was this the same man Bollier had encountered?

Consulting the evidence from the Lockerbie trial, Dornstein found
Maltese immigration records that included Mas'ud's Libyan passport
number: 835004. If this was the technical expert, perhaps he was the
person who had actually made the Lockerbie bomb. "I remember
there was a black colonel," Bollier told Dornstein. "Dark skin, yes." In
his recollection, however, the man was short. "Do you remember his
name?" Dornstein asked. Bollier didn't. "Was the dark-skinned man
called Abu Agila Mas'ud?"

"No," Bollier replied. (In an email, Bollier told me that any suggestion that he was linked to the destruction of Pan Am 103 is a "despi-
cable accusation" and a "fictional idea." His email address, which I
discovered on his website, is Mr.Lockerbie@gmail.com.)

Everywhere Dornstein went in Libya, he asked people if they
knew of Mas'ud. Nobody said yes. "We kept hitting brick walls," Ali
Zway recalled. "We weren't even sure he existed." The name sounded
as if it could be a nom de guerre or an alias, Tim Grucza said, adding,
"He seemed like a ghost." As it happened, Scottish investigators had
also come across the name. But in 1999, when some of them were permitted to enter Libya and question government ministers, the officials
refused to confirm or deny that Mas'ud existed.

• • •

When a bomb ripped through the La Belle discotheque in Berlin on
April 5, 1986, the walls caved in and the dance floor collapsed into
the basement. Three people were killed and 229 were injured; two
American servicemen died, and more than 50 were wounded. Afterward, the National Security Agency intercepted communications
indicating that the attack had been carried out by spies operating out
of the Libyan embassy in East Berlin. A few years later, after Germany reunited, a Berlin prosecutor named Detlev Mehlis accessed
files revealing that the Stasi had been tracking the La Belle terrorists
before and after the attacks. Mehlis identified one of the key perpetrators: Musbah Eter, a baby-faced Libyan operative who had been
posted in East Berlin. But Eter had fled the country. Then, one day
in 1996, Eter walked into the German embassy in Malta and turned
himself in. Before leaving Berlin, he had fallen in love with a German
woman and fathered a daughter, and now he was looking for a way

back to Germany, even if it meant serving time in prison. Mehlis flew to Malta to debrief Eter. They met for beers at a Holiday Inn, and Eter gave a full confession. In 2001, he was convicted of the La Belle bombing, along with three associates.

After Dornstein's pursuit of perpetrators in Libya came up empty, he widened his purview to look at the broader community of Libyan terrorists who had been operating during the 1980s. He decided to consult the Stasi files about the La Belle bombing. At the spy agency's former headquarters, in an imposing edifice in East Berlin, he found that intelligence reports were archived on hundreds of thousands of little cards. Examining the surveillance files for the La Belle disco bombers, Dornstein discovered, along with the names of Eter and his co-conspirators, several references to Abu Agila Mas'ud—the bomb technician. He had apparently arrived in Berlin before the attack, and after the blast he had stayed in room 526 of Berlin's Metropol Hotel. Mas'ud employed code names and aliases, the files noted. But the Stasi knew the number of his Libyan passport: 835004. It was a perfect match for the number that Dornstein had found in the Maltese immigration records.

"When the Americans investigated Lockerbie, they had suspects, but they didn't know the roles everyone played," Dornstein said. "The Stasi knew who was who. They knew that Mas'ud showed up in Berlin right before La Belle." Dornstein tracked down Mehlis, the German prosecutor, who told him that Musbah Eter, the La Belle terrorist, had spoken about Mas'ud when he confessed at the Holiday Inn in Malta. According to Eter, Mas'ud had brought the La Belle bomb to the Libyan embassy in East Berlin and instructed him on how to arm it. Mehlis showed Dornstein a piece of stationery from the Holiday Inn, upon which Eter had written "AbuGela" alongside the German word "Neger" (Negro).

Dornstein learned that Eter had been released from a German prison and had stayed in Berlin, where he ran a restaurant. Eter is a diminutive man in his fifties, with a streak of white in his black hair and a fondness for ascots. When Dornstein met him, in late 2012, he was working with the new rebel government in Libya to find medical care in Germany for veterans of the revolution. Dornstein did not initially make it clear to Eter that he was the brother of a Lockerbie victim or that he was making a film about the attack. Instead, he asked genial questions about the work that Eter was doing for Libyan war veterans. Eter introduced Dornstein to his daughter, who was now in her twenties and did not appear to know about her father's past.

But Eter made little effort to keep secrets from Dornstein. At one point, he took the camera crew on a walking tour of the East Berlin neighborhood where he used to live and pointed out the old Libyan embassy. It now houses offices and a bike shop. Eter flagged down a German man who worked in the building and told him that he had once worked in the old embassy. The man said, brightly, "I heard a rumor that the La Belle disco bombing was carried out from this building."

"It's no rumor!" Eter replied, even more brightly. "It was organized in this building!"

With the man's help, he gained access to the complex and climbed to the second floor. He then muttered something in Arabic, which Dornstein later had translated: "What we did was wrong, and I admit it. If I could go back in time, I wouldn't have done it."

For Dornstein, meeting Eter was revelatory. "I had been trying to construct the world of Libyan intelligence in the 1980s from spare parts, and now suddenly here was this guy who had actually lived it," he said. "It was as if you'd read all the *Harry Potter* books, then you got to sit down with a guy who actually went to Hogwarts." Dornstein knew that he had to be careful. His research suggested that Eter might have worked as an assassin during his early years in Berlin. Many young functionaries in the Qaddafi regime were sent to Europe with instructions to execute Libyan dissidents in exile. (Qaddafi referred to these dissidents as "stray dogs.") The more Dornstein asked Eter about his past, the more Eter came to suspect that the film might not be focused on his philanthropic efforts.

One night in December, Eter asked Dornstein to dinner. The camera crew was not invited. Dornstein was hoping that Eter might disclose something important, so he decided to wear his hidden camera. He expected to meet at a restaurant in central Berlin and was surprised when Eter gave him the address of a small apartment on the outskirts of the city. Dornstein felt nervous, but relaxed a bit when he arrived and found that Eter had arranged for a generous spread of Middle Eastern food accompanied by fresh pita bread dusted with flour. They were joined by a German-language translator, and while Dornstein launched into questions about Eter's life and legal status, Eter ate silently, drinking red wine and watching Dornstein with a wary eye. Eventually, he explained his discomfort: he had begun to doubt that Dornstein was just a filmmaker. "Are you FBI?" he asked. "CIA?"

This was not the first time that Dornstein had been accused of being a spy—it was a routine assumption on his visits to Tripoli—but he broke out in a cold sweat. Underneath his shirt, he felt the surgical tape on his chest start slipping. Whenever this happened, the hidden camera's lens tilted toward the ceiling, ruining the shot, and Dornstein had developed a habit of smoothing the front of his shirt with his palms to put the camera back in place. He did this, and explained that he was not a spy. Eter seemed to settle down, and Dornstein helped himself to a piece of pita bread and smoothed his shirt again. After a while, he glanced down and discovered, to his horror, that each time he pressed his palms against his black shirt he was smearing flour from the pita bread in a ring around the hidden camera. It looked like a big white target.

"Can I use the bathroom?" Dornstein blurted.

"Are you recording this?" Eter demanded.

"No," Dornstein said, growing flustered. "Can I use the bathroom?"

Eter indicated a door just off the room where they were eating. Dornstein wanted to get rid of the camera, but unwiring himself and pulling the receiver out of his boot would take some effort, and the bathroom door was made of frosted glass. Besides, where could he ditch the camera? The bathroom had no window to throw it out of. He composed himself, dusted off his shirt, and rejoined Eter and the translator. "I still feel sick talking about it," he told me.

Eter did not challenge him again that night. But Dornstein feels guilty about having made the clandestine recording. "He had been honorable in his dealings with me," he said. He has not used the hidden camera since.

The topic that Dornstein was most determined to discuss with Eter was Abu Agila Mas'ud. In one of their discussions, Eter acknowledged having known the bomb expert. "Is he still alive?" Dornstein asked. Eter said that he was.

• • •

When Dornstein was organizing the Dave Archives, he made an upsetting discovery. After he annotated the journals, he sought out friends whom David had mentioned, to ask them about his brother. In one of these conversations, a friend mentioned, as if Ken had always known, that David had been sexually abused as a child. "David told me everything," Ken said to me. "But he didn't tell me this." The perpetrator was the older brother of one of David's childhood friends, and as Ken dug into this secret episode, he learned that years later David had confronted the man. David didn't hit him or call the police. But he wanted to face the abuser, who was now married with children of his own. "He wanted to make the guy uncomfortable in front of his family," Ken told me. "He delivered the message, the vengeance message: 'I know what you did.'"

At Brown, Ken had majored in philosophy and had read Robert Nozick on the difference between retribution and revenge. He was especially drawn, he told me, to "the idea that there's an odd bond between the victim and the perpetrator. They're locked in a relationship, and the role of the avenger is to deliver a message. 'I know who you are. I know what you did.'" As he tried to sort through his sense of irresolution about his brother's death, he kept returning to Nozick's formulation. When we talked in his study in Somerville, Dornstein quoted Elie Wiesel: "Sometimes it happens that we travel for a long time without knowing that we have made the long journey solely to pronounce a certain word, a certain phrase, in a certain place. The meeting of the place and the word is a rare accomplishment." It might seem abstract and philosophical, Dornstein said, but this is the way he came to understand his role as avenger. He surveyed books about Jews tracking down Nazis, and Israelis hunting the terrorists who attacked the 1972 Munich Olympics. His reckoning, he told me, would come not in an act of retribution but in the delivery of a message: "Twenty-five years ago, on a day of your choosing, you put a bomb in an airplane, and the course of my life changed. Now, on a day of my choosing, I will come to your home and I will knock on your door and say, 'I was on the other side of that act.' "

When Dornstein and I started having conversations about his film, in the fall of 2014, his obsessions had coalesced around Abu Agila Mas'ud. If Eter was correct that Mas'ud was still alive, Dornstein wanted to track him down. Others might disagree with his conclusions: Swire, for instance, still believes that Megrahi, who died in 2012, was innocent, and he thinks that the bomb originated not in Malta but in London. ("I welcome Ken's terrific efforts to get to the truth," Swire told me, adding that he has never ruled out the possibility that Qaddafi and his regime were involved.) The prosecution made various missteps during Megrahi's trial, such as putting unreliable witnesses on the stand, some of whom were paid by the U.S. government. But Dornstein told me, "That doesn't make Megrahi innocent."

Whenever there is a calamitous terrorist attack, alternative theories take shape in the gaps in the available evidence. During the 1980s, the world of Middle Eastern terrorism was filled with conspiracies, so there are plausible scenarios in which the Palestinians or the Syrians or the Iranians were involved with the Libyans in planning Lockerbie. Radical groups sometimes collaborated, trading hardware and expertise. "Endless names and intrigue," Dornstein told me. "You can't even hold it in your head."

Some might be tempted to dismiss Dornstein as a kook. Having a personal connection to a tragedy is a special qualification—and a kind of mandate—but emotional investment can also be blinding. When someone spends twenty-five years investigating an incident, his objectivity can be imperiled. Ken's sister, Susan, told me that she has never felt any desire to know the details of the Lockerbie attack or the identities of the men who carried it out. "I could care less if you find the guy who did it," she said. "The killers themselves, they have zero meaning to me. It wasn't directed at David. It was a random attack of violence. They weren't specifically targeting him." She stressed that she had always been supportive of Ken's investigations, but added, "I don't know if it's healthy anymore. It would be sad for Ken to give David up, because then who else is keeping him alive? If you close the book, he's gone. But after twenty-five years we have families. We have people who rely on us. We need to move on."

At one point, Dornstein told me, he asked Swire if he could imagine a time when the quest for the truth was behind him. David has now been dead for longer than he was alive, and Dornstein wondered if he might still be seeking answers when he was Swire's age. Part of him wanted Swire to discourage him from such a future. Swire acknowledged that his campaign had always been "a way of dealing with the loss of a dearly loved daughter." But he said that he had no plans to stop. "I suppose you have to parse the harm it's doing to you, and to those who love you, against the good that it might produce in the end if you crack it," he said.

One day this spring, Dornstein emailed me a video clip. It was the footage from Libyan state television of Megrahi's triumphant homecoming in 2009. I played the clip, and he narrated over the phone. As onlookers strained to touch Megrahi's sleeve, the first person up the stairs to greet him was Said Rashid, one of the alleged Lockerbie plotters. After disembarking, Megrahi climbed into a waiting SUV, where he was embraced by the man behind the wheel—Abdullah Senussi, Qaddafi's intelligence chief and one of the alleged masterminds of the plot. Megrahi had always maintained that he had no involvement in the bombing of Flight 103, but here he was, embracing some of the other prime suspects. "It's like a reunion," Dornstein exclaimed. "A belated victory party for the Lockerbie plotters." He had me play the footage a second time, and after Megrahi's embrace with Senussi, Dornstein said, "Okay, now pause it." I immediately noticed something. Less than a second passes between the embrace with Senussi and the moment the car drives away, but in that instant a third man, who was previously obscured in the shadows of the backseat, leans forward, clasps Megrahi's hand, and kisses him on the cheek. The video captures him for only an instant. He wears a white suit, his head is virtually bald, and his skin is very dark.

• • •

Dornstein decided to send the video to Eter's lawyer, in the hope that Eter would look at it. In Berlin, Dornstein had witnessed Eter's affection for his Westernized daughter and wondered if Eter might be worried about his legacy, trying to atone for the evil he had done. Eter also had a more self-interested motivation: he was attempting to secure permanent immigration status in Germany. If he could furnish valuable information, it might help his cause. The lawyer agreed to show Eter the video and ask him if the man in the backseat of the SUV was Abu Agila Mas'ud. Several days later, the answer came back: It was difficult to tell. The lighting wasn't great. But Eter was 80 percent sure that it was.

Dornstein now knew Mas'ud's name, his passport number, and what he looked like. With a video image of his face, there might be a real possibility of finding him. But what then? Libya had slipped into civil war and was much more dangerous than it had been on Dornstein's earlier trips. The rebels had rounded up Qaddafi loyalists and were holding show trials in Misrata and Tripoli. Former senior officials had been photographed in prison cells, in blue uniforms, looking sullen. Abdullah Senussi, the former intelligence chief, had fled to Mauritania, but Libya secured his return. After the murder of the U.S. ambassador Christopher Stevens in Benghazi in September 2012, Libya was considered extremely dangerous for Americans. Setting up a private meeting with Mas'ud would be very difficult. But Dornstein had noticed that on at least two recent occasions the United States had sent covert military snatch teams into Libya to pick up suspects and remove them from the country. In 2014, *The Washington Post* published video of an early-morning raid in which U.S. special-operations forces suddenly materialized on the streets of Tripoli, surrounded the car of Nazih Abdul-Hamed al-Ruqai—who was wanted in connection with the 1998 bombings of U.S. embassies in Kenya and Tanzania—and whisked him away in a white van. The abduction took less than sixty seconds, and several weeks later al-Ruqai was arraigned in a federal court in Manhattan. (He died, reportedly of liver cancer, before he could stand trial.) "Maybe they could do one of these raids and get Mas'ud," Dornstein suggested to me.

Technically, the case had never been closed in the United States, but it wasn't clear if anyone was actively pursuing it. Dornstein presented his findings to Richard Marquise, a retired FBI agent who was one of the lead investigators on the Lockerbie case. Marquise was impressed. "He showed me a bunch of stuff I'd never seen," he told me. "Declassified CIA documents! I knew the information in them, but I'd never seen these documents." Marquise told me that investigators had heard stories about Mas'ud. "We always suspected that he was the guy that armed the bomb," he said. "But we could never get any more information on him. The Scottish police couldn't get the Libyans to admit that he *existed,* and we weren't sure about the name. We thought maybe it was a pseudonym."

After Dornstein laid out his evidence, Marquise called the FBI. "I've got some information you should be aware of," he said. "Maybe we'll get some more indictments." Shortly after Marquise relayed Dornstein's findings to the bureau, Musbah Eter was summoned to a meeting at the U.S. embassy in Berlin. When I spoke with Dornstein in June 2015, he seemed cautiously optimistic, explaining that the Justice Department had interviewed Eter in Germany and appeared to be pursuing this new lead in the case. "I think the U.S. is pushing," Dornstein said. Eter had told U.S. officials that Mas'ud and Megrahi were both involved in Lockerbie, and that he had heard Mas'ud speak of traveling to Malta to prepare the attack. Even if the Obama administration did not want to send a special-ops team into Libya to capture Mas'ud, Eter had raised the possibility that he could try to lure him out of the country.

This was common in international law enforcement: when a suspect is hiding out in a nation where he enjoys protection, a skillful ruse can trick him into traveling to a country where he can be arrested. It might be a risky proposition for Eter. But he seemed willing to entertain any plan that would help secure his immigration status. He would also be helping the Germans: Mas'ud was wanted in connection with the La Belle disco bombing as well as with Lockerbie.

As the U.S. government was dealing with Eter, Dornstein was turning his footage into a film. He had a title—"My Brother's Bomber"—but what he didn't have was an ending. *Frontline* wanted to air the documentary, in three parts, in the fall, and this deadline exposed the tension between Dornstein's roles as grieving brother and documentary filmmaker. He had always been a storyteller: as an adolescent, before David's death, he had wanted to be a comedy writer, and he had never shied away from showmanship. In *The Boy Who Fell Out of the Sky,* he withholds, until page 73, the fact that the woman he eventually married had first dated his brother. ("An admission: I am leaving out important parts of this story," he writes.) His friend Richard Suckle, who is now a producer in Hollywood, assured me that, though the impetus for Dornstein's film might have been therapeutic, at a certain point his narrative instincts would take over. "I think it goes beyond emotional catharsis," Suckle said. "Nobody ever got to the bottom of it, all the thousands of people who worked on the investigation. It's about being the guy that got to the finish line when nobody else did."

Dornstein knew that if he revealed his discovery about Mas'ud in the film, Mas'ud would likely go into hiding, short-circuiting any government effort to capture him. In July, Dornstein said to me, "In terms of the timing, the question is, at what point do I want to finish my film and get what I came for? I have to ask myself, 'Tell me again what you are in this for?' How much do I care about actually getting him, or would I be satisfied with something short of that? Because when I publish, it's over. I'm in an odd position, because I initiated what has now become an official process—and I could also be the person to sabotage it."

When I asked Dornstein if it was important to him that Mas'ud face justice, he said that it was not his paramount concern. He reminded me of Nozick's concept of revenge. "Do I think he would have anything interesting to tell me?" Dornstein said. "I don't. I don't even think he has interesting reasons for doing what he did." The crucial thing was to deliver a message. "I've been thinking about this person for so long," he said. "And for so long it seemed as though he might not exist at all. It would be enough for me to say his name and have him turn his head. Me proving he exists is the checkmate."

Dornstein had only Eter's word that Mas'ud was still alive, and he wanted what hostage negotiators call "proof of life." Then, one day last summer, Eter's lawyer sent Dornstein a grainy digital photograph of several men—one of whom, in the background, had very dark skin. All the men, Dornstein noticed, were wearing blue uniforms. On his computer, Dornstein began searching for photographs from the recent show trials in Libya. Pulling up a series of shots from Getty Images, he found a higher-resolution version of the scene depicted in the grainy photograph. In the foreground was the lined and scowling face of Abdullah Senussi, the former intelligence chief. Over his shoulder, against the wall, was a bald man with very dark skin. To Dornstein, he looked a lot like the man who had greeted Megrahi in the SUV.

Upon making the discovery, Dornstein called me, very excited. As his investigation progressed, he had taken to using an encrypted cellphone program, and he insisted that we switch to a secure line before he relayed the news. "I found it kind of incredible," he said. "Eter said it's confirmed that the guy is alive, but there was never any sense that he was in *jail*."

Dornstein sent one of the high-resolution images back to Berlin. Not long afterward, the lawyer relayed Eter's response: "One hundred percent. It's him."

This was a huge development in Dornstein's quest, but he fretted that the identification was still less than airtight. He knew that Eter, given his immigration issues, was not an entirely disinterested witness. (When I reached Eter in Berlin, he declined to answer questions for this article.) After some further study, Dornstein found a researcher at Human Rights Watch, Hanan Salah, who was based in Nairobi and had been closely monitoring the trials in Libya. He reached her on Skype, and they spoke for an hour about the political situation in Libya and the general tenor of the trials. Then Dornstein told her that he was trying to confirm the identity of a defendant he had seen in a photograph. "Do you want to tell me the name?" she said. "Yes," Dornstein said, and he typed the name Abu Agila Mas'ud.

For a moment, Salah was silent while she consulted the charge sheet. Then she said, "There's no one with that name."

"Do you feel you have the full list?" Dornstein stammered.

"Yeah," Salah said, her voice conveying that she knew this was not the answer he wanted to hear.

"Okay, well, that's very helpful," Dornstein said. "Because maybe this person who is telling me this . . . isn't right. For whatever reason—"

"Oh, wait," she interrupted. "Wait, wait, wait. I have a name. It's just written slightly differently . . . Abuajila Mas'ud."

Dornstein was elated. A woman with no connection to the Lockerbie story had identified the dark-skinned man on trial in Libya as the same person who appeared in the CIA files, the Stasi files, and the Maltese immigration records. For years, Mas'ud had been a ghost, a passport number. Now there was a charge sheet and a high-resolution photograph. "He's Defendant No. 28," Salah said.

"Do you know what the charge is?" Dornstein asked.

Salah consulted her trial notes. "It seems to be . . . bomb making," she said.

• • •

Mas'ud stood accused of using remote-detonated explosive devices to booby-trap the cars of Libyan opposition members in 2011, after revolution broke out. According to the charge sheet, which Dornstein had someone translate from Arabic, Mas'ud was not Libyan by birth: he had been born in Tunisia in 1951. "It changes things for me," Dornstein told me. "The guy's in jail. He was always the under-the-radar guy, and now he's in a show trial." He added, "There couldn't have been any better confirmation that it was him than those charges." Most striking to Dornstein was the fact that the bomb maker had not abandoned his career: decades after La Belle and Lockerbie, Mas'ud had continued to play a deadly role for Qaddafi. Presumably, there were other, more recent victims of his bombings—other family members, like Dornstein, who felt aggrieved. "It brings the whole thing into the messy present," he said.

When I asked Brian Murtagh, the former lead U.S. prosecutor, about Dornstein's findings, he became slightly defensive. Investigators knew about Mas'ud years ago, Murtagh told me, but because he was so obscure, he remained a "could-have-been": "Did we think, 'Gee, if he's the technical guy, maybe he put the bomb together'? Sure. But we didn't have a picture of the guy." Murtagh argued that Dornstein, as a journalist, had certain advantages over government investigators. "For an FBI agent to go to the places where Ken has gone, he would have to have permission from the Libyan government and the authorization of the State Department. Journalists don't have to play by the same rules," he said. "We have jurisdiction to prosecute out the ying-yang, but if you can't *find* the person, your jurisdiction doesn't amount to a whole lot."

There was a certain grim poetry in the Libyan trials: Mas'ud might have evaded justice for arming the bomb that blew up Pan Am Flight 103, yet when he was finally put on trial in Libya, it was for bomb making. At the same time, the outcome was frustrating, in that the trials, which were held in Tripoli, afforded little due process. Dornstein's commitment had always been more to truth than to justice, and it seemed unlikely that any truth about Mas'ud's role in Lockerbie would emerge from these proceedings.

Meanwhile, Dornstein was racing to finish his film. "Everyone keeps asking, 'Do you have your ending?'" Tim Grucza said. Dornstein's research suggested that Mas'ud was likely being held in a prison in Misrata. His needs as a filmmaker and his desire for emotional catharsis both seemed to be pointing in the same direction. Grucza, who had covered many wars, was ready to go to Misrata. But Dornstein hesitated. "It's completely lawless now," he said of Libya. After doing some research on the ground, Suliman Ali Zway, the fixer, counseled against an expedition, explaining that it would be one thing to take the risk if Mas'ud was living in a private home—but he was in prison. "We're never going to get access," Ali Zway said. Finally, Dornstein concluded that it was "too much risk for too little reward."

On July 28, 2015, Mas'ud was sentenced to ten years. In early September, Dornstein called me and said, "A situation has developed." He had managed to get in touch with a middleman, in Malta, who said that he was a representative of the Libya Dawn militias—the rebel coalition that had administered the trials. The middleman had made a proposal: "Essentially, I have what seems to be a pretty high-level invitation to go to Malta, then fly on a chartered plane to Tripoli, interview Mas'ud, and get out." This was a seductive offer, but there were reasons to be wary. Why would Libya Dawn facilitate such a meeting? It is an Islamist group, but it was now fighting ISIS, and Dornstein speculated that Libya Dawn saw the invitation as a way of currying favor with the United States. "They're trying to show that they're a reasonable horse to back," he said. The security situation in Libya remained precarious. Even if Libya Dawn guaranteed safe passage, there were many ways to end up in serious trouble. In Tripoli and Misrata, the traffic alone posed a danger: "You're sitting next to a flatbed truck with a bunch of guys with guns. You could get carjacked and have nowhere to run."

Eventually, Dornstein decided that Libya was simply not safe. It would be unfair to his wife and children to undertake such a risk on behalf of his dead brother. More than once in our conversations,

Dornstein referred to the story of Tantalus, who, in Greek mythology, reaches for fruit that will forever elude his grasp. He had spent more than $350,000 making the film, maxing out credit cards and getting a home-equity loan. Even after he appeared to decide not to go to Libya, he revisited the issue with me: "Let's say I did talk my way into the prison and got in front of this guy. I can't imagine that on a first meeting he's going to say, 'I'm so impressed with your detective work, I'm going to tell you everything.' In the Hollywood version, that's what happens, but not in this version. This isn't *Fitzcarraldo*. I'm not Werner Herzog in the jungle." He continued, "There's a legitimate tension in the whole film between backward-looking things and forward-looking things. But this is a film that ends with me returning to my family and putting all this behind me." The documentary would appear in three installments on *Frontline* in September and October 2015.

When I asked Ali Zway if he believed there was any final reckoning that might be enough for Dornstein, he said, "For Ken? It's never enough." Mas'ud is one man on Dornstein's list, he pointed out. "I'm sure that Ken has many more names. And now that he's found one, he'll want to find more. I don't think he'll ever get closure. There's always something missing."

Once, when Dornstein was in college, he wanted to visit Yellowstone National Park. He didn't have any money to get there, and his father was disinclined to fund the trip. But David wrote him a check for $300. Ken knew that David didn't have any money to speak of, either, so he never cashed the check. But he held on to it for years.

In 2006, after Ken published his book, he declared that he was done with Lockerbie. But he wasn't. When he and Geismar first started dating, he used to talk to her about the need to "continue" Dave. Can such a project ever end? On a cinematic level, Dornstein's decision to return to his family rather than risk being killed in Libya makes for a good ending. But will it be so simple in life? For the next ten years, Mas'ud would be sitting in a jail cell in Libya, and I wondered if Dornstein would be able to keep that thought at bay, even after completing a book and a film. When I met Geismar, I asked her if her husband might soon clear his Lockerbie files out of the attic. "That's a good question," she said. "For so long, he's had a foot in the past and a foot in the present. He's been the prisoner and the jailer at the same time. I'm all about emotional closure. But all of this work he's done, I think it's about the process more than the result." She smiled, her face full of sadness and compassion. "Maybe this is a door that never gets closed."

In December 2020, thirty-two years after the Lockerbie bombing, the U.S. Department of Justice charged Abu Agila Mas'ud with making the bomb. The U.S. government sought his extradition from Libya so that he could face trial in the United States. Ken Dornstein has moved on to make a variety of films on a range of subjects that have nothing to do with Lockerbie.

THE EMPIRE OF EDGE

How a doctor, a trader, and the billionaire Steven A. Cohen got entangled in a vast financial scandal. (2014)

AS DR. SID GILMAN APPROACHED the stage, the hotel ballroom quieted with anticipation. It was July 29, 2008, and a thousand people had gathered in Chicago for the International Conference on Alzheimer's Disease. For decades, scientists had tried, and failed, to devise a cure for Alzheimer's. But in recent years two pharmaceutical companies, Elan and Wyeth, had worked together on an experimental drug called bapineuzumab, which had shown promise in halting the cognitive decay caused by the disease. Tests on mice had proved successful, and in an initial clinical trial a small number of human patients appeared to improve. A second phase of trials, involving 240 patients, was near completion. Gilman had chaired the safety-monitoring committee for the trials. Now he was going to announce the results of the second phase.

Alzheimer's affects roughly five million Americans, and it is projected that as the population ages, the number of new cases will increase dramatically. This looming epidemic has added urgency to the scientific search for a cure. It has also come to the attention of investors, because there would be huge demand for a drug that diminishes the effects of Alzheimer's. As Elan and Wyeth spent hundreds of millions of dollars concocting and testing bapineuzumab, and issued hints about the possibility of a medical breakthrough, investors wondered whether bapi, as it became known, might be "the next Lipitor." Several months before the Chicago conference, *Barron's* published a cover story speculating that bapi could become "the biggest drug of all time."

One prominent investor was known to have made a very large bet on bapi. In the two years leading up to the conference, the billionaire hedge-fund manager Steven A. Cohen had accumulated hundreds of millions of dollars' worth of Elan and Wyeth stock. Cohen had started his own hedge fund, SAC Capital Advisors, with $25 million in 1992 and developed it into a $14 billion empire that employed a thousand people. The fund charged wealthy clients conspicuously high commissions and fees to manage their money, but even after the exorbitant surcharge investors saw average annual returns of more than 30 percent. SAC made investments in several thousand stocks, but by the summer of 2008 the firm's single largest position was in Wyeth, and its fifth largest was in Elan. All told, Cohen had gambled about three-quarters of a billion dollars on bapi. He was famous for making trades based on "catalysts"—events that might help or hurt the value of a given stock. Sid Gilman's presentation of the clinical data in Chicago was a classic catalyst: if the results were promising, the stocks would soar, and Cohen would make a fortune.

Gilman had not wanted to make the presentation. Seventy-five years old and suffering from lymphoma, he had recently undergone chemotherapy, which left him completely bald—like the "evil scientist in an *Indiana Jones* movie," he joked. But Elan executives urged Gilman to participate. He was a revered figure in medical circles, the longtime chair of neurology at the University of Michigan's medical school. In Ann Arbor, a lecture series and a wing of the university hospital were named for him. His CV was forty-three pages long. As a steward for the fledgling drug, he conveyed a reassuring authority.

But soon after Gilman began his thirteen-minute presentation, accompanied by PowerPoint slides, it became clear that the bapi trials had not been an unqualified success. Bapi appeared to reduce symptoms in some patients but not in others. Gilman was optimistic about the results; the data "seemed so promising," he told a colleague. But the investment community was less sanguine about the drug's commercial prospects. One market analyst, summarizing the general feeling, pronounced the results "a disaster."

The Chicago conference was indeed a catalyst, but not the type that investors had expected. It appeared that Cohen had made an epic misjudgment. When the market closed the following day, Elan's stock had plummeted 40 percent. Wyeth's had dropped nearly 12 percent. By the time Gilman made his presentation, however, SAC Capital no longer owned any stock in Elan or Wyeth. In the eight days preceding the conference, Cohen had liquidated his $700 million position in the two companies and had then proceeded to "short" the stocks—to bet against them—making a $275 million profit. In a week, Cohen had reversed his position on bapi by nearly $1 billion.

Gilman and Cohen had never met. The details of the clinical trials had been a closely guarded secret, yet SAC had brilliantly anticipated them. Cohen has suggested that his decisions about stocks are governed largely by "gut." He is said to have an uncanny ability to watch the numbers on a stock ticker and intuit where they will go. In the assessment of Chandler Bocklage, one of his longtime deputies, Cohen is "the greatest trader of all time."

But federal authorities had a different explanation for SAC's masterstroke. More than four years after the Chicago conference, in December 2012, prosecutors in New York indicted a young man named Mathew Martoma, who had worked as a portfolio manager for Cohen. They accused him of using confidential information about bapi to engineer the most lucrative insider-trading scheme in history. According to the indictment, Martoma had been receiving secret details about the progress of the clinical trials for nearly two years and, ultimately, obtained an early warning about the disappointing results of the second phase. His source for this intelligence was Sid Gilman.

• • •

In 1977, after completing medical school at UCLA and teaching at Harvard and Columbia, Gilman was recruited to run the neurology department at the University of Michigan. He moved to Ann Arbor with his first wife, Linda, and their two sons. Gilman's marriage unraveled in the early 1980s, and the older son, Jeff, developed psychological problems. Jeff committed suicide in 1983, overdosing on pills in a hotel room near campus. Gilman had experienced tragedy before: his father had walked out on the family when he was a boy, and his mother later committed suicide. After Jeff's death, Gilman seems to have dealt with his despair by throwing himself into his job. "The man worked himself to distraction," one of his many protégés, Anne Young, who went on to become the chief of neurology at Massachusetts General Hospital, told me.

In 1984, Gilman married a psychoanalyst named Carol Barbour, but they never had children, and though his surviving son, Todd, attended the University of Michigan, they eventually became estranged, leaving him with no ties to his former family. Over the years, however, Gilman became a father figure to dozens of medical residents and junior colleagues. "Helping younger people along—that was a constant," Kurt Fischbeck, a former colleague of Gilman's who now works at the National Institutes of Health, told me. Gilman was "incredibly supportive" of younger faculty, Young said. "He would go over grants with us, really putting an effort into it, which is something chairs rarely do."

One day in 2002, Gilman was contacted by a doctor named Edward Shin, who worked for a new company called the Gerson Lehrman Group. GLG, as it was known, served as a matchmaker between investors and experts in specialized industries who might answer their questions. "It was kind of ridiculous that the hedge fund business got so much information by asking for favors . . . when they would certainly pay," the company's chief executive, Mark Gerson, told *The New York Times*. Shin proposed that Gilman join GLG's network of experts, becoming a consultant who could earn as much as $1,000 an hour. Gilman was hardly alone in saying yes to such a proposal. A study published in *The Journal of the American Medical Association* found that by 2005 nearly 10 percent of the physicians in the United States had established relationships with the investment industry—a seventy-five-fold increase since 1996. The article noted that the speed and the extent of this intertwining were "likely unprecedented in the history of professional-industrial relationships." Gilman read the article, but disagreed that such arrangements were objectionable. In an email to Shin, he explained that investors often offered him a fresh perspective on his own research: "Although remuneration provides an incentive, the most attractive feature to this relationship (at least for me) is the exchange."

Gilman's university salary was about $320,000 a year, a sum that went a long way in Ann Arbor. As he took on more paid consultations, he began supplementing his income by hundreds of thousands of dollars a year. Acquaintances did not notice any abrupt change in his lifestyle: Gilman wore elegant clothes, but otherwise he and his wife appeared to live relatively modestly. "He was not a flashy guy who reveled in expensive toys," Tim Greenamyre, a former student, who now runs the Pittsburgh Institute for Neurodegenerative Diseases, told me. Gilman counseled Greenamyre and other colleagues to avoid even the appearance of a conflict of interest in their professional dealings, and he made a point of telling people that he never invested in pharmaceutical stocks. The consulting, he later maintained, was simply "a diversion."

In the summer of 2006, Gilman received a call from Mathew Martoma, who explained that he had recently joined SAC and was focusing on health-care stocks. They spoke about Alzheimer's remedies, and specifically about bapineuzumab. Although Martoma had no medical background, he was attuned to the scientific intricacies at play. His mother and his wife, Rosemary, were both physicians, and he had a long-standing interest in Alzheimer's, dating back to his childhood, in Florida, when he volunteered as a candy striper at a local hospital. He and Gilman talked for more than two hours. Afterward, Martoma asked GLG to schedule another consultation.

SAC was a notoriously intense place to work. Its headquarters, on a spit of land in Stamford, Connecticut, overlooking the Long Island Sound, were decorated with art from Cohen's personal collection, including *Self,* a refrigerated glass cube, by Marc Quinn, containing a disembodied head sculpted from the artist's frozen blood. It was nearly as frigid on the twenty-thousand-square-foot trading floor, which Cohen kept fiercely air-conditioned; employees were issued fleece jackets with the SAC monogram, for keeping warm. The atmosphere was hushed, with telephones programmed to blink rather than ring, but a curious soundtrack could be heard throughout the building. As Cohen sat at his sprawling desk, before a flotilla of flat-screen monitors, and barked orders for his personal trades, a camera—the "Steve cam"—was trained on him, broadcasting his staccato patter to his subordinates. Cohen is not a physically imposing man: he is pale and gnomish, with a crooked, gap-toothed smile. But on the Steve cam he was Oz.

When SAC first approached Martoma about a job, he was ambivalent. He was living in Boston, working happily at a small hedge fund called Sirios Capital Management. He knew that careers at SAC followed a starkly binary narrative. Portfolio managers were given a pot of money. If their investments were consistently profitable, they became very rich very quickly. If their investments lost money, they were out of a job. Contracts at SAC contained a "down and out" clause, so it was prosper or die. Cohen likened his traders to elite athletes; for many years, he paid a psychiatrist who had worked with Olympic competitors to spend several days a week at SAC, counseling employees about mastering their fears. He hired high achievers who were accustomed to grueling pressure. Martoma had studied bioethics at Duke, graduating summa cum laude. After a year working at the National Institutes of Health, where he co-authored a paper, "Alzheimer Testing at Silver Years," in the *Cambridge Quarterly of Healthcare Ethics,* he was admitted to Harvard Law School. He departed a year later, during the dot-com boom, and launched a start-up. Next, he obtained an MBA from Stanford. SAC was another brand-name institution, a strong allure for someone like Martoma. After visiting the office in Stamford and spending a day shadowing Cohen on the trading floor, he accepted the job.

SAC relied on portfolio managers to devise novel investment ideas. In a marketplace crowded with hedge funds, it had become "hard to find ideas that aren't picked over," Cohen complained to *The Wall Street Journal* in 2006. In the business, a subtle but crucial informational advantage was called "edge." Richard Holwell, a former federal judge in New York who presided over high-profile securities-fraud cases, told me that in order to evaluate a technology stock, hedge funds sent "people to China to sit in front of a factory and see whether it was doing one shift or two." He added, "An edge is the goal of every portfolio manager." When Cohen was asked about edge during a deposition in 2011, he said, "I hate that word." But SAC's promotional materials boasted about the firm's "edge," and Cohen provided his employees with every research tool that might offer a boost over the competition.

The eat-what-you-kill incentive structure at SAC put a damper on collegiality. Employees with edge had no motivation to share it with one another. But every good idea was shared with Cohen. Each Sunday, portfolio managers sent a memo to an email address known as "Steve ideas," in which they spelled out their most promising leads, weighted by their level of conviction. Martoma had always been avid about research, and he was impressed by SAC's resources. At his disposal was a boutique firm full of former CIA officers who could monitor the public statements of corporate executives and evaluate whether they were hiding something; SAC also had a "buffet plan" with the Gerson Lehrman Group, giving Martoma unrestricted access to thousands of experts. From his first days in Stamford, he was interested in the investment potential of bapi. He contacted GLG with a list of twenty-two doctors he hoped to consult, all of whom were involved in the clinical trials of the drug. Most declined, citing a conflict of interest; clinical investigators had to sign confidentiality agreements that constrained their ability to talk about the progress of the trials. But Sid Gilman accepted, noting, in his response to GLG, that he would "share only information that is openly available." On the Sunday after the initial conversation with Gilman, Martoma sent an email to Steve Cohen, suggesting that SAC buy 4.5 million shares of Elan stock and noting that his conviction level was "High."

• • •

Martoma was born Ajai Mathew Thomas in 1974 and grew up in Merritt Island, Florida. His parents had emigrated from Kerala, in southern India, during the 1960s. They were Christian; the name Martoma, which the family adopted around the turn of the millennium, is a tribute to the Mar Thoma Syrian Church, an Orthodox denomination that is based in Kerala. Mathew's father, Bobby, was a stern man with a sharp nose and a clipped mustache. He owned a dry-cleaning business and placed enormous pressure on his son to succeed. Mathew obliged, excelling in school and starting a lawn-mowing operation in which he outsourced the actual mowing to other kids. The oldest of three brothers, he seems to have taken naturally to the role of family standard-bearer. Childhood photographs show him grinning, with his hair neatly parted, in a tiny three-piece suit.

When Martoma's father first came to America, he was admitted to MIT, but he could not afford to attend. He retained a fascination with Cambridge, however, and prayed daily that his oldest son would go to Harvard. Martoma graduated from high school as co-valedictorian, but he ended up going to Duke. Shortly after Mathew's eighteenth birthday, Bobby presented him with a plaque inscribed with the words "Son Who Shattered His Father's Dream."

During college, Martoma volunteered in the Alzheimer's wing of the Duke Medical Center and developed an interest in medical ethics. Bruce Payne, who taught Martoma in a course on ethics and policy making, remembers him as "creased and pressed—very pre-professional." Payne wrote a recommendation letter for Martoma's application to business school at Stanford, praising his subtle readings of Sissela Bok's book *Lying* and Albert Camus's *Plague*. Martoma was unusually adept at cultivating mentors. "He was ambitious; he wanted to make something of his life," Ronald Green, who supervised Martoma during his year at NIH and is now a professor at Dartmouth, told me. "To some extent, I felt like Mathew was an adopted son."

At Stanford, Martoma was introduced to a young pediatrician from New Zealand named Rosemary Kurian. Strikingly beautiful, she was studying for her medical boards so that she could practice in the United States. She had grown up in a sheltered family and had never dated before. But she felt an immediate bond with Mathew: her parents were also from Kerala, and she, too, felt both very Indian and very Western. "I was just enamored with how lovely he was," she told me recently. "And he seemed to be very respectful of my parents." Her mother and father endorsed the relationship, and in 2003 Mathew and Rosemary were married, in an Eastern Orthodox cathedral in Coral Gables, Florida. By the time they moved to Connecticut, they had one child and Rosemary was pregnant with a second. She stopped working, but she was very involved in advancing Mathew's career. "Mathew didn't just do that job by himself," she told me, with a smile. He worked perpetually. "It was heads-down, tails-up, 24/7 kind of work."

Martoma rose at 4:00 a.m. to keep up with the European health-care markets, then worked until the market in New York closed. After spending a few hours with the children, he put in another shift, sitting in bed with his laptop while Rosemary fell asleep beside him. He had numerous investment prospects, but bapi was the most promising, and it became an obsession. "As a portfolio manager, you live by your ups and downs," Rosemary said. "These stocks, they're your babies, and you're following them and you're nurturing them." The fixation became a running joke, and her conversations with him were often punctuated by the word "Bapsolutely!"

Rosemary never met Sid Gilman, but throughout the fall of 2006 Martoma arranged frequent consultations with him about bapi. Much later, in court, Gilman recounted this phase in their relationship as a kind of intellectual seduction. They spoke for hours about the trials for various Alzheimer's drugs. "Every time I told him about a clinical trial, he seemed to know a good deal about it," Gilman testified. "The more I told him about each of the trials, the more he wanted to know." Gilman found himself wishing that his students in Ann Arbor were as bright and curious as Martoma. That October, Gilman had plans to visit New York on other business, and Martoma arranged to meet with him at SAC's offices in Manhattan. In an email to GLG, Martoma specified that he wanted the meeting "to be with just me and dr. gilman alone." The appointment was at lunchtime, and when Gilman was shown into the room, he was pleased by a small courtesy—an array of sandwiches. Martoma walked in, broad shouldered and genial, with close-cropped black hair and long eyelashes that gave his face a feline aspect. He was "very, very friendly," Gilman recalled. Martoma complimented him on "the previous consultations we had."

According to GLG's records, Gilman and Martoma had forty-two formal consultations over two years. Gilman consulted with many other investors during this time, and Martoma spoke to many other doctors, but neither spoke to anyone else with nearly the same frequency that they did with each other. It seemed to Gilman that Martoma shared his passion for Alzheimer's research and regarded the efforts to create an effective drug as much more than a matter of financial interest. In emails, Martoma had a tendency to slip into the first-person plural, using "we" when discussing how medical professionals treated people with the disease. Gilman also got the impression that Martoma wanted to be friends. Martoma proposed that they have coffee after meetings of the American Academy of Neurology. He talked to Gilman about his family's emigration from India and about how he and Rosemary had had their children in rapid succession. In emails, he sent his best wishes to Gilman's "better half." Gilman called Martoma "Mat," but even when they were speaking almost daily, Martoma always addressed him as "Dr. Gilman." Once, when Gilman was traveling in Istanbul, he forgot about a scheduled consultation. Unable to reach him, Martoma had his assistant make multiple calls to try to track the doctor down. Eventually, a hotel employee discovered Gilman by himself, reading, and alerted him to the calls. "I was in a foreign country, and he couldn't find me," Gilman testified. "It was touching."

Later, Gilman had trouble pinpointing just when his relationship with Martoma crossed into illegality. But he recalled a moment when Martoma asked, repeatedly, about the side effects that one might expect to see from bapi. "I didn't quite recognize it for what I think it was, which was an attempt to find confidential information," Gilman said. Initially, he offered theoretical responses, but Martoma "persisted in wanting to know what really happened," and finally the answers "slipped out." Gilman told him how many patients and how many placebo cases had experienced each adverse effect. While he was talking, Martoma periodically asked him to slow down so that he could transcribe the numbers.

• • •

In 1942, lawyers in the Boston office of the Securities and Exchange Commission learned that the president of a local company was issuing a pessimistic forecast to shareholders and then offering to purchase their shares. What the president knew, and the shareholders didn't, was that earnings were on track to quadruple in the coming year. He had edge, which allowed him to dupe his own shareholders into selling him the stock at far below its real value. Later that year, the SEC established Rule 10b-5 of the Securities Exchange Act, making insider trading a federal crime. At the time, one of the commissioners remarked, "Well, we're against fraud, aren't we?"

In the ensuing decades, however, enforcement of this prohibition has been inconsistent. Some academics have suggested that insider trading is effectively a victimless crime and should not be aggressively prosecuted. At least privately, many in the financial industry agree. But in 2009, when Preet Bharara took over as U.S. Attorney for the Southern District of New York, with jurisdiction over Wall Street, he made it a priority to curb this type of securities fraud. The problem had become "rampant" in the hedge-fund industry, Bharara told me, in part because of a prevailing sense that the rewards for insider trading were potentially astronomical—and the penalty if you were caught was relatively slight. "These are people who are in the business of assessing risk, because that's what trading is, and they were thinking, 'The greatest consequence I will face is paying some fines,'" Bharara said. His strategy for changing their behavior was to throw a new variable into the cost-benefit equation: prison. Agents from the FBI and the SEC began asking investment professionals to identify the biggest malefactors. Peter Grupe, who supervised the investigations at the FBI, told me that all the informants were "pointing in the same direction—Stamford, Connecticut."

Rumors about insider trading had circulated around Steve Cohen since his first years in the business. As a young trader at a small investment bank called Gruntal & Company, he was deposed by the SEC in 1986 about suspicious trades surrounding General Electric's acquisition of RCA. Cohen asserted the Fifth Amendment and was never indicted, but during the 1990s, as his fund became extraordinarily profitable, observers and rivals speculated that he must be doing something untoward. Like Bernard Madoff's investment firm, SAC enjoyed a level of success that could seem suspicious on its face. "A lot of people assumed for years that SAC was cheating, because it was generating returns that didn't seem sustainable if you were playing the same game as everyone else," the manager of another hedge fund told me.

When Cohen was growing up, as one of eight children in a middle-class family in Great Neck, New York, his father, who owned a garment factory in the Bronx, brought home the *New York Post* every evening. Cohen read the sports pages, but noticed that there were also "these other pages filled with numbers." In an interview for Jack Schwager's book *Stock Market Wizards,* he recalled, "I was fascinated when I found out that these numbers were prices, which were changing every day. I started hanging out at the local brokerage office, watching the stock quotes. When I was in high school, I took a summer job at a clothing store, located just down the block from a brokerage office, so that I could run in and watch the tape during my lunch hour. In those days, the tape was so slow that you could follow it. You could see volume coming into a stock and get the sense that it was going higher. You can't do that nowadays; the tape is far too fast. But everything I do today has its roots in those early tape-reading experiences."

Cohen was never a "value investor"—someone who makes sustained commitments to companies that he believes in. He moved in and out of stocks quickly, making big bets on short-term fluctuations in their price. "Steve has no emotion in this stuff," one of his portfolio managers said in a deposition last year. "Stocks mean nothing to him. They're just ideas, they're not even *his* ideas . . . He's a trader, he's not an analyst. And he trades constantly. That's what he loves to do." The business model at SAC, though, was based not on instinct but on the aggressive accumulation of information and analysis. In fact, as federal agents pursued multiple overlapping investigations into insider trading at hedge funds, it began to appear that the culture at SAC not only tolerated but encouraged the use of inside information. In the recent trial of Michael Steinberg, one of Cohen's longtime portfolio managers, a witness named Jon Horvath, who had worked as a research analyst at SAC, recalled Steinberg telling him, "I can day-trade these stocks and make money by myself. I don't need your help to do that. What I need you to do is go out and get me edgy, proprietary information." Horvath took this to mean illegal, nonpublic information—and he felt that he'd be fired if he didn't get it.

When Cohen interviewed job applicants, he liked to say, "Tell me some of the riskiest things you've ever done in your life." In 2009, a portfolio manager named Richard Lee applied for a job. Cohen received a warning from another hedge fund that Lee had been part of an "insider-trading group." SAC's legal department warned that hiring Lee would be a mistake, but Cohen overruled them. (Lee subsequently pleaded guilty to insider trading.)

White-collar criminals tend to make soft targets for law enforcement. "The success rate at getting people to cooperate was phenomenal," Peter Grupe told me. Most of the suspects in insider-trading investigations have never been arrested, nor have they contemplated the prospect of serious jail time. When Michael Steinberg was waiting for the jury in his trial to pronounce a verdict, he fainted in open court. So the authorities approached hedge-fund employees, one by one, confronting them with evidence of their crimes and asking them what else they knew. Because the suspects weren't anticipating being under surveillance, the FBI could tail them for weeks. Then, one day, as a suspect headed into a Starbucks and prepared to place his usual order, an agent would sidle up and place the order for him.

The tactics echoed the approach the FBI had used to dismantle the New York Mob. The plan was to arrest low-level soldiers, threaten them with lengthy jail terms, and then flip them, gathering information that could lead to arrests farther up the criminal hierarchy. Over time, agents produced an organizational chart with names and faces, just as they had with La Cosa Nostra. At the top of the pyramid was Steve Cohen.

In 2010, FBI agents approached a young man named Noah Freeman who had been fired by SAC and was teaching at a girls' school in Boston. Freeman became a key witness. Asked in court how often he had attempted to obtain illegal edge, he replied, "Multiple times per day." According to an FBI memo, "Freeman and others at S.A.C. Capital understood that providing Cohen with your best trading ideas involved providing Cohen with inside information." When Martoma first came to SAC, his due-diligence report had noted his "industry contacts" and his personal "network of doctors in the field." Through the fall of 2007, he acquired more and more Elan and Wyeth stock, and Cohen followed his lead, supplementing the money that Martoma was investing from his own portfolio with funds from Cohen's personal account. That October, Martoma emailed Cohen that bapi was on track to start phase III trials soon, and that they would make up "the MOST COMPREHENSIVE ALZHEIMER'S PROGRAM to date."

SAC had a proprietary computer system, known as Panorama, that allowed employees to monitor the company's holdings in real time. Employees checked Panorama incessantly, and many noticed the scale of the bet that Martoma, a relatively junior portfolio manager, was making—and the fact that Cohen was backing him. Because of the open plan in the Stamford office and the simulcast from Cohen's desk, people could watch as Martoma approached the boss and murmured recommendations. A portfolio manager named David Munno, who had a PhD in neuroscience, was skeptical about bapi's prospects. He didn't like Martoma, and didn't understand the source of his conviction. At one point, he wrote to Cohen, wondering whether Martoma actually knew something about the bapi trial or simply had "a very strong feeling."

"Tough one," Cohen replied. "I think Mat is the closest to it."

It's impossible to know exactly how Martoma buttressed Cohen's confidence in bapi. Portfolio managers at SAC often wrote detailed explanations to support trading recommendations, but when it came to bapi, Cohen and Martoma preferred to talk. Martoma's emails to his boss often consisted of a single line: "Do you have a sec to talk?" "Do you have a moment to speak when you get in?" Whenever Munno pressed Cohen on how Martoma knew so much about bapi, Cohen responded cryptically. "Mat thinks this will be a huge drug," he wrote to Munno at one point. On another occasion, he explained simply that "Mat has a lot of good relationships in this area."

A second portfolio manager, Benjamin Slate, shared Munno's concerns, suggesting, in one email, that it was "totally unacceptable to bet ½ billion dollars on alzheimers without a real discussion." In a message to Slate a month before the Chicago conference, Munno complained that Martoma was telling people he had "black edge." In subsequent legal filings, SAC has claimed that Munno and Slate coined the term "black edge" as "humorous commentary." But, according to filings by the Department of Justice, "black edge" was "a phrase meaning inside information."

Initially, Gilman might have "slipped" when he divulged secret details to Martoma, but as their friendship continued, the malfeasance became more systematic. Whenever Gilman learned about a meeting of the safety-monitoring committee, Martoma scheduled a consultation immediately afterward, so that Gilman could share whatever new information he had obtained. Apart from consultation fees, Gilman did not receive any additional remuneration from Martoma, yet he slid into ethical breaches with an ease verging on enthusiasm. At one point, Gilman proposed outright deception, suggesting to Martoma that they supply the Gerson Lehrman Group with fraudulent pretexts for meetings, in order to deflect suspicion.

On June 25, 2008, Gilman sent an email to Martoma with the subject line "Some news." Elan and Wyeth had appointed him to present the results of the phase II clinical trials at the International Conference on Alzheimer's Disease, in July. Martoma scheduled a consultation, informing GLG, inaccurately, that he and Gilman would be discussing therapies for multiple sclerosis. Up to this point, Gilman had been given access to the safety results of the trials, but he had been "blinded" to the all-important efficacy results. Now, in order to present the findings, Gilman would be "unblinded." Two weeks later, Elan arranged for a private jet to fly him from Detroit to San Francisco, where the company had offices. He spent two days with company executives, crafting his conference presentation. When he returned to Michigan, an Elan executive sent Gilman an email titled "Confidential, Do Not Distribute." It contained an updated version of the twenty-four-slide PowerPoint presentation that would accompany his remarks. After downloading the slideshow, Gilman received a call from Martoma. They spoke for an hour and forty-five minutes, during which, Gilman later admitted, he relayed the contents of the presentation.

But the material was complicated—too complicated, perhaps, to convey over the phone. Martoma announced that he happened to be flying to Michigan that weekend; a relative had died, but he had been too busy to attend the funeral, so he was going belatedly to pay his respects. Could he swing by?

"Sure, you can drop in," Gilman replied.

Two days later, Martoma flew from JFK to Detroit, took a taxi to Ann Arbor, and met with Gilman for an hour in his office on campus. He flew back to New York that evening, without having visited his family. Rosemary picked him up at the airport. The next morning, Sunday, Martoma emailed Cohen, "Is there a good time to catch up with you this morning? It's important." Cohen emailed Martoma a phone number, and at 9:45 a.m. Martoma called him at home. According to phone records introduced in court, they spoke for twenty minutes. When the market opened on Monday, Cohen and Martoma instructed Phil Villhauer, Cohen's head trader at SAC, to begin quietly selling Elan and Wyeth shares. Villhauer unloaded them using "dark pools"—an anonymous electronic exchange for stocks—and other techniques that made the trades difficult to detect. Over the next several days, SAC sold off its entire position in Elan and Wyeth so discreetly that only a few people at the firm were aware it was happening. On July 21, Villhauer wrote to Martoma, "No one knows except me you and Steve."

Martoma said nothing to Gilman about the sell-off, and a week later he flew to Chicago for the conference, bringing along Rosemary and their children, as he often did when he traveled. Gilman also did not know that Martoma had cultivated a second source connected to the clinical trials—Joel Ross, a New Jersey doctor who had been involved in the efficacy tests. Ross had plans to attend a dinner the night before Gilman's presentation, at which he and other principal investigators would be shown the full data from the trials. Martoma met Ross in the lobby of the hotel immediately after the dinner. But Ross was mystified by their interaction. He was still moderately optimistic about bapi, having seen real improvements in the patients he was supervising, but Martoma was more skeptical. "He was always very detail oriented," Ross later said. But now Martoma already seemed to know every detail of the results that Ross had only just learned himself at the dinner, moments earlier. Ross was unnerved: it was as if Martoma had been "in the room."

As Gilman made his presentation the next evening, word of the ambiguous results hit the news wires. Tim Jandovitz, a young trader who worked for Martoma, watched in dismay as the news appeared on his Bloomberg terminal in Stamford. He checked Panorama, which showed that SAC still held huge positions in Elan and Wyeth. Jandovitz believed that both he and Martoma had just lost more than $100 million of Steve Cohen's money—and, along with it, their jobs. The next morning, he braced himself and went to the office. But when he consulted Panorama, he saw that the Elan and Wyeth shares had vanished. Some time later, Martoma informed Jandovitz that SAC no longer owned the stock. The two men had worked closely together, and Jandovitz was hurt that he had been left out of the loop. Martoma explained that the decision to sell had been kept secret on "instructions from Steve Cohen."

People outside the firm were equally startled to learn that SAC had turned a potential disaster into a windfall. "TELL ME MARTOMA GOT OUT OF ELAN," a friend of Jandovitz's, who worked at J. P. Morgan, said in an instant message. Jandovitz replied, "w/out getting into detail, wed and this week have been GREAT for us."

"I LOVE IT," his friend wrote.

Jandovitz agreed: "Stuff that legends are made of."

That year, Martoma received a bonus of $9.3 million. The last time he saw Gilman—before the two men met again in court—was the day after the presentation, when Martoma invited Gilman to lunch at a Chicago hotel. "Did you hear about what happened to Elan stock?" Martoma said, adding that it had plummeted. The market does not like a drug that helps only half the people who receive it, he explained.

Several months later, at the end of September 2008, Gilman sent Martoma an email with the subject heading "How are you?"

> Hi Mat. I haven't heard from you in awhile and hope that all is well with you and your family. I hope that you have not been too terribly set back by the great turmoil in the markets plus the disappointing drop in Elan stock . . . Anyway, no need to call, I have nothing new; I just wonder how you are faring.

Martoma never responded.

• • •

Regulators at the New York Stock Exchange monitor millions of transactions. Six weeks after the Alzheimer's conference, investigators flagged the huge reversal by SAC before Gilman's presentation and alerted the Securities and Exchange Commission. In the summer of 2009, Charles Riely, an attorney at the SEC, and Neil Hendelman, an investigator, began combing through hundreds of phone records, trying to identify a link between an insider at one of the drug companies and SAC. It took more than a year of investigation, but one day Riely and Hendelman were looking through Gilman's phone records and came across the cell-phone number of Mathew Martoma. Sanjay Wadhwa, who oversaw the SEC investigation, told me, "That's when we said, 'This is probably the guy.'"

By that time, federal authorities had been investigating Steve Cohen for years. But Cohen was a more elusive target than perhaps they had imagined. He described his firm as having a "hub and spokes" structure, with him at the center, pulling in information, while his specialized portfolio managers ran their accounts with a degree of autonomy. This meant that the authorities could arrest and flip low-level suspects who might describe the crooked culture of the place, but these employees would not necessarily be in a position to testify that Cohen knowingly traded on inside information. In the summer of 2009, the FBI obtained a wiretap on Cohen's home, a thirty-five-thousand-square-foot mansion in Greenwich, but the tap yielded no incriminating evidence. According to a person involved in the investigation, Cohen spent most of the month that it was operational in a house that he owned in the Hamptons. For a time, the agency wanted to place an informant in Cohen's company, and groomed a stock trader who had once worked at SAC to seek employment there again. But Cohen rejected the overture, explaining, in a 2011 deposition, that "rumors from people on the street" indicated that the trader was wearing a wire.

In most white-collar cases, the authorities subpoena reams of internal communications, but this approach had limited utility with SAC, whose legal department warned employees not to "compose or send any electronic communication, or leave any voice mail message, if you wouldn't want it . . . read by regulators." On one occasion in July 2009, a new portfolio manager sent Cohen an instant message saying that he was going to short Nokia on the basis of "recent research." He apologized for this oblique rationale but explained that he had just gone through SAC's compliance training—"so I won't be saying much." Anytime a written exchange approached potentially incriminating territory, Cohen insisted on oral communication. "I am getting coffee on tues afternoon with the guy who runs north American generics business," a colleague once informed him. Cohen's reply: "Let's talk later."

Even when there appeared to be ironclad evidence that Cohen had received and acted upon inside information, his lawyers went to impressive rhetorical lengths to challenge it. One day in 2008, Jon Horvath, the analyst, sent an email to two colleagues about an upcoming earnings report from Dell. His source, he wrote, was "a 2nd hand read from someone at the company." One of the colleagues forwarded the email to Cohen's personal research trader, who forwarded it to Cohen—and then telephoned him. Two minutes after the call, Cohen began liquidating his position in Dell, which was worth $10 million.

Yet when this trade became a focus in the Steinberg trial, Cohen's lawyers argued that Cohen's decision to sell Dell was independent: although the "2nd hand read" email was sent to his in-box, Cohen "likely never read" it. He received a thousand emails each day, the lawyers elaborated; he sat at a desk with seven monitors, and it was on the far left monitor that his Outlook in-box appeared. Moreover, the Outlook window was behind two other programs, and the window was minimized, allowing Cohen to see only five emails at a time: "Cohen would have had to turn to the far left of his seven screens, minimize one or two computer programs, scroll down his e-mails, double-click into the 'second-hand read' e-mail to open it, read down three chains of forwards, and digest the information." (Steinberg was ultimately charged with insider trading in the Dell case and convicted; he was sentenced to three and a half years in prison, but he appealed. In 2015, after a court decision narrowed the definition of insider trading, the government dropped all charges against him.) In theory, Steinberg could have testified against his boss to avoid the prospect of jail time, but he might not have been able to produce any additional evidence that Cohen had knowingly traded on inside information. Moreover, Steinberg was an old friend of Cohen's who had worked with him for more than a decade and was therefore unlikely to betray him.

Martoma had no such loyalty to Cohen. After receiving his enormous bonus in 2008, he lost money in 2009. In 2010—down and out—he was fired. In an email, a former colleague disparaged him as a "one trick pony with Elan." Martoma and his family moved to Boca Raton, where he and Rosemary bought a large house in a waterfront community for $1.9 million. Neither of them had a job, and they focused instead on their kids (they had a third child in 2009) and on charity, establishing the Mathew and Rosemary Martoma Foundation and giving it an endowment of $1 million. Martoma's best friend from Duke, Tariq Haddad, who is now a cardiologist in Virginia, told me that Mathew has always been passionate about philanthropy. "He's given 10 percent of his life savings away," he said. "Over a million dollars, he's donated."

On the evening of November 8, 2011, the Martomas returned home from running errands to discover two FBI agents in their front yard. One of them, B. J. Kang, had been a key figure in the investigation of

Steve Cohen. Kang has a buzz cut and a brusque demeanor, and he is known for carrying his service weapon—and several magazines of extra ammunition—with a regularity that may not be entirely necessary for an agent on the hedge-fund beat. "Get inside the house," he told Rosemary. "This has nothing to do with you."

"I'm staying right here," she replied. "Whatever you have to say to Mathew, you can say to me."

Kang turned to Martoma. "Do you want to tell her or should I?"

Martoma looked unsteady. Then he said, "You can go ahead and tell her if you like."

Rosemary was confused and terrified. She had no idea what this was about. According to Rosemary, Kang then said, "We know what you did at Harvard."

Martoma fainted.

• • •

When Martoma was accepted at Harvard Law School, his father was so happy that he insisted on driving his son in a U-Haul all the way from Florida to Massachusetts. Martoma, who at the time was still using his birth name, did well in his first year. He was an editor on the *Harvard Journal of Law & Technology,* and he co-founded the Society on Law and Ethics. In the fall of his second term, he sent applications for judicial clerkships to twenty-three judges. But when a clerk for one of the judges scrutinized Martoma's transcript, something looked off, and the clerk got in touch with the registrar at Harvard. On February 2, 1999, the registrar confronted Martoma. His transcript had apparently been doctored: two Bs and a B plus had all been changed to As. (A remaining B plus, an A, and an A minus were left unchanged.) Martoma initially insisted that "it was all a joke." But the school referred the matter to Harvard's Administrative Board, which recommended expulsion. He fought the decision vociferously, hiring a lawyer and taking two polygraph examinations. There had been a misunderstanding, Martoma explained: he had altered his transcript not for the judges but for his parents. He brought the faked transcript home over winter break, and they were ecstatic. (The panel evaluating his case noted that Martoma was "under extreme parental pressure to excel.") But, after showing his parents the transcript, Martoma continued, he had to leave town abruptly, so he asked one of his younger brothers to compile the clerkship applications that he had left out in his bedroom. Unwittingly, the brother picked up a copy of the forged transcript, and included it in the mailing for the judges. Martoma had discovered the mistake before being confronted by the registrar, he insisted, and had sent emails to the secretaries of two professors from whom he had sought recommendations, asking them not to send the letters, "as I am no longer looking for a clerkship."

The Administrative Board remained dubious, because the secretaries did not receive the emails until the night of February 2—hours after Martoma had been questioned by the registrar. The emails were time-stamped February 1, and Martoma maintained that there had been some sort of server delay, because he had definitely sent them the previous day. His mother, father, and brother all testified before the board and backed his account. Martoma even turned over his laptop to a company called Computer Data Forensics, which produced a technical report for the Administrative Board analyzing the metadata of the emails in which he asked to withdraw the recommendations. The firm found that the emails had indeed been sent on February 1.

Nevertheless, Harvard finalized the expulsion. While contesting his dismissal, Martoma had moved to an apartment complex in Framingham, Massachusetts, where he became friends with a young MIT graduate named Stephen Chan. The two began eating dinner together and training in martial arts at a local gym. Eventually, they started a business. Martoma's parents took out a second mortgage to assist the enterprise, and Martoma and Chan hired several employees. Martoma told the employees that he was a Harvard-trained lawyer. The name of the company was Computer Data Forensics. Martoma had supplied Harvard with a forensic report issued by his own company. The partnership between Martoma and Chan ended, acrimoniously, not long afterward, with Martoma taking out a restraining order against Chan, and Martoma's parents were forced to mediate with disgruntled employees (who had not been paid). Bobby Martoma, incensed with his son, called him "a complete liability." Later that year, Martoma applied to business school at Stanford. Soon after being accepted, he stopped calling himself Ajai Mathew Thomas and legally adopted his current name. Stanford surely would not have accepted him had it known of his expulsion from Harvard, but because Stanford will not comment on the case, it is impossible to know whether Martoma mischaracterized his year in Cambridge or left it out of his academic history altogether. To Ronald Green, his former supervisor at the NIH, he explained his departure from Harvard by pointing to the entrepreneurial opportunities available at that time. "The way I understood it, he dropped out to start a business, and it was booming," Green told me.

When I asked Rosemary Martoma when she learned about the expulsion, she said that Mathew had confided it to her early in their relationship. "I'm a full-disclosure person," she explained. But the incident was a source of humiliation for Martoma and for his family, and it became a closely held secret. Even his best friend, Tariq Haddad, always believed that Martoma dropped out of law school; he learned the truth only recently, after Martoma was indicted. Martoma always feared exposure of the Harvard incident, Rosemary said: "It was like a dagger that had been hanging over his head." (SAC performed background checks on prospective employees, but it is not known whether the firm detected this blemish in Martoma's record. Of course, SAC could have learned of it and hired him anyway; forging a law school transcript and mailing it to twenty-three federal judges demonstrates impressive comfort with risk.)

When Martoma regained consciousness, Agent Kang told him that the FBI knew about "the trade in 2008." Both Rosemary and Mathew immediately understood what he meant. The other agent, Matt Callahan, hung back, but Kang was aggressive. "Your whole life is going to be turned upside down," he said. "You're going to lose all your friends, and your children are going to grow up hating you, because you're going to live your years in a jail cell." According to Rosemary, Kang said that the government would "crush" Martoma unless he cooperated. "We want Steve Cohen," Kang said.

Martoma was not an ideal star witness: if Cohen's lawyers could find a path of escape through a minimized Outlook window, imagine what they might do to Martoma's credibility on the stand by bringing up his Harvard career. Then again, criminal kingpins are often convicted on the testimony of morally dubious underlings. The key witness who put away John Gotti was Sammy "the Bull" Gravano, who had confessed to nineteen murders. A rap sheet was practically a prerequisite to testify against Whitey Bulger. And Martoma clearly possessed a dogged instinct for self-preservation. His parents still called him by his birth name, Ajai, which in Hindi means "Undefeatable."

But then something surprising happened. Martoma refused to cooperate.

· · ·

Agent Kang had already paid a visit to Sid Gilman. At an initial meeting at the university, and in several subsequent conversations, investigators asked Gilman if he had supplied confidential information about bapineuzumab to Martoma. Gilman repeatedly lied to them. "I was intensely ashamed," he explained later. "I had betrayed my colleagues, myself, my university." Kang told Gilman that he was a minor player in this saga—a "grain of sand"—and that the person the authorities were really after was Steve Cohen. Eventually, Gilman agreed to tell the government everything, in exchange for a promise not to prosecute him. Would Martoma flip next? In criminal cases where cooperation is a possibility, a defendant's attorney goes to prosecutors with a "proffer," explaining what the client might offer in exchange for lenient treatment. But, despite warnings from Agent Kang that if Martoma went to trial the FBI would "ruin his life," Martoma's attorneys never broached the notion of a plea deal. Here was a hedge funder who might finally deliver Steve Cohen and, because of his enormous profits from the bapi trade, would face extensive jail time if he didn't. Yet Martoma was intransigent. Eventually, a team of FBI agents returned to Boca Raton and, in front of the children, marched him out of his house in handcuffs.

In financial and law-enforcement circles, many wondered why Martoma accepted the role of fall guy. One explanation suggested to me by numerous people was that a numbered account had been set up for the Martomas in some tropical banking haven. But this scenario struck me as unlikely. Suppose that Cohen did seek to witness tamper in this way. Even if he did so in the billionaire's fashion—through

multiple intermediary layers of deniability—wouldn't he be handing Martoma the ammunition for a lifetime of blackmail? If someone
promised Martoma $10 million not to testify about securities fraud,
what would stop him from renegotiating on the spot, by demanding
twenty million not to testify about obstruction of justice on top of
securities fraud? Even so, Cohen's money was an inescapable factor
in the case. After working briefly with a criminal-defense attorney
named Charles Stillman, Martoma chose to retain Goodwin Procter,
a major law firm with very high fees. But Martoma was not paying for
his lawyers: SAC was. So the attorneys advising Martoma on whether
he should risk a jail sentence or testify against Cohen were sending
their bills to Cohen's company.

After the U.S. Attorney's office announced an indictment of Martoma, Cohen convened a company-wide meeting at SAC and said that
he was furious about the behavior of "a handful of employees." Martoma was the eighth person who had worked for Cohen to be charged
with insider trading—the largest number of individuals from any U.S.
financial institution to be criminally charged in recent years. Even if
Martoma didn't turn on Cohen, the company was clearly in trouble. In
March 2013, lawyers for SAC agreed to pay $616 million to the SEC in
order to settle civil insider-trading charges. Several months later, the
SEC launched a separate case against Cohen personally, charging him
with "failure to supervise" subordinates and alleging that he received
"highly suspicious information that should have caused any reasonable hedge-fund manager . . . to take prompt action." In the summer
of 2014, the Department of Justice announced a criminal indictment
of SAC—though not of Cohen directly—alleging that the company
had become a "magnet for market cheaters" and that Cohen had presided over insider trading "on a scale without known precedent in the
hedge-fund industry." Not long afterward, the firm pleaded guilty to
the criminal charges, agreeing to pay a historic fine of $1.8 billion.

Cohen had always greeted allegations of impropriety at SAC with
bored disdain. When a lawyer asked him in a deposition in 2011 about
Rule 10b-5—the federal regulation against insider trading—Cohen
claimed not to know what it said. The lawyer pointed out that Cohen's
own compliance manual at SAC spelled out the rule. Cohen responded

that he didn't know what the compliance manual said, either. The lawyer was incredulous: "You don't know, sitting here today as the head of the firm, what your compliance manual says?"

"That's right," Cohen said. "I've read it. But if you're asking me what it says today, I don't remember."

Not long after SAC announced its settlement with the SEC, the news broke that Cohen had bought Picasso's *Le rêve* for $155 million—the second-highest price in history for a painting. While he was at it, he bought a new house in East Hampton, a waterfront property worth $60 million.

• • •

The trial of Mathew Martoma began in January 2014 and lasted a month. Blizzards had deposited huge snowbanks around the federal courthouse in downtown Manhattan, and every morning Mathew and Rosemary Martoma arrived in a chauffeured car and clambered, with their lawyers, over cordons of dirty snow. They had brought the children with them to New York and were staying at a midtown hotel. Mathew's mother and father had come from Florida for the trial, and they sat in the front row, bundled in winter coats and scarves and looking solemn. Rosemary's parents sat beside them. "Ladies and gentlemen, the case is not about scientific testing and it is not about trading," the government's lead lawyer, Arlo Devlin-Brown, told the jury. "The case is about cheating."

Martoma, wearing a dark suit, watched impassively as a parade of former SAC colleagues testified; Rosemary smiled when she agreed with a witness and flared her nostrils when she didn't. She wore eye-catching clothes, becoming an attraction for the tabloid photographers who clustered at the base of the courthouse steps. An article in *Bloomberg Businessweek* remarked on her poise in the courtroom and the defiant smile she maintained when she and Mathew walked in and out of the courthouse, hand in hand, "as if she's walking a red carpet."

The government presented dozens of emails that Martoma sent to Cohen and other colleagues, and called on Joel Ross, the doctor from New Jersey, to recount how he shared inside information with Martoma. But the heart of the case was the testimony of Sid Gilman, who in the second week made his way, slowly, to the stand. Gilman had resigned from the University of Michigan, and administrators had scrubbed all traces of him from the institution: the wing of the hospital, the lecture series, the university's website. His federal grant support disappeared, his former colleagues wanted nothing to do with him, and he was banned from the campus. He had lately been advising patients at a free clinic. "I had given a great deal to that university, and I am suddenly ending my career in disgrace," he said. Gilman still dressed elegantly, his shirt and tie cinched tightly around his neck, accentuating his large, round head. But he was eighty-one and visibly frail. During five days of testimony, he looked marooned in the witness box, a shipwrecked man.

Several lawyers suggested to me that Martoma's attorneys should never have let the case go to trial, because the evidence against him was so conclusive that he didn't stand a chance. But his defense team, a pair of lean and intense litigators, Richard Strassberg and Roberto Braceras, relentlessly attacked Gilman's credibility as a witness. Gilman had apparently told prosecutors that he had emailed a copy of the PowerPoint presentation to Martoma. But, the defense team pointed out, the prosecutors had failed to find any trace of that email. At times, Gilman just seemed confused. Asked about the population of Ann Arbor, he said that it was fifteen hundred. (The population exceeds a hundred thousand.) Some of Gilman's colleagues speculated that after decades of studying neurodegenerative disorders, he was now succumbing to cognitive decline himself. Of course, this may be a generous interpretation of actions that many who knew him found inexplicable. "Nobody could believe it," Anne Young told me. "To jeopardize his career for a hundred thousand dollars or so is insane."

Martoma, Strassberg told the jury, was "the quintessential American success story," whereas Gilman was a confused old man who had been coached by the government. When speaking to Gilman, Strassberg combined the elevated volume you might use to address someone who is hard of hearing with the patronizing tone you might employ with a ten-year-old. If this was a strategy, it backfired. Every time Strassberg asked whether Gilman hadn't heard or understood something that he said, Gilman bristled. "You're slurring your words," the old doctor snapped at one point.

Martoma's lawyers suggested that the information Gilman shared with Martoma was already publicly available. "There is nothing nefarious or improper about trying to get edge," Braceras argued. "That was the job." The lawyers challenged the government's narrative of a special relationship between Gilman and Martoma, observing that Gilman had consultations with scores of other investors. But former colleagues of Gilman's told me that the government's story was plausible. "Sid was a mentor to so many people, and enjoyed that role, and was good at it," Tim Greenamyre said. "I could certainly see how, if someone was cunning and perceptive, they could pick up on that, and take advantage of it."

As Gilman answered questions on the stand, day after day, he looked, above all, lonely. His son Todd lived nearby, in New Haven, but they had hardly spoken for years. On his final day of testimony, Gilman was asked what set Martoma apart from the other investors he had dealt with. "He was personable," Gilman replied. After a pause, he said, "And he, unfortunately, reminded me of my first son. In his inquisitiveness. His brightness. And, sadly, my first son was very bright also, and committed suicide."

• • •

One matter that was not illuminated at trial was the substance of the twenty-minute phone call that Martoma had with Cohen on the Sunday morning after his trip to Michigan. If Martoma took the stand, prosecutors would attack his credibility by introducing evidence of his expulsion from Harvard Law School, so he elected not to testify in his own defense. Steve Cohen wasn't called to testify, either. In 2012, he had been asked about the phone call during his deposition with the SEC. He said only that Martoma was "getting uncomfortable with the Elan position." Asked whether he inquired why Martoma had grown uncomfortable, Cohen said that he remembered having done so—but that he could not recall Martoma's answer.

A second theory about why Martoma didn't flip on Cohen was that any conversation the two of them had that day would have been deliberately opaque. Cohen would never be so foolish as to sit and listen while a subordinate laid out the full provenance of an illegal tip. At some firms, Judge Holwell told me, there is an unwritten "don't ask, don't tell" policy, where the fact that a piece of information came from an insider would be conveyed not in so many words but with a facial expression, a tone of voice, or coded language (say, a conviction level of nine). The sociologist Diego Gambetta, in his book *Codes of the Underworld,* explains that people engaged in criminal conduct often evolve an elaborate semiotics to communicate with one another, because they cannot speak openly about their plans. One federal official who has investigated SAC told me, "In the Mob, sometimes it's just an expression. One expression means 'Kill him.' Another expression means 'Don't kill him.' How do you bring that to a jury?"

After deliberating for three days, the jury convicted Martoma of two counts of securities fraud and one count of conspiracy. Rosemary wept as the verdict was read. The guidelines for his sentence would be based not just on the $9.3 million bonus he had received from SAC in 2008 but also on the $275 million profit that SAC had made on the bapi trades. Yet Cohen was not charged with those trades, or even named as an unindicted co-conspirator. The judge, Paul Gardephe, went so far as to ask the attorneys to avoid discussing Cohen altogether, because he had not been charged with any crime. "General questions about how Steve Cohen conducted his trading, I think, are very dangerous," he told them. "They represent a risk of opening the door to a broader examination of how Steve Cohen did business . . . And I think we all agree that that is not a path we want to go down." (In a subsequent ruling, Gardephe left little doubt about his own views, concluding that Cohen's trades in July 2008 "were based on inside information that Martoma had supplied.") During the trial, Cohen was photographed at a Knicks game, sitting courtside with the art dealer Larry Gagosian. According to a recent article in *New York,* Cohen told his children that he felt betrayed by his subordinates. "People in the company have done things that are wrong, and they're going to pay for what they did," he said. "I didn't do anything wrong."

Before Judge Gardephe delivered his sentence, Martoma's family sent him 143 letters from friends and supporters, pleading for leniency. "We pressed him to excel until he maxed out," Bobby Martoma wrote. "As a father, I wonder . . . whether I was wrong to dream as I did." On September 8, 2014, Gardephe sentenced Martoma to nine years

in federal prison. Delivering the sentence, he invoked the deception
at Harvard and suggested that there was a "common thread" between
that transgression and this case: an "unwillingness to accept anything
other than the top grade, the best school, the highest bonus—and the
willingness to do anything to achieve that result."

· · ·

A few days after the sentencing, I took an elevator to the twenty-sixth
floor of a skyscraper on Forty-Second Street to meet with Rosemary
and Mathew Martoma. I walked into a glass-walled conference room
that seemed to hover over midtown. Martoma was there, wearing a
neat V-neck sweater. He shook my hand, smiled warmly, and thanked
me for coming. But he did not want to talk. Rosemary explained that
she would speak on his behalf. She was wearing a cream-colored
blouse, tan slacks, and a tiny gold crucifix around her neck, and after
Mathew left the room, we talked for nearly four hours.

Things were looking dire for the Martomas. The government
would likely take possession of their house in Boca Raton, and Judge
Gardephe had ordered them to forfeit the millions of dollars that they
have spread across several bank accounts, which would clear out their
savings while still falling well short of the $9 million that they have
been ordered to pay the U.S. government. When I consulted the tax
returns of the Mathew and Rosemary Martoma Foundation, I discovered that the couple had not, in fact, given $1 million to charity.
Instead, after parking that sum in their tax-exempt nonprofit, they
had given away smaller amounts to various charities. In 2011, they
gave away only $3,000; this included a check to the Florida chapter of
the Alzheimer's Association, in the amount of $210. All the remaining
money in the foundation will now go to the government.

When I asked Rosemary why Mathew didn't flip on Cohen, her
answer did not match any of the prevailing theories. "He's innocent,"
she said. Martoma could not plead guilty to a crime he did not commit. Outside the courthouse, after the sentencing, Bobby Martoma
had told me much the same thing, invoking the Ten Commandments
and bellowing, "Thou shalt not bear false witness!" The government's
case was a fiction, Rosemary assured me. "At SAC, there's an expectation that you're using the resources to formulate a hypothesis, and

that's what he did," she said. But Gilman had admitted to violating his own confidentiality agreement, I pointed out. He might have had "little mini brain infarcts, where he was slipping on things he shouldn't have," Rosemary said. But these were "irrelevant to Mathew's trading." Gilman had lost everything. Why would he lie on the stand about having committed these crimes? Because, Rosemary explained, when he was initially interviewed by FBI agents, he lied to them, and at that point they had him on obstruction of justice. So the prosecutors could make him say anything they wanted. "His story was coerced," she said.

She told me about her grandfather, a lawyer in India who had worked alongside Mahatma Gandhi in the struggle for independence. British authorities threw her grandfather into prison, where he contracted cholera and other ailments, from which he never fully recovered. Rosemary noted the "parallels" between her grandfather's martyrdom and her husband's. Rosemary's mother, in a letter to Judge Gardephe, elaborated: "Mathew has given Rosemary courage by reminding her of her grandfather's suffering for a noble principle, and that he too is standing for a noble principle, that is sticking to the truth."

While Rosemary and I spoke, Mathew retreated to an inner room in the law offices where we were meeting. Periodically, Rosemary left me alone in the conference room and went to confer with him. It was a discomfiting interview scenario, with Martoma lurking in the wings like Polonius. People who maintain their innocence after a criminal conviction are often desperate to get their stories out, and each time Rosemary disappeared to debrief Mathew on our conversation, I half expected him to walk back in with her and tell me that he had been railroaded by the feds. But he never came. They had arranged for a single chicken-salad sandwich to be delivered, and it sat on a sideboard, wrapped in plastic. Eventually, alone in the conference room, I ate it.

When Rosemary returned, she spoke at length about the duplicity of Sid Gilman. "He's a strange man, and he compromised his values to save himself," she said. The notion that Gilman and Martoma had a special relationship was "far-fetched"—a fabrication of the prosecutors that Gilman had parroted. "There is no relationship outside of a cordial consulting relationship," she said, mocking the notion that Gilman was genuinely moved by Martoma having arranged lunch at their initial meeting in New York. She looked at me pointedly and said, "I mean, were you touched when we served a sandwich to you?"

Throughout our conversations, Rosemary was quick, animated, and intelligent. But her account stood at odds with what I had witnessed during the monthlong trial and had encountered in my reporting. She stressed that when Mathew visited Michigan that summer weekend before the 2008 Alzheimer's conference, it was indeed because a relative had died. "Did he see Gilman while he was there?" I asked. "I don't think he has a specific memory of it," she replied. Early in our conversation, I had asked if Martoma felt vindicated by his acceptance at Harvard Law School, having been denied admission at Harvard College. After one of her visits with him, Rosemary returned to the room and said that she needed to correct one point: "Mathew *did* get into college at Harvard."

"As an undergrad?" I asked.

"Yeah," she said. "He was admitted and chose to go to Duke instead."

This struck me as hard to believe. I asked why Martoma, the very opposite of a rebellious kid, might defy his father's deepest wish. She responded, vaguely, that Duke "was southern" and "felt a little bit more comfortable to him." I wondered if, on this and other points, Rosemary was simply lying to me. But as our conversation progressed, it became clear that she ardently believed in her husband. She reminisced about her medical residency in Boston, when she would be on call overnight and Mathew would sleep in the hospital with her so that she wouldn't be alone. She pointed to the many letters written to Gardephe as evidence of the degree to which Mathew remained a beloved friend and a role model for his extended family. "Every Indian parent I've known, they take the weight of their children on their shoulders," she said. "When you look into the eyes of all the four parents that are left behind, every single heart is broken." Mathew's mother had told him recently that she wished she could serve his prison sentence for him, Rosemary said. She added, "I've said that to him, too."

Within this close-knit family, it seemed crucial to maintain that

Martoma was going to prison for a crime that he did not commit, and it occurred to me that there might be one final explanation for his unwillingness to accuse Cohen of criminality. In order to implicate Cohen in a conspiracy, Martoma would have had to plead guilty and admit to being part of that conspiracy himself. Could it be that Martoma was prepared to leave his wife and family and spend the better part of a decade in prison for the sake of preserving their illusion that he was an honorable man? I thought of Gilman on the stand, abandoned by his friends and colleagues, while the first few pews in the courtroom were filled by Martoma's extended family—by people who believed in him.

Martoma was scheduled to begin his sentence, at a federal prison in Miami, in a month. When I asked how Rosemary and the children would manage, she said, "I'm not sure." The children are nine, seven, and five. "They understand Daddy's going to jail," she said. "I mean, as an adult, I'm having a hard time understanding it." Neither side of the family has any savings to give them, she said, adding, "There is not, and never was, and never will be, any discussion of Steve Cohen taking care of us."

By April, SAC had ceased to exist, and Cohen's company was rechristened Point72 Asset Management. Under an agreement with the government, it would be limited to investing Cohen's personal fortune of roughly $9 billion. Cohen announced that he would institute more robust compliance measures to prevent insider trading and that he had hired the Silicon Valley security company Palantir Technologies to monitor his traders. He had also reportedly banned certain kinds of instant messaging at the firm. When I asked Preet Bharara about the ultimate failure of his multiyear effort to catch Cohen, he responded, through a spokesman, that his office brings charges against "those for whom there is sufficient proof."

After Martoma's conviction, Stanford Business School rescinded its original offer of admission, effectively stripping him of his degree. "What to make of the early interest in ethics?" his Duke professor Bruce Payne asked. "A hugely ambitious guy wanting to know the exact contours of the boundaries that might limit him? Or an anchor to the windward for self-protection by someone already willing to break the rules to his own advantage? If it was the latter, I was conned, and conned quite effectively."

When I asked Rosemary about the future, she cried. "I don't have the answers, but you know it is my goal to find them," she said. "And I do pray that America will give us a chance to survive. And to thrive."

While Mathew Martoma served his sentence, Rosemary started a nonprofit called KidsMates, to support children facing adversity, particularly children with a parent who is incarcerated. Steve Cohen settled the SEC's civil case against him in 2016; he was barred from investing outside money, but only until 2018. He remains one of the richest people on Wall Street. In 2020, he bought a controlling interest in the New York Mets.

A LOADED GUN

A mass shooter's tragic past. (2013)

AMY BISHOP, A NEUROBIOLOGIST at the University of Alabama in Huntsville, sat down at the conference table just moments before the faculty meeting began. It was three o'clock on February 12, 2010, and thirteen professors and staff members in the biology department had crowded into a windowless conference room on the third floor of the Shelby Center for Science and Technology. The department chair, a plant biologist named Gopi Podila, distributed a printed agenda. Bishop was sitting next to him, in a spot by the door. Inside her handbag was a gun.

Bishop was forty-four, with a long, pale face framed by dark hair that she wore in a pageboy, her bangs slashed just above her small blue eyes. She was normally a vocal participant in departmental meetings, but on this occasion she was silent, and she appeared to be brooding. There was an obvious explanation: a year earlier, the department had denied Bishop's bid for tenure, and her protracted and increasingly desperate efforts to appeal the decision had been fruitless. When the semester ended, she knew, her job would end as well. Much of Podila's agenda concerned plans for the next semester, so there was another plausible reason for Bishop's withdrawn manner: she didn't really need to be there.

A biochemist named Debra Moriarity watched Bishop from across the table. Moriarity knew all about Bishop's tenure woes; they had developed a friendship since Bishop had arrived on campus as an assistant professor in 2003. They often talked about their families: Bishop had four children (her oldest, Lily, was a student at Huntsville); Moriarity had recently become a grandmother. Moriarity had voted against Bishop's receiving tenure, and Bishop knew it, but they had remained cordial, and Bishop had confided in Moriarity about her professional despair. "My life is over," she had said at one point. Moriarty reassured her that she would find another position. "It's just a matter of the fit," Moriarty said. During the meeting, she made a mental note to ask Bishop how her search for a new job was going.

For fifty minutes, Bishop said nothing. Then, just as the meeting was concluding, she stood up, pulled out the gun, a 9 mm Ruger semiautomatic, and shot Podila in the head. The blast was deafening. She fired again, hitting a department assistant, Stephanie Monticciolo. Next, Bishop turned and shot Adriel Johnson, a cell biologist. People screamed and ducked for cover, but Bishop was blocking the only door. Moriarty did not fully register what was happening until she saw Bishop—her jaw set, her brow furrowed—train the gun on a fourth colleague, Maria Ragland Davis, and shoot her.

Moriarty dived under the table. With gunshots ringing out above her, she flung her arms around Bishop's legs, looked up, and screamed, "Amy, don't do this! Think of my daughter! Think of my grandson!" Bishop looked down—then turned the gun on Moriarty.

Click. Moriarty, in terror, stared at the gun. *Click.* The weapon had jammed. Moriarty crawled past Bishop and into the hallway; Bishop followed her, repeatedly squeezing the trigger. As Bishop tried to fix the gun, Moriarty scrambled back into the conference room, and another colleague barricaded the door. The room, a prosecutor later said, looked "like a bomb went off. Like a war zone." Six people had been shot, three of them fatally. The entire episode had lasted less than a minute.

Bishop went downstairs to a ladies' room, where she rinsed off the gun and stuffed it, along with her bloodstained plaid blazer, into a trash can. Then she walked into a lab and asked a student if she could borrow his cell phone. She called her husband, Jim, who often picked her up after class, and said, "I'm done." When she left the Shelby Center, through a loading dock in the back, a sheriff's deputy apprehended her.

Satellite news trucks began arriving to report on the tragedy. By 2010, mass shootings in America had nearly lost their capacity to shock. Although it was only February, there had already been fifteen other shootings that year involving three or more victims. But

Amy Bishop's case was notable in that she did not fit the profile of a mass shooter: women very rarely commit such killings. Bishop had been a high achiever since childhood. An accomplished violinist in her youth, she had received a PhD from Harvard and had completed postdoctoral work at the Harvard School of Public Health. Her marriage appeared to be stable. She had no criminal record and no history of substance abuse.

After massacres involving gun violence, from Columbine High School in 1999 to Sandy Hook Elementary School in 2012, one of our national rituals is to search for some overlooked sign that the shooters were capable of such brutality. "This is not a whodunit," Amy Bishop's court-appointed lawyer, Roy Miller, observed after the Huntsville attack: Bishop left nine living witnesses to her crime. The question was why. After the shooting, the press initially focused on Bishop's professional disgruntlement. (A headline in *The Chronicle of Higher Education* asked, "Is Tenure a Matter of Life or Death?") But Miller suggested that the problem was more complicated. "There are people in our community who are walking time bombs," he said, adding, "They are so hard to identify."

The morning after Bishop was taken into custody, the sheriff's department in Huntsville received a phone call from a man named Paul Frazier, who said that he was the chief of police in Braintree, Massachusetts—the Boston suburb where Bishop had grown up. Frazier said, "The woman you have in custody, I thought you'd want to know: she shot and killed her brother back in 1986."

• • •

The Bishop family home in Braintree, at 46 Hollis Avenue, is a gabled Victorian with a gracious covered porch. It was built in the nineteenth century by a dentist who ran his practice from a cottage on the property. The front lawn is dominated by a giant copper beech whose knuckled branches are sturdy enough to support climbing children. When Amy's little brother, Seth, was a boy, he would ascend the tree, then panic, unable to get back down. His mother, Judy, would issue branch-by-branch instructions until he reached the ground.

Judy, whose maiden name was Sanborn, came from an old New

England family in Exeter, New Hampshire, where her grandfather had owned a shoe factory. She met her husband, Sam, at the New England School of Art, in Boston. He was in many ways her opposite: born Sotir Papazoglos, he was raised by immigrants in a Greek enclave of Somerville. He joined the U.S. Air Force in 1954 and later changed his name to Sam Bishop. Judy was a gregarious woman with a curly blond mane and a raucous sense of humor; Sam was taciturn and burly, with an Old World reserve. "I chased him until he caught me," Judy liked to say.

In 1964, they moved to Iowa City, where Sam did graduate work in fine arts at the University of Iowa, painting during the day and working as a janitor at night. The next year, Judy gave birth to Amy. She was a bright, emphatic child who arranged her toys in elaborate formations, as if they were perpetually on parade. The family eventually returned to Massachusetts, where Sam got a teaching job in the art department at Northeastern University. They settled in Braintree in 1968, and Seth was born later that year.

Braintree is a middle-class suburb just south of Boston, at the edge of the Blue Hills. During the postwar years, it became a beachhead for Irish and Italian families fleeing the city's grittier precincts. (When I was growing up in Dorchester, a few miles away, people from Braintree and nearby towns used to joke that they were OFD, originally from Dorchester, with a distinctly Bostonian nostalgia—proud to be from there, but also proud to have left.)

Braintree could seem clannish, but Judy's affability won people over. She got involved in civic life, joining the town meeting, the local governing body, and drawing editorial cartoons for the local paper. Deb Kosarick, a nurse who rented the cottage from the Bishops and grew close to the family, told me, "She was like the town spokesperson. If you had a question, you'd call her."

Amy was asthmatic, and her childhood was punctuated by trips to the emergency room. Her early attraction to science was a by-product of this affliction: she resolved to find a cure. She started playing the violin in the third grade, and Seth asked Sam and Judy if he could play, too. It has been suggested that there was a rivalry between the siblings, and Amy certainly possessed a competitive streak. But those who knew them at the time insist that the Bishop kids were close. "She doted on her little brother," Kathleen Oldham, who was close friends with Amy in Braintree, said. "They both loved music, loved science. She seemed to enjoy having someone younger to collaborate with."

Amy recently called me from the Alabama prison where she is incarcerated. Maintaining that she and her brother always had "a good relationship," she reminisced about childhood excursions to the beach with him and about spending time together at her grandmother's summer house on Lake Winnipesaukee, in New Hampshire. "Seth and I loved each other," she said.

Siblings can be confederates just as easily as rivals, particularly when they feel at odds with their milieu. "Braintree is a jock town," one of Judy's friends told me, and in this context the gangly, studious Bishops could seem exotic. When they practiced the violin on summer evenings, their shrill arpeggios elicited, among neighbors, a mixture of curiosity and envy. "Amy was kind of a loner," Judy's friend recalled. "But in a town like Braintree, a bright kid is apt to be."

Seth was shy, too, but less aloof. "Seth would sit and talk with you," Deb Kosarick remembers. "He'd pull up a chair. Amy was more of a breeze-through kind of person." He plunged into new hobbies with enthusiasm. "Seth liked to find out how things worked," his best friend, Paul Agnew, told me. Their friendship grew out of a shared fascination with trains: they tinkered with a model railroad that Seth had constructed in his attic, and sneaked past "No Trespassing" signs into a local Conrail yard, where they could examine the mammoth locomotives up close. On his bike, Seth ventured beyond Braintree; with a pen and a map, he charted ambitious expeditions through surrounding communities. Sometimes Judy would be driving, miles from home, and see a solitary rider pedaling up ahead, only to discover that it was her son.

I spoke with some of Seth's friends, now men in their forties, and more than one started crying at the mention of his name. They attested to his mischievous vitality and his self-possession. Once, in middle school, he was surrounded in the cafeteria by classmates who taunted him for carrying his violin and suggested, mockingly, that he play it. Seth removed the instrument from its case, raised his bow, and began to play, beautifully, until the bullies were cowed into silence. "He called their bluff," Agnew, who observed the episode, remembered.

During his senior year of high school, Seth began dating a boisterous, diminutive junior named Melissa Tatreau. Amy, who had moved into Boston to attend Northeastern, did not seem to approve of the relationship. "I got the impression she thought I wasn't good enough," Melissa told me. Seth's family was inviolable, Melissa was learning— "a unit."

One night in 1985, the Bishops returned home from the wake of Sam's father to find the curtains billowing out of an open first-floor window. Thieves had ransacked their house, stealing Judy's wedding ring, a pair of silver cups commemorating the births of Seth and Amy, and other valuables, and stuffing them into pillowcases stripped from the children's beds. The family was distraught. Judy wrote a letter to the local paper, pleading for the return of their keepsakes. Sam drove to nearby Canton, where he visited a sporting-goods store and purchased a twelve-gauge shotgun. Judy and Amy objected to having the gun in the house, but Sam kept the weapon, unloaded, in his bedroom closet, with a box of shells on a nearby dresser.

More than a year later, on December 6, 1986, the Braintree police received a frantic 911 call from Judy Bishop. Her daughter had shot her son, she said. Soon afterward, she told the police that she had witnessed the whole thing. It was an accident.

• • •

The chief of the Braintree Police Department, John Vincent Polio, was an acquaintance of Judy Bishop's. He had joined the force in 1950 and rose to the top job in 1962, acquiring a reputation for being cunning, controlling, and eccentric. Polio had a gleaming bald head and hooded, skeptical eyes, and he wore pin-striped suits and colorful ties. He had made his name as a reformer and a moralist, shutting down pornographic theaters and unlicensed gambling parlors. He set about upending the cozy quid pro quos that can distinguish small-town life, banning practices like "ticket fixing," in which local grandees who were stopped for speeding could call in a favor at the department and get the ticket expunged. "Between pols and cops, there gets to be a symbiotic relationship," he once observed. "Like suckers feeding on sharks."

Polio was especially determined to curb police corruption. Once, in 1974, he received a tip that two of his own officers were planning to burglarize a local restaurant, the Mai Tai, and he arrested the men himself. He was hard on his subordinates, even the honest ones, and one local resident who knew Polio told me, "He had a crew that didn't like him very much."

One of the young officers in the department was Paul Frazier, who went on to become chief himself, and later informed authorities in Alabama about Seth Bishop's death. "Polio didn't trust anybody," Frazier told me when I met him. Yet, as embattled as Polio felt, Frazier said, "I would bet he was the most powerful person in this town."

We were sitting in Frazier's office, in a back corner of the police station. He was preparing to retire, but had agreed to talk about the Bishop case. "This used to be Polio's office," Frazier said with a smile, adding, "but it didn't look like this." Polio was something of an autodidact, and he had helped design the police station—a squat complex of striated brown stone. Keeping the drapes of his office closed, he would sit in the amber light of a single bulb above his desk and glower at visitors, Frazier recalled, "like he was J. Edgar Hoover."

On the morning of December 6, 1986, Judy Bishop got up while it was still dark. With the rest of the family asleep upstairs, she left the house and drove, as she did most days, to nearby Quincy, where she stabled an elderly gelding. She usually spent a few hours exercising the horse and cleaning out the stable. It later became a significant question when, exactly, she returned to the house, but she was definitely there by just after 2:00 p.m., when she called the police.

The station is less than two miles from the Bishop house, so officers quickly arrived at the scene. Judy met them at the front door, her clothing spotted with blood. She directed them to the kitchen. Seth lay in a crimson slick on the floor, bleeding to death from a chest wound. Amy, who was twenty-one at the time, wasn't there.

As paramedics tried to revive her son, Judy spoke to the police. Seth had just returned home from the grocery store, she said, and she was in the kitchen with him when Amy came downstairs, carrying Sam's shotgun.

Judy told the officers, "Amy said to me, 'I have a shell in the gun, and I don't know how to unload it.' I told Amy not to point the gun at anybody." But, as Amy swung the weapon around to show it to her brother, Judy said, "the gun fired." The kitchen was small, and Amy had been standing close to her brother, so the shot hit Seth point-blank. When he collapsed, Judy told the police, Amy fled.

The officers put out a bulletin, and not long afterward Amy was picked up outside an auto-body shop in town. She was taken to the police station, where a lieutenant named James Sullivan interviewed her. That morning, Amy had been alone in the house; after her mother had left for the stables, her father and her brother had also gone out. "She stated that she loaded the shotgun because she had been worried about 'robbers' coming into the house," Sullivan wrote afterward. Seth had once taught her how to load the weapon, she said—but not how to unload it. So she loaded several shells, but as she was trying to figure out how to remove them, she accidentally fired a shot, shattering a vanity mirror and blasting a hole in her bedroom wall. When she heard Seth come home, she went downstairs and asked him to help her unload it, at which point, Sullivan wrote, "she turned and the shotgun went off." He added, "I asked her if she shot her brother on purpose and she stated no."

Amy told the police that her father had left the house that morning after a family "spat." Later, in Sam's own interview with law enforcement, he described it as "a disagreement with Amy" over "a comment that she had made." He left at around 11:30 a.m. and browsed for Christmas presents at the South Shore Plaza, a nearby mall. When he returned home, Hollis Avenue was aglow with emergency lights.

Sam hurried to the hospital and was there at 3:08 p.m., when Seth was pronounced dead. He was eighteen. As Seth's thin body was pushed past Sam on a gurney, Seth seemed to turn his head and gaze up at his father. "They keep saying he was dead, but he didn't seem dead to me," Sam later recalled. "He looked at me."

That evening, Amy was released from the police station, and Judy and Sam took her home. "Due to the highly emotional state of Amy Bishop, it had generally been impossible to question her while she was at the Braintree Police Department," a subsequent report maintained. So Amy had been "released to the custody of her parents with further investigation to follow." While the family was out, some neighbors had scrubbed Seth's blood from the kitchen floor, to spare them the task.

Deb Kosarick, the nurse renting the cottage, arrived home around suppertime, and she joined Judy in the kitchen. Amy had gone upstairs and climbed into her parents' bed. Sam had retreated to his study. Kosarick's grandfather had been a police officer in a small town in Massachusetts, and Kosarick, knowing a bit about law enforcement, was surprised that Amy had been released so quickly. As Judy relayed the horror of what had happened, Kosarick noticed specks of blood and tissue still clinging to the kitchen appliances. "You can't be in here," she said to Judy, gently escorting her from the room.

"When death comes to a young person . . . the community as a whole stops for just a second, attempting to catch its breath," a friend of Judy's, Vincent Martino, wrote in the local paper. In the days after Seth died, people came by the Bishops' house to drop off Chinese food or to express condolences. Scores of mourners attended Seth's wake, at the All Souls Church. His body was in an open casket, and Sam and Judy clung to their daughter. "Amy looked like a zombie," her friend Kathleen Oldham recalls. "She was catatonic."

A medical examiner ruled Seth's death an accident, pending a police investigation. Two days after the shooting, Chief Polio told *The Boston Globe,* "Every indication at this point in time leads us to believe it was an accidental shooting." But the ultimate responsibility to investigate fell to the district attorney. Eleven days after the killing, Brian Howe, a state trooper working with the DA's office, along with two Braintree police officers, interviewed the Bishops at the house on Hollis Avenue. In Howe's final report on the case, dated March 30, 1987, he concluded that Seth's death was the result of "the accidental discharge of a firearm."

• • •

When I spoke to Amy on the phone, she said that she was "horrified" by her brother's death. She insisted that it had been an accident, but said that she nevertheless felt "guilty." For months after the shooting, she crawled into bed with her parents. During the day, friends had to coax her to leave the house. Today, a young person who had witnessed—or been responsible for—the violent death of a sibling would almost certainly receive therapy. But Amy received no counseling or psychiatric evaluation after Seth's death. Her father was not a big believer in psychiatry, and Amy told me that she had not wanted to confront what had happened. "I was very insular, sticking to the house and trying to get over things," she recalled. "I felt terrible. I didn't want to *explore* feeling terrible." The Bishops chose not to move, so Amy continued to eat meals in the kitchen where her brother had died and to walk past his bedroom, which her parents had left intact, with its Revolutionary War wallpaper and a handmade sign above the door—an old woodworking project that bore the chiseled letters "S-E-T-H."

Amy returned to Northeastern, but for a time she lived at the house in Braintree. After finishing classes for the day, she would go to Sam's office on campus and wait for him to drive her home. Eileen Sharkey, Sam's longtime secretary and a friend of the family's, said that Amy seemed to deflect her grief by becoming a dedicated student; she earned excellent grades. Sam grew more somber and withdrawn. "Judy focused on keeping Sam going, and on saving Amy," Sharkey said. "Judy's purpose was to save her family."

Occasionally, Judy would be out driving and spot a boy riding his bike up ahead. Maybe there's been a terrible mistake, she would think, overcome by excitement. But then she would pull alongside and see that it was not her son.

As Amy moved on with her life, graduating from Northeastern and enrolling in the PhD program in genetics at Harvard, in 1988, she seldom spoke of her brother. Brian Roach, a college classmate, said, "You just knew: don't bring it up."

One person who attended Seth's wake was Jim Anderson, a student at Northeastern whom Amy had met in a campus group devoted to Dungeons & Dragons and other role-playing games. After dating for a few years, they got married in 1989, in a simple ceremony at the church where the Bishops had held Seth's wake.

Sam Bishop had told his daughter that one way to overcome her loss was to create life herself. In 1991, she gave birth to Lily, who was followed by two more daughters, Thea and Phaedra. Friends describe Amy as a loving, if high-strung, mother. She bought organic food, encouraged her children to play instruments, and fretted over whether they were adequately challenged in school. Amy found the PhD program difficult and distinguished herself less at Harvard than she had at Northeastern. But in 1993, after revising her thesis, she was awarded a degree, and began the first of several postdoctoral appointments. For a time, Amy, Jim, and the children lived in the cottage on Hollis Avenue—a convenient arrangement, because Amy trusted only Judy to babysit. But in 1996, Sam and Judy sold the house and moved to Ipswich, thirty-five miles to the north. "Too many ghosts," Sam said.

In 2001, Amy had a baby boy. She named him Seth. Few of her friends were aware of the significance of the name. "I knew her when she was pregnant," her friend Gail Doktor recalled. "Imagine having a whole conversation about baby names with someone who is sidestepping the fact that she's going to name her baby after her brother—who she killed." In an eerie coincidence, Amy's son was born on what would have been her brother's thirty-third birthday.

• • •

Amy had written poetry in college, and later took up fiction. She became friends with Gail Doktor through a local writers' group. Amy eventually produced three novels, dark thrillers in the Michael Crichton vein, but they were never published. Like Bishop, the books' protagonists are of Greek extraction, dream of an illustrious career in science, and are haunted by the death of a child they once knew. For several of Amy's characters, procreation offers a symbolic redemption. One of her protagonists is seized by a fear that her baby might grow up to resemble a boy named Luke, who died. Amy writes, "She wondered whether she could survive her boy's childhood, if she could, without crying, watch her child that looked like Luke run and play." (Amy acknowledged to me that "there are some parallels" between her life and her novels, but cautioned, "I try to keep it a fictionalized account.")

Amy was a divisive figure in the writing group. She boasted that she was working with a literary agent to secure a book deal, and she liked to mention that she was distantly related, on her mother's side, to the novelist John Irving. She had little patience for the gently constructive language of a writing workshop, and could be brusque and disparaging. "Kill it," she would say of a plot element that she found wanting. She was proud of her PhD, and the status conferred by a

Harvard education was a leitmotif in her books. (Her writing colleagues did not know that Amy had been considered a weak doctoral
candidate. "This is local scandal No. 1," someone who was familiar
with her graduate work at Harvard told me. "She should never have
got a degree.")

As brittle and imperious as Bishop could be, she also could be a
warm and considerate friend. Many people told me about her quick,
barbed humor. Gail Doktor used to call her Crazy Amy, in affectionate
acknowledgment of her volatility. "People vibrate at different speeds,"
Doktor said. "And Amy vibrated at a high frequency." When Doktor's
daughter was given a diagnosis of cancer, Amy sent along clips about
new courses of treatment; occasionally, she clutched Doktor's hands
and said a prayer.

Amy had discovered religion after Seth's death, while she was still
in college, and began attending a local evangelical church. This might
have seemed an anomalous development for a budding Harvard scientist; moreover, Sam was lapsed Greek Orthodox, and Judy was a Uni-
tarian whose church, Sam joked, was more like "a debate society." But
Amy's novels reveal a deep preoccupation with the concept of deliv-
erance from sin. The protagonist of *Easter in Boston* wonders whether
"any amount of calling on the Lord Jesus would erase her sins." The
central figure in *The Martian Experiment* finds solace only at the end,
when a friend tells her, "Jesus loves you no matter what you've done."
(Amy told me that she accepts Christ as her Savior, and she has been
reading the Bible in prison.)

One Saturday morning in 2002, Amy, Jim, and the children went
for breakfast at a crowded IHOP in Peabody, Massachusetts. When
they requested a booster seat for Seth, a waitress told them that the
last one had just been given to another party. "But we were here first!"
Amy protested. She approached the offending customer—a woman
sitting down to breakfast with her own kids—and launched into an
expletive-laced rant. "I am Dr. Amy Bishop!" she shrieked repeatedly,
according to a police report. A manager asked Amy to leave the restaurant, and she complied—after walking back to the woman with
the booster seat and punching her in the head. Amy was arrested,
but the charges against her were dropped, and never appeared on her
permanent record.

At the time, Amy was still doing postdoctoral research; it was clear to those who knew her well that she was under a great deal of pressure to succeed in a demanding profession that can be inhospitable to women, while also caring for four young children. The stress of reconciling one's desire to have a family with the imperatives of an elite job is a recurring theme in the novels. "We will be regarded as leaders in our fields just because of the name on our diplomas," a pompous scientist says to one heroine. "And you want to change nappies, wipe snotty noses, and shovel green glop into a baby's mouth like any fat, stupid Hausfrau?"

Several people who know the family noted that Amy was, effectively, the sole breadwinner: Jim never obtained an advanced degree and worked only sporadically, often in laboratory jobs that he secured through Amy's assistance. In *Easter in Boston,* the heroine, Elizabeth, is married to Jack, a computer programmer who can't hold a job in his field and ends up working at Radio Shack; she describes him as "ambition-challenged" and a "flaccid, bed-loving loser." Amy once told one of her Alabama colleagues that her husband was "too smart to work."

In Amy's third novel, *Amazon Fever,* about a Harvard postdoctoral fellow, Olivia White, who must save the planet from a deadly retrovirus, the University of Alabama in Huntsville is described as the "M.I.T. of the South." When Amy accepted a tenure-track job there and the family relocated, in 2003, the move seemed to promise some financial stability. She and Jim began to collaborate on the invention of an automated cell incubator; David Williams, the president of the university, predicted to a local paper that the device would "change the way biological and medical research is conducted." But because Amy was pursuing patents rather than writing papers, her publication record was scant, and she appears not to have heeded repeated warnings that failing to publish more could jeopardize her prospects for tenure. She fared no better in the classroom, where she would occasionally inform pupils that they were not as bright as students at Harvard. She abruptly dismissed several graduate students from her lab. Others requested to be transferred.

Amy had always been anchored, to some extent, by her friends and family in Massachusetts, but as her career began to drift in Huntsville, she grew increasingly isolated, and stopped returning their phone calls and emails. She was prone to erratic, at times bizarre behavior. In 2009, she published an article in the *International Journal of General Medicine*, an online publication widely regarded as a vanity press, and listed four co-authors: Jim, Lily, Thea, and Phaedra. "We were going to do a lot of work side by side and bring the kids in on it," Jim later explained to *Wired*. "Like the Curies did."

That spring, Amy's tenure was denied. At least one member of her committee expressed a concern that she was "crazy," telling *The Chronicle of Higher Education* that he had first worried about her mental health "five minutes after I met her." Amy filed a series of appeals, eventually hiring a lawyer. And she began to fixate on what she considered the cautionary tale of Douglas Prasher, a molecular biologist whose research funding dried up in 1992, when his tenure prospects at the Woods Hole Oceanographic Institution seemed in doubt. Prasher ultimately abandoned science. Then, in 2008, two scientists with whom he had collaborated won the Nobel Prize in Chemistry, based in part on Prasher's research. By that time, Prasher was living in the Huntsville area, where he drove a courtesy van for a local Toyota dealership. Amy told her husband that she was worried she might have a similar fate.

Since childhood, Amy had suffered from severe allergies, which could manifest themselves as hives or eczema. In the months before the shootings in Alabama, she told me, she was under tremendous stress, and she began to hallucinate. Shortly after Seth's death, she said, she started to "hear voices," and since then they had continued, off and on, coinciding occasionally with allergy attacks. "Sometimes they're scary and sometimes they're not," she said of the voices, but she refused to elaborate.

One day, Amy drove to the university and parked in front of the administration building. Sitting in her car, she called the office of the president and announced her intention to come upstairs to discuss her case. She was told that President Williams would not meet with her, and that she should not even enter the building. According to an affidavit written by Amy in prison, which was described in a recent court filing, she then saw Williams and the provost, Vistasp Karbhari, hurriedly leave the building, escorted by police. Amy telephoned Debra Moriarity. "They act like I'm going to walk in and shoot somebody," she said.

A week before the killings, Amy's husband accompanied her to Larry's Pistol & Pawn, a firing range on the edge of town, for target practice. They brought along a 9 mm Ruger that Jim had acquired, more than a decade earlier, in Massachusetts; a friend had bought the weapon in New Hampshire and given it to him, illegally, allowing Jim to circumvent the waiting period that Massachusetts imposes on gun permits. It remains unclear whether Jim had concerns about entrusting Amy with a firearm; he refused repeated requests for an interview. But Amy occasionally described her husband to friends as "a Svengali." Several people who knew them during these years suggested to me that when Amy felt injured or humiliated by some professional slight, Jim tended not to soothe his wife's outrage but to fan it. One close friend of the couple told me, "Amy was a narcissist. She had a deep desire to be reaffirmed, and that was the way that Jim held power over her."

When Jim called Judy Bishop to tell her that the police had taken Amy into custody, she asked, "Jim, did you have a *gun* in the house?"

• • •

Not long after Amy Bishop shot her colleagues in Huntsville, authorities in Massachusetts released decades-old documents about the death of her brother. The original police reports—several dozen yellowed pages, some covered in handwritten jottings, some of them typed—contain revelations that call into question the 1987 state police report that declared the killing an accident.

When Seth fell to the floor and Amy ran out of the kitchen, she left the house through the back door, taking the shotgun with her. She crossed Hollis Avenue and cut through a wooded area, emerging in an alley that dead-ended at the body shop of Dave Dinger Ford, an auto dealership. Because it was a Saturday, the place was closed, but a few off-duty mechanics were hanging out there. According to the mechanics, Amy came inside, holding the shotgun. She said that she needed a car and demanded that they turn over some keys. The men ran, and Amy was outside Dinger Ford when Ronald Solimini—a cop who had been sent from the Bishops' house to look for a young woman wearing a jean jacket and carrying a shotgun—came across her.

Amy looked "frightened, disoriented," Solimini noted in his report, but "she kept both her hands on the shotgun." Solimini approached her slowly, trying to reason with her. But she wouldn't put down the weapon.

As he was talking, Solimini noticed that another officer, Tim Murphy, was approaching Amy from behind, his .38 revolver drawn. Solimini continued to talk as Murphy crept closer, until he was just a few feet behind Amy. Then Murphy shouted, "Drop the rifle! Drop the rifle! Drop the rifle!" According to Murphy's report, Amy complied. The officers handcuffed her, recited her *Miranda* rights, and took away her gun.

One afternoon not long ago, I visited a friend who is knowledgeable about firearms and spent an hour loading and firing the same model of 12-gauge Mossberg that Amy Bishop used that day. A pump-action shotgun is loaded by "racking the slide"—a thrust-and-pull gesture, familiar from action films, that emits a satisfying mechanical *shuck*. The Mossberg that Amy carried could hold up to five rounds. Shotgun rounds are brass-and-plastic cylinders densely packed with gunpowder and tiny pellets, or shot. When the trigger is pulled, the shot explodes out of the weapon, but the casing—the shell—remains inside the gun. If one of these spent shells is in the chamber, racking the slide will, in a single fluid motion, eject the old shell out of the side of the gun and push a fresh round into the chamber.

As I racked the shotgun, fired it, and racked it again, one detail from the police reports nagged at me. At the house on Hollis Avenue, the officers had discovered a cardboard box of twenty-five rounds on Amy's bed. Four rounds were missing. She had fired one of them in her bedroom. (The police recovered the spent shell on the bedroom floor.) A second round had killed Seth. They discovered a third round in Amy's jacket pocket. And, when the police examined the shotgun after taking it from Amy, they found the fourth round. It was in the chamber, ready to fire. After you have fired a pump-action shotgun, the only way to chamber another round is to pump it again. So at some point after shooting Seth and before being arrested, Amy must have racked the slide, jettisoning the shell that had killed her brother and loading a fresh one in its place.

When Amy arrived at the Braintree police station, she was taken to the booking room. Pointing a loaded weapon at anybody is grounds for a felony charge of assault, and brandishing a gun in front of a police officer is an affront to law enforcement that is seldom taken lightly. So why did the police let Amy Bishop go?

Soon after the Alabama massacre, Paul Frazier, the Braintree chief of police, offered an unsettling answer. At a press conference, he was unambiguous in his assignment of blame. One of the lieutenants had been booking Amy, he explained, when he was informed that the police chief had ordered her release.

A reporter asked Frazier who the chief had been at the time.

"John Polio," he replied.

• • •

"It was all Polio's decision," Frazier told me. Amy was being questioned at the station when Judy Bishop arrived. According to Ronald Solimini, who had returned to the station by then, Judy demanded to see the chief, shouting, "Where's John V.?"

When I asked Frazier how Judy came to be on a first-name basis with the chief, he said, "She was a big supporter of his." In the mid-1980s, he reminded me, Judy had been a member of the town meeting, the local representative body. Polio, who was in his early sixties at the time, had been "quietly working" members of the group in the hope of raising the mandatory retirement age of police officers, which was sixty-five.

In this telling, the famously incorruptible Polio ended up granting the ultimate political favor. For years afterward, Frazier told me, officers in the department whispered among themselves about the decision to let Amy go. It was an open secret in the station house, Frazier said, and knowledge of this transgression cast in a different light Polio's prohibition on ticket fixing and other forms of small-bore police corruption. "If he can fix a murder, I can fix a ticket" was the prevailing attitude, Frazier said. "It was a miscarriage of justice," he concluded. "Just because it was a friend of his."

By the time these new details emerged, Polio was eighty-seven and still living in Braintree. When reporters showed up at his front door, they found a frail old man with concave cheeks, wearing a white baseball cap that said "#1 Grandpa." He invited them in.

Polio said that in his recollection Seth and Amy had been "horsing around" with the family shotgun when it went off. "The mother was saying her version of how it happened, and her version was that it was an accident," Polio recalled. He said that it was "outlandish" to suggest that there had been any sort of cover-up. Polio refused to accept responsibility for the decision to let Amy go without charging her. "I didn't tell anybody to release her," he said.

Bill Delahunt, who was then the district attorney for Norfolk County, which includes Braintree, and who went on to serve seven terms in Congress, told me that if he had been aware of the incident at Dinger Ford, he would have charged Amy with assault, which likely would have triggered a psychiatric evaluation. "It might have had a totally different result in terms of what happened in her life," he said. Delahunt blamed Brian Howe, the state trooper who had written the final police report calling Seth's death an accident, for omitting an account of the standoff with the police.

But when I tracked down Howe, who is now retired and living in Georgia, he told me that he hadn't included the aftermath of the shooting in his report because he hadn't known about it. He said that he had asked the Braintree police for their original reports, but they had not been turned over. Although Delahunt told me that Howe should have been more diligent in his investigation, he, too, placed the ultimate responsibility on the Braintree Police Department—and, in particular, on Polio. "They never would have released Amy without the imprimatur of Polio," Delahunt said. "They would have been afraid to."

The newly disclosed evidence reframed the public persona of Amy Bishop. After the Alabama shootings, the media had initially portrayed her as an oddity, a "nutty professor" whose actions were an extreme expression of the pressures of academic life. Now she was depicted as something more malevolent and familiar: the bad seed. Seth's death, in this reckoning, was only the first entry in a catalog of unheeded warnings. There was the episode at IHOP, and another case, in 1993, in which Amy and her husband had been questioned by the Bureau of

Alcohol, Tobacco, and Firearms. Amy's postdoctoral adviser at Harvard, Paul Rosenberg, with whom she had apparently had some dispute, received a suspicious package in the mail one day. Rosenberg opened it carefully—the Unabomber was active in those years—and narrowly circumvented the trigger mechanism attached to a pair of six-inch pipe bombs. The case remains unsolved, and charges were never brought against Amy or her husband. But they were both identified as suspects. They were living in the cottage on Hollis Avenue at the time, and authorities searched the place while Sam and Judy looked on. Law-enforcement interviews revealed that Amy and Jim had spoken to friends about how one might build a pipe bomb. And Amy had once given her college friend Brian Roach a strange birthday present: ten pounds of potassium permanganate, which can be used to make explosives. (Roach told me that it was "just a joke.")

In the weeks after the Alabama shootings, several former colleagues and neighbors came forward, describing various altercations with Amy, mostly over trivial matters. Jimmy Anderson Sr., Amy's father-in-law, told a reporter that he had seen "the Devil in her eyes."

"People kept sweeping her bad behavior under the rug, and now we're paying a tremendous price," one trustee of the University of Alabama told *The Huntsville Times*. Even Roy Miller, Amy's lawyer, believed that there was a telling pattern of violence. "Something is wrong with this lady," he said. "Her history speaks for itself."

As this new interpretation of Amy Bishop's past took hold, Judy Bishop began her own metamorphosis in the public eye. The grief-stricken mother transformed into a manipulative schemer who had subverted the law in order to protect her wayward child. In this new interpretation, Judy resembled the Joan Crawford character in *Mildred Pierce*, a strenuously doting mother who covers up a string of misdeeds, including murder, committed by her daughter, with disastrous results.

Euripides describes motherhood as "a potent spell," and the human instinct to protect one's children can inspire awe. One winter day in northern Quebec some years ago, a polar bear wandered into a village and approached a seven-year-old Inuit child. The child's mother threw herself at the seven-hundred-pound animal, and held it off until a hunter arrived and shot it.

Of course, it's one thing to save your children from certain death and another to shield them from criminal prosecution. But most parents would likely recognize the impulse to cover for a child's transgressions, whether or not they might actually do so themselves. Several years ago, an Atlanta elementary school teacher named Sheila Michael was sentenced to eight years in prison for concealing her twenty-two-year-old daughter's involvement in a hit-and-run accident that killed five people. While a manhunt was under way for the driver who caused the accident, Michael persuaded a mechanic to mask the damage to the family car. It emerged in court that her daughter had wanted to confess, but Michael had told her not to, because, as the judge observed, "you did not want to lose her."

Had Judy Bishop, witness to the death of her own son, made a similar calculation?

Cold cases are hard to investigate under the best of circumstances, and the shooting of Seth Bishop was especially difficult because it had not been treated as a crime to begin with. Neither the Braintree police nor the state police had run much of an investigation. None of the physical evidence had been retained; even the Mossberg shotgun had vanished after the ballistics tests. There were a few perfunctory crime-scene photographs, but the Bishop house had not been subjected to a comprehensive investigation; in any case, the integrity of the scene had been compromised by the sympathetic neighbors who had wiped away the blood.

There was another problem: by 2010, the statute of limitations had long since expired on any crimes that Amy might be charged with in relation to the confrontation at Dinger Ford. The only crime that had no statute of limitations was murder, but to convict Amy of that, prosecutors would have to prove that she had intentionally killed her brother.

One day, as investigators were reviewing the crime-scene photographs, they stumbled on a possible clue. In one of the pictures taken in Amy's room, a copy of the *National Enquirer* was visible on the floor. Someone in the district attorney's office ordered the issue from the Library of Congress, and investigators saw that much of it was devoted to the murder of the parents of Patrick Duffy, an actor on *Dallas*. On November 18, 1986, two young assailants had killed Duffy's parents in the Montana bar that they owned. They used a 12-gauge shotgun and fled the scene, brandishing the weapon in an attempt to steal a getaway car. This might have seemed like a tenuous basis for divining Amy's mental state on the day of the shooting, but investigators wondered if Amy had seen the article as a kind of instruction manual. William Keating, the district attorney at the time, suggested to the *Globe* that the photograph could be used to prove intent.

In April 2010, local authorities opened an inquest into Seth's death. Twenty witnesses appeared at a redbrick courthouse in Quincy. Tom Pettigrew, one of the mechanics who had encountered Amy at Dinger, described her holding the shotgun, saying, "Put your hands up!"

Solimini, the cop, recalled how strange it was to hear Judy Bishop ask for Polio by his first name. "I never heard *anybody* call him John," he said. Kenneth Brady, a sergeant who was in the station that day, testified that he, too, heard Judy ask for the chief. James Sullivan, the lieutenant who questioned Amy, said that he had actually written the words "murder" and "assault with a dangerous weapon" on the charging sheet. But because the officers were later instructed to release Amy, she was never charged with those crimes.

According to Sullivan, whom I spoke with recently, his interrogation of Amy came to an "abrupt halt" when Judy Bishop entered the booking room, in a conspicuous breach of protocol. One of the captains on duty told him that Judy Bishop had spoken to Polio and explained that the shooting had been an accident—and Polio believed her.

"I was like, *what?*" Sullivan told me. He recalled complaining to the captain, "If we let every person go because their mother didn't think they committed a crime, there would be no point in arresting anyone." But he was told that Polio had ordered the release, and that he was "to obey that order."

At the inquest, Sergeant Brady testified that after Amy was reunited with her mother, they embraced: "Mrs. Bishop stated that she had lost her son today, and she didn't want to lose her daughter."

When Sam Bishop took the stand, he denied that the "spat" with Amy had been serious. "I didn't leave there thinking we had some terrible disagreement," he said. The robbery in the summer of 1985 had been "traumatic" for Amy, he explained, which was why she dug out the gun and loaded it. "She was sitting in that Victorian house," he said. "She was afraid. And she made a terrible mistake in acting on that fear." He had brought along a photograph of Seth and Amy, to remind the judge that "they're real people." The picture, which was taken around Halloween, just a few months before Seth died, captured the siblings grinning at each other, carving a small pumpkin on a kitchen table blanketed in newsprint.

• • •

"I left the house at about six in the morning and I was gone until two o'clock," Judy said when she took the stand. "I pulled in to the driveway and Seth pulled in right behind me." She helped him carry groceries inside; then Amy came downstairs and asked for help unloading the shotgun. At that point, Judy said, Seth reached for the gun, Amy turned, and "it fired." Amy had one hand on the barrel and one hand on the stock: "She didn't even have her hand on the trigger."

As the mother of the victim and an eyewitness to the shooting, Judy was a powerful presence on the stand. She recounted hearing her son say, "Oh, no, Mom," before he collapsed to the floor. "The blood was just—it just came in a wave," she said. "My shoes were full of blood. My hair was full of blood." She concluded by saying, "I just would add that it was the worst day of our lives."

Judy denied having any sort of friendship with John Polio, and insisted that she never asked for him at the station. Polio and his wife, Ginny, testified, and they, too, said that Judy and the chief had not been close friends. I recently met with Ginny Polio at a coffee shop in Braintree, and she made a surprising claim: although the officers at the station had not known it, the chief had actually been in the building that day. Polio had designed his office to have its own entrance, through a private garage, so that his subordinates would not know whether he was there. "Part of my job is to have the most evasive schedule I can," he once said. "Knowing cops the way I do, they have to realize that Daddy may be around at any time."

Ginny was also at the station that day, she told me; before marrying Polio in 1999, she had been his secretary. She recalled that a captain, Ted Buker, discovered Polio in his office and told him, "Chief, you know Judy Bishop, the town meeting member? Her daughter, Amy, shot her brother. Her mother said it was an accident." According to Ginny, Buker didn't mention the incident at Dinger Ford, and said that he intended to turn the case over to the state police and the district attorney. In Ginny's rendering, Polio replied, "Do it." He never spoke with Judy Bishop; he never ordered Amy's release. (Ted Buker is no longer alive.)

Ginny is a small woman with a flinty gaze. She remains incensed by what she regards as a concerted effort by veterans of the Braintree police to smear her husband. Polio died in December 2010, weakened, Ginny believes, by the ordeal of defending himself. He was buried with a police escort, but when family members were organizing a wake, they requested that Paul Frazier stay away.

After the inquest, the case was referred to a grand jury, and on June 16, 2010, Amy Bishop was indicted for the first-degree murder of her brother. Sam and Judy released a statement. "We cannot explain or even understand what happened in Alabama," they wrote. "However, we know that what happened 23 years ago to our son, Seth, was an accident."

Two days after the Massachusetts indictment was announced, Amy, in jail in Alabama, popped the blade out of a safety razor and slashed her wrists. When I asked her about this incident, she told me that she had tried to end her life once before, after Seth's death. That time, she said, she hadn't known what she was doing; by 2010, she had experience teaching anatomy and physiology. "I slashed longitudinally, over the radial artery," she said. She collapsed in her cell, bleeding, and survived only because a prison guard discovered her. Roy Miller, her lawyer, told me, "Another four minutes, and she would have been dead."

• • •

One morning last fall, I drove north from Boston to the blustery coastal town of Ipswich. In a quiet subdivision, I stopped at a gray clapboard house set back from the road. Sam Bishop met me at the door.

I had been speaking with Judy for some time, in phone conversations during which her voice often warbled and thickened with tears, and we'd exchanged a series of emails. Whether despite or because of their anguish and isolation, Judy and Sam remain very close. They share an email address, which meant that it was sometimes difficult for me to ascertain who, precisely, was writing.

"Every time I go to the doctor, I've lost another inch," Judy said, straining as she retrieved a photo album from a high shelf. She was in their living room, an airy space with exposed beams and artwork, by both of them, on the walls. She was wearing an oversized Mark Eckō T-shirt that was tagged with fake graffiti. Her hair, which was still voluminous, had turned translucent white. "Growing old," she said with a smile. "It's not for sissies."

We flipped through the photo album, and Judy showed me pictures of her children's birthday parties; of Seth and Amy flying balsawood airplanes in the back yard; of Seth on his way to the prom, grinning, in his red Camaro. Then the images of Seth ceased, and as Judy turned the pages, we saw a pressed flower; a poem, in Greek, by Sam's mother; and the faded program from Seth's memorial service.

"What the Bishops have gone through really is a Greek tragedy," their friend Eileen Sharkey had told me. "One child destroys another by accident, then is destroyed herself, and the parents are left to watch as every little thing that could be salvaged from Seth's death—Amy's attempt to have a normal life—is torn away."

Judy had prepared a lunch of tuna sandwiches, and as we ate at the kitchen table, Sam said that during the weeks after the Alabama shooting, TV crews had set up klieg lights outside their home and shone them through the windows, so that at midnight it felt like the middle of the day. They did not dispute the horror of what Amy had done in Alabama, though they didn't dwell on it, either. "She's a brilliant, brilliant girl, and she just snapped," Judy said. But the Bishops expressed a righteous fury over what they perceive to be the opportunistic score settling of authorities in Massachusetts. "They were out to find some way to nail Polio," Judy said. She is offended by the notion that these men would presume to tell her how her own son died. "I was there!" she exclaimed. "I saw it happen. It changed my life."

The Bishops told me that Frazier had lied in his February press conference. At that event, Frazier had not only suggested a conspiracy between Judy Bishop and Chief Polio; he had erroneously claimed that the morning argument had been between Amy and Seth. Judy scoffed at Frazier's implication that she was politically powerful in Braintree: she had been a member of the town meeting, but that body consisted of some 240 people. The Bishops believe that Solimini also lied at the inquest when he conjured Judy asking to see Polio and invoking his first name. "We are damaged people—we'll never be the same," Judy said, her voice rising. "What they did is unforgivable. And I hope they burn in hell."

"Okay, Judy," Sam said gently. He had been nervously thumbing through a folder of documents, and he began to pull out copies of the original police reports, each underlined and annotated. He had discovered a U.S. Army report suggesting that a military version of the 12-gauge Mossberg, when dropped on its muzzle, can occasionally misfire. But when he presented the report at the inquest, Sam said, it was ignored. (In fact, the officer who examined the gun after Seth's death mentioned the report when he testified—but he added that he had personally "shock tested" the weapon, and it had not misfired.)

Sam explained that the kitchen in the house on Hollis Avenue was a very tight space. He stood up from the table and mimed sweeping the shotgun around, as Amy would have done to show it to Seth. "I have a feeling she may have banged it," he said, speculating that if the stock had hit a cabinet or a counter, that might account for the misfire.

When I asked about the family "spat," Sam said that he had woken at around ten that morning, but did not come downstairs until around eleven thirty. "I almost tripped on something in the hallway," he said. He doesn't remember what it was, but he reprimanded Seth and Amy and told them to pick up their belongings. "And they responded, Amy especially," he said. But they resolved the matter amicably. "I didn't think anything of it," Sam insisted.

On the subject of Amy's moods, Judy said, "She had her father's temper."

"Did Amy and Sam ever butt heads?" I inquired.

"Oh, yeah," Judy said, eyeing her husband and chuckling. Sam said nothing.

In the Bishops' view, the Dinger Ford incident has been overblown. "She was in shock!" Sam said, though he could not explain why Amy had racked the slide again after leaving the house. In any case, Judy pointed out, if Amy was looking for a getaway car, she didn't need to go waving a shotgun around. Judy's car was in the driveway. The keys were hanging by the kitchen door.

One thing that particularly angers the Bishops is the fact that Frazier and other members of the department—who supposedly were so troubled by the decision to release Amy in 1986—said nothing about the matter until the news arrived from Alabama in 2010. The Bishops have a point: dozens of cold cases were reopened in Massachusetts during those years. Fear of John Polio might account for a reluctance to speak out while he was still in power, but he retired in 1987. "There was nothing said for twenty-five years," Sam said. "Now, all of a sudden, everyone's got the answer?" (When I asked Frazier about the inaction of the Braintree police, he said, "That's a good question." After a pause, he ventured, "We just never thought we could resurrect the case.")

Amy's parents blame her suicide attempt in prison squarely on the indictment in Massachusetts. But when I asked them whether Amy had ever tried to kill herself before that incident, Judy said, "No."

"Well, she cut herself . . . ," Sam began.

Judy corrected him: Amy had been "carving pumpkins," she said, and "she stabbed herself right here"—she tapped her wrist. "That was *not* a suicide attempt." They took Amy to the hospital, where a doctor stitched her up.

"She was saying she wanted to see how sharp the knife was," Sam explained.

"It wasn't a suicide attempt," Judy said again.

• • •

Roy Miller, an Alabama native with a croaky drawl, has been practicing law in the Huntsville area for nearly four decades. After the court assigned him to be Amy Bishop's lawyer, he spent eighteen months preparing an insanity defense. Amy had asked for the death penalty. "The woman wants to die," Miller told me. The alternative would likely be life without parole, and Amy, who was incarcerated at the county jail in Huntsville, would probably be transferred to the Julia Tutwiler Prison for Women, a notoriously brutal institution in central Alabama. A 2012 complaint filed with the Justice Department alleged that the prison was marked by "frequent and severe officer-on-inmate sexual violence." When I asked Miller about Tutwiler, he said, "It is *antediluvian* down there." Amy told a friend that she didn't want to spend the rest of her life in "a tiny little box."

But Sam and Judy persuaded her that even if she wished to be executed, capital cases are often so attenuated that it could be decades before an execution happened. So she entered a plea of not guilty by reason of insanity. The defense hired a series of prominent psychiatrists to evaluate Amy, but it would not be an easy case to make. Juries in Alabama have exhibited a notable distaste for the insanity defense. "Someone essentially is caught in the act and the next thing you know they are insane," Rob Broussard, the district attorney prosecuting Amy, has remarked. "The public sees insanity defenses for what they're worth, which is not much."

Amy told me that though she is "horrified" by what she calls "the UAH incident," she has no memory of the killings. Moments after the shootings, as police officers shoved her into a cruiser, she told them, "It didn't happen . . . They're still alive." It is difficult to know whether this partial amnesia is genuine or a tactic. She told me that though she remembered shooting Seth by accident, she didn't recall anything that happened at Dinger Ford. When I asked her why she had racked the shotgun after shooting her brother, she said, "I don't remember that at all." I pointed out that her periods of memory loss seemed to coincide with her gravest misdeeds. She responded, "After traumatic events, people often remember nothing."

The Alabama case was further complicated by the fact that several of the people she shot, including Gopi Podila, the department head, had actually voted *for* her tenure; the bloodshed could not be explained simply as an act of vengeance. Amy's parents, and her friends, tend to refer to Seth's death as "the accidental shooting" with a robotic insistence that can sometimes feel like spin. When it comes to the shootings in Alabama, they often employ the passive voice, as though Amy had no agency in the matter. Once, when I was talking with her friend Brian Roach, he referred to "the accident in Alabama."

Amy told me that she is being treated with the antipsychotic Haldol, and that she has paranoid schizophrenia. But Roy Miller said that she had not received so definitive a diagnosis and that, in any case, it could be difficult to sustain in court the notion that Amy was beset by extreme delusions. She had, by and large, lived a well-adjusted life. She earned a PhD and raised four children without major incident.

When I asked Judy if she had been aware that Amy sometimes heard voices, she said, "Absolutely not." She added that if such a thing were true, Amy "wouldn't tell her father or me."

Amy did not shed her imperiousness in jail. She joked to Miller that her vocabulary was deteriorating because of the company that she was forced to keep and that her IQ was dropping. "She has a tremendous sense of humor," Miller said, noting that it occasionally got her into trouble. "They had her in a cell with one of these real fat ladies from one of these real country burgs," Miller told me. "This lady, she didn't have any teeth." The cellmate had a pair of false teeth that on one occasion she placed on the windowsill. A passing guard spotted the dentures and asked Amy and her cellmate who owned them. Amy grinned at the guard and said, "Let me give you a hint."

"She got chewed out for that," Miller said, with a dry laugh.

"I punched out a girl. Three girls, actually," Amy told me, explaining that the county jail was "rowdy." She insisted that in all three cases she had acted in "self-defense." After one verbal dispute in the mess hall, another inmate beat her mercilessly with a cafeteria tray.

Amy's trial was scheduled for September 24, 2012. But two weeks before that date Miller approached the prosecution about the possibility of a deal. Amy was willing to plead guilty to capital murder in exchange for a commitment by prosecutors that they would not seek the death penalty. She would spend the rest of her life in prison, without the possibility of parole. It is not entirely clear what drove this reversal, but Miller told me that if they went to trial, there would have been a "1 percent chance" that they could have convinced a jury that Bishop was not guilty by reason of insanity. He also said that a battery of psychiatric tests had proved inconclusive: the defense had no satisfying evidence that Bishop was insane.

The prosecutors agreed to the deal. One afternoon in September, I went to the Madison County Courthouse, in downtown Huntsville, to watch Bishop plead guilty. Dozens of policemen had congregated for the arrival of the most notorious murderer in the county's history. The courtroom was full of spectators, but Amy had asked her family to stay away. As she was led in, everyone craned their necks to catch a glimpse. She wore a red jumpsuit and flip-flops over white socks. The shackles around her ankles jingled like sleigh bells as she shuffled past. She had lost weight: her eyes were sunken, and her pale forearms looked like Popsicle sticks. But she held her head high, flaring her nostrils a little, appraising the room with a residual trace of her anxious hauteur.

When a defendant pleads guilty in a capital-murder case in Alabama, the state must present an abbreviated version of its evidence in court, and Amy sat quietly, clasping and unclasping her hands, while the prosecution described her crimes. As photographs of her slaughtered colleagues were projected, she buried her head in her arms like a schoolchild, her dark hair spilling onto the table. When the judge asked Amy if she agreed to plead guilty and waive any right to appeal, she addressed the court for the first and only time, saying, in a soft voice, "Yes." She was subsequently moved to Tutwiler.

The next question was whether Amy might still face a murder trial in Massachusetts. That would be a disastrous turn for the Bishops, who would have to relive once more the trauma of Seth's death, and face uncomfortable questions about Amy's actions at Dinger Ford and the circumstances of her release. Yet it might also pose a problem for the prosecutors. It was one thing to indict Amy; many litigators will tell you that it is not difficult to secure an indictment from a grand jury. But trying her for first-degree murder would oblige the prosecution to present a case involving an alleged crime that took place more than a quarter of a century earlier. Some of the people who might be called to testify were now elderly, with faulty memories. Many others were dead. Almost all the original physical evidence was missing, including the apparent murder weapon, and the only eyewitness to the event was the mother of both the victim and the shooter—and she would no doubt be summoned as the star witness for the defense.

There was also the matter of motive. While some accounts suggested that there had been animosity between Amy and her brother, I was unable to identify a single person who knew the siblings and could testify to that; the prosecutors would likely face a similar challenge. Paul Frazier had asserted in his press conference that the quarrel on the morning of December 6 had been between Amy and Seth, but all the other evidence indicated that it had actually been between Amy and her dad.

A few days after Amy's guilty plea, the Norfolk County district attorney's office released a statement announcing that it would not seek her extradition, because Massachusetts does not have the death penalty; given that Amy is serving life without parole in Alabama, the statement explained, "the penalty we would seek . . . is already in place."

Then the case took an unexpected turn. Amy let it be known, through a public defender named Larry Tipton who was representing her in Massachusetts, that she *wanted* to be tried for Seth's death. She had always insisted that the shooting was an accident, and she appeared to resent the implication of the withdrawn indictment. "She wants to use a trial to help demonstrate that she's innocent," Tipton said.

"I want the truth to come out," Amy told me. "I want that for me, for my parents, for closure."

• • •

When violence suddenly ruptures the course of our lives, we tend to tell ourselves stories in order to make it more explicable. Confronted with scrambled pieces of evidence, we arrange them into a narrative. Faced with the same tragic facts, those who concluded that Amy Bishop murdered her brother and those who concluded that she didn't both took messy events and turned them into a story. But neither story was especially convincing.

The caricature of Amy as the demonic sister who sought inspiration in the pages of the *National Enquirer* before murdering her brother in cold blood is too facile, as is the cynical narrative of a secret hand-shake between John Polio and Judy Bishop that kept the truth buried for decades. In the months that I spent talking with people in Braintree, I came to believe that there had indeed been a cover-up, but that it had been an act not of conspiracy but of compassion. In small towns, in particular, some degree of denial about what happens behind the closed doors of one's neighbors can come to seem not merely exigent but humane. "I've always believed it was an accident," Amy's friend

Kathleen Oldham told me. Then, echoing a sentiment that I heard countless times, she added, "And I've always said, if it wasn't, I didn't want to find out." Some of the police officers in Braintree knew the Bishop family. Judy knew the parents of some of the younger cops, through the town meeting. It might have seemed that the most charitable way to address the confounding tragedy at Hollis Avenue was simply to move on—a parochial gesture of mercy and denial that had an incalculable cost, decades later, in Alabama.

The counter-narratives put forward by the Bishops and by Ginny Polio are also unsustainable. However much Chief Frazier and his colleagues loathed John Polio, the notion that they would fabricate evidence and invent misgivings simply to defame him seems dubious. Again, there is a more humane and logical explanation for the zeal with which the authorities in Braintree pried open this painful case in 2010: for officials there, the inquest offered a way to purge past misconduct and exorcise an old form of government. "This wasn't just about a shooting that happened twenty-three years ago," the town's mayor, Joe Sullivan, told me. "It was about Braintree today."

Whatever sympathy one might feel for the Bishops, there was no denying the anomalies in their account of that Saturday. One afternoon, I went to see someone who knows the family but had asked that I not use her name. "I'm going to tell you something that I haven't told anyone in twenty years," she said.

In the 1980s, Judy Bishop had a close friend named Saran Gillies, a local woman who was active in Braintree politics. On the day that Seth was shot, Gillies was planning to go to Judy's house for tea, but Judy had called her to cancel. "There's been a terrible fight here," Judy told Gillies, according to the woman, whom Gillies telephoned immediately afterward. "It's bad." Sam had gone off "in a huff." Shortly thereafter, Gillies learned that Seth Bishop had been shot.

"Saran and I put it together," the friend told me. When Amy heard Seth return with the groceries, they surmised, she must have "thought it was her father coming home." The hypothesis that these two women secretly shared was that Amy had no intention of killing her brother. What she might have intended, when she descended the stairs with the shotgun, was to kill her father.

Of course, this was just another speculative narrative about murky events, and Gillies died several years ago. Yet this theory might explain how a fight between Sam and Amy, and not Seth and Amy, had left Seth dead. It would also explain a key discrepancy in the timing of the story that the Bishops have related. At the inquest, and in Judy Bishop's interviews with me, she insisted that she was at the stables from 6:00 a.m. until roughly 2:00 p.m., and that she arrived home just as Seth returned from the grocery store. But when Brian Howe, the state trooper, interviewed the Bishops shortly after Seth's death, Amy told him that when she came downstairs with the shotgun, she had the impression that her mother had been home "for a while." In the same set of interviews, Sam Bishop told Howe and the two officers with him that he had expected Judy home between eleven o'clock and noon. In her statement, Judy said that she had "returned to the residence to see if there was anything for lunch." Seth was home when she got there, Judy told Howe, and "stated that he would go to the store to pick up some food so that [we] could all have lunch."

According to this account, delivered shortly after the shooting, Judy came home not after Seth returned from the grocery store but before he had left. There is a good reason that Sam and Judy Bishop would be uncomfortable with such a timeline: in their telling, Amy took out the shotgun in the first place because she had been home alone for several hours.

At the inquest, the firearms expert who had examined the 12-gauge Mossberg testified that it normally takes five pounds of pressure on the trigger in order to fire the gun.

"You're saying the only way it could have gone off accidentally, even if her finger was on the trigger, was if someone was actually pulling it?" he was asked.

"Trying to pull the gun out of her hands," he responded. "Yeah."

None of this necessarily indicates that Amy intended to kill her father. She could have been waving the gun around, angry with Sam and wanting to make a demonstration. When I was about fourteen, I once had an argument with my father. It was about some trivial matter—I don't remember what—but I was furious. We were staying by the ocean, and my father would swim every day, taking long laps parallel to the beach. As he swam that day, I started skipping rocks. I saw him approaching, and continued to pick stones from the sand and hurl them at the waves. Then, suddenly, I heard a howl. My father staggered out of the water, disoriented and alarmed. I hadn't meant to hit my father—I had intended simply to frighten him, to assert myself somehow. Apart from the shock, it did him no real harm. But it could have. When I told my mother this story recently, she surprised me by saying, "You know, in all these years, your father has never told me about that."

After I heard the story about Saran Gillies, I went back through Amy's novels, looking for any further clues that they might hold, and I made a startling discovery. In her first book, *The Martian Experiment,* Abigail White, the protagonist, is haunted by an incident from her childhood. Early in the novel, Abigail is playing with Kathy, a friend from school, and Kathy's younger brother, Luke. The two girls quarrel, and Kathy throws a rock at Abigail. Overcome by fury, Abigail spies a fist-sized rock on the ground and "fires" it into the air, "hoping to make Kathy dodge away in fear." The rock sails toward Kathy, but it misses her—and lands, instead, on the head of her little brother, Luke.

"He fell back like a toy soldier," Amy writes. "He never knew what hit him." Abigail is stunned, "dreading what horror her rock, meant to scare Kathy, had visited upon Luke." He slips into a coma and dies, and his parents conclude that he must have had an aneurysm.

The passage echoed what seemed to be the most plausible account of Seth's death: in a fit of anger, a young woman wields a dangerous weapon, intending to frighten one person, but ends up killing another. Abigail is tormented by her actions, and she eventually tries to confess to her grandmother, whom she calls, in the Greek style, Yaya—the name that Amy used with her own grandmother. "I killed Luke," she says. In a firm whisper, Yaya tells her, "The boy is with God. He knows you are sorry."

Later, Abigail's father enters her room, thinking that she is asleep, and kisses her on the forehead. "That one kiss told her that the decision was made and final." The family will say nothing of her possible responsibility for the death.

When I posed the alternative hypothesis of that day to Amy, she hurried off the phone. The next day, she called back. She denied that the argument with her father had been serious, and offered a different account of it: she had finished a pot of coffee, and Sam had been irritated because "he had to make another pot." She said, "So I'm not sure where that phone call when Mom said we had a fight came from, because we didn't," adding, "Our family always had a very nice relationship."

In a recent book, *Far from the Tree,* Andrew Solomon writes, in a discussion about how parents cope with children who have killed, "There's a fine line between heroic love and willful blindness." Parental denial may be driven by compassion, Solomon argues, but it can also be profoundly confusing for the child. If the child has committed a terrible crime, the parent may refuse to confront it because that feels like the surest strategy for restoring a stable existence. But that very refusal may actually be further destabilizing. In Solomon's view, it can be "alienating—even traumatic" when parents refuse to acknowledge the horrible things that their children have done. In her novel *Amazon Fever,* Amy Bishop describes the father of her heroine as "willfully blind," and wonders whether that blindness might make him, on some level, "complicit." The passage made me wonder about Sam. Had he considered that Amy might have been intent on shooting him? And had he and Judy ever discussed this possibility?

I decided to talk to Judy about the alternative theory, although I wondered if there was much point. "There are only two people who really know what happened in that house," the woman who related the theory to me said. "And I think Judy has buried it and come up with something she can deal with." She paused. "And bless her for that."

She was not alone in this feeling. In speaking with people in Braintree, I was often asked if I had children, as if that might be some prerequisite for grasping the moral calculus at play. "I've never asked Sam and Judy what happened in the house that day, because I don't want them to lie to me," Judy's friend Deb Kosarick told me. "And you know what? To protect my kids, I'd lie, too. I'd lie on a stack of Bibles."

• • •

The day before Thanksgiving, I went to see the Bishops again. It was a bitterly cold morning, and smoke curled from their chimney. On December 6, they had plans to visit Seth's grave, which is in New Hampshire. It was an annual pilgrimage, and for years Amy had joined them. She would speak to the grave, telling Seth about her life and her children. Even today, she will occasionally call her parents and tell them that Seth has visited her in her jail cell—that he talks to her, and sits on the edge of her bed. Until very recently, Amy told me, she spoke of her brother "in the present tense, or not at all."

Amy seems unlikely to prevail in her request for a trial in Massachusetts. The decision is up to the district attorney, who appears disinclined to proceed. She has also appealed her conviction in Alabama. This move—which baffled her parents, given that she had pleaded guilty and waived her right to an appeal—also has little chance of success. "The worst thing about prison is being separated from my children," she told me. Jim, who still lives in Huntsville, has custody of the kids. She speaks to them on the phone as often as she can. Her daughter Phaedra is in the process of selecting colleges. Amy is encouraging her to apply to Harvard.

Sam made coffee, and we sat at the kitchen table. When I asked Judy about where she had been on December 6, she reiterated that she had been at the stables all morning and did not return home until approximately 2:00 p.m., just as Seth was getting back with the groceries.

I pointed out that in her original statement to police officials she had said that she had come home before Seth left to buy groceries.

"That's not true," Judy said.

"Those weren't *statements*," Sam said. Brian Howe and two other officers had interviewed them; the three of them then compiled their notes into a summary report. Perhaps the summary was mistaken. In any case, Sam told me, he had told the men that he had expected Judy to return at eleven thirty or twelve simply because that was the time she normally came home from the stables.

"All I know is what happened," Judy said. "I left the barn. I drove in the driveway. Seth pulled in right behind me."

"I wasn't thinking about trying to get some *alibi* for anyone," Sam said, growing flustered. "We had a funeral. We had a burial. We had a daughter who was totally depressed. They asked the questions. We weren't thinking of the time. They *heard* things, the three of them."

I asked Judy whether she had made plans to have tea with Saran Gillies that day—plans that she broke, because of the fight between Sam and Amy.

"What?" she said. "That's not true."

I explained that I had heard this from someone who knew Gillies well.

"Holy God, look at these people!" Judy exclaimed, her voice rising.

I then told the Bishops the story about my father and the rock. "Is there any scenario where Amy was angry with Sam," I began, "and she came down with the gun, and she was waving it, and—"

"Absolutely not," Judy said. She moved from the table to an adjacent couch by the fire.

I asked why Gillies would tell someone that she had plans with Judy that day if she didn't.

"I don't think she did," Judy said. "Someone is saying something that isn't true." She began to cry. "All these people that are talking about it, they weren't there," she said.

"It's over, Judy," Sam said.

"It *isn't* over," she said.

"I know, but there's nothing we can do about it."

"Amy was a good, good girl. We lived a decent life," Judy told me. "All I know is what happened. I was there." She looked at me intently, her eyes glazed with tears. "I was there," she repeated. "I was *there*." She held her stare, unblinking, until, eventually, I grew uncomfortable and looked away.

Amy Bishop is still serving her life sentence in Alabama. In May 2020, she was awarded second place in Pen America's Prison Writing Contest for a short story she wrote called "Man of Few Words." Eleven months later, her son, Seth—a violinist, like his mother and the uncle with whom he shared a name—was shot to death. He was twenty. The shooter, Vincent Harmon, was a friend of his. Harmon, who was eighteen, was charged with reckless murder.

THE HUNT FOR EL CHAPO

Inside the capture of the world's most notorious drug lord. (2014)

ONE AFTERNOON IN DECEMBER 2013, an assassin on board a KLM flight from Mexico City arrived at Amsterdam's Schiphol Airport. This was not a business trip: the killer, who was thirty-three, liked to travel, and often documented his journeys around Europe on Instagram. He wore designer clothes and a heavy silver ring in the shape of a grimacing skull. His passport was an expensive fake, which he had used successfully many times. But moments after he presented his documents to Dutch customs, he was arrested. The U.S. Drug Enforcement Administration had filed a Red Notice with Interpol—an international arrest warrant—and knew that he was coming. Only after the Dutch authorities had the man in custody did they learn his real identity: José Rodrigo Aréchiga, the chief enforcer for the biggest drug-trafficking organization in history, Mexico's Sinaloa cartel.

To work in the Mexican drug trade is to have a nickname, and Aréchiga went by the whimsically malevolent handle El Chino Ántrax. He supervised the armed wing of the Sinaloa—a cadre of executioners known as Los Ántrax—and coordinated drug shipments for the cartel's leader, Joaquín Guzmán Loera, who was known as El Chapo, or Shorty. Aréchiga was a *narcotraficante* of the digital age, bantering with other criminals on Twitter and posting snapshots of himself guzzling Cristal, posing with exotic pets, and fondling a gold-plated AK-47. Guzmán, who is fifty-seven, typified an older generation. Obsessively secretive, he ran his multibillion-dollar drug enterprise from hiding in Sinaloa, the remote western state where he was born, and from which the cartel takes its name. The Sinaloa cartel exports industrial volumes of cocaine, marijuana, heroin, and methamphetamine to America; it is thought to be responsible for as much as half the illegal narcotics that cross the border every year. Guzmán has been characterized by the U.S. Treasury Department as "the world's most powerful drug trafficker," and after the killing of Osama bin Laden in 2011, he became perhaps the most wanted fugitive on the planet. Mexican politicians promised to bring him to justice, and the United States offered a $5 million reward for information leading to his capture. But part of Guzmán's fame stemmed from the perception that he was uncatchable, and he continued to thrive, consolidating control of key smuggling routes and extending his operation into new markets in Europe, Asia, and Australia. According to one study, the Sinaloa cartel is now active in more than fifty countries.

On several occasions, authorities had come close to catching Guzmán. In 2004, the Mexican Army descended on a dusty ranch in Sinaloa where he was holed up, but he had advance warning and fled along a rutted mountain track in an all-terrain vehicle. Three years later, Guzmán married a teenage beauty queen named Emma Coronel and invited half the criminal underworld of Mexico to attend the ceremony. The army mobilized several Bell helicopters to crash the party; the troops arrived, guns drawn, to discover that Guzmán had just departed. American authorities have no jurisdiction to make arrests in Mexico, so whenever DEA agents developed fresh intelligence about Guzmán's whereabouts, all they could do was feed the leads to their Mexican counterparts and hope for the best. In Washington, concerns about the competence of Mexican forces mingled with deeper fears about corruption. A former senior Mexican intelligence official told me that the cartel has "penetrated most Mexican agencies." Was Guzmán being tipped off by an insider? After a series of near misses in which Chapo foiled his pursuers by sneaking out of buildings through back doors, officials at the U.S. embassy in Mexico City took to joking, bitterly, that there is no word in Spanish for "surround."

Guzmán developed "a Zorro-like reputation," Gil Gonzalez, who pursued him in Mexico for the DEA, told me. In dozens of *narco-corridos,* the heraldic Mexican ballads that glorify traffickers, singers portrayed Guzmán as a country boy turned cunning bandit who had grown rich but not soft, his *cuerno de chivo,* or "goat horn"—Mexican slang for an assault rifle with a curved magazine—never far from his side. Yet Guzmán himself remained maddeningly obscure. Only a few photographs of him circulated publicly. A famous series taken after an arrest in 1993 shows a stocky, dark-eyed, square-jawed young man standing awkwardly in a prison yard; he gazes at the camera with a shyness that seems at odds with his fearsome reputation.

Chapo escaped eight years later, and had been on the run ever since. Because he might have had plastic surgery to alter his appearance, the authorities could no longer be sure what he looked like. One *narcocorrido* captured the predicament: "Only he knows who he is / So go looking for someone / Who looks just like him / Because the real Chapo / You'll never see again."

The authorities tried to track Guzmán by monitoring telephone lines. Narcotics smuggling necessitates regular phone communication between farmers and packers, truckers and pilots, accountants and enforcers, street dealers and suppliers. But traffickers at the top of the hierarchy maintain operational security by rarely making calls or sending emails. Guzmán was known to use sophisticated encryption and to limit the number of people he communicated with, keeping his organization compartmentalized and allowing subordinates a degree of autonomy, as long as the shipments kept running on time. "I never spoke to him directly," one former Sinaloa lieutenant told me. "But I knew what he wanted us to do." The Sinaloa cartel is sometimes described as a "cellular" organization. Structurally, its network is distributed and has more in common with a terrorist organization like al-Qaeda than with the antiquated hierarchies of the Cosa Nostra. When the cartel suffers the loss of a major figure like El Chino Ántrax, it can reconstitute itself—but not without a few phone calls among the leadership.

At the DEA, which taps hundreds of phone lines and email accounts associated with traffickers, the process of applying pressure to a criminal organization and then monitoring furtive attempts at outreach is known as "tickling the wires." When El Chino Ántrax was arrested in Amsterdam, the cartel was still coping with two other high-level losses: in November, the twenty-three-year-old son of one of Guzmán's closest associates was arrested while trying to cross the border in Nogales; in December, Mexican troops in a helicopter shot and killed another key cartel enforcer, on a stretch of highway by the

Sea of Cortés. As the cartel attempted to regroup, authorities on both sides of the border intercepted scores of phone calls, texts, and emails. They learned that Guzmán would soon be coming to Culiacán, the state capital of Sinaloa, for a meeting with his sons Alfredo and Iván—ascendant traffickers who were both close friends of El Chino Ántrax's. The DEA presented an intelligence dossier to authorities in Mexico, and in mid-January a special-forces unit of commandos from the Mexican Marines, or SEMAR, began to assemble at a forward operating base near the resort town of Los Cabos, along the southern tip of the Baja Peninsula. The marines, who are the Mexican equivalent of Navy SEALs, were joined by a small group of American advisers. Mexican authorities code-named the mission Operation Gargoyle. Its object was to capture Guzmán.

According to *The Dallas Morning News,* the government of Mexico's president, Enrique Peña Nieto, informed the marines and their American partners that they would have approximately three weeks to bring down the drug lord. A U.S. official involved in planning the operation told me that this was true. Fighting drug traffickers in Mexico has become a matter of triage, and the unit was soon to be redeployed to battle another cartel, the Knights Templar, in the restive state of Michoacán. (Eduardo Sánchez, the chief spokesman for the government of Mexico, denied that any such time limit was in place. "There was no window," he said.)

As the marines and their advisers moved into Los Cabos, they tried not to attract attention. A battleship anchored off the coast was used as a decoy, so that curious observers might conclude that the sudden influx of commandos was part of a standard naval exercise. But one reason that Guzmán had remained at large so long was his unparalleled network of informants. One person involved in the operation told me, "As soon as we landed, he knew."

• • •

Guzmán had always been a master of escape. Born in the mountain village of La Tuna, in Mexico's wild and craggy Sierra Madre Occidental, he was the oldest child of a subsistence farmer who dabbled in the drug trade. For generations, Sinaloan ranchers had cultivated cannabis and opium, and children were taken out of elementary school to assist in the harvest. Guzmán left school for good in third grade, and in the 1970s, in spite of his illiteracy, he became an apprentice to two drug chieftains: Amado Carrillo Fuentes, who owned a fleet of airplanes and was known as the Lord of the Skies; and Miguel Ángel Félix Gallardo, a police officer turned drug baron who ran the Guadalajara cartel and was known as El Padrino—the Godfather.

Guzmán started as a kind of air-traffic controller, coordinating cocaine flights from Colombia. But he was clever and aggressive and quickly began to acquire power. One night in November 1992, Guzmán's henchmen massacred six people at a crowded discotheque in Puerto Vallarta. They severed the telephone lines so that nobody could call for help, then walked inside and opened fire on the dance floor. The targets were Tijuana-based traffickers whom Guzmán was challenging for control of the lucrative smuggling routes through Baja California. They were in the bathroom when the shooting started, and fled without being harmed. The next spring, the traffickers arranged for their own hit men to murder Guzmán at the international airport in Guadalajara. As gunfire erupted, Guzmán scrambled out of his vehicle and crawled to safety. Seven people were killed, including Archbishop Juan Jesús Posadas Ocampo. (The gunmen apparently mistook him for Guzmán.)

Posadas's murder caused a political uproar, and it was not long before Guzmán, who had gone into hiding, was picked up by authorities in Guatemala and turned over to Mexico. He was sentenced to twenty years in prison, on charges of conspiracy, drug trafficking, and bribery, and ended up in Puente Grande, in Jalisco, which was considered one of the most secure prisons in Mexico. Behind bars, Guzmán consolidated both his empire and his reputation. He bought off the prison staff and enjoyed a life of relative luxury: he conducted business by cell phone, orchestrated regular visits from prostitutes, and threw parties for favored inmates that featured alcohol, lobster bisque, and filet mignon. While he was there, the Mexican attorney general's office subjected him to psychological interviews. The resulting criminal profile noted that he was "egocentric, narcissistic, shrewd, persistent, tenacious, meticulous, discriminating, and secretive."

One day in January 2001, a prison administrator pulled aside a makeshift curtain that Guzmán had draped across the entrance to his cell and shouted, "He's escaped!" A subsequent investigation determined that Guzmán had hidden in a laundry cart pushed by a paid accomplice. But many in Mexico speculate that he didn't have to bother with subterfuge. Guzmán controlled Puente Grande so thoroughly by the time of his exit that he might as well have walked out the front door. Criminal charges were eventually brought against seventy-one people who worked at the prison, including the warden.

If Chapo's escape suggested that the Mexican political system had been corroded by drug money, his subsequent years as a fugitive did little to diminish this impression. He retreated to Sinaloa and expanded his operations, launching violent turf wars with rival cartels over control of prized entry points along the U.S. border. The sociologist Diego Gambetta, in his 1993 book, *The Sicilian Mafia*, observes that durable criminal enterprises are often woven into the social and political fabric of a community, and part of their "intrinsic tenacity" is their ability to offer certain services that the state does not. Today on the streets of Culiacán you see nightclubs, fortified villas, and an occasional Lamborghini. Chapo and other drug lords have invested and laundered their proceeds by buying hundreds of legitimate businesses: restaurants, soccer stadiums, day-care centers, ostrich farms. Juan Millán, the former state governor of Sinaloa, once estimated that 62 percent of the state's economy is tied up with drug money.

Sinaloa remains poor, however, and Badiraguato, the municipality containing Guzmán's home village, is one of the most desperate areas in the state. There had always been some sympathy for the drug trade in Sinaloa, but nothing deepens sympathy like charity and bribes. Eduardo Medina-Mora, Mexico's ambassador in Washington, described Guzmán's largesse in the state: "You are financing everything. Baptisms. Infrastructure. If someone gets sick, you provide a little plane. So you have lots of local support, because you are Santa Claus. And everybody likes Santa Claus." Mexico's municipal police were poorly trained, poorly paid, and poorly equipped, rendering them susceptible to bribery. "In practical terms, organized crime literally privatized the municipal police forces across many parts of the country," one senior Mexican official told me.

Guzmán's influence over the public sector was not confined to law enforcement. Last year, a former bodyguard for the current governor of Sinaloa, Mario López Valdez, released a series of YouTube videos in which he described accompanying López Valdez, who had just taken office, on a trip to meet with Guzmán. In one video, the bodyguard played a recorded conversation in which the governor appeared to instruct his subordinates not to antagonize the Sinaloa cartel—and, instead, to crack down on its rivals. López Valdez insisted that the recording was doctored. Last August, the bodyguard was discovered beside a road in Sinaloa. He had been decapitated.

As long as Guzmán remained in the mountains, the inhospitable terrain and the allegiance of locals appeared to guarantee his safety. In 2009, Dennis Blair, President Barack Obama's national intelligence director, met with Guillermo Galván, who was then Mexico's secretary of defense. Galván told him that everybody knew, roughly, where Guzmán was. The challenge was taking him into custody. According to a diplomatic cable that was later released by WikiLeaks, Galván explained that Guzmán was believed to move among a dozen or so ranches and to be protected by up to three hundred armed men. The peaks of the Sierra Madre Occidental are steep and jagged, and the roads that vein their contours often taper to a single dirt track. An armored convoy would be spotted by Guzmán's lookouts well before it arrived at its destination. And if a Black Hawk helicopter was dispatched to attack his outpost, he would hear it thundering across the valley from miles out, leaving plenty of time to flee.

More recently, however, intelligence collected by Mexican authorities and the DEA indicated that Guzmán might be changing his habits. There is a saying in the Mexican drug trade that it is better to live one good year than ten bad ones. Many young men enter the industry expecting to enjoy a decadent life for a short time before being incarcerated or killed. Young narcos behave recklessly: they go to nightclubs, they race Bentleys, and they post pictures of themselves online with their co-conspirators (and with the occasional dead body). The only traffickers in Sinaloa who beat the odds are those who are content to follow a more austere life in the mountains. Until lately, Guzmán had taken that approach. But because he was tired, or married to a much younger woman, or overconfident of his ability to escape, Guzmán began spending time in Culiacán and other cities. "Here's a guy who has made hundreds of millions of dollars in the drug trade, and he's living like a pauper up in the mountains," Mike Vigil, a former DEA agent who worked in Mexico for many years, told me. "He likes the fiestas. He likes the music. He likes to dance." Another law-enforcement official speculated that though Guzmán was accustomed to a rustic life, Emma Coronel was not. "She's not much of a mountain person," he said, adding that they had twin daughters and, even though Guzmán was a fugitive, his wife was adamant that he be present in the girls' lives: "She would go out of her way to maintain that family life."

Guzmán had other weaknesses. "He loves the gourmet food," a DEA official told me. From time to time, he would be spotted at an elegant restaurant in Sinaloa or in a neighboring state. The choreography was always the same. Diners would be startled by a team of gunmen, who would politely but firmly demand their telephones, promising that they would be returned at the end of the evening. Chapo and his entourage would come in and feast on shrimp and steak, then thank the other diners for their forbearance, return the telephones, pick up the tab for everyone, and head off into the night.

It has been reported, erroneously, that Guzmán used a satellite phone; in fact, his favored communication device was the BlackBerry. Like many narcos, he was suspicious of satellite phones, because most of the companies that manufacture them are American and the devices are relatively easy for law-enforcement officials to compromise. But the BlackBerry is made by a Canadian company, and Guzmán felt more comfortable using one. This trust was misplaced: by early 2012, the DEA had homed in on Guzmán's BlackBerry, and could not only monitor his communications but also use geolocation technology to triangulate his signal. That February, the agency confirmed that Guzmán had traveled to Los Cabos for a liaison with a prostitute. He had been married at least three times, and he had relationships with many mistresses; nevertheless, he appears to have had an unflagging appetite for paid companionship. (Numerous current and former officials noted Guzmán's prodigious consumption of Viagra. "He ate it like candy," one said.) The DEA agents who monitored his emails and texts marveled at the extent to which his communications seemed focused not on managing his multinational empire but on juggling the competing demands of his wife, his ex-wives (with whom he remained cordial), his girlfriends, and his paid consorts. "It was like *Peyton Place*," a former law-enforcement official who kept track of the communications told me. "It was a nonstop deal."

After authorities traced the BlackBerry signal to a mansion on a cul-de-sac in a wealthy enclave near the coast, Mexican troops burst through the front door of the building. Whether Guzmán had been alerted in advance remains unclear, but he had enough time to sneak out the back of the property; he went to an adjacent resort, where he blended into a crowd of vacationers before moving on. Over the next three days, the authorities pursued him as he moved around the city, desperately trying to arrange an escape route to the mountains. At one point during the chase, Guzmán must have realized that his BlackBerry had been compromised, and decided to turn this setback to his advantage. He met up with a subordinate and gave him the BlackBerry. Someone involved in the operation said of Guzmán, "He took us for a ride." The authorities, unaware of the handoff, chased the signal around Los Cabos, until they finally pounced on the sacrificial subordinate. While they were occupied with arresting him, Chapo made it into the desert, where a private plane picked him up and flew him back to the safety of the Sierra Madre.

• • •

"He changed it up after Los Cabos," one U.S. law-enforcement official told me, adding a line worthy of a *narcocorrido:* "He's an illiterate son of a bitch, but he's a street-smart motherfucker." Rather than switch BlackBerrys, as he had done in the past, Guzmán now appeared to stop communicating altogether. Like bin Laden, he might have chosen to rely on couriers. But a courier system is too inefficient for the fast pace of the narcotics trade, and so, as U.S. and Mexican authorities eventually discovered, Chapo devised an elaborate solution. In the past, he had occasionally restricted his contact with others in the cartel by relaying his commands through a proxy. For a time, a woman known as La Voz (the Voice) served as his gatekeeper, sending and receiving messages on his behalf. After Los Cabos, Guzmán reinstated this arrangement, but with additional precautions. If you needed to communicate with the boss, you could reach him via BBM, BlackBerry's instant-messaging application. (Guzmán had apparently learned to read and write well enough to communicate in the short-hand of instant messages.) Your message would go not directly to Guzmán, however, but to a trusted lieutenant, who spent his days in Starbucks coffee shops and other locations with public wireless networks. Upon receiving the message, the lieutenant would transcribe it onto an iPad so that he could forward the text using Wi-Fi—avoiding the cellular networks that the cartel knew the authorities were trolling. The transcribed message would be sent not to Guzmán but to a second intermediary, who, also using a tablet and public Wi-Fi, would transcribe the words onto *his* BlackBerry and relay them to Guzmán. Although Guzmán continued to use a BlackBerry, it was almost impossible to track, because it communicated with only one other device. When he received your message, his reply would be relayed back to you through the same indirect means. Many members of the cartel did not realize that when they wrote to the boss and received an answer, every word had been transmitted via two intermediaries. This is sometimes described as a "mirror" system, and it is fiendishly difficult for authorities to penetrate (especially when the transcribers keep moving from one Wi-Fi hot spot to another). Nevertheless, by studying the communications patterns of the cartel, analysts at the Special Operations Division of the DEA eventually grasped the nature of the arrangement. They resolved to focus on the small ring of logistical facilitators surrounding Guzmán, to identify the mirrors that he was using, and, ultimately, to target their communications.

In early February of this year, when the special-forces unit from SEMAR began making forays into Sinaloa, it was the first time that Mexico's marines had ever pursued such a significant operation in the state. Unlike the Mexican Army—which tended to move slowly, and always informed state authorities before conducting an operation, even when those authorities were corrupt—the marines were nimble and secretive. They mobilized rapidly, on Black Hawk helicopters, and did not ask permission before initiating raids. The marines pursuing Guzmán had seen intense combat in recent years, battling the Zetas cartel in northeast Mexico. They were veterans of a 2009 firefight that had killed a former associate of Guzmán's, Arturo Beltrán Leyva, during a raid in Cuernavaca. One of the marines in the unit, a young officer from Tabasco named Melquisedet Angulo Córdova, was killed in the shoot-out. He was buried with full military honors. Shortly after his funeral, gunmen charged into a home where his family had gathered to mourn, and murdered his mother, his brother, his sister, and his aunt. The warning could not have been clearer. Yet, according to people who know the unit, the marines grew more determined to bring down the traffickers. They now made a fetish of secrecy. Whenever they were photographed in public, they followed the custom of other elite security forces in Mexico and wore black masks over their faces. They implemented clever safeguards against penetration by the cartels. Apart from the admiral who commanded them and a few senior personnel, none of them knew where they were headed or who their target might be until they boarded a Black Hawk to undertake the mission. Several days before an operation, the commandos were obliged to surrender their cell phones, to protect against leaks.

The first important arrest of Operation Gargoyle occurred on February 13, when the unit apprehended a group of Sinaloa assassins on a highway outside Culiacán. The marines confiscated the men's phones and sent them off for analysis. Because cartel members frequently shed phones, a single device can offer an intelligence windfall if it contains current numbers for other members of the organization. In American debates over the National Security Agency's warrantless collection of "metadata," this is one reason that many authorities have been quick to defend these techniques; a constellation of dialed phone numbers can be used to build a "link chart" exposing the hierarchy of an organization.

Using information extracted from the phones collected in the arrest, the marines and the DEA began to focus on a trafficker named Mario Hidalgo Argüello. A plump-cheeked man with a droopy mustache and a crooked boxer's nose, he was a veteran of Mexico's special forces who had switched sides to work for the traffickers. Within the cartel, he was known as El Nariz—the Nose. Now that Guzmán was spending more time in urban areas, his entourage had become very small. Nariz was part of this privileged circle, serving as Guzmán's personal assistant and errand boy. In Culiacán, Guzmán rarely spent consecutive nights in the same bed. He rotated from house to house and seldom told those around him—even Nariz—where his next destination was, until they were en route. Guzmán had a personal chef, an attractive young woman who accompanied him everywhere he traveled. He is said to have feared poisoning and sometimes made his underlings taste food before he would eat it. But one DEA agent said of the chef, "She's absolutely a great cook. So maybe the whole personal-chef thing was more hedonism than paranoia." Guzmán also liked take-out food, and on the night of February 16 he sent Nariz out to pick up an order.

Guzmán's life had become largely nocturnal, and he ate dinner very late. That evening, he was sleeping at a safe house that belonged to his ex-wife Griselda López. By the time Nariz left work, it was already past midnight. Nariz returned to his own house in Culiacán, and discovered that the commandos from SEMAR had been waiting for him. Under questioning by the marines, Nariz admitted that Guzmán was hiding in the city, and gave the address. "He flipped right away," an American law-enforcement official told me.

Just before dawn, the marines arrived at a cream-colored two-story house on Río Humaya Street, in the middle-class neighborhood of Libertad. There were bars on the windows, but that was standard in Culiacán. The marines readied their weapons and produced a battering ram, but when they moved to breach the front door, it didn't budge. A wooden door would have splintered off its hinges, but this door was a marvel of reinforced steel—some of the marines later likened it to an air lock on a submarine. For all the noise that their efforts made, the door seemed indestructible. Normally, the friction of a battering ram would heat the steel, rendering it more pliable. But the door was custom-made: inside the steel skin, it was filled with water, so that if anyone tried to break it down, the heat from the impact would not spread. The marines hammered the door again and again, until the ram buckled and had to be replaced. It took ten minutes to gain entry to the house.

The marines streamed through a modest kitchen and into a series of windowless rooms. They noticed surveillance cameras and monitors everywhere. A gaudy oil painting of a bucking bull, stuck full of swords but still defiant, hung on one wall. But there was nobody in the house. In a bathroom on the ground floor, they discovered a bathtub that had been raised from its base, on hydraulic lifts, at a forty-five-degree angle, revealing a dark opening leading to a steep set of stairs: a tunnel.

• • •

In the early days of Guzmán's career, before his time at Puente Grande, he distinguished himself as a trafficker who brought an unusual sense of imagination and play to the trade. Today, tunnels that traverse the U.S.-Mexico border are a mainstay of drug smuggling: up to a mile long, they often feature air-conditioning, electricity, sophisticated drainage systems, and tracks, so that heavy loads of contraband can be transported on carts.

Guzmán invented the border tunnel. A quarter of a century ago, he commissioned an architect, Felipe de Jesús Corona-Verbera, to design a grocery store that served as a front company, and a private zoo in Guadalajara for his collection of tigers, crocodiles, and bears. By this point, Guzmán was making so much money that he needed secure locations in which to hide it, along with his drugs and his weapons. So he had Corona-Verbera devise a series of *clavos*, or stashes—secret compartments under the beds in his homes. Inevitably, a bolder idea presented itself: If you could dig a *clavo* beneath a house near the U.S. border, why not continue digging and come out on the other side? Guzmán ordered Corona-Verbera to design a tunnel that ran from a residence in Agua Prieta, immediately south of the border, to a cartel-owned warehouse in Douglas, Arizona. The result delighted him. "Corona made a fucking cool tunnel," he said.

Since then, U.S. intelligence has attributed no fewer than ninety border tunnels to the Sinaloa cartel. When the marines began breaking into the house on Río Humaya Street, Guzmán was inside, as was a bodyguard. As the battering ram clanged against the door, they moved quickly into the ground-floor bathroom. Chapo activated the escape hatch by pushing a plug into an electrical outlet by the sink while flicking a hidden switch on the side of the vanity mirror. Suddenly, the caulk around the rim of the bathtub broke, and the tub rose from its tiled frame. The caulk had camouflaged the escape hatch; even the bodyguard might have been unaware of its existence before Guzmán turned on the hydraulic lift.

They scrambled down the steps into a narrow passage. The space was lit, but very tight, and they moved quickly, knowing that they had only a slight head start on the marines. They reached a small portal resembling the door of a bank safe, where the tunnel they were in connected to the main sewer system of Culiacán; crawling through this opening, they entered a cylindrical tunnel. The passage was unlit and less than five feet high; nevertheless, they splashed through the dirty, shallow water at high speed, as if Guzmán had rehearsed this escape. By the time the commandos entered the tunnel, Guzmán had been running for more than ten minutes.

A tunnel is an exceedingly dangerous environment in which to stalk someone who is armed: if he should turn and fire at you, he doesn't even need to aim—one of the ricocheting bullets will likely hit you. But the marines did not hesitate. In the streets of Culiacán, meanwhile, dozens of troops were in position, ready to pursue Guzmán when he returned above ground. In the sky, a covert U.S. drone looked down on the city, poised to track the fugitive if he emerged from a manhole and fled through the streets.

Meanwhile, Chapo ran through the sewers, like Harry Lime in *The Third Man*. The tunnel forked, and at one juncture the marines were momentarily flummoxed, unable to tell which path he had taken. Then they spotted a tactical vest on the ground—Guzmán or the bodyguard must have shed it—and charged onward in that direction. Eventually, the marines emerged at a storm drain by the banks of a muddy river, more than a mile from the point where Guzmán had entered the tunnel. Once again, he had vanished.

• • •

Two days later, on February 19, President Obama, who was visiting Mexico City, held a press conference with President Peña Nieto. Obama praised the "excellent cooperation between the United States and Mexico" on criminal-justice issues. When Peña Nieto came into office in 2012, many Washington officials had doubts about his determination to fight the cartels. His predecessor, Felipe Calderón, had launched an unprecedented assault against drug trafficking, deploying fifty thousand troops to battle the traffickers in the streets; the armed forces pursued a "kingpin strategy," seeking to dismantle drug syndicates by killing or capturing their leaders. Calderón's approach received strong financial and material support from Washington. But the campaign was a resounding failure: the death toll in Mexico spiraled as the cartels fought daylight gun battles with the authorities and among themselves. In Ciudad Juárez, one of the flash points in the conflict, the annual murder rate jumped from about three hundred in 2007 to more than three thousand in 2010. The carnage might have been somewhat redeemed had Calderón succeeded in curtailing the *narcotraficantes*. But, as Ioan Grillo observes in his recent book, *El Narco*, "In the drug business, it seems, a war economy functions perfectly well." The flow of narcotics across the border never diminished significantly, and as cartels like Sinaloa and the Zetas vanquished smaller competitors, they consolidated territorial control, growing more powerful and more grotesque in the process. "Corpse messages"—piles of dismembered bodies—were left on major street corners.

Mexican voters who went to the polls in 2012 were weary of the violence; Peña Nieto, a youthful-looking former governor who represented the Partido Revolucionario Institucional, or PRI, which had dominated Mexican politics for much of the past century, promised a fresh start. He pledged to focus not on attacking the cartels but on reducing the killing—though his plan for achieving this met with skepticism. In the past, PRI officials had largely countenanced drug trafficking, in exchange for well-placed bribes, and it wasn't clear if Peña Nieto was sincere about pursuing a different path. For years, U.S. law-enforcement officers had chafed at the pretense that they were merely "advising" their Mexican counterparts in the fight against the narcos; some of them wanted American armed forces to have wide operational latitude on the ground, as they once had in Colombia. Calderón had come closer to tolerating such a scenario than any previous Mexican head of state had. But Peña Nieto indicated that he preferred to maintain greater distance. When young Mexican officers study their nation's military history, the curriculum dwells, inescapably, on the many invasions by the United States; the prospect of an overbearing American law-enforcement presence south of the border offended many Mexicans' sense of sovereignty. Soon after Peña Nieto assumed office, he declared that all initiatives led or assisted by the United States must be routed through an office in Mexico's Ministry of the Interior, which became known as "the single window."

It was especially surprising, then, when Peña Nieto's administration began capturing or killing some of the country's most brutal drug kingpins, often in close collaboration with the United States. Last July, the authorities arrested Miguel Ángel Treviño Morales, one of the leaders of the Zetas, who sometimes burned his victims alive. The next month, military operatives apprehended the leader of the Gulf cartel—El Pelón, or Baldy—who was known for blindfolding his enemies and torturing them to death. For Peña Nieto, establishing rhetorical distance from the gringos might have created the political latitude for him to collaborate with them.

At the time of the Obama meeting, the SEMAR unit was still pursuing Guzmán in Culiacán. (This was a departure: Mexican armed forces had generally retreated to their bases following a failed attempt to apprehend him.) After the marines emerged from the sewers without capturing him, they discovered that the house on Río Humaya Street was connected not just to Culiacán's sewer system but, through the sewers, to six other houses, each similarly furnished and appointed, and each with its own bathtub escape hatch. Guzmán had been shuttling nightly among these houses. Information from one of Guzmán's captured associates led the marines to a nearby warehouse, where they uncovered a cache of heavy weaponry and more than three tons of cocaine and methamphetamine. Some of the drugs had been concealed inside plastic cucumbers and bananas, in preparation for a surreptitious journey across the border.

The marines knew that in addition to the safe houses and the escape routes, Guzmán had aides who could provide him with a new BlackBerry or a ride out of town. So SEMAR occupied each safe house it discovered, and focused on pursuing the men in Guzmán's entourage, on the theory that if they cut him off from his support network, he would no longer have a place to hide. What had started as a covert operation became overt as Mexican forces attempted to heighten the pressure on Chapo. Eduardo Sánchez, the government spokesman, told me that authorities established conspicuous roadblocks "so that Mr. Guzmán could feel that we were after him."

Soon after the escape in the tunnel, the marines arrested Manuel López Osorio, another former special-forces officer who had joined Guzmán's inner circle; he went by the name El Picudo (Pointy Nose). He, too, became cooperative under questioning and gave up a significant detail. Picudo said that he had picked up Guzmán and the bodyguard by a storm drain on the outskirts of Culiacán. He had driven them south of the city, where they met up with another aide and switched vehicles. According to Picudo, the bodyguard Guzmán was traveling with was his most trusted employee: Carlos Hoo Ramírez, who was called El Cóndor.

The marines knew who Cóndor was, and raided his house in Culiacán. It was empty. They had also been monitoring his Black-Berry communications, but the device appeared to be turned off. Suddenly, on February 20, it came to life: he was sending a text. The authorities traced the signal and saw that it came from the port city of Mazatlán, 140 miles to the southeast. In light of the debacle in Los Cabos, the SEMAR operators and their American colleagues worried that Guzmán might have already left Mazatlán. He enjoyed considerable protection in the city, where he had often received shipments from India and China of the precursor chemicals used to manufacture meth. But it would be folly to move from one major population center to another, and judging from Guzmán's past behavior, he was probably already back in the Sierra Madre. By this point, federal authorities in Mexico City had learned about the botched operation in Culiacán, and the three-week window before the SEMAR unit would be redeployed was nearly closed. But, if Cóndor was so indispensable to the drug lord, capturing him could provide valuable intelligence and squeeze Guzmán even further. So the marines flew down to the coast.

• • •

Mazatlán is a resort town popular with retirees from the United States and Canada. It has long been a corridor for narcotics trafficking, but as uncontested Sinaloa territory it has been spared the severe internecine violence that has plagued more disputed areas. On the night of Friday, February 21, about forty marines assembled in the city, along with a small contingent of agents from the DEA, the U.S. Marshals Service, and the Department of Homeland Security. The marshals, who specialize in locating fugitives, had been able to trace the signal on Cóndor's BlackBerry to the Miramar, a white twelve-story hotel-condominium building with three columns of half-moon balconies overlooking the Pacific.

Geolocation technology can trace a signal to a given city block or building, but not necessarily determine where in the building the device is situated. So, in the early hours of Saturday morning, the marines fanned out, forming a perimeter around the property. Someone consulted the registry and discovered that two apartments had been rented the previous day. A team of marines climbed to the sixth floor and burst into one of the apartments, where they discovered two groggy tourists, who were recovering from an evening of partying. (One of them, an American, thought that their room had been stormed because they had been smoking marijuana. The marines were perplexed when he produced, from his wallet, a California medical-marijuana card.)

Meanwhile, on the fourth floor, a team of six marines approached apartment 401, where they discovered Cóndor standing guard and holding an assault rifle. He raised his weapon only for a moment, since it was obvious that he was outnumbered. Guzmán's decision to jettison his huge security force had allowed him to move around quickly and inconspicuously, but he was left essentially defenseless. The commandos needed no battering ram as they crashed through a flimsy wooden door, shouting, "Marines!" They entered a two-bedroom apartment with potted plants, cheap furniture, and a white tile floor. In one bedroom, the marines found two women: the chef and a nanny, who had been sleeping with Guzmán's two-year-old twins, Emali and María Joaquina. A pink Pack 'n Play—which matched the girls' miniature pink suitcases—had been set up. The marines raced to the master bedroom in the back, where they discovered Emma Coronel, who had been sleeping. "Don't kill him!" she shrieked. Guzmán had scrambled out of bed in his underwear, grabbed an assault rifle, and darted into a small bathroom. "Don't kill him!" Coronel pleaded again. "He's the father of my children!"

The standoff lasted only a few seconds, with the marines bellowing and Coronel screaming. Then Chapo shouted, "Okay, okay, okay, okay!" and extended his empty hands through the bathroom doorway.

It had been a stunningly swift operation: less than three minutes after the marines stormed the apartment, Guzmán surrendered. No one would have imagined such a legendary outlaw going out in anything but a firefight. But SEMAR had developed a reputation as an outfit that shoots first and asks questions later. "They notoriously kill everybody in the room when there is the slightest provocation," an American law-enforcement official who has worked with SEMAR told me. With his wife and daughters present, Guzmán might have realized that the only way to spare their lives was to surrender.

When the marines searched the Miramar apartment, they found a blue vinyl wheelchair: Guzmán had entered the building pretending to be a frail old man. But when they took him into custody, they discovered that he looked much as he had in the earlier photographs. His teeth were a little pearlier; he'd had them capped. His hair and his mustache were still thick and jet-black. (In the house on Río Humaya Street in Culiacán, the marines discovered a bottle of hair dye.) They got him dressed in a pair of black jeans and a white shirt, then escorted him out of the building and around the corner to a dirt soccer field, where he was placed on a Black Hawk and transported to a nearby naval base. A Learjet then took him to Mexico City.

As the marines frog-marched El Chapo out of a hangar at the airport, journalists photographed him looking furtively at his captors. His face was bruised and swollen, which SEMAR attributes not to any rough handling but to dings that he had received while sprinting through the dark tunnels beneath Culiacán. The marines also noticed bruises and cuts on his feet, and learned that when he fled the house on Río Humaya Street, he didn't have time to grab his shoes; he had run through the tunnels barefoot.

Guzmán was gruff but respectful with his captors. He had been planning to leave for the mountains that day, he told them. If the marines had arrived just a few hours later, he would have been gone. "I can't believe you got me," he said.

• • •

At eleven forty-two that morning, Peña Nieto announced the capture on Twitter: "I acknowledge the work of the security agencies of the Mexican state in pulling off the apprehension of Joaquín Guzmán

Loera in Mazatlán." U.S. officials had already leaked the news to the Associated Press, but Peña Nieto wanted to be certain that his troops had the right man. In the summer of 2012, Mexican authorities announced that they had captured Guzmán's son Alfredo, and held a press conference in which they paraded before the cameras a sullen, pudgy young man in a red polo shirt. A lawyer representing the man then revealed that he was not Guzmán's son at all, but a local car dealer named Félix Beltrán. Guzmán's family chimed in, with barely suppressed glee, that the young man in custody was not Alfredo. In another recent case, officials in Michoacán announced that they had killed the infamous kingpin Nazario Moreno, a triumph that was somewhat undercut by the fact that Moreno—who was known as El Más Loco, or "the Craziest One"—had supposedly perished in a showdown with government forces in 2010. (DEA agents now joke that El Más Loco is the only Mexican kingpin to have died twice.) Fingerprints and a DNA swab confirmed that the man captured at the Miramar was indeed Guzmán. It was a huge victory for Peña Nieto and for the DEA, if largely a symbolic one. Nobody had any illusions that the arrest would slow down the drug trade. "If you kill the CEO of General Motors, General Motors will not go out of business," a Mexican official told me. Guzmán's genius was always architectural, and the infrastructure that he created will almost certainly survive him. Five weeks after Guzmán's apprehension, two new drug tunnels were discovered in Sinaloa territory, starting in Tijuana and emerging in the industrial outskirts of San Diego.

Some believe that even before Guzmán's capture his role in the organization had become largely symbolic. "He was a nonexecutive chairman," Ambassador Medina-Mora told me. "An emblematic figure." Even so, the arrest signified a powerful reassertion of the rule of law in Mexico. Alejandro Hope, a former senior official in Mexican intelligence, told me that the message of Operation Gargoyle is simple and resounding: "No one is beyond sanction." Yet almost as soon as Peña Nieto's government took Guzmán into custody, questions arose about its ability to hold him. According to a memo sent to Attorney General Eric Holder a few hours after the Mazatlán raid, Guzmán is the subject of indictments in Arizona, California, Texas, Illinois, New York, Florida, and New Hampshire. The morning after his capture, Michael McCaul, the Texas Republican who chairs the House Homeland Security Committee, announced that Guzmán should be extradited to America, telling ABC, "There is a history here—he escaped from a prison in 2001." A federal prosecutor in New York declared that Guzmán should be tried in New York. The head of the DEA office in Chicago vowed, "I fully intend for us to have him tried here." But Mexico's attorney general, Jesús Murillo Karam, was quick to object. Guzmán still needed to complete his original twenty-year sentence, and then face multiple new charges, before the Mexican government would consider turning him over to the United States. He announced that Mexico has "no intention" of extraditing Guzmán, citing a concern that other Mexican officials raised with me: that American authorities might flip Guzmán and grant him a reduced sentence in exchange for his cooperation. The United States has a history of "reaching deals with criminals," Murillo Karam noted. This opposition to extraditing El Chapo could also be driven by less noble concerns: flipping Guzmán might provide the American government with evidence against top Mexican officials.

In a story that aired on the Televisa network, the Mexican journalist Carlos Loret de Mola reported that during the flight from Mazatlán to Mexico City, Guzmán told the marines that he had killed between two and three thousand people. If this figure includes not just individuals he murdered personally but people he authorized subordinates to kill, it is surely a gross underestimate. Nobody knows exactly how many people have been killed in Mexico's drug wars over the past decade, but between the dead and the disappeared the number likely exceeds eighty thousand. As both the instigator and the victor of some of the bloodiest battles on the border, Guzmán bears responsibility for an appalling proportion of these atrocities. His victims were overwhelmingly Mexican; one reason that the drug war has been so easy for most Americans to ignore is that very little of the violence visited upon Mexico has spilled into the United States. During the years when Juárez was the most dangerous city on the planet—and a resident there had a greater statistical likelihood of being murdered than someone living in the war zones of Afghanistan or Iraq—El Paso, just across the border, was one of the safest cities in America. Given this record, it makes intuitive sense that Guzmán should answer for his crimes where the worst of them were committed. But the Mexican officials I spoke with acknowledge that the criminal-justice system in their country is fragile, and that corruption remains endemic. Last summer, an old friend of Guzmán's, Rafael Caro Quintero, was released in the middle of the night from the prison where he had been serving a forty-year sentence for murdering a DEA agent. He was sprung on a technicality by a panel of Mexican judges, under circumstances that struck many observers as suspicious. The U.S. Justice Department furiously objected that Caro Quintero still faced charges in America and declared that the Mexicans should extradite him. But he had already disappeared into the mountains.

The prospect of a similar dead-of-night release for Chapo may not be far-fetched. The level of distrust between U.S. and Mexican officials on this issue is pronounced; indeed, one theory I heard for the Americans' decision to leak the news of Guzmán's capture to the Associated Press was that going public would foreclose any possibility of Mexican authorities quietly letting him go. "Once bitten, twice shy," Ambassador Medina-Mora told me, maintaining there was no possibility that his country would risk the political embarrassment of allowing its most notorious convict to escape a second time.

But there are plausible scenarios short of actual escape that would be troubling. According to the U.S. Treasury Department, Caro Quintero continued to operate his drug business during his years in prison, much as Guzmán did while he was at Puente Grande. Guzmán is ostensibly being held "in isolation" at Mexico's most secure prison, Altiplano, about fifty miles west of Mexico City. He is permitted visits not just with his lawyer but also with members of his family, many of whom have been implicated in the activities of his cartel. Shortly after the arrest in Mazatlán, Guzmán's son Alfredo lashed out on Twitter. "The Government is going to pay for this betrayal—it shouldn't have bitten the hand that feeds it," he wrote. "I just want to say that we are not beaten. The cartel is my father's and will always be my father's. GUZMAN LOERA FOREVER." His brother Iván vowed revenge: "Those dogs that dared to lay a hand on my father are going to pay."

• • •

One curious feature of Guzmán's capture was the fact that he was betrayed, in rapid succession, by at least two of his closest aides: Nariz and Picudo. Had either one refused to cooperate, Guzmán would likely remain free today. I was impressed, initially, by the speed with which the marines had elicited leads from these subordinates, both of them ex-members of Mexico's special forces who had been hardened by years in the cartel. One U.S. law-enforcement official told me that it is not unusual for cartel members to start cooperating as soon as they are captured. "There's very little allegiance once they're taken into custody," he said.

But when I raised the subject with a former DEA agent who has spoken to Mexican counterparts involved in the operation, he had a different explanation. "The marines tortured these guys," he told me matter-of-factly. "They would never have given it up, if not for that." The DEA refused to comment on the torture allegation. However, two senior U.S. law-enforcement officials told me that though they had no specific knowledge of the Mexican authorities using torture in the operation, they "wouldn't be surprised." Eduardo Sánchez, the spokesman for the Mexican government, denied the allegation and maintained that in this and other operations "federal officials, agents, and officers perform their duties strictly within the applicable legal framework and with utmost respect for human rights." But the Mexican armed forces have been implicated before in the use of torture as an interrogation technique in the pursuit of drug traffickers. A 2011 Human Rights Watch report found that members of Mexico's security services "systematically use torture to obtain forced confessions and information about criminal groups," and documented the use of such techniques as "beatings, asphyxiation with plastic bags, waterboarding, electric shocks, sexual torture, and death threats." The broad employment of brutal techniques, coupled with the high profile and the urgency of the hunt for Guzmán, makes it seem all the more plausible that Mexican authorities used unsavory, and illegal, means to pursue him.

What will become of the Sinaloa cartel remains unclear. Chapo's top associates, Ismael Zambada and Juan José Esparragoza, are both older than he is and seem unlikely to assume day-to-day management.

Guzmán's sons would appear to be candidates, but as the coddled children of a wealthy trafficker they may be more enamored of the narco-lifestyle than of the business itself. "The drug trade is one of the few really meritocratic sectors in the Mexican economy," Alejandro Hope said. "Being the son of Chapo Guzmán doesn't necessarily guarantee you'll be his successor."

But the question of who will inherit the Sinaloa cartel may be somewhat beside the point, because, well before Guzmán's capture, the landscape of crime in Mexico had begun to shift. Whereas Sinaloa is a traditional drug cartel, focusing chiefly on the manufacture and export of narcotics, newer groups, such as the Zetas and the Knights Templar, have diversified their moneymaking activities to include extortion, human trafficking, and kidnapping for ransom. With cocaine consumption declining in the United States, and marijuana on a path toward widespread legalization, a Darwinian logic is driving the cartels' expansion into more parasitic varieties of crime. Organizations that once concentrated exclusively on drugs now extract rents from Mexico's oil industry and export stolen iron ore to China; the price of limes in U.S. grocery stores has doubled in the past few years because the cartels are taxing Mexico's citrus farmers. "We don't have a drug problem—we have a crime problem," more than one Mexican official told me, and as the criminal syndicates continue to evolve, this dynamic could end up rendering organizations like Guzmán's obsolete. The prohibition of narcotics might have created a monster, but, as Alejandro Hope pointed out, even if you decriminalized all drugs tomorrow, the monster would find a way to survive. "You can't legalize kidnapping," he said.

Some speculate that Guzmán wasn't really captured against his will: seeing that his time had come, he chose to enjoy a quiet retirement behind bars. One by-product of the culture of corruption in Mexico is a reflexive cynicism about any official story put out by the government. Several years ago, a fearless journalist named Anabel Hernández published a book about the Sinaloa cartel, called *Los señores del narco*. (It was recently published in English, under the title *Narcoland*.) Hernández argued that Guzmán's influence was so pervasive, and the Mexican political system so thoroughly rotted by graft, that the whole Chapo saga could be interpreted as a grand charade.

Guzmán was "imprisoned" at Puente Grande, but he was actually running the place. He "escaped," when in reality, Hernández suggests, the president of Mexico at the time, Vicente Fox, personally authorized his release, in exchange for a colossal bribe. (Fox has angrily denied this accusation.) Guzmán spent years as a "fugitive," though everyone knew where he was, and the authorities were simply lying when they claimed that they "could not catch him." Hernández's book sold more than a hundred thousand copies in Mexico—her taste for conspiracy and her tone of bitter knowingness struck a chord. So it should come as no surprise that many observers believe that Guzmán's "capture" in Mazatlán was a theatrical event directed by the drug lord himself. When I reached Hernández and asked her what she made of the arrest, she challenged the very premise of my question. "*If* Chapo Guzmán has been captured," she said. "*If* that is the real story." She is not convinced that the man who was photographed in Mazatlán, and whose DNA was tested, is the real Chapo. When Guzmán was questioned in prison by authorities, he, too, seemed to suggest a case of mistaken identity. He maintained his innocence, his rote replies taking on a smug absurdity:

Q: May the deponent say to which organization he belongs.

A: I don't belong to any cartel . . . I am a farmer.

His products were not cocaine, heroin, marijuana, and meth, Guzmán insisted, but corn, sorghum, beans, and safflower. He made 20,000 pesos a month, he continued, or about $18,000 a year. In a poll of Mexicans conducted after the arrest, half the respondents said that Guzmán was more powerful than the government of Mexico; in Culiacán, in the days after his capture, hundreds of protesters took to the streets, holding signs demanding his release.

Guzmán's wife, Emma Coronel, was born in California, and she retains U.S. citizenship. After the raid in Mazatlán, the authorities let her go, along with her daughters, and she has since disappeared from public view. She was only seventeen when she caught Chapo's eye, in 2006, while competing in a beauty contest at the annual Festival of Coffee and Guava, in her home state of Durango. Her uncle Ignacio "Nacho" Coronel was one of Chapo's closest associates at the time, and when the cartel boss conveyed his interest, she might have had little choice but to indulge it. A *norteño* band, Los Alegres del Barranco, was playing at the festival. Like Chapo, the band members came from the Badiraguato area, and they had found success playing *narcocorridos* about the cartel. They are rumored to have performed at private parties for Guzmán and his associates; they even toured the United States, with gigs in Los Angeles, Las Vegas, and Miami. After the raid, Los Alegres posted a new single, "La captura de Joaquín," on YouTube. A jaunty guitar-and-accordion number, it's not so different from their other ballads, apart from the words. "They don't know what they've done, and what kind of trouble they've got themselves in, the people who ordered my arrest," the band sings, assuming the voice of the kingpin. "It won't be long before I return to La Tuna and become a fugitive again. That's what the people want."

As predicted, Chapo did escape again. In July 2015, he vanished from Altiplano, fleeing through an underground tunnel that his confederates had dug from a house a mile away from the prison. The tunnel had lighting and air-conditioning and led directly into the cell where he was being held. It featured an ingenious motorcycle that had been mounted on a rail, so that this time the kingpin would not have to escape on his bare feet. After another epic manhunt, Chapo was recaptured in 2016 and swiftly shipped to the United States, where he stood trial in Brooklyn and was sentenced to life in prison. He is serving his sentence at ADX, in Florence, Colorado, the most secure federal prison in the United States. Emma Coronel attended her husband's trial. In 2021 she was arrested at Dulles Airport and subsequently pleaded guilty to helping Chapo run his drug empire. She is serving a three-year sentence.

WINNING

How Mark Burnett resurrected Donald Trump
as an icon of American success. (2019)

EXPEDITION ROBINSON, A SWEDISH reality-television program, premiered in the summer of 1997 with a tantalizing premise: sixteen strangers are deposited on a small island off the coast of Malaysia and forced to fend for themselves. To survive, they must cooperate, but they are also competing: each week, a member of the ensemble is voted off the island, and the final contestant wins a grand prize. The show's title alluded to both *Robinson Crusoe* and *The Swiss Family Robinson,* but a more apt literary reference might have been *Lord of the Flies.* The first contestant who was kicked off was a young man named Sinisa Savija. Upon returning to Sweden, he was morose, complaining to his wife that the show's editors would "cut away the good things I did and make me look like a fool." Nine weeks before the show aired, he stepped in front of a speeding train and killed himself.

The producers dealt with this tragedy by suggesting that Savija's turmoil was unrelated to the series—and by editing him virtually out of the show. Even so, there was a backlash, with one critic asserting that a program based on such merciless competition was "fascist television." But everyone watched the show anyway, and Savija was soon forgotten. "We had never seen anything like it," Svante Stockselius, the chief of the network that produced the program, told the *Los Angeles Times* in 2000. *Expedition: Robinson* offered a potent cocktail of repulsion and attraction. You felt embarrassed watching it, Stockselius said, and yet "you couldn't stop."

In 1998, a thirty-eight-year-old former British paratrooper named Mark Burnett was living in Los Angeles, producing television. *Lord of the Flies* was one of his favorite books, and after he heard about *Expedition: Robinson,* he secured the rights to make an American version.

Burnett had previously worked in sales and had a knack for branding. He renamed the show *Survivor*.

The first season was set in Borneo, and from the moment it aired on CBS in 2000, *Survivor* was a ratings juggernaut: according to the network, 125 million Americans—more than a third of the population—tuned in for some portion of the season finale. The catchphrase delivered by the host, Jeff Probst, at the end of each elimination ceremony, "The tribe has spoken," entered the lexicon.

Burnett had been a marginal figure in Hollywood, but after this triumph he, too, was rebranded, as an oracle of spectacle. Les Moonves, then the chairman of CBS Television, arranged for the delivery of a token of thanks—a champagne-colored Mercedes. To Burnett, the meaning of this gesture was unmistakable: "I had arrived." The only question was what he might do next. A few years later, Burnett was in Brazil, filming *Survivor: The Amazon*. His second marriage was falling apart, and he was staying in a corporate apartment with a girlfriend. One day, they were watching TV and happened across a BBC documentary series called *Trouble at the Top*, about the corporate rat race. The girlfriend found the show boring and suggested changing the station, but Burnett was transfixed. He called his business partner in L.A. and said, "I've got a new idea."

Burnett would not discuss the concept over the phone—one of his rules for success was to always pitch in person—but he was certain that the premise had the contours of a hit: *Survivor* in the city. Contestants competing for a corporate job. The urban jungle! He needed someone to play the role of heavyweight tycoon. Burnett, who tends to narrate stories from his own life in the bravura language of a Hollywood pitch, once said of the show, "It's got to have a hook to it, right? They've got to be working for someone big and special and important. Cut to: I've rented this skating rink."

In 2002, Burnett rented Wollman Rink in Central Park for a live broadcast of the season 4 finale of *Survivor*. The property was controlled by Donald Trump, who had obtained the lease to operate the rink in 1986, and had plastered his name on it. Before the segment started, Burnett addressed fifteen hundred spectators who had been corralled for the occasion, and noticed Trump sitting with Melania Knauss, who was then his girlfriend, in the front row. Burnett prides himself on his ability to "read the room": to size up the personalities in his audience, suss out what they want, and then give it to them. "I need to show respect to Mr. Trump," Burnett recounted, in a 2013 speech in Vancouver. "I said, 'Welcome, everybody, to Trump Wollman skating rink. The Trump Wollman skating rink is a fine facility, built by Mr. Donald Trump. Thank you, Mr. Trump. Because the Trump Wollman skating rink is the place we are tonight and we love being at the Trump Wollman skating rink, Mr. Trump, Trump, Trump, Trump, Trump." As Burnett told the story, he had scarcely got offstage before Trump was shaking his hand, proclaiming, "You're a genius!"

Cut to: June 2015. After starring in fourteen seasons of *The Apprentice,* all executive produced by Burnett, Trump appeared in the gilded atrium of Trump Tower on Fifth Avenue to announce that he was running for president. Only someone "really rich," Trump declared, could "take the brand of the United States and make it great again." He also made racist remarks about Mexicans, prompting NBC, which had broadcast *The Apprentice,* to fire him. Burnett, however, did not sever his relationship with his star. He and Trump had been equal partners in *The Apprentice,* and the show had made each of them hundreds of millions of dollars. They were also close friends: Burnett liked to tell people that when Trump married Knauss in 2005, Burnett's son Cameron was the ring bearer.

Trump had been a celebrity since the 1980s, his persona shaped by the best-selling book *The Art of the Deal.* But his business had foundered, and by 2003 he had become a garish figure of local interest—a punch line on Page Six. *The Apprentice* mythologized him anew, and on a much bigger scale, turning him into an icon of American success. Jay Bienstock, a longtime collaborator of Burnett's and the showrunner on *The Apprentice,* told me, "Mark always likes to compare his shows to great films or novels. All of Mark's shows feel bigger than life, and this is by design." Burnett has made many programs since *The Apprentice,* among them *Shark Tank,* a start-up competition based on a Japanese show, and *The Voice,* a singing contest adapted from a Dutch program. In 2018, he became the chairman of MGM Television. But his chief legacy is to have cast a serially bankrupt carnival barker in the role of a man who might plausibly become the leader of the free world.

"I don't think any of us could have known what this would become," Katherine Walker, a producer on the first five seasons of *The Apprentice*, told me. "But Donald would not be president had it not been for that show." Tony Schwartz, who wrote *The Art of the Deal*, which falsely presented Trump as its primary author, told me that he feels some responsibility for facilitating Trump's imposture. But, he said, "Mark Burnett's influence was vastly greater," adding, "*The Apprentice* was the single biggest factor in putting Trump in the national spotlight." Schwartz has publicly condemned Trump, describing him as "the monster I helped to create." Burnett, by contrast, has refused to speak publicly about his relationship with the president, or about his curious, but decisive, role in American history.

• • •

Burnett is lean and lanky, with the ageless, perpetually smiling face of Peter Pan and eyes that, in the words of one ex-wife, have "a Photoshop twinkle." He has a high forehead and the fixed, gravity-defying hair of a 1950s film star. People often mistake Burnett for an Australian, because he has a deep tan and an outdoorsy disposition and because his accent has been mongrelized by years of international travel. But he grew up in Dagenham, on the eastern outskirts of London, a milieu that he has recalled as "gray and grimy." His father, Archie, was a tattooed Glaswegian who worked the night shift at a Ford automobile plant. His mother, Jean, worked there as well, pouring acid into batteries, but in Mark's recollection she always dressed immaculately, "never letting her station in life interfere with how she presented herself."

As an only child, Mark grew up watching American television shows such as *Starsky & Hutch* and *The Rockford Files*. At seventeen, he volunteered for the British army's Parachute Regiment; according to a friend who enlisted with him, he joined for "the glitz." The Paras were an elite unit, and a soldier from his platoon, Paul Read, told me that Burnett was a particularly formidable special operator, both physically commanding and a natural leader: "He was always super keen. He always wanted to be the best, even among the best." (Another soldier recalled that Burnett was nicknamed the Male Model, because he was reluctant to "get any dirt under his fingernails.") Burnett served in Northern Ireland and then in the Falklands, where he took part in the 1982 advance on Port Stanley. The experience, he later said, was "horrific, but on the other hand—in a sick way—exciting."

When Burnett left the army, after five years, his plan was to find work in Central America as a "weapons and tactics adviser"—not as a mercenary, he later insisted, though it is difficult to parse the distinction. Before he left, his mother told him that she'd had a premonition and implored him not to take another job that involved carrying a gun. Like Trump, Burnett trusts his impulses. "Your gut instinct is rarely wrong," he likes to say. During a layover in Los Angeles, he decided to heed his mother's admonition, and walked out of the airport. He later described himself as the quintessential undocumented immigrant: "I had no money, no green card, no nothing." But the California sun was shining, and he was eager to try his luck. Burnett is an avid raconteur, and his anecdotes about his life tend to have a three-act structure. In Act 1, he is a fish out of water, guileless and naive, with nothing but the shirt on his back and an outsized dream. Act 2 is the rude awakening: The world bets against him. It's impossible! You'll lose everything! No such thing has ever been tried! In Act 3, Burnett always prevails.

Not long after arriving in California, he landed his first job—as a nanny. Eyebrows were raised: a commando turned nanny? Yet Burnett thrived, working for a family in Beverly Hills, then one in Malibu. As he later observed, the experience taught him "how nice the life styles of wealthy people are." Young, handsome, and solicitous, he discovered that successful people are often happy to talk about their path to success. Burnett married a California woman, Kym Gold, who came from an affluent family. "Mark has always been very, very hungry," Gold told me recently. "He's always had a lot of drive." For a time, he worked for Gold's stepfather, who owned a casting agency, and for Gold, who owned an apparel business. She would buy slightly imperfect T-shirts wholesale, at $2 apiece, and Burnett would resell them, on the Venice boardwalk, for $18. That was where he learned "the art of selling," he has said. The marriage lasted only a year, by which point Burnett had obtained a green card. (Gold, who had also learned a thing or two about selling, went on to co-found the denim company True Religion, which was eventually sold for $800 million.)

One day in the early 1990s, Burnett read an article about a new kind of athletic event: a long-distance endurance race, known as the Raid Gauloises, in which teams of athletes competed in a multiday trek over harsh terrain. In 1992, Burnett organized a team and participated in a race in Oman. Noticing that he and his teammates were "walking, climbing advertisements" for gear, he signed up sponsors. He also realized that if you filmed such a race, it would make for exotic and gripping viewing. Burnett launched his own race, the Eco-Challenge, which was set in such scenic locations as Utah and British Columbia, and was televised on various outlets, including the Discovery Channel. Bienstock, who first met Burnett when he worked on the *Eco-Challenge* show in 1996, told me that Burnett was less interested in the ravishing backdrops or in the competition than he was in the intense emotional experiences of the racers: "Mark saw the drama in real people being the driving force in an unscripted show."

By this time, Burnett had met an aspiring actress from Long Island named Dianne Minerva and married her. They became consumed with making the show a success. "When we went to bed at night, we talked about it; when we woke up in the morning, we talked about it," Dianne Burnett told me recently. In the small world of adventure racing, Mark developed a reputation as a slick and ambitious operator. "He's like a rattlesnake," one of his business competitors told *The New York Times* in 2000. "If you're close enough long enough, you're going to get bit."

Mark and Dianne were doing far better than Mark's parents ever had, but he was restless. One day, they attended a seminar by the motivational speaker Tony Robbins called "Unleash the Power Within." A good technique for realizing your goals, Robbins counseled, was to write down what you wanted most on index cards, then deposit them around your house, as constant reminders. In a 2012 memoir, *The Road to Reality*, Dianne Burnett recalls that she wrote the word "family" on her index cards. Mark wrote "more money."

• • •

As a young man, Burnett occasionally found himself on a flight for business, looking at the other passengers and daydreaming: If this plane were to crash on a desert island, where would I fit into our new society? Who would lead and who would follow? "Nature strips away the veneer we show one another every day, at which point people become who they really are," Burnett once wrote. He has long espoused a Hobbesian worldview, and when he launched *Survivor*, a zero-sum ethos was integral to the show. "It's quite a *mean* game, just like life is kind of a mean game," Burnett told CNN in 2001. "Everyone's out for themselves."

On *Survivor*, the competitors were split into teams, or "tribes." In this raw arena, Burnett suggested, viewers could glimpse the cruel essence of human nature. It was undeniably compelling to watch contestants of different ages, body types, and dispositions negotiate the primordial challenges of making fire, securing shelter, and foraging for food. At the same time, the scenario was extravagantly contrived: the castaways were shadowed by camera crews, and helicopters thundered around the island, gathering aerial shots. Moreover, the contestants had been selected for their charisma and their combustibility. "It's all about casting," Burnett once observed. "As a producer, my job is to make the choices in who to work with and put on camera." He was always searching for someone with the sort of personality that could "break through the clutter." In casting sessions, Burnett sometimes goaded people, to see how they responded to conflict. Katherine Walker, the *Apprentice* producer, told me about an audition in which Burnett taunted a prospective cast member by insinuating that he was secretly gay. (The man, riled, threw the accusation back at Burnett and was not cast that season.)

Richard Levak, a clinical psychologist who consulted for Burnett on *Survivor* and *The Apprentice* and worked on other reality-TV shows, told me that producers have often liked people he was uncomfortable with for psychological reasons. Emotional volatility makes for compelling television. But recruiting individuals for their instability and then subjecting them to the stress of a televised competition can be perilous. When Burnett was once asked about Sinisa Savija's suicide, he contended that Savija had "previous psychological problems." No *Survivor* or *Apprentice* contestants are known to have killed themselves, but in the past two decades several dozen reality-TV participants have. Levak eventually stopped consulting on such programs, in part because he feared that a contestant might harm himself. "I would think, jeez, if this should unravel, they're going to look at the personality profile and there may have been a red flag," he recalled.

Burnett excelled at the casting equation to the point where, on season 2 of *Survivor*, which was shot in the Australian outback, his castaways spent so much time gossiping about the characters from the *previous* season of *Survivor* that Burnett had to warn them, "The more time you spend talking about the first *Survivor*, the less time you will have on television."

But Burnett's real genius was in marketing. When he made the rounds in L.A. to pitch *Survivor*, he vowed that it would become a cultural phenomenon, and he presented executives with a mock issue of *Newsweek* featuring the show on the cover. (Later, *Survivor* did make the cover of the magazine.) Burnett devised a dizzying array of lucrative product-integration deals. In the first season, one of the teams won a care package that was attached to a parachute bearing the red-and-white logo of Target. "I looked on *Survivor* as much as a marketing vehicle as a television show," Burnett once explained. He was creating an immersive, cinematic entertainment—and he was known for lush production values, and for paying handsomely to retain top producers and editors—but he was anything but precious about his art. Long before he met Trump, Burnett had developed a Panglossian confidence in the power of branding. "I believe we're going to see something like the Microsoft Grand Canyon National Park," he told *The New York Times* in 2001. "The government won't take care of all that—companies will."

• • •

Seven weeks before the 2016 election, Burnett, in a smart tux with a shawl collar, arrived with his third wife, the actress and producer Roma Downey, at the Microsoft Theater in Los Angeles for the Emmy Awards. Both *Shark Tank* and *The Voice* won awards that night. But his triumphant evening was marred when the master of ceremonies, Jimmy Kimmel, took an unexpected turn during his opening monologue. "Television brings people together, but television can also tear us apart," Kimmel mused. "I mean, if it wasn't for television, would Donald Trump be running for president?" In the crowd, there was laughter. "Many have asked, 'Who is to blame for Donald Trump?'" Kimmel continued. "I'll tell you who, because he's sitting right there. *That guy.*" Kimmel pointed into the audience, and the live feed cut to a close-up of Burnett, whose expression resolved itself into a rigid grin. "Thanks to Mark Burnett, we don't have to watch reality shows anymore, because we're living in one," Kimmel said. Burnett was still smiling, but Kimmel wasn't. He went on, "I'm going on the record right now. He's responsible. If Donald Trump gets elected and he builds that wall, the first person we're throwing over it is Mark Burnett. The tribe has spoken."

Around this time, Burnett stopped giving interviews about Trump or *The Apprentice.* He continues to speak to the press to promote his shows, but he declined an interview with me. Before Trump's presidential run, however, Burnett told and retold the story of how the show originated. When he met Trump at Wollman Rink, Burnett told him an anecdote about how, as a young man selling T-shirts on the boardwalk on Venice Beach, he had been handed a copy of *The Art of the Deal* by a passing rollerblader. Burnett said that he had read it and that it had changed his life; he thought, "What a legend this guy Trump is!" Anyone else hearing this tale might have found it a bit calculated, if not implausible. Kym Gold, Burnett's first wife, told me that she has no recollection of him reading Trump's book in this period. "He liked mystery books," she said. But when Trump heard the story, he was flattered.

Burnett has never liked the phrase "reality television." For a time, he valiantly campaigned to rebrand his genre "dramality"—"a mixture of drama and reality." The term never caught on, but it reflected Burnett's forthright acknowledgment that what he creates is a highly structured, selective, and manipulated rendition of reality. Burnett has often boasted that for each televised hour of *The Apprentice,* his crews shot as many as three hundred hours of footage. The real alchemy of reality television is the editing—sifting through a compost heap of clips and piecing together an absorbing story. Jonathon Braun, an editor who started working with Burnett on *Survivor* and then worked on the first six seasons of *The Apprentice,* told me, "You don't make anything up. But you accentuate things that you see as themes." He readily conceded how distorting this process can be. Much of reality

TV consists of reaction shots: one participant says something outrageous, and the camera cuts away to another participant rolling her eyes. Often, Braun said, editors lift an eye roll from an entirely different part of the conversation.

The Apprentice was built around a weekly series of business challenges. At the end of each episode, Trump determined which competitor should be "fired." But, as Braun explained, Trump was frequently unprepared for these sessions, with little grasp of who had performed well. Sometimes a candidate distinguished herself during the contest, only to get fired, on a whim, by Trump. When this happened, Braun said, the editors were often obliged to "reverse engineer" the episode, scouring hundreds of hours of footage to emphasize the few moments when the exemplary candidate might have slipped up, in an attempt to assemble an artificial version of history in which Trump's shoot-from-the-hip decision made sense. During the making of *The Apprentice,* Burnett conceded that the stories were constructed in this way, saying, "We know each week who has been fired, and, therefore, you're editing in reverse." Braun noted that President Trump's staff seems to have been similarly forced to learn the art of retroactive narrative construction, adding, "I find it strangely validating to hear that they're doing the same thing in the White House."

Such sleight of hand is the industry standard in reality television. But the entire premise of *The Apprentice* was also something of a con. When Trump and Burnett told the story of their partnership, both suggested that Trump was initially wary of committing to a TV show, because he was so busy running his flourishing real-estate empire. During a 2004 panel at the Museum of Television and Radio in Los Angeles, Trump claimed that "every network" had tried to get him to do a reality show, but he wasn't interested: "I don't want to have cameras all over my office, dealing with contractors, politicians, mobsters, and everyone else I have to deal with in my business. You know, mobsters don't like, as they're talking to me, having cameras all over the room. It would play well on television, but it doesn't play well with them."

The Apprentice portrayed Trump not as a skeezy hustler who huddles with local mobsters but as a plutocrat with impeccable business instincts and unparalleled wealth—a titan who always seemed to be climbing out of helicopters or into limousines. "Most of us knew he was a fake," Braun told me. "He had just gone through I don't know how many bankruptcies. But we made him out to be the most important person in the world. It was like making the court jester the king." Bill Pruitt, another producer, recalled, "We walked through the offices and saw chipped furniture. We saw a crumbling empire at every turn. Our job was to make it seem otherwise."

Trump maximized his profits from the start. When producers were searching for office space in which to stage the show, he vetoed every suggestion, then mentioned that he had an empty floor available in Trump Tower, which he could lease at a reasonable price. (After becoming president, he offered a similar arrangement to the Secret Service.) When the production staff tried to furnish the space, they found that local vendors, stiffed by Trump in the past, refused to do business with them.

More than 200,000 people applied for one of the 16 spots on season 1, and throughout the show's early years the candidates were conspicuously credentialed and impressive. Officially, the grand prize was what the show described as "the dream job of a lifetime"—the unfathomable privilege of being mentored by Donald Trump while working as a junior executive at the Trump Organization. All the candidates paid lip service to the notion that Trump was a peerless businessman, but not all of them believed it. A standout contestant in season 1 was Kwame Jackson, a young African American man with an MBA from Harvard who had worked at Goldman Sachs. Jackson told me that he did the show not out of any desire for Trump's tutelage but because he regarded the prospect of a nationally televised business competition as "a great platform" for career advancement. "At Goldman, I was in private-wealth management, so Trump was not, by any stretch, the most financially successful person I'd ever met or managed," Jackson told me. He was quietly amused when other contestants swooned over Trump's deal-making prowess or his elevated tastes, when they exclaimed, on tours of tacky Trump properties, "Oh, my God, this is so rich—this is, like, really rich!" Fran Lebowitz once remarked that Trump is "a poor person's idea of a rich person," and Jackson was struck, when the show aired, by the extent to which Americans fell for the ruse. "Main Street America saw all those glittery things, the helicopter and the gold-plated sinks, and saw the most successful person in the universe," he recalled. "The people I knew in the world of high finance understood that it was all a joke."

This is an oddly common refrain among people who were involved in *The Apprentice:* that the show was camp, and that the image of Trump as an avatar of prosperity was delivered with a wink. Somehow, this interpretation eluded the audience. Jonathon Braun marveled, "People started taking it seriously!" When I watched several dozen episodes of the show recently, I saw no hint of deliberate irony. Admittedly, it is laughable to hear the candidates, at a fancy meal, talk about watching Trump for cues on which utensil they should use for each course, as if he were Emily Post. But the show's reverence for its pugnacious host, however credulous it might seem now, comes across as sincere. Did Burnett believe what he was selling? Or was Trump another two-dollar T-shirt that he pawned off for eighteen? It's difficult to say. One person who has collaborated with Burnett likened him to Harold Hill, the traveling fraudster in *The Music Man,* saying, "There's always an angle with Mark. He's all about selling."

Burnett is fluent in the jargon of self-help, and he has published two memoirs, both written with Bill O'Reilly's ghostwriter, which double as manuals on how to get rich. One of them, titled *Jump In! Even if You Don't Know How to Swim,* now reads like an inadvertent metaphor for the Trump presidency. "Don't waste time on overpreparation," the book advises. At the 2004 panel, Burnett made it clear that with *The Apprentice* he was selling an archetype. "Donald is the real current-day version of a tycoon," he said. "Donald will say whatever Donald wants to say. He takes no prisoners. If you're Donald's friend, he'll defend you all day long. If you're not, he's going to kill you. And that's very American. It's like the guys who built the West." Like Trump, Burnett seemed to have both a jaundiced impression of the gullible essence of the American people and a brazen enthusiasm for how to exploit it. *The Apprentice* was about "what makes America great," Burnett said. "Everybody wants one of a few things in this country. They're willing to pay to lose weight. They're willing to pay to grow hair. They're willing to pay to have sex. And they're willing to pay to learn how to get rich."

At the start of *The Apprentice,* Burnett's intention may have been to tell a more honest story, one that acknowledged Trump's many stumbles. Burnett surely recognized that Trump was at a low point, but, according to Walker, "Mark sensed Trump's potential for a comeback." Indeed, in a voice-over introduction in the show's pilot, Trump conceded a degree of weakness that feels shockingly self-aware when you listen to it today: "I was seriously in trouble. I was billions of dollars in debt. But I fought back, and I won, big league."

The show was an instant hit, and Trump's public image, and the man himself, began to change. Not long after the premiere, Trump suggested in an *Esquire* article that people now liked him, "whereas before, they viewed me as a bit of an ogre." Jim Dowd, Trump's former publicist, told Michael Kranish and Marc Fisher, the authors of the 2016 book *Trump Revealed,* that after *The Apprentice* began airing, "people on the street embraced him." Dowd noted, "All of a sudden, there was none of the old mocking," adding, "He was a hero." Dowd, who died in 2016, pinpointed the public's embrace of *The Apprentice* as "the bridge" to Trump's presidential run. The show's camera operators often shot Trump from low angles, as you would a professional basketball player, or Mount Rushmore. Trump loomed over the viewer, his face in a jowly glower, his hair darker than it is now, the metallic auburn of a new penny. (*Apprentice* employees were instructed not to fiddle with Trump's hair, which he dyed and styled himself.) Trump's entrances were choreographed for maximum impact and often set to a moody accompaniment of synthesized drums and cymbals. The "boardroom"—a stage set where Trump determined which candidate should be fired—had the menacing gloom of a *Godfather* movie. In one scene, Trump ushered contestants through his rococo Trump Tower aerie and said, "I show this apartment to very few people. Presidents. Kings." In the tabloid ecosystem in which he had long languished, Trump was always Donald, or the Donald. On *The Apprentice,* he finally became Mr. Trump.

"We have to subscribe to our own myths," the *Apprentice* producer Bill Pruitt told me. "Mark Burnett is a great mythmaker. He blew up that balloon and he believed in it." Burnett, preferring to spend time pitching new ideas for shows, delegated most of the daily decisions about *The Apprentice* to his team, many of them veterans of *Survivor* and *Eco-Challenge.* But he furiously promoted the show, often with Trump at his side. According to many of Burnett's collaborators, one of his greatest skills is his handling of talent—understanding their desires and anxieties, making them feel protected and secure. On interview tours with Trump, Burnett exhibited the studied instincts of a veteran producer: anytime the spotlight strayed in his direction, he subtly redirected it at Trump. Burnett, who was forty-three when season 1 aired, described the fifty-seven-year-old Trump as his "soul mate." He expressed astonishment at Trump's "laser-like focus and retention." He delivered flattery in the ostentatiously obsequious register that Trump prefers. Burnett said he hoped that he might someday rise to Trump's "level" of prestige and success, adding, "I don't know if I'll ever make it. But you know something? If you're not shooting for the stars, you're not shooting!" On one occasion, Trump invited Burnett to dinner at his Trump Tower apartment; Burnett had anticipated an elegant meal and, according to an associate, concealed his surprise when Trump handed him a burger from McDonald's.

Trump liked to suggest that he and Burnett had come up with the show "together"; Burnett never corrected him. When Carolyn Kepcher, a Trump Organization executive who appeared alongside Trump in early seasons of *The Apprentice,* seemed to be courting her own celebrity, Trump fired her and gave on-air roles to three of his children, Ivanka, Donald junior, and Eric. Burnett grasped that the best way to keep Trump satisfied was to ensure that he never felt upstaged. "It's Batman and Robin, and I'm clearly Robin," he said.

Burnett sometimes went so far as to imply that Trump's involvement in *The Apprentice* was a form of altruism. "This is Donald Trump giving back," he told the *Times* in 2003, then offered a vague invocation of post-9/11 civic duty: "What makes the world a safe place right now? I think it's American dollars, which come from taxes, which come because of Donald Trump." Trump himself had been candid about his reasons for doing the show. "My jet's going to be in every episode," he told Jim Dowd, adding that the production would be "great for my brand." It was. Season 1 of *The Apprentice* flogged one Trump property after another. The contestants stayed at Trump Tower, did events at Trump National Golf Club, sold Trump Ice bottled water. "I've always felt that the Trump Taj Mahal should do even better," Trump announced before sending the contestants off on a challenge to lure gamblers to his Atlantic City casino, which soon went bankrupt. The prize for the winning team was an opportunity to stay and gamble at the Taj, trailed by cameras. *The Apprentice* was so successful that by the time the second season launched, Trump's lackluster tie-in products were being edged out by blue-chip companies willing to pay handsomely to have their wares featured on-screen. In 2004, Kevin Harris, a producer who helped Burnett secure product-integration deals, sent an email describing a teaser reel of Trump endorsements that would be used to attract clients: "Fast cutting of Donald—'Crest is the biggest' 'I have worn Levis since I was 2' 'I love M&Ms' 'Unilever is the biggest company in the world' all with the song over the top." Burnett and Trump negotiated with NBC to retain the rights to income derived from product integration, and split the fees. On set, Trump often gloated about this easy money. One producer remembered, "You'd say, 'Hey, Donald, today we have Pepsi, and they're paying three million to be in the show,' and he'd say, 'That's great, I just made a million five!'"

Originally, Burnett had planned to cast a different mogul in the role of host each season. But Trump took to his part more nimbly than anyone might have predicted. He wouldn't read a script; he stumbled over the words and got the enunciation all wrong. But off the cuff he delivered the kind of zesty banter that is the lifeblood of reality television. He barked at one contestant, "Sam, you're sort of a disaster. Don't take offense, but everyone hates you." Katherine Walker told me that producers often struggled to make Trump seem coherent, editing out garbled syntax and malapropisms. "We cleaned it up so that he was his best self," she said, adding, "I'm sure Donald thinks that he was never edited." However, she acknowledged, he was a natural for the medium: whereas reality-TV producers generally feel obliged to amp up personalities and events, to accentuate conflict and conjure intrigue, "we didn't have to *change* him—he gave us stuff to work with." Trump improvised the tagline for which *The Apprentice* became famous: "You're fired."

NBC executives were so enamored of their new star that they instructed Burnett and his producers to give Trump more screen time. This is when Trump's obsession with television ratings took hold. "I didn't know what demographics was four weeks ago," he told

Larry King. "All of a sudden I heard we were No. 3 in demographics. Last night, we were No. 1 in demographics. And that's the important rating." The ratings kept rising, and the first season's finale was the No. 1 show of the week. For Burnett, Trump's rehabilitation was a satisfying confirmation of a populist aesthetic. "I like it when critics slam a movie and it does massive box office," he once said. "I love it." Whereas others had seen in Trump only a tattered celebrity of the 1980s, Burnett had glimpsed a feral charisma.

• • •

On June 26, 2018, the day the Supreme Court upheld President Trump's travel ban targeting people from several predominantly Muslim countries, Secretary of State Mike Pompeo sent out invitations to an event called the Ministerial to Advance Religious Freedom. If Pompeo registered any dissonance between such lofty rhetoric and Trump administration policies targeting certain religions, he didn't mention it. The event took place the next month at the State Department in Washington, D.C., and one of the featured speakers was Mark Burnett. In 2004, he had been getting his hair cut at a salon in Malibu when he noticed an attractive woman getting a pedicure. It was Roma Downey, the star of *Touched by an Angel,* a long-running inspirational drama on CBS. They fell in love, and married in 2007; together, they helped rear Burnett's two sons from his second marriage and Downey's daughter. Downey, who grew up in a Catholic family in Northern Ireland, is deeply religious, and eventually Burnett, too, reoriented his life around Christianity. "Faith is a major part of our marriage," Downey said in 2013, adding, "We pray together."

For people who had long known Burnett, it was an unexpected turn. This was a man who had ended his second marriage during a live interview with Howard Stern. To promote *Survivor* in 2002, Burnett called in to Stern's radio show, and Stern asked casually if he was married. When Burnett hesitated, Stern pounced. "You didn't survive marriage?" he asked. "You don't want your girlfriend to know you're married?" As Burnett dissembled, Stern kept prying, and the exchange became excruciating. Finally, Stern asked if Burnett was "a single guy," and Burnett replied, "You know? Yeah." This was news to Dianne, Burnett's wife of a decade. As she subsequently wrote in her memoir, "The 18-to-34 radio demographic knew where my marriage was headed before I did."

Years ago, Burnett told *Esquire* that religion was "a waste of time." Dianne Burnett told me that when she was married to him, he had no interest in faith. "But you know what? People change," she continued. "So I'll give him the benefit of the doubt." When Burnett met Downey, he reinvented himself. Having made a fortune producing television that was often exploitative, he announced that he would now focus exclusively on "family-friendly franchises," declaring, "You don't need to be mean to create drama." Burnett and Downey launched a production company that has specialized in Christian-themed programming, including a $100 million remake of *Ben-Hur.* (It flopped.) Burnett has spoken enthusiastically to colleagues about the role that prayer and religious devotion now play in his life. He and Downey describe themselves as "the noisiest Christians in Hollywood."

Kym Gold told me she thinks that Burnett tends to adapt to his current partner. Before he married Gold, who is Jewish, he took a six-week course in Judaism. "I've never known Mark to be religious," Gold observed. But she noted that "people close to him have said, 'He follows the wind.'" Rick Warren, the evangelical pastor, is a friend of Burnett's. "Mark is not at all the person he was a decade ago," he told me. "Hollywood is built on money, sex, power, and fame. I would say that none of those things are driving forces for him anymore." Warren assured me, unprompted, that Burnett is sincere in his Christianity—that he is a "genuine believer" who has committed to being an "ambassador" for his faith. Others who know Burnett noted to me that the Christian community is itself a significant viewer demographic. Burnett talks with colleagues about the "faith audience" and describes the Christian community as "the largest army on earth." In 2013, he and Downey produced *The Bible,* a History Channel miniseries that, Burnett claims, was watched by a hundred million people. The Good Book, in Burnett's words, is "the ultimate period piece."

At the State Department, Burnett mentioned religious intolerance "throughout the Middle East," genocide in Darfur, and the persecution of religious minorities in Myanmar. "I'm simply a TV producer," he said, noting that he was "far less educated" than his audience. But he was good at communicating with the masses, he went on. He explained his formula for storytelling: "K-I-S-S—'Keep it simple, stu-pid.'" Burnett said that when he and Downey travel, strangers some-times "ask her to lay her hands upon them," as if she were actually an angel. This, he confided, is "the power of media." He suggested that his position in Hollywood gave him some leverage when it came to pressing politicians to do the right thing, because, "in the end, nobody wants to look bad in the media." But Burnett did not cite any contro-versial White House policies that he hoped to change; he didn't even mention Trump's name.

Burnett had remained close to the president. At the National Prayer Breakfast in 2017, he introduced Trump, saying that there "has never been a single bad word between us" and describing their fourteen-year friendship as "one of the greatest relationships of my life." Over the years, Burnett and Downey have given to Democratic causes, and in 2008 they donated the maximum contribution to Barack Obama's campaign. But Burnett has never been especially political. One long-time *Apprentice* staff member told me that Burnett did not welcome the idea of losing his star to a presidential campaign, noting, "Trump running for president cost Mark a lot of money. He made millions on *The Apprentice,* and Trump killed the franchise." By the time Trump announced his campaign, ratings for *The Apprentice* had fallen, and the show had been repackaged as *The Celebrity Apprentice.* The contestants were now D-list celebrities, including Gary Busey, the zonked-out actor, and Gene Simmons, the repellent front man of Kiss. There were the same business challenges and boardroom eliminations, but the stakes felt conspicuously lower. A lot of the drama in the origi-nal *Apprentice* had stemmed from the idea that for aspiring entrepre-neurs competing on the show could be a career-defining opportunity. For the aging, Botoxed cohort on *The Celebrity Apprentice,* their very presence on the show was a tacit admission that their best days were behind them. Still, everyone gamely pretended to take it seriously. Describing the show in one public appearance, Donald Trump Jr. said that it could be intimidating for Trump's children to pass judgment on someone "as accomplished as a Gene Simmons."

In the opening episode of season 11, the theatrical tension of the boardroom was suddenly punctured by an electronic trill. "Whose cell phone?" Trump growled.

"How do I turn this off?" Busey stuttered, fumbling with the tiny buttons.

"Gary, turn your cell phone off!" Trump said. It is strange to watch this kind of malarkey now and consider that only a few years later one of these men would be president.

"Donald mentioned a number of times, 'Maybe I'll run for president one day,'" Burnett told *The Washington Post* in January 2016. "And sad to say, politics is kind of a TV show." When Burnett was asked whether he supported Trump's candidacy, he deflected the question, retreating behind his conceit that politics is simply entertainment by other means. "I have no idea about the politics," he said, adding, "I have had great fun—great fun—watching it."

After Trump won the election, he turned to his old friend for advice on the inaugural festivities. Like a starlet who keeps returning to a favorite director, Trump had always loved the way that Burnett made him look. Burnett was summoned to New York for a consultation with the president-elect and another Trump confidant, the financier Tom Barrack. Burnett pitched a few Riefenstahlian notions: a parade up Fifth Avenue; a televised helicopter ride ushering Trump from Manhattan to D.C. Barrack, who became the chairman of the inaugural committee, later said that Burnett was actively involved in producing the inauguration, adding, "Mark is a genius, and the president-elect loves him." I spoke to several people who recalled Burnett telling them that he was busy working on the inauguration. A Democratic political operative who was involved in a back-channel campaign to dissuade big-name stars from appearing at the event told me that Burnett had tried to enlist musicians to perform. "Mark was somebody we were actively working against," the operative said. Trump's wish list included Elton John, Aretha Franklin, and Paul Anka—who, he hoped, would sing "My Way"—but they all claimed to be otherwise engaged. The event ended up with sparse crowds and a feeble roster of performers. Burnett eventually played down his role in the inauguration. His representatives told me that "he did not produce" the event. One person who knows Burnett pointed out, "It wasn't successful, so he probably doesn't want to be associated with it."

• • •

On October 8, 2016, the day after *The Washington Post* released the *Access Hollywood* tape in which Trump was caught on a hot mike bantering about grabbing women's crotches, Bill Pruitt tweeted, "As a producer on seasons 1 & 2 of #theapprentice I assure you: when it comes to the #trumptapes there are far worse." In other interviews, Pruitt said that during his time on *The Apprentice* he'd heard Trump make not only sexist statements but also racist ones. This was not so difficult to imagine. Trump's natural idiom is vulgarity, and the targets of his ire—the football player Colin Kaepernick, "shithole countries," any African American journalist who asks him a tough question—are clearly not chosen at random. Part of what was mesmerizing about him, to Mark Burnett and, ultimately, to the American people, was his compulsion for offensive talk. But in the heightened political atmosphere of an impending Trump presidency, the notional existence of more "Trump tapes" assumed a potent urgency. Last summer, Omarosa Manigault Newman, the former *Apprentice* contestant and aide to the president, reignited such speculations when she claimed to have heard a tape, recorded during the period when *The Apprentice* was made, in which Trump said the n-word. Manigault Newman produced a recording of her own, taken surreptitiously, of a conversation with two aides from the Trump campaign, in which they appeared to discuss the existence of such a tape. On the recording, one of the aides, Lynne Patton, says that she raised the issue with Trump and that he said he had no recollection of using such language. "No, he said it," Katrina Pierson, the other aide, interjects. "He's embarrassed."

On August 13, 2018, Trump denied that he had ever used racial slurs, tweeting, "@MarkBurnettTV called to say that there are NO TAPES of the Apprentice where I used such a terrible and disgusting word as attributed by Wacky and Deranged Omarosa." This was a peculiar thing to tweet: If Trump had never uttered the epithet, why would he need to be assured by Burnett that there were no tapes of him doing so? The tweet was also notable because, when the *Access Hollywood* tape leaked, Burnett had taken his most definitive step toward distancing himself from Trump. In a statement, he had said, "Given all of the false media reports, I feel compelled to clarify a few points. I am not now and have never been a supporter of Donald Trump's candidacy. I am NOT 'Pro-Trump.' Further, my wife and I reject the hatred, division and misogyny that has been a very unfortunate part of his campaign." Trump generally answers such criticism with a hyperventilating rebuttal, but he didn't fire back at Burnett—at least not publicly—and their friendship does not appear to have suffered. Scarcely two months after issuing his statement about not being "Pro-Trump," Burnett attended a fundraiser for the president-elect at Cipriani in New York, and in January 2017 he and his two sons flew to Washington for the inauguration.

Burnett might have wanted to downplay his friendship with the president, but Trump felt no similar compunction. In March 2018, at a rally in Richfield, Ohio, he announced, "I got a call from Mark Burnett! He did *The Apprentice;* he's a great guy. He said, 'Donald, I called just to say hello and to tell you, did you see Roseanne's ratings?'" (Roseanne Barr, a rare Trump supporter in Hollywood, had just rebooted her sitcom.) "I said, 'Mark, how big were they?' 'They were unbelievable! Over eighteen million people!'" When I asked Burnett's representatives about the president's characterizations of his exchanges with Burnett, they declined to either confirm or deny their accuracy.

Burnett's reluctance to discuss the Trump presidency is dismaying to many people involved with *The Apprentice,* given that Trump has succeeded in politics, in part, by borrowing the tropes of the show. Jonathon Braun pointed out to me that when Trump announced his candidacy, in 2015, he did so in the atrium of Trump Tower and made his entrance by descending the gold-colored escalator—choreography that Burnett and his team had repeatedly used on the show. After Trump's announcement, reports suggested that people who had filled the space and cheered during his speech had been hired to do so, like TV extras, for a day rate of $50. Earlier this year, the White House started issuing brief video monologues from the president that strongly evoke his appearances on Burnett's show. Justin McConney, a former director of new media for the Trump Organization, told *New York* that whenever Trump works with camera people, he instructs them, "Shoot me like I'm shot on *The Apprentice.*"

Randal Pinkett, who won season 4 of *The Apprentice,* told me that he had watched Trump's campaign with a growing sense of dread. Pinkett had long since concluded that Trump was racist. When

Trump named Pinkett, who is African American, the winner, he asked him if he would consider sharing the title with another contestant, a white woman. Pinkett declined. "The only conclusion I can draw is that he didn't want to see a black man be the sole winner of his show," he told me. In a recent interview with *Vanity Fair,* Trump's former lawyer Michael Cohen said Trump told him that he had not chosen Kwame Jackson, the Goldman Sachs banker, to win in season 1, because "there's no way I can let this black fag win."

As a winner, Pinkett went to work for the Trump Organization. "The closer I got to Donald, the less I liked what I saw," he recalled. "It's like a person with bad breath." After Pennsylvania legalized casino gambling in 2004, Trump applied for a license to build a casino in a predominantly African American community. "The community hated Donald," Pinkett said. So the company dispatched Pinkett as an advocate. Upon returning, he said, "I'm not going out there again to represent you folks." The Trump Organization was using him like a prop, he felt, and he did not want to sell a project that the community so roundly opposed. The casino was never built. Even the grand prize on *The Apprentice* was a bit of a fake, Pinkett told me. His Trump Organization job was actually paid for by NBC. "It wasn't even his money!" he said.

When Trump announced his campaign, Pinkett and Kwame Jackson decided to make a public statement opposing him. "This wasn't about policy or politics; this was about fitness for office," Jackson recalled. "This was about basic American character and decency." They reached out to scores of former contestants and planned a press conference. In the end, apart from Pinkett, Jackson, and two other contestants, nobody showed up. In a statement, Trump said, "How quickly they forget. Nobody would know who they are if it weren't for me."

"I think the reality for Mark Burnett is he's a Hollywood guy," Jackson told me. "He probably feels that if he torpedoes Donald Trump, he'll torpedo a part of his own legacy. And it's funny, because he has enough money and enough power in Hollywood that he could actually afford to speak up." Burnett's silence "is abdication," Jackson said. "It's collusion. It's being complicit, just like an Ivanka Trump. I'm very disappointed in Mark for that."

• • •

A recent piece in *The Ankler,* a widely read online newsletter about Hollywood, noted that Burnett "has spent the past couple years reigning over his corner of resistance territory with nary the slightest hint of backlash." Donald Trump was a folk devil in Hollywood, and everyone in the industry knew about Burnett's close association with the president, yet no prominent liberals were refusing to work with Mark Burnett. It's one thing to "take brave stands on the red carpet," the article observed. "But you wouldn't want to go so crazy as to . . . get on the wrong side of a mid-sized ministudio." Burnett was recruited to the television arm of MGM in 2015 by Gary Barber, the company's chairman and CEO. Barber, a former accountant, had brought the studio back from bankruptcy, slashing costs and shepherding profitable titles like the James Bond franchise. In his effort to build up MGM, Barber wanted to augment the studio's television business. So he bought Burnett's company and enlisted him to oversee television production. Ostensibly, Barber and Burnett got along. But, whereas Mark Burnett Productions had been characterized by profligate dazzle, Barber was thrifty and monitored every expense. The chairman of MGM's board is Kevin Ulrich, a financier whose private-equity fund holds a controlling stake in the company. People who know Ulrich describe him as someone who relishes the flashy perquisites of Hollywood moguldom. Whereas Barber liked to spend weekends quietly tending to the racehorses he owns, Ulrich liked going to parties and premieres. Barber was interested in selling the studio—a move that Ulrich opposed. According to several sources, Burnett began cultivating Ulrich, inviting him to events and introducing him to celebrities. Then, last March, MGM's board informed Barber that he had been fired; he had just signed a contract extension, so the studio would pay him $260 million to leave.

Despite this payment, he was incensed. Three months after Barber's ouster, Burnett was promoted to chairman of television at MGM. Barber declined to speak with me, but a friend of his said that he was "blindsided" by his ouster: Burnett had made an alliance with Ulrich and got Barber kicked off the island. As a younger man, Burnett made it known that he wasn't content to be the producer of a few hit shows—

he wanted to run a television studio one day. According to someone who has worked closely with him, Burnett had always felt like an outsider, "because in the reality-TV business, you're never part of the true Hollywood." He had long aspired to transition to scripted television and films but did not have much talent for such storytelling. At MGM, he would oversee both scripted and unscripted shows, including the acclaimed series *Fargo* and *The Handmaid's Tale*. He had now achieved such a level of power that even in reflexively liberal Hollywood his association with Trump was discussed mostly in whispers. Many people who spoke to me for this piece would not do so on the record, citing fears of being blacklisted.

Nevertheless, *The Apprentice* continues to dog Burnett. In 2017, when he took the stage at the Producers Guild of America Awards to accept the award for Outstanding Producer of Competition Television, there were boos in the audience. In September, he skipped the Emmy Awards, though *The Voice* and *Shark Tank* were nominated; the night before the ceremony, however, he and Downey attended the annual gala for the Motion Picture & Television Fund at a hotel in Century City. Walking into the event, they had a confrontation with the actor Tom Arnold.

Arnold, a wild-eyed industry veteran best known for his role in the 1994 film *True Lies* and for a former marriage to Roseanne Barr, had been on a quest to uncover damaging *Apprentice* outtakes of Donald Trump. He had even launched a gonzo TV show, produced by Vice, called *The Hunt for the Trump Tapes*. As Arnold relates on the show, he and Trump knew each other for years, because they had occupied "the same level of Hollywood." Indeed, in 2010, Burnett had emailed Arnold, "Is there any way I can get you to do Celeb Apprentice? . . . I do think that Celeb Apprentice has an awesome brand. Trump really wants you. I want you." Arnold was, in his own estimation, a prankster and a marginal celebrity. It disturbed him to think that someone just like him might be entrusted with managing the country.

What precisely happened in Century City is a matter of dispute, but there was a scuffle between Arnold and Burnett. Soon afterward, Roma Downey tweeted a photograph of the back of her hand, writing, "Got this bruise tonight when Tom Arnold tried to ambush my husband Mark and me at a charity event. Is your TV show worth it Tom? Please stop."

Some observers wondered whether a bruise could have emerged that quickly. Arnold himself offered a very different account on Twitter: "Mark Burnett just went apeshit & choked me at this huge Emmy party then he ran away with his torn Pink shirt & missing gold chain. I'm waiting for LAPD." It might seem improbable that Burnett, the smiling glad-hander, would physically attack someone. But it would not be unprecedented. His second wife, Dianne Burnett, told me that one day, in Santa Monica, Mark left her and one of their sons in the car in order to fetch frozen yogurt. While he was gone, a vagrant began aggressively banging on the car window, presumably in search of a donation. When Burnett returned, Dianne recalled, he punched the man in the face, knocking him down, then drove away. Hours after the Century City event, *TMZ* published an account by an eyewitness, who said that "Mark had his hands on Tom's throat, and Tom was tearing at Mark's shirt and ripping off his crucifix." The authorities have declined to press charges against Burnett, and several people close to him characterized Arnold as a puerile stunt artist who cornered Burnett in a bit of performance art in order to promote his lousy show. That may well be true, but there is a certain cosmic poetry in the notion that the only person in Hollywood willing to antagonize Burnett about his relationship with Trump is a figure like Tom Arnold. Someone who has worked with Burnett told me, "Mark created the *world* in which Tom Arnold is the only guy who can go after him. Tom Arnold is trolling Mark Burnett just like Donald Trump trolled all his opponents. And he's doing it for a reality show!"

• • •

After season 1 of *Survivor,* a contestant named Stacey Stillman sued CBS and Burnett, claiming that he had improperly shaped the competition by whispering to contestants about whom they should vote to eliminate. In a deposition, another cast member said that Burnett "believed that certain people would make a better TV show than others, and he did what he could to have influence over those people staying on the island." Burnett denied any wrongdoing, and the suit was ultimately settled. One consequence of the lawsuit was that when it came time to make *The Apprentice,* producers tried to have cameras on Donald Trump from the moment he walked onto the set until the moment he left—and all that footage was preserved. When MGM bought Burnett's company, it assumed ownership of those outtakes, and after the *Access Hollywood* tape leaked, it had to contend with public demands to unseal the *Apprentice* tapes. Marvin Putnam, a lawyer who represents MGM, told me, "Mark Burnett cannot release the tapes. Period. Even if Mark Burnett wanted to release the tapes, Mark Burnett cannot release the tapes." Putnam explained that the contracts that Trump and other cast members signed contained standard industry stipulations limiting the manner in which outtakes and other footage could be used. These are binding obligations, which means that if MGM were to violate them—by releasing footage not just of Trump but of anyone who appeared with him on-screen—the studio could be sued. Brian Edwards, the president of television operations at MGM, who has worked with Burnett for more than a decade, pointed out that even without such legal constraints Burnett couldn't release the tapes; if he did, talent would refuse to work with him in the future. "If everybody in reality television knew that their outtakes were going to be made public at the first sign of pressure, what do you think would happen to the business?" Edwards asked.

Neither Putnam nor Edwards would comment on whether MGM possesses tapes in which Trump says something offensive; nor would they say how much, if any, of the archive has been reviewed. Over the fourteen seasons hosted by Trump, nearly two hundred hours of *The Apprentice* aired on NBC. If Burnett indeed shot three hundred hours of footage for each episode, there could be some sixty thousand hours of outtakes to sift through. Most of the former *Apprentice* staffers I spoke to recalled hearing Trump speak coarsely about women. "He wasn't going around saying 'pussy, pussy, pussy' all the time," Walker said. But he regularly made comments about the bodies of female contestants and female staffers. One *Apprentice* employee told me, "He'd say, 'How about those boobs? Wouldn't you like to fuck her?'" Even so, Braun said he doubted that there was any *Apprentice* tape in which Trump uses the n-word. "I was the supervising editor on the first six seasons," he said. "I didn't watch every frame, but in everything I saw, I didn't hear him saying anything so horrible." Braun noted that editors on reality shows often amuse themselves by compiling "gag" reels of a cast member's most off-color or embarrassing moments. The producers may be barred, legally, from airing such outtakes, but that doesn't stop editors from sharing them internally. Tom Arnold told me that he has seen one such reel from *The Apprentice,* in which Trump uses the n-word. But Braun, who is dismayed that Trump is president, is dubious. "If there was a tape, it would have spread like wildfire," he said. Another *Apprentice* staffer made the same point: "If somebody had the goods, it would have leaked long ago. There were no Trump fans on the set. I don't know a single person who worked on the show who voted for Trump."

Whenever Trump appeared on the show, the staffer explained, there were "at least a hundred people watching him," with a dozen cameras capturing every angle. Live feeds were transmitted to executives not just at NBC but at corporations sponsoring the episode. The staffer continued, "In the *Access Hollywood* tape, Donald was on a bus. He thought he was alone. He never thought he was alone in the boardroom. It was a *set.*" To Braun, the hunt for the tapes feels like a distraction. "We've seen that it doesn't matter," he said. "He now says plenty of things that are outwardly racist, misogynist, and fascist. It just doesn't hurt him." After Manigault Newman made her claims about the *Apprentice* tapes, *The Economist* conducted a survey and found that 77 percent of white Trump voters felt that "it is possible that a person who uses the 'N-word' while in office can still be a good President." More than a third of white Trump voters admitted to using the word themselves.

. . .

One day in the fall of 2018, Burnett got a call from his first wife, Kym Gold, with whom he remains friendly. Gold was upset about what was happening in the country, and asked Burnett to intervene with Trump. "We had it out," she told me. "I said, 'You've got to help our children, for the future and safety of this country.'" Gold implored Burnett, "Tell him this is not a reality show. This is real life. You're the president. You're saying things you cannot say—to reporters, to other world leaders." Burnett heard her out. "I'm not into politics," he told her. "I'm not even on Twitter." But he said that he had no intention of speaking out against Trump or of releasing any tapes. "I'm just a guy who produces shows," he insisted.

Burnett may not be a policy maven, but he has long been fascinated with political star power. In 2010, he launched *Sarah Palin's Alaska* on TLC, announcing, "With a dynamic personality that has captivated millions, I can't think of anyone more compelling than Sarah Palin to tell the story of Alaska." At the time, Burnett contended that the show was "completely nonpolitical." *The Daily Beast* disagreed, suggesting that it "may qualify as the earliest, most expensive presidential campaign ad ever made." Burnett and Trump have licensed the *Apprentice* format to dozens of other countries, and Burnett once noted that, increasingly, tycoons cast in the Trump role are "people with political aspirations." At least half a dozen hosts have held political office, including João Doria, the governor-elect of São Paulo State, who is an ally of Jair Bolsonaro, Brazil's strongman president-elect. In 2017, Kevin O'Leary, one of the hosts of *Shark Tank,* announced his intention of running for prime minister of Canada, as a member of the Conservative Party, noting that he and Trump had "both worked for Mark Burnett, and we both got famous on reality television." Burnett joked to more than one person that he was no longer simply a TV producer but a producer of political leaders. (Four months later, O'Leary dropped out of the race and returned to the show.)

For nearly two decades, Burnett has also spoken about his desire to make a television show with Vladimir Putin. In 2001, he sought to enlist Putin in a project called *Destination Mir,* a reality competition in which the winner would be sent into space. The idea was scuttled after Russia decommissioned the Mir space station. In 2015, Burnett expressed an interest in building a reality show featuring Putin—not so much a program about politics, Burnett suggested, as a hymn to the glory of Russia, "the humans, the nature, the animals of the nation." Burnett's myopia about politics may be selective, but that does not mean it is feigned. He would hardly be the first Hollywood chieftain with a dim grasp of current events beyond Los Angeles, but even by industry standards he can seem remarkably disconnected. Shortly after the mass shooting at Marjory Stoneman Douglas High School in Parkland, Florida, in February 2018, Burnett attended a regular meeting of television executives at MGM. At one point, someone mentioned the marketing plan for a project in the studio's film division: a remake of *Death Wish,* starring Bruce Willis. The movie, about an armed vigilante, was unabashedly pro-gun; Breitbart eventually hailed it as an "NRA Public Service Announcement." Someone asked whether MGM would be altering the rollout of the film, in light of the shooting. "What shooting?" Burnett said, according to someone outside MGM who was briefed on the meeting. When his incredulous colleagues wondered how he could not have been aware of the Parkland massacre, Burnett said, "I don't know what you're talking about," adding, "I'm not on social media."

For all Burnett's talk about being nonpolitical, his reluctance to disavow the president may stem, in part, from a fear of alienating Trump's constituents. Like Republican lawmakers or evangelical pastors, Burnett is beholden to a faction of the public that, in many instances, thinks the president can do no wrong. "The moment you go political, you turn half of the nation against you," Rick Warren told me. "And, when you're trying to reach as many people as you can, you don't want to do that." The dilemma is compounded, Warren pointed out, when the occupant of the White House is so vindictive. "You know the way this president chews up people?" Warren said. "There's a fine line in what you can say."

Katherine Walker suggested that part of the reason Burnett seems so unfazed by the role he has played in the Trump saga may be that he is British. "There is something to being American and having these visceral reactions that Mark doesn't have," she said. "He just doesn't get it on that level. I don't think he has the same sense of 'Oh, my God, what have I done?'" For many Americans, the Trump presidency evokes a painful feeling of dispossession, as cherished norms and national institutions are eviscerated. "People are making it seem like Mark's ignoring evil," Walker continued. "But I think it's more benign than that—and scarier, in a way. He doesn't care. He just wants to stay out of it."

• • •

"Mark is extremely smart," Richard Levak, the psychologist who consulted for Burnett on *The Apprentice,* told me. "Mark has an eye for casting, and he cast Donald Trump." I asked Levak what kind of personality profile he might have prepared for Trump as a candidate for the show. He said he would have noted "the energy, the impulsiveness, the inability to articulate a complete thought because he gets interrupted by emotions, so when he speaks, it's all adjectives—'great,' 'huge,' 'horrible.'" What made Trump so magnetic as a reality-television star was his impulse to transgress, Levak continued, and it is the same quality that has made a captive audience of the world. "That somebody can become that successful while also being that emotionally undisciplined—it's so macabre that you have to watch it," he said. "And you keep waiting for the comeuppance. But it doesn't come." There has likely never been a man who, in his own lifetime, has been as widely spoken and written about as Donald Trump. Politics has never been so spellbinding. "It's the reason people watch a schoolyard fight," Levak said. "It's vicariously watching someone act out and get away with it." Burnett once remarked that *Lord of the Flies* is so absorbing because all the characters are suddenly transported into a world in which "the rules are changed, and convention, law, and morality are suspended." It's an apt paraphrase of the Trump presidency.

On Sunday afternoons, Burnett likes to pour himself a generous glass of wine and stroll out onto the balcony of his seven-thousand-square-foot home off the Pacific Coast Highway in Malibu. He and Downey refer to the property, which was undamaged by the recent wildfires, as the Sanctuary. It is an exquisite spot, with white couches facing an unbroken view of the ocean. Burnett likes to reflect on the fact that his mansion is not far from one of the homes where, as a young immigrant, he worked as a nanny.

He *is* on social media, as it happens. He seldom tweets, but he's active on Instagram. Along with family snapshots and photographs of Burnett palling around with celebrities and religious figures, there are a couple of videos he has taken of himself relaxing on the balcony. "Lazy Sunday afternoon," Burnett says in one of them. He is barefoot, wearing a T-shirt that says "Spiritual Gangster." He gestures at his expansive view, with undisguised satisfaction, and says, "Look at this. Wow." He pans the camera across the sky, which is just starting to bruise red and violet in the twilight. "So grateful," Burnett says. He often expresses wonderment at how blessed he is, and at the magnitude of his success—which, these days, he ascribes to "God's favor."

When I remarked to Jonathon Braun that Burnett seems eerily untroubled by the legacy of his own creation, he said that for Burnett the presidency was just another game. "I think it's a game for Trump, too," Braun said. "It's a game for the audience. I think the voters like it. They're enjoying the spectacle. It's in the soul of who Mark is. They're kindred spirits. There are no major causes driving them—it's just about playing a game and winning it." Years ago, when Burnett did publicity for *Survivor,* interviewers tried to figure out how the contestants had fared that season. Of course, he could not reveal such secrets. So when they asked Burnett who would win the game, he told them, "Me."

Burnett stayed at MGM. He never released any tapes from The Apprentice, *and as of this writing he never delivered the studio a real hit. Trump lost his bid for reelection in 2020, but seventy-four million people voted for him. He retreated to Mar-a-Lago, to plot his comeback. If he doesn't run for president again, it will almost certainly involve television, and if it involves television, it could very well involve Mark Burnett.*

SWISS BANK HEIST

*The computer technician who exposed a
Geneva bank's darkest secrets.* (2016)

A FEW DAYS BEFORE Christmas in 2008, Hervé Falciani was in a
meeting at his office in Geneva when a team of police officers arrived
to arrest him. Falciani, who was thirty-six, worked for HSBC, then
the largest bank in the world. He was on the staff of the company's
private Swiss bank, which serves clients who are wealthy enough to
afford the minimum deposit—half a million dollars—required to
open an account. Falciani had been at HSBC for eight years, initially
in Monaco and then in Geneva. He was a computer technician who
helped supervise security systems for the handling of client data. He
had grown up in Monaco, where as a young man he had worked as a
croupier at the Casino de Monte-Carlo, and developed an excellent
poker face. As the Swiss police escorted him from the building, he
insisted that he had done nothing wrong.

Officers questioned Falciani at a nearby station. They were investigating a data theft from the bank. Since 1713, when the Great Council of Geneva banned banks from revealing the private information of
their customers, Switzerland had thrived on its reputation as a strong-
hold of financial secrecy. International elites could place their fortunes beyond the reach of tax authorities in their own countries. For
Swiss wealth managers, who oversaw more than $2 trillion in interna-
tional deposits, the promise to maintain financial privacy was akin to
a religious vow of silence. Switzerland is the home of the numbered
account: customers often specify that they prefer not to receive statements, in order to avoid a paper trail. In light of these safeguards, the
notion of a breach at HSBC was shocking. Police officials told Falciani
that someone calling himself Ruben al-Chidiak had stolen client data
from the bank. They weren't sure how much information had been

taken or how the theft had been engineered. But they suspected that Chidiak was a pseudonym—and that the real culprit was Falciani. Falciani told the police that his job was to protect data: How could they accuse him of compromising such information?

As darkness fell, he asked to go home. His wife, Simona, would be worried about him. The investigators released him, but instructed him to return for further questioning the next morning. Falciani walked through streets strung with Christmas lights to his apartment in a dingy building on the Rue des Mouettes. He and Simona packed a few bags, bundled their three-year-old daughter, Kim, against the cold, and prepared to flee the country.

Despite his protests, Falciani had stolen the data. When the Falcianis walked out of their apartment, they left the keys in the door. Falciani rented a car, and they drove through the Alps. The next morning, as Swiss investigators assembled at the police station in Geneva, Falciani was approaching the South of France. He left the rental car at the airport in Nice. His wife and daughter went on to Italy, for a visit with Simona's family; Falciani traveled to his parents' home in Castellar, a hill town near the French-Italian border.

W. Somerset Maugham once described the Côte d'Azur as "a sunny place for shady people," and Falciani, who was now a fugitive, hunkered down in Castellar. As a precaution, he had not traveled with the stolen data, instead uploading the information to remote servers. He now downloaded the files onto his laptop. The Swiss had asked French authorities to help track down Falciani, and at dawn on January 7, 2009, gendarmes raided his parents' house. The prosecutor in Nice who handled the case, Éric de Montgolfier, told me that authorities in Switzerland were so eager to seize Falciani's computer that they sent a Swiss prosecutor to accompany the gendarmes. The French police arrested Falciani and seized his MacBook Pro and his iPhone. But when he was out of earshot of the Swiss prosecutor, on the way to the police station in nearby Menton, he told the gendarmes that his computer contained information of possible interest to the French state: names, account numbers, account balances. The hard drive held evidence, he said, of "tax evasion committed by French people." Falciani had obtained sixty thousand files relating to tens of thousands of HSBC clients from nearly every country. An HSBC lawyer later described Falciani's crime as "the largest robbery of a bank ever committed in the world."

Falciani's flight to France coincided with the onset of the global financial crisis. Many countries were scrambling to secure revenues and crack down on citizens whose fortunes were stashed in offshore tax havens. Years before the leak, in April 2016, of the Panama Papers—a cache of documents from Mossack Fonseca, a law firm in Panama City that specializes in the creation of anonymous shell companies—there was ample evidence that the global plutocracy has many outlets for dissimulation in the realm of personal finance. "Only the little people pay taxes," the billionaire Leona Helmsley once remarked, to her housekeeper. In 1989, the housekeeper recounted the exchange to a New York jury, and Helmsley spent eighteen months in prison. Most tax evasion, however, goes unpunished. According to a 2012 study by James Henry, a former chief economist at McKinsey who now advises the Tax Justice Network, the world's wealthiest people salt away at least $21 trillion beyond the reach of tax authorities. In his book *The Hidden Wealth of Nations,* the economist Gabriel Zucman offers a lower, yet still enormous, estimate: $7.6 trillion, or 8 percent of the world's personal financial wealth. Zucman calculates that "the fraud perpetuated through unreported foreign accounts each year costs about $200 billion to governments throughout the world."

The data that Falciani stole could function as a treasure map, enabling a country like France to recover some of that lost revenue. Montgolfier said, "When you have so many French people with Swiss accounts"—he raised his eyebrows and his shoulders in a synchronized Gallic shrug—"it has . . . a *perfume* of fraud."

The Swiss prosecutor demanded that Montgolfier turn over Falciani's laptop, but he demurred. "We'll look at the computer," he said. "Then we'll decide if we return it." To the Swiss government, Falciani was merely a thief, but the French saw him differently. "I would characterize him as a bit messianic," Montgolfier told me. "There was the context of the world crisis, provoked by finance and all these big banks enabling tax evasion, and this guy just wanted to set the world free of those behaviors." In a memoir recently published in Europe, *Earthquake on Planet Finance,* Falciani writes of his motives: "I wanted a different world for my daughter. I didn't want her to grow up in a reality where money rules, where the abuse of power and the constant bypassing of the rules was the norm." As if to underline the incendiary implications of Falciani's data, Montgolfier placed the laptop in a safe. While French authorities deliberated about how to proceed, Falciani spent the night in a holding cell in Menton. But the next morning, in a gesture that indicated a shift in Falciani's status, his guards surprised him with coffee and croissants.

•   •   •

When I first met Falciani, on a winter day at the Place d'Italie in Paris in 2014, he had been living under police protection, fearful that his life was endangered because of the information he had exposed about unscrupulous elites. He often traveled with three bodyguards, who were provided by the French state, but when we met, Falciani arrived alone, on a fold-up scooter. He had proposed a curious venue for our meeting: Hippopotamus, a chain restaurant that caters to French children, with a cartoon mascot and colorful menus featuring an array of tiny steak frites. Falciani ordered a slice of cheesecake. He was dressed in the manner of a Tarantino assassin: white shirt, skinny black tie, aggressively tailored black suit. He is soap-star handsome, with a dimpled chin, olive skin, and what one French newspaper described as "a commercial smile." His sideburns tapered to a sliver.

"My father worked in a bank," Falciani said, in accented English. As a child in Monaco, which is one of Europe's oldest tax havens, he often accompanied his father to work and marveled at the discreet power of the institution. The bank was immaculate, and everybody spoke in hushed tones. It reminded Falciani of a church. After business hours, he liked to dash through the carpeted hallways.

As Falciani grew older, he noticed that the flow of money into Monaco was affected by political events. When war ravaged Lebanon during the 1980s, wealthy Lebanese moved their families, and their fortunes, to the principality. When François Mitterrand came to power in France, the country's aristocrats, fearful of new taxes, stashed their money in Monaco banks. Sometimes suitcases filled with cash arrived for deposit, and Falciani watched his father count the money by hand. The names of clients were never mentioned.

Falciani studied math and physics at the University of Nice, then began working in the Casino de Monte-Carlo, initially on the gaming floor and later in the casino's internal bank, which extends lines of credit to wealthy clients. In 2000, he joined HSBC. Around the time he started working there, an employee named Stephen Troth, who had handled celebrity clients in Monaco, was discovered to have skimmed millions of dollars from their accounts. "It was a very simple scheme," Falciani told me, adding that he had followed the scandal closely. When the fraud was revealed, the Monaco branch determined that it needed to improve the security of its internal network, and Falciani was one of the employees who worked on devising better systems. In 2006, he was transferred to the private bank in Geneva, where he undertook a similar project. He was excited about this new challenge, he recalled: "I had great expectations."

HSBC, or the Hong Kong and Shanghai Banking Corporation, traces its origins to 1865 and its early success to the opium trade. The bank has grown substantially over the past two decades—it now has nearly fifty million customers—and it has acquired a reputation for being less than scrupulous, even by the loose standards of international banking. In 2012, a U.S. Senate investigation concluded that HSBC had worked with rogue regimes, terrorist financiers, and narcotraffickers. The bank eventually acknowledged having laundered more than $800 million in drug proceeds for Mexican and Colombian cartels. Carl Levin, the Michigan lawmaker who chaired the Senate investigation, said that HSBC had a "pervasively polluted" culture that placed profit ahead of due diligence. In December 2012, HSBC avoided criminal charges by agreeing to pay a $1.9 billion penalty. The company's CEO, Stuart Gulliver, said that he was "profoundly sorry" for the bank's transgressions. No executives faced penalties.

The private bank in Geneva had become part of HSBC in 1999, when the company, which is headquartered in London, acquired Republic National Bank from the estate of Edmond Safra, the Lebanese-born financier. Safra had split his time between homes in Geneva, Monaco, and the Riviera town of Villefranche-sur-Mer, where he owned a palatial villa that had once belonged to King Leopold II of Belgium. Many of Safra's clients had been Russians who were alleged to have criminal ties. As a U.S. prosecutor once remarked,

"Republic always had some very interesting customers who find the government looking at them, more so than maybe other banks." When Falciani arrived in Geneva, he told me, he realized that HSBC was engaged in a "gigantic swindle." Clients were not only placing their fortunes in accounts that were "undeclared" to tax authorities; HSBC bankers were actively assisting clients in hiding their money, by setting up shell companies and sham trusts in the British Virgin Islands and Panama. In some instances, the bankers were handing customers $100,000 bricks of U.S. bills, allowing money to be smuggled back home. In a subsequent investigation by French prosecutors, an HSBC client said that the bank had instructed him to "make a company in Panama, which should open an account at HSBC in Lugano, into which I should transfer all my holdings, in order to not be hit by this tax."

Like many Swiss banks, HSBC offered "hold mail" accounts, refraining from sending any statements or other mail to clients. One might suppose that the inconvenience of such an arrangement would make it attractive only to the rare client who fetishized privacy, but nearly fifteen thousand clients chose this method—roughly half of the account holders at HSBC's Swiss bank. Another client questioned in the subsequent investigation recalled that when he wanted to make a deposit, he would meet his account manager in a public place. "I would give him an envelope holding my money, in cash," he explained. "And a few days later he would tell me by phone that the funds had been credited to my account in Switzerland." HSBC has numerous offices in Paris, but, according to the French investigation, when the Swiss bankers visited clients there, they preferred to meet in cafés; in a similar spirit of concealment, account holders used pay phones when making calls to Switzerland. One client pointed out that the furtive face-to-face meetings offered "a bit of reassurance about the money I had in Switzerland, since I had no documents or anything that attested to my having an account."

Although the conduct that Falciani witnessed might have been illegal, it was fairly standard practice for Swiss banks at the time. A 2014 U.S. Senate report describes a Credit Suisse banker traveling to America to meet a client for breakfast at a Mandarin Oriental hotel, and passing along an issue of *Sports Illustrated* in which account statements were concealed between the pages. Swiss banks routinely dispatched emissaries to cultivate new clients at art shows and regattas, and the illegality of the service was implicit in the pitch: if you bank with us, your fortune will not be taxed. It is not illegal for a person or a corporation to hold a Swiss bank account, or to engage in tax "avoidance"—skirting tax requirements through gymnastic accounting and the exploitation of loopholes. But tax evasion, in which wealth is actively concealed from authorities, is illegal, and the behavior of Swiss bankers often suggested that they knew they were crossing the line. According to testimony in a 2014 criminal trial in Florida, representatives of the Swiss bank UBS, who traveled to such events as Art Basel to recruit clients, carried encrypted laptops that were configured with an emergency password, so that they could erase the hard drive with a few keystrokes. An unnamed Swiss banker, speaking to *The New York Times,* recalled telling colleagues, "We all have one foot in prison." He observed to the paper, "Maybe that's why we were all paid so much."

Most Swiss banks had compliance procedures designed to prevent tax evasion, money laundering, and other financial crimes. But Sue Shelley, who until 2013 was an HSBC executive vice president in charge of compliance in Luxembourg and who worked closely with the Geneva bank, told me that "compliance really took a backseat" to making profits. Shelley found that when compliance officers raised too many questions about large deposits with dodgy origins, they risked being sidelined. Compliance was often perceived as "a business-prevention department," and as a result the division was chronically understaffed. "We kept finding more and more red flags that we didn't have the resources to address," she said. When I asked Falciani about compliance at the bank, he said, "They just do a few checks." He said that he tried to sound the alarm internally and was ignored—a claim that the bank disputes. To Falciani, the bankers at HSBC were little more than crooks in pinstripes. "I spent too many years waiting for something to change," he told me. Eventually, he took matters into his own hands.

· · ·

It started with the gradual accumulation of client data. In theory, this should have been impossible: one principle of security at Swiss banks is that client information is distributed in "cellular" fashion, so that no individual has access to too much data. The bank's computer system was "subdivided into airtight compartments," Falciani maintains, and each employee was instructed not to wonder about what was happening beyond his own computer screen. In order to preserve the anonymity of accounts, only a few employees knew the identity behind any account number. But, like Edward Snowden, with whom he feels a strong affinity, Falciani was a systems guy. His technical expertise allowed him to outmaneuver the bank's security software. In Geneva, he was working on a new customer-relations management system. One day, as he harvested data from the bank's internal network, he says, he stumbled upon information to which he should not have had access: not just the names and account numbers of customers, but also the confidential notes that HSBC bankers maintained about their meetings with clients. "I'd never heard about this sort of flaw in the computer system," Falciani later told the investigators. The data was being updated in real time; it seemed that he had stumbled into a wormhole that held the bank's deepest secrets. He even came across the details of his own account with the bank.

At this point, another computer technician might have hastened to inform his superiors about the vulnerability. Falciani did not. Nobody knows exactly how Falciani purloined such a staggering volume of sensitive data. Alexandre Zeller, who at the time was the head of HSBC's Swiss operations, has spoken of the theft as if it were a magic trick. In a deposition provided to French investigators, Thibaut Lestrade, a technician with the French tax administration, praised Falciani's wizardry: "It wouldn't have been enough to just press a button and copy a whole grouping of data. There were data that came from several different systems which, I suspect, were not made to be connected to one another." A confidential investigative file compiled by Swiss authorities notes that Falciani has "a certain talent for computing" and describes him as "an autodidact" who is "passionate about the exploration of data and the establishment of links within them."

When I asked Falciani how he had avoided triggering digital

alarms, he explained that he had help from a shadowy league of like-minded professionals. "We started to work out a strategy," he said.

"Who is 'we'?" I asked.

"The Network," he replied.

"How many people are in the Network?"

He smiled cryptically. "I don't want to give too much detail."

According to Falciani, the Network was a loose confederation of "anti-tax-evasion crusaders," consisting of law-enforcement officers, lawyers, and spies. He told me that the Network not only helped him to steal the data; it facilitated his escape to France. HSBC, which conducted an internal investigation after Falciani became a fugitive, maintains that his story about the Network is a ruse, and that he had only one co-conspirator: a thirty-four-year-old Lebanese woman named Georgina Mikhael, who had become a technical administrator at HSBC in September 2006.

Mikhael, who has since returned to Beirut, has a throaty voice, large dark eyes, and caramel-colored hair. She and Falciani worked in adjacent offices, and they became close. They would leave the building to get coffee or to exercise together at the gym. Mikhael knew that Falciani was married, but she sensed that he was unhappy in his marriage, and he looked at her, she later said, as if he could "devour me with his eyes." Before long, they had embarked on an affair.

• • •

The prosecutor in Nice, Éric de Montgolfier, discovered that the files on Falciani's hard drive were encrypted—an unintelligible compost of names, nationalities, account numbers, and deposit amounts. So French authorities established a task force to decode the information, calling it Operation Chocolate. ("A dumb name," a French official acknowledged. "But we weren't going to call it Operation HSBC.") In February 2009, twenty specialists assembled at a hotel in Nice and set to work, in close consultation with Falciani, who provided passwords to decrypt the information and advice on how to organize it. By the end of the summer, they had extracted a list of a hundred thousand names that were connected to HSBC accounts. Éric Woerth, the French budget minister at the time, announced that the French government had recovered the names of three thousand taxpayers who held undeclared accounts in Switzerland, remarking, "This is the first time we have this kind of information: accurate, with names, account numbers, and amounts on deposit. This is exceptional."

Swiss officials threatened to halt a series of unrelated intergovernmental initiatives if the French refused to return the data. The Swiss newspaper *Le Temps* characterized the clash over Falciani's files as "a diplomatic earthquake." One Swiss justice official sent Montgolfier an intemperate letter saying that Falciani had not merely damaged the bank; he had attacked the Swiss state. "It was extraordinary," Montgolfier said. "To harm HSBC was to harm Switzerland."

The agitation of the Swiss should not have been surprising. By the time Falciani handed the HSBC data to the French, the Swiss tradition of financial secrecy was coming under assault. In 2007, an American banker who had worked for UBS in Geneva, Bradley Birkenfeld, approached U.S. authorities with information about how the bank had helped thousands of Americans evade taxes. Birkenfeld himself had provided a variety of "concierge" tax-evasion services: he once bought diamonds for an American client, then smuggled them into the United States inside a toothpaste tube. "This was an orchestrated money-laundering, tax-evasion machine," Birkenfeld told me. "In Switzerland, you can do whatever you want. You want to walk in the door with a hundred million dollars? You can deposit it. Have a nice day. Never pay taxes again." Although the European Central Bank plans to eliminate the €500 note, given that high-denomination bills are perhaps most useful to criminals, Switzerland still has a 1,000-franc note (roughly $1,000). "They have the largest currency denomination in the world—what does that tell you?" Birkenfeld said. "One time, in Geneva, I took a 1,000-Swiss-franc note and bought a pack of gum. The guy behind the counter didn't blink an eye."

As a result of Birkenfeld's leak, UBS was forced to turn over to the IRS the details of more than forty-five hundred clients with undeclared accounts, and the bank eventually paid a fine of $780 million. In 2008, Switzerland's finance minister, Hans-Rudolf Merz, warned other countries that if the world tried to crack down on Swiss bank secrecy, it was liable "to break its teeth." When the Group of Twenty met in London in 2009, offshore accounts and tax evasion were high on the agenda for the first time, under the rubric "The End of Bank

Secrecy." Neutrality is another cherished Swiss tradition, but now Switzerland's closest neighbors were tabulating the ways in which bank secrecy had enriched the country at the expense of others. As Nicholas Shaxson suggests in his book *Treasure Islands: Uncovering the Damage of Offshore Banking and Tax Havens,* the Swiss banking industry was predicated on the idea that "it is perfectly OK for one jurisdiction to exercise its sovereign right to get rich by undermining the sovereign laws and rules of other places."

In this political context, the Falciani list posed an existential threat to the Swiss economy. The files had ended up in the possession of the French, but they contained incriminating details related to HSBC clients around the world. It was not long before other governments began asking the French to share information. Early in 2010, tax authorities in the U.K. asked if British taxpayers were on the list, and officials in Paris turned over several thousand names. That May, police in Italy announced that they had received details about Italian account holders. The scandal unfolded while Italy's prime minister at the time, Silvio Berlusconi, was being investigated for tax fraud, and leaks to the press revealed that many prominent Italians were on the list, from a Roman princess to the jeweler Gianni Bulgari. The Italian press called it the *elenco della vergogna*—the list of shame. French authorities also shared portions of the list with Argentina, Russia, Canada, Australia, Sweden, Belgium, Spain, Germany, and India (where the hidden funds were described as "black money").

Scandals erupted in each country, but the biggest aftershock was felt in Greece, which was already suffering from the global economic crisis. In 2010, Christine Lagarde, who at the time was the French finance minister, shared two thousand names on Falciani's list with her Greek counterpart, George Papaconstantinou. According to a study by scholars at the University of Chicago and Virginia Tech, in 2009 Greek taxpayers failed to declare as much as €28 billion—roughly 12 percent of the country's gross domestic product. Greece had amassed a giant debt, and to reduce it, Papaconstantinou had enacted severe austerity measures, cutting pensions and wages and raising taxes, even though many Greeks were in desperate financial straits. Yet, when Papaconstantinou learned the names of wealthy Greeks who were hiding their fortunes offshore, the government took no action. In 2012, the Greek magazine *Hot Doc* published a version of the list. Papaconstantinou's successor, Evangelos Venizelos, initially claimed ignorance. Then he announced that he had discovered a memory stick containing Falciani's data in an office drawer, and had given it to authorities. When prosecutors requested a fresh copy of the Greek list, from Paris, and compared it with the data provided by Venizelos, they found that three names were missing from the memory stick. All were relatives of Papaconstantinou, who was convicted of tampering with the list and given a suspended sentence.

Although the Swiss government appears to have quickly understood the possible repercussions of the Falciani list, the management at HSBC was slow to comprehend the extent of its predicament. Alexandre Zeller, the head of the private bank in Switzerland, downplayed the data loss, claiming that only ten or so clients were affected. Zeller did not understand that the breach was of historic dimensions until December 2009, when the French finally shared the complete list with the Swiss. HSBC executives were shocked when Falciani was subsequently hailed across Europe as the "Edward Snowden of banking," in part because they had become convinced that he was something decidedly more sinister.

• • •

The Swiss Bankers Association, an industry group, maintains an international alert system that allows participating banks to issue security bulletins to other banks. The system is monitored by Swiss police, and in February 2008 an officer noticed a posting from a woman named Samira Harb, who worked at Bank Audi in Lebanon. Harb explained that she had recently met with a man who was looking to sell a database containing what appeared to be private-client information from a Swiss bank. In a subsequent interview with Swiss authorities, Harb said that she had been taken aback by the man's presentation and had pointed out to him that "my name could have been on the list if I had an account." The man was aggressive. Opening a Mac laptop, he showed her a spreadsheet containing account numbers, addresses, and job titles. When Harb asked him how he had obtained this information, he was evasive, saying that he had used "IT techniques." Harb declined the man's offer, but held on to his business card. It identified him as Ruben al-Chidiak. He was traveling with an associate, a Lebanese woman named Georgina Mikhael.

In Bern, a Swiss federal prosecutor named Laurence Boillat opened an investigation. There was no record of a Ruben al-Chidiak in Switzerland, and the name had a fictitious ring. But Georgina Mikhael was working at HSBC in Geneva. Boillat placed Mikhael under surveillance, including a wiretap on her cell phone. She did not appear to be communicating with Chidiak, but Boillat determined that she was having an affair with a married colleague, Hervé Falciani. Mikhael exchanged more than five hundred phone calls and text messages with Falciani. During an instant-message chat on Skype, she seemed to be asking about the transfer of client information onto a memory stick. "Have you committed a sin?" she wrote. "You have to be careful baby." Toward the end of 2008, the surveillance revealed that Mikhael was planning to leave her job and return to Beirut. Boillat and a team of investigators confronted Mikhael at her office. She immediately confirmed that Chidiak was actually Falciani, and pledged to cooperate.

Mikhael told the investigators that Falciani had intended to use his database not to expose tax evasion but to make money. They were in love, she explained. He told her that he wanted to leave Simona. "I thought that Hervé was serious, and that we could imagine a future together," she said. But Falciani told her that he needed to raise money in order to finance a divorce. (Simona was aware of the relationship, Mikhael told the investigators, adding, "I don't know if she knows the story of the data.") Private banks routinely attempt to poach wealthy clients. Mikhael told the investigators that she and Falciani had traveled to Beirut to sell the data on HSBC customers to another bank. Before departing, they had created a company, based in Hong Kong, named Palorva—a mash-up of "Palomino," which was Mikhael's nickname, and "Hervé." They set up a website and posted a motto: "Business is the art of extracting money from another man's pocket without resorting to violence." The website said that Palorva could help banks recruit new customers by scouring public databases for information. Falciani felt that he should have an alias, Mikhael said. Wanting "a name that would be familiar to his Lebanese interlocutors," he decided that Ruben al-Chidiak sounded plausibly Arab. They printed business cards—Chidiak was identified as Palorva's "sales manager"—and in

February 2008 they flew to Lebanon, using Simona Falciani's HSBC credit card to buy the tickets.

In addition to Bank Audi, they met with four other banks, but made no sales. According to Mikhael, Falciani traveled at all times with a can of Mace and a knife. (He denies this, saying, "That's not my style.") When I asked Falciani if he had an affair with Mikhael, he said yes, but added, "It was nothing special." In Beirut, the couple strolled along the Corniche, and Mikhael introduced Falciani to her family. "Georgina thought we were going to settle in Lebanon," Falciani subsequently testified in a deposition in France. "I let her think I had the same idea." But once they returned to Switzerland, the relationship soured. Mikhael noticed that each time a new young woman started working at the bank, Falciani followed her around "exactly like he did with me." Eventually, she told Swiss investigators, she "realized that he wasn't ready to leave his wife." At one point, she sent him an email: "The deal we made doesn't say that you should never call me!! Apparently you've been having great weekends." Falciani, it seems, had begun seeing other women. Later, when Swiss investigators analyzed his cell phone, they found a contact listed as "Myriam government." Was this a liaison from a foreign-intelligence service? Was it someone from the Network? When they looked up the number and summoned the woman for an interview, they discovered that Myriam was a philosophy student and a part-time secretary from Geneva—"a romantic conquest" of Falciani's, as one investigator put it. (Apparently, Falciani, mindful that his wife or his mistress might inspect his contact list, had added "government" to throw off suspicion.)

Mikhael eventually concluded that Falciani was "a liar, a born manipulator, a seducer, a pickup artist." Falciani told me that he never intended to sell files in Beirut. On the contrary, he had known about the warning system maintained by the Swiss Bankers Association and had set up meetings in Beirut with the express intention of triggering the alert system, in order to lure Swiss authorities into exposing HSBC's criminality. "It was a trap," he said.

Why fabricate a false identity? Falciani told me that his friends in the Network had developed suspicions about Georgina Mikhael and her sudden appearance in Geneva. "This girl was maybe not there only for her," Falciani said. "She had no banking experience at all."

"Who did you think she was working for?" I asked.

Falciani cast a theatrical glance around Hippopotamus before leaning toward me and whispering, "Hezbollah."

I looked at him with bewilderment. There were times when Falciani reminded me of Chuck Barris, the host of *The Gong Show*, who, in his 1984 memoir, *Confessions of a Dangerous Mind*, claimed that he had secretly led a double life as a CIA assassin. In order to determine whether Mikhael was a Hezbollah spy, Falciani said, he tested her by seeing if she had the means to secure him "a real fake identity"—a Lebanese passport and an identity card with a pseudonym. His actions sounded bizarre, Falciani allowed, but you had to understand that during this period dangerous people were coming to Geneva and taking a great interest in him. He said, "You have read about the kidnapping?"

One night in August 2007, Falciani was walking in Geneva's Champel district when a van suddenly pulled alongside him. Men inside the vehicle "threw me in, holding a gun to my head," he recalled. "I found myself in the basement of a church, in front of two men. A big red-headed guy that speaks impeccable French and a super-tough brown-haired guy." They were Mossad agents, and the Israeli government needed his assistance. An Islamist mole had apparently infiltrated HSBC. Would he help expose the infiltrator? He accepted the mission.

At least this is the version that Falciani told the French newspaper *Nice Matin*. When I pressed him about the episode, his story shifted. "My friends organized the kidnapping," he said. It was staged by the Network.

So the kidnappers weren't actually Mossad agents?

"It was real fake," Falciani replied. "Like a real fake identity." He conceded that in the HSBC saga "you have a lot of real fake things."

In 2010, Swiss prosecutors asked Mikhael about the Mossad story. "I'm convinced that this story is pure invention," she said. She has initiated a defamation suit against Falciani in Paris, insisting that she is neither a terrorist nor a spy, and arguing that Falciani's allegations are "worthy of a crime novel." (Through a lawyer, Mikhael declined to speak with me, but the lawyer reiterated that she has never been a member of Hezbollah, noting that she is Christian.)

In Paris, I met with Christian Eckert, the French budget minister, who wrote a report on Falciani and his revelations. The French government has not only vaunted Falciani's information; it has fought a significant international battle to protect him from prosecution by the Swiss. Eckert acknowledged that Falciani "has a tendency to romanticize his stories a little." But he insisted that financial authorities had confirmed "the authenticity of the information that he gave." Even if Falciani wasn't always a reliable narrator, the French government had no buyer's remorse. When I alluded to Georgina Mikhael's contention that Falciani is merely a con man and a common thief, Eckert grimaced as if he'd swallowed a bad oyster, and muttered, "Salope"—the French word for "bitch."

• • •

Until recently, it seemed impossible to shame the Swiss into breaking their tradition of banking secrecy. In the 1990s, when U.S. investigators came looking for looted assets that had been stolen from Jews during World War II, the Swiss government stonewalled. But by 2012, Falciani's revelations and other pressures threatened to overwhelm the Swiss resistance to transparency. In 2010, the U.S. Congress passed a law requiring banks overseas to submit to the IRS the names and account details of American clients. The Organisation for Economic Co-operation and Development, meanwhile, amended a convention on mutual administrative assistance in tax matters so that Swiss banks could be obligated to divulge client information. In February 2012, prosecutors in New York indicted Wegelin & Company, the oldest bank in Switzerland, for money laundering and abetting tax evasion. The bank was effectively put out of business. Chancellor Angela Merkel infuriated Swiss officials when she announced that the German government would happily pay a Swiss bank employee who was offering to sell information about secret accounts held by German taxpayers. "If these data are relevant, we should aim to get hold of them," she said. This established a frightening precedent for Swiss banks. Oswald Grübel, the chief executive of UBS, said, "If governments are in the market of buying illegal data, that changes the world."

On June 30, 2012, Falciani traveled to the southern port of Sète, where he boarded a Morocco-bound ferry that would make a stop in

Spain. His reasons for going to Spain have never been clear. I heard a rumor in Paris that there was a woman there. But Falciani, characteristically, offered me a more intriguing explanation. During the summer of 2012, the U.S. Senate concluded the investigation revealing that HSBC had engaged in money laundering and facilitated the operations of Mexican drug cartels. According to Falciani, he had been an instrumental source for this investigation, and he was advised by supporters in the U.S. government to leave France. "There was a lot of risk in that period for people to kill me," Falciani told me. (A staff member who was involved in the Senate inquiry told me that Falciani was not a source for the investigation.)

Early the next morning, the ferry arrived in Barcelona. When Falciani disembarked and presented his passport to Spanish immigration officials, he was arrested. He had been safe in Paris, because he had a French passport and France rarely extradites its own citizens. But Switzerland had issued a Red Notice—an international arrest warrant—with Interpol, and the Spanish elected to honor it. This placed Spanish authorities in a slightly awkward position, given that in 2010 they had requested Falciani's list from the French. Madrid tax inspectors had subsequently conducted a series of investigations into prominent Spaniards who had used HSBC to mask their wealth. Emilio Botín, the head of Banco Santander, was exposed as an account holder and was obliged, along with other members of his family, to pay nearly $300 million in back taxes.

Falciani hired a lawyer to challenge the extradition. Pending the resolution of his case, he was sent to Valdemoro prison, south of Madrid. Falciani was cavalier about this interlude, telling me, "It's tough for my family, you know, but I'm kind of Superman—for me, it's okay." He passed the days playing racquetball with members of ETA, the militant Basque separatist group. A priest lent him a book about Julian Assange, which he read with great interest.

At an extradition hearing in April 2013, Falciani appeared in thick glasses and a preposterous brown wig. The disguise was for his own safety, he explained in his memoir: "My only fear was that someone might take me out before my arrival at the court." In arguing that he should not be returned to Switzerland, Falciani volunteered to assist the Spanish government in its battle against tax fraud, saying,

"The fight for financial transparency is fundamental." A month later, a Spanish court ruled against extradition. Because the principle of bank secrecy does not exist in Spanish law, the court argued, violating that secrecy in Switzerland was not a crime in Spain.

Falciani insists that the five and a half months he spent in the Spanish jail was part of his grand design. "I knew I would be imprisoned," he told me. "But I had to flee the threats that I was exposed to and take up the fight against financial secrecy."

But why would Spain be safer than France? Visibly impatient with my failure to grasp his logic, he said, "Because *I would be in jail*."

Upon his release, Falciani returned to France, where he was given police protection. Montgolfier, the prosecutor in Nice, told *Le Temps* that Swiss attempts to discredit Falciani should be dismissed. "No one seems to doubt what we have in our hands," he said. "We cannot question the data." Falciani told me that his house had been broken into and that as a consequence of his notoriety Simona, who had remained in Italy with Kim, was fired from her job as a clerk in a shoe store. In interviews, he has adopted a tone of menace toward his antagonists. "I have become more dangerous," he told *Le Monde* in 2013.

The French government says that it has never paid Falciani for his information, and he denies having been paid by any of the governments that have used his data to pursue tax cheats. But if Falciani had been compensated, such a transaction would not be without precedent. In 2006, a former employee of LGT Group, a private bank in Liechtenstein, offered the details of hundreds of accounts to German intelligence services—and received a reported €5 million in return. Some German officials voiced discomfort with the quid pro quo, and with Angela Merkel's endorsement of such deals. Kurt Lauk, the president of the business council of the Christian Democrats, said, "We are signaling to these data thieves: we will buy what you steal."

• • •

Georgina Mikhael has observed of Falciani, "He has an enormous imagination. Overflowing." His outlandish stories about secret agents and a network of hackers opposed to tax evasion seem like the fantasies of a paranoiac or the ramblings of a fabulist. But in March 2008, before fleeing Geneva, he had sent emails to British and German intelligence agencies, announcing, "I have the whole list of clients of one of the world's top five private banks." (The agencies did not pursue this opportunity.) He also contacted a French revenue inspector named Jean-Patrick Martini. During the summer of 2008, Falciani arranged a secret meeting with Martini in a French village across the Swiss border. Martini brought along a psychologist, who helped him come to the conclusion that Falciani seemed credible about the provenance of his data. In a subsequent deposition, Martini testified, "He said there had been fraud, that the bank was complicit in a fair number of irregularities, and that it was important to put a stop to it. I always had the conviction that he was acting out of pure civic duty."

After Falciani crossed into France in December 2008, he met Martini again, at a café in the Nice airport, and turned over CDs containing the HSBC data. When Montgolfier and his team raided the apartment of Falciani's parents, they did not realize that another French official already possessed a copy of the list. Georgina Mikhael has said that Falciani's overtures to foreign governments were simply a hedge on his efforts to sell the data: if he failed to make a deal with a bank, he would seek a buyer in the intelligence community. He was aware that Germany had paid millions to the leaker from LGT Group, the Liechtenstein bank. In *Falciani's Tax Bomb,* a 2015 documentary by the British filmmaker Ben Lewis, Mikhael says that it was the Liechtenstein deal that "gave him the idea to sell the data to secret services."

Of course, someone can have a desire to expose wrongdoing and also want to be rewarded for his trouble. Government agreements with whistle-blowers often look morally confused. In 2009, Bradley Birkenfeld, the American banker who leaked documents about illegal activity at UBS, was sent to prison for his role in the conspiracy. He served two and a half years. (Though UBS paid a fine, no other executive went to jail for the misconduct that Birkenfeld exposed.) Upon Birkenfeld's release, he received a government reward of $104 million—the largest ever paid by the IRS.

In airport terminals around the world, HSBC posts advertisements that emphasize its reach across continents and cultures. An image appears twice, with different captions: a tattooed arm is labeled "trendy" in one picture and "traditional" in the next, suggesting that the cosmopolitan traveler needs a global bank that grasps differences in cultural perception. As Falciani's fortunes rose and fell, we kept in touch through Skype, and I often thought of those ads. In France, Falciani looked like a whistle-blower; in Switzerland, he looked like a thief. "I was taken in by his charm," Mikhael says in the documentary. "But I am still amazed that the whole world has been charmed by him."

In December 2014, Swiss prosecutors indicted Falciani for industrial espionage and data theft. After the charges were announced, he seemed unruffled. He couldn't understand why anyone questioned the purity of his motives. "I did everything straight," he told me.

· · ·

One day in early 2014, someone dropped off a memory stick at the reception desk of *Le Monde* in Paris. It contained a copy of Falciani's data. Until that point, bits of the list had become public, but no media outlet possessed a complete copy. Overwhelmed by the amount of information, the editors of *Le Monde* joined with the International Consortium of Investigative Journalists to comb through it. In February 2015, the project, Swiss Leaks, resulted in dozens of articles in newspapers around the world. The novelty and importance of the list lay more in its magnitude than in its confirmation of individual venality. Nevertheless, it was bracing to put human faces—many of them famous—on the story. *The Guardian* and other Swiss Leaks participants revealed that the Falciani list included politicians, arms dealers, and people linked to terrorist financing and to the trade in blood diamonds. Stuart Gulliver, the CEO of HSBC, acknowledged that the list had become "a source of shame."

Exposed clients sometimes offered comical responses. The French chef Paul Bocuse said that he had "forgotten" about an account containing €2.2 million. David Bowie explained to *The Guardian* that although he lived in Manhattan, he had been a legal resident of Switzerland since 1976. One person whose name ended up on the list, John Malkovich, sued *Le Monde,* saying that he has never had an undeclared account at HSBC. There were serious consequences for a few of the named clients. For example, a French court sentenced Arlette Ricci, the seventy-three-year-old heiress to the Nina Ricci fortune, to a year in prison for tax fraud. But the vast majority of people identified as holding undeclared accounts were not prosecuted. Instead, they appear to have settled with their respective governments, in a series of quiet amnesties.

Nearly three thousand accounts were held by U.S. taxpayers. When I met with Christian Eckert, the French budget minister, he showed me official documentation indicating that in early 2010 U.S. authorities had requested French assistance in securing the American names on the list. In May 2012, four IRS agents and a prosecutor from the Department of Justice flew to Paris and interrogated Falciani about his database. "I remain at your disposal," he said, according to a transcript of the meeting.

The Department of Justice declined to comment on its questioning of Falciani, and the IRS denied my request, under the Freedom of Information Act, for details about its possible use of the list to pursue tax violators. But in 2009 the IRS introduced a plan allowing U.S. citizens with undeclared accounts to volunteer the details to the government and pay outstanding taxes, without fear of criminal penalties. IRS officials maintain that they have collected more than $8 billion through this program, and it stands to reason that some people who settled in this fashion were on Falciani's list. Indeed, there is evidence that U.S. authorities have used the list to pursue cases against American taxpayers. According to an affidavit in a federal case against a New Jersey couple, Eli and Renee Chabot, the government received a CD in April 2010 containing a portion of Falciani's list, and the data revealed that the Chabots had several million dollars at HSBC Switzerland in accounts associated with a company called Pelsa Business Inc. The Chabots refused to turn over information to the IRS about the accounts. Last year, an appeals court held that this was not a permissible invocation of the Fifth Amendment. But the case against them may face complications. In the Falciani documentary, Victor Song, a former enforcement officer at the IRS, says that a determination was made by the Department of Justice that Falciani's information would be inadmissible in U.S. courts, because it had been "stolen from a bank in Europe."

● ● ●

Last November, at a federal court in Bellinzona, Switzerland, a prosecutor named Carlo Bulletti argued that Falciani was no crusader. "The whole construct of the White Knight is a tissue of lies," he said. Falciani was being tried in absentia for industrial espionage and data theft. A former supervisor of Falciani's testified that he had grumbled about the cost of living in Geneva and complained about his salary, which never exceeded $130,000. Laurent Moreillon, a lawyer for HSBC, called Falciani a "data robber" and noted that the breach had been devastating for the bank, had created embarrassment for account holders, and had precipitated numerous divorces.

Falciani's attorney, Marc Henzelin, denied that his client had attacked a financial fortress. The data practically "fell into his pocket," leaving Falciani feeling "troubled" by the vulnerability of the bank's internal software. Henzelin acknowledged that the trip to Beirut wasn't a "very glorious episode," but he suggested that Falciani had overplayed the intrigue. "All this is part of a movie script, but not very serious," he insisted. Falciani had gone to Lebanon to sell data, Henzelin said, but only with material harvested from the internet. "There is no indication that the data he wanted to sell in Beirut were precisely data from HSBC Switzerland," Henzelin argued. The prosecution claimed that the privacy of thousands of honorable clients had been violated, but, as Henzelin pointed out, this was hard to reconcile with the damning particulars of the list. Of 628 Indian names on the list, only 79 had declared their assets to the Indian government. The proportion was similar for Argentina and Greece. Gabriel Zucman, the economist, estimates that 80 percent of assets in offshore havens are undeclared. Tax evasion wasn't incidental to HSBC's Swiss bank, Henzelin concluded; it was the bank's raison d'être.

Switzerland has been hard on those who violate bank secrecy: Rudolf Elmer, a former employee of the Swiss bank Julius Bär, was tried in 2011 for sharing information about tax evasion and other improprieties with WikiLeaks. Elmer was imprisoned for two hundred days, some of it in solitary confinement; he says that his family was harassed by detectives working for the bank. In Swiss society, to violate the covenant of secrecy is to risk not just prison but also ostracism.

During the trial, Falciani taunted prosecutors by speaking at a

conference in Divonne, a French spa town a mile from the Swiss border. The title of the conference was "Investigative Journalism in the
Time of WikiLeaks." Falciani arrived unshaven, his dark hair slicked
back, dressed in a black blazer and jeans. He had a tan, and as flash-
bulbs popped, he had the self-conscious demeanor of a movie star at
a premiere. "My action continues to be fruitful," Falciani declared.
"I'm working with administrations and investigators." Although he
had remained in France, he had joined a new Spanish political party,
Partido X, and stood for election in the European Parliament in 2014
on an anticorruption-and-transparency platform. (The party won no
seats.) He was also promoting *Earthquake on Planet Finance,* in which
he related his adventures and called for greater accountability in the
international financial system.

The book is an extraordinary document. Falciani writes that
the Network consists of "about 100 people working toward the same
objective." He claims that while he was fleeing Switzerland, he was
contacted by Network operatives on a keyboardless phone, "white in
color and the size of a credit card, so slim that one could hide it in the
pages of a book." The device sounds like something Apple will be selling a decade from now, but Falciani describes it as proprietary Network technology. In Beirut, he "was always running the risk of being
kidnapped." In Spain, powerful enemies could have "faked an accident
to eliminate me." He describes secret meetings on railway platforms
and bodyguards who watch over him so discreetly that nobody but
Falciani ever seems to notice them.

At a press conference, a reporter asked Falciani how Simona had
coped with his troubles. "She is courageous, she has never failed," he
said, adding, unprompted, "I never had any mistresses." Noting that
he no longer lived with his family, he initially called it "a life-style
choice," then explained that he was trying to protect their safety. "We
communicate by Skype," he said. The hotel where the event took
place was also a casino. Falciani seemed at ease there.

A few days later, in Bellinzona, the attorneys and the presiding
judge spent the morning debating whether, in light of Falciani's decision to boycott his own trial, his remarks in Divonne were admissible
in lieu of testimony. (They were not.) On November 27, 2015, Falciani

was convicted of aggravated industrial espionage and sentenced to five years in prison. HSBC released a statement celebrating the verdict and noted that the bank "has always maintained that Falciani systematically stole clients' information in order to sell it."

It was the harshest sentence ever delivered in Switzerland for the violation of bank secrecy. But the authorities were clearly waging a rearguard battle. Marc Henzelin, Falciani's attorney, noted that his client was being prosecuted while Switzerland succumbed to international pressure to dismantle bank secrecy altogether. "It is not Falciani who is being judged," Henzelin said. "It is *Switzerland*." Eckert, the French budget minister, told me, "I think the Swiss are now convinced that secret banking doesn't have much of a future."

The French are pursuing a criminal case against HSBC over the Falciani revelations and have indicted the bank for direct marketing to nationals, money laundering, and facilitating tax fraud. But in Switzerland authorities dropped an investigation of HSBC after the bank agreed to apologize for "organizational deficiencies" and pay a conspicuously manageable fine of $43 million. (Last year, HSBC's net profits exceeded $13 billion.)

When I asked Birkenfeld, the former UBS banker, about the penalty HSBC paid in Switzerland, he laughed. "I had friends who worked at HSBC who handled accounts that were larger than that," he said. The system is rigged, Birkenfeld exclaimed: "The Swiss government can't investigate the bank. They would be investigating themselves!"

• • •

A few days after Falciani's sentencing, I visited Geneva. The city felt scrubbed and prosperous. As dusk fell, neon signs bearing the logos of Swiss banks and watch companies glowed over the lake, which looked as clear as glass. HSBC had recently relocated from an old lakeside palace that it inherited from Edmond Safra to a row of handsome whitewashed buildings. No executives would meet with me, but a beleaguered-seeming British press spokesman escorted me through a series of sleek glass interiors to a conference room on a high floor and assured me that the bank has changed. HSBC has nearly tripled its number of compliance officers, to nine thousand, and has ceased operations in a dozen countries. "The number of accounts has been managed down," he said.

Where will the profits that HSBC is forfeiting go? To other banks, he said, or other countries. Money has a tendency to move, and Switzerland is hardly the only tax haven. If it becomes impractical to hide fortunes there, the money could migrate to Singapore or, for that matter, to America. Shruti Shah, the vice president of Transparency International U.S.A., recently found that in such states as Delaware and Nevada it is easier to establish an anonymous shell company than it is to obtain a library card. It seems unlikely that reforming the Swiss banking sector will diminish the widespread practice of tax evasion, because wealthy clients can simply transfer their money to a more lax jurisdiction or convert their cash to art or gold or some other easily laundered asset. The *Times* recently observed that fighting tax evasion by striking deals with an individual banking haven is like "plugging one hole in a colander."

Whether the culture at HSBC has actually changed is open to debate. After the bank was implicated in servicing drug cartels and sanctioned regimes, the U.S. Justice Department appointed an independent monitor to assess HSBC's efforts at reform. Last summer, the monitor reported that employees continued to display a lack of cooperation with internal audits. Managers maintained the same approach to in-house compliance: "discredit, deny, deflect, and delay."

Sue Shelley, the former compliance chief in Luxembourg, began her career at Midland Bank in Liverpool when she was a teenager, ripping up old checkbooks. After Midland merged with HSBC in 1992, she created a compliance department for HSBC's operation in the Cayman Islands. She arrived in Luxembourg in 2009 and was struck by the lax precautions at the private bank—and by its reaction to the Falciani leak. "The steps that I saw taken were more about protecting data, making it harder for employees to take data out, than they were about the underlying issue, which was tax evasion," she told me. In a series of reports, Shelley raised concerns to management and the board of directors about suspicious clients and transactions and about the permissive culture at the bank. In response, Shelley said, she was "bullied, isolated, and ignored." By 2013, she had become consumed by stress, feeling that she was both aggravating superiors with her warnings and failing to catch other irregularities. Shelley had what she describes as "a bit of a nervous breakdown." While she was home recuperating, HSBC fired her without explanation.

Shelley had been at the bank for thirty-six years. She is certain that the reason she was fired is that she refused to ignore compliance issues. In 2014, she won an improper-termination lawsuit. Her story echoes that of Carolyn Wind, who oversaw compliance and money-laundering prevention for HSBC's U.S. operations, and was fired in 2007. Wind told a Senate subcommittee that she lost her job because she had pushed for "additional compliance resources."

In April 2016, the Falciani list was dwarfed by the Panama Papers leak. An anonymous source released eleven and a half million documents relating to the practices of Mossack Fonseca, exposing the financial dealings of a dozen current and former heads of state, and underscoring how extensively the global elite uses shell companies and tax havens to obscure its wealth. The leak documented that HSBC and its subsidiaries had created some twenty-three hundred shell companies that had been registered by Mossack Fonseca. According to a *Guardian* report, HSBC helped to keep open the Swiss bank accounts of Rami Makhlouf, the financier cousin of the Syrian dictator, Bashar al-Assad, after hostilities in Syria intensified. (Makhlouf's family has been blacklisted by the U.S. government since 2007.)

At one point, several senior HSBC executives were summoned to a committee of the House of Commons in London to address improprieties at the bank. Asked why no top executives had been fired after the recent string of scandals, Douglas Flint, the group chairman, said that he was "a great supporter of individual responsibility" but felt that in this instance it would be inappropriate "for a single individual to be responsible." Stuart Gulliver, the CEO, said that since taking over in 2011, he had implemented "root and branch" reforms. But it was hard to see him as an agent of change. When committee members inquired how he chose to receive his personal compensation from the bank, Gulliver acknowledged that for many years he was paid through an anonymous shell company that he had set up in Panama—through Mossack Fonseca. Gulliver insisted that he had always paid his taxes and that he employed the Panamanian shell simply for "privacy." But he admitted his "inability to convince anyone that these arrangements were not put in place for reasons of tax evasion."

Falciani remains in Paris, and the week the Panama Papers were released, I spoke with him over Skype. He welcomed the leak, he told me, but he was dubious about the prospects of broader change. The banking industry, he said, will make the minimum reforms necessary in order to quell outrage. Then executives will figure out how to game the new regulatory environment. Bankers, Falciani observed, have a great "ability to adapt."

He mentioned the huge sum that Bradley Birkenfeld had been awarded for blowing the whistle on UBS, and said that France needed to follow America's lead and create incentives for whistle-blowers. Falciani seemed a bit glum, and it struck me that one problem with adopting the vestments of a transparency advocate in order to stay out of a Swiss prison cell is that you are obliged to keep wearing them. I asked Falciani if it had been worth it to upend his life. He hesitated, then said yes. "It used to be that when people thought of Switzerland, it was chocolate, watches, and rich people," he said. "Now it is also corruption."

Falciani ended up settling in Spain, under security protection sponsored by the United Nations. In 2018, he was rearrested in Madrid, because Swiss authorities had continued to push for his extradition. But a Spanish court once again refused to turn him over. When he was arrested, Falciani was about to give a speech at a university. The title of the speech was "When Telling the Truth Is Heroic."

THE PRINCE OF MARBELLA

The decades-long battle to catch an elusive
international arms broker. (2010)

PALACIO DE MIFADIL, ONE OF several homes owned by the wealthy Syrian arms merchant Monzer al-Kassar, is a white marble mansion overlooking the resort town of Marbella, on the southern coast of Spain. Surrounded by lush grounds and patrolled by three mastiffs, it has a twelve-car garage and a swimming pool shaped like a four-leaf clover. One sunny morning in 2007, two Guatemalans, named Carlos and Luis, arrived at the front gate. One of Kassar's associates ushered the men between curving marble staircases into the grand salon. Kassar was expecting them. He had agreed to sell them several million dollars' worth of weapons for the Revolutionary Armed Forces of Colombia—the South American narco-insurgent organization known as the FARC, which the U.S. government considers a terrorist group.

Since moving to Spain some thirty years earlier, Kassar had become one of the world's most prolific arms dealers. Although he owned an import-export company that conducted legitimate business, he had also developed a reputation as a trafficker willing to funnel munitions to rogue states and armed groups in defiance of international sanctions and embargoes. He has been accused of many transgressions: fueling conflicts in the Balkans and Somalia, procuring components of Chinese anti-ship cruise missiles for Iran, supplying the Iraqi Army on the eve of the U.S. invasion in 2003, and using a private jet to spirit $1 billion out of Iraq and into Lebanon for Saddam Hussein. A 2003 United Nations report branded him an "international embargo buster." In 2006, when Iraq's new government released its list of most wanted criminals, Kassar was No. 26. (He was "one of the main sources of financial and logistics support" for the insurgency, an Iraqi official said.) Authorities claimed that Kassar had been involved in smuggling drugs, financing terrorist groups, and ordering the assassination of various rivals and witnesses against him. Expelled from England, and convicted in absentia on terrorism charges in France, for supplying explosives that were used in a 1982 attack on a restaurant in the Jewish Quarter in Paris, he had been a wanted man for thirty years.

Kassar liked to playfully deny the charges against him, saying that he had never dealt drugs ("I don't even smoke cigarettes!") and claiming that he had long since retired from the arms trade. But, along with Persian carpets and silk flowers, the grand salon was decorated with framed photographs that showed him posing with Saddam Hussein's psychopathic son Uday, and with Kassar's longtime friend Abu Abbas, the former head of the Palestine Liberation Front, who was responsible for hijacking the Italian cruise ship the *Achille Lauro* in 1985. "How do I know who's good and who's bad?" Kassar would say of his associates. "The bad people for you may be the good people for me."

Kassar lived in Marbella with his wife, Raghdaa, and their four children. Ostentatiously well mannered and stylishly dressed, he projected a roguish cosmopolitanism: he spoke half a dozen languages, had half a dozen passports, and maintained a fleet of Mercedes sedans, along with a private jet that he piloted himself. If his houseguests were smokers, he offered them specially rolled Cuban cigars with a band that read "M. al-Kassar" and bore a tiny photograph of his son. He often visited the casino in nearby Puerto Banús to play blackjack, always paying for his chips with the same dog-eared check, which was returned to him once he had collected his winnings. He showed it off to friends, as an indication of his skill as a gambler. "I would see him in a local bar or disco, and it was obvious that he didn't have a care in the world," Sam Wyman, a former CIA official who was stationed in the Middle East and Spain, told me. Over the years, Kassar had developed powerful links with various governments and their intelligence services, whose agents often intersect with the underworld. The result was a degree of impunity. "He was a protected person, in some respects, by virtue of his relationships," Wyman said. These connections, coupled with strong legal counsel, had allowed Kassar to avoid significant jail time. In the Arab world, he was known as the Peacock. In Europe, the press called him the Prince of Marbella.

"Bienvenidos!" Kassar said as he entered the salon. A handsome man in his early sixties, with a strong nose, hooded eyes, and close-cropped gray hair, he was dressed in a tailored blue suit and wore an Hermès belt with a buckle in the shape of an H. "What would you like to drink? Tell me." He asked about his visitors' trip and called Carlos "little brother."

"We need to talk," Carlos said. He and Luis were interested not just in machine guns and rocket-propelled grenade launchers, he explained, but also in surface-to-air missiles, which could be used to shoot down American helicopters in Colombia. Kassar assured them that he would be able to get what they needed. "Just look at what's happening in Iraq," he said. "They're good for everything, for all those helicopters." As Kassar's aging white poodle, Yogi, wandered in and out of the room, the men discussed the dangers of conducting business over the phone. Kassar instructed his guests to call him on a special line, saying, "I have the most secure phone in the world."

At one point, Carlos complained that the United States was interfering in the FARC's activities in Colombia. "Uh-huh," Kassar murmured sympathetically. "All over the world," he said. This statement was more apt than Kassar might have realized, because, as he negotiated the deal, every word that he said was being recorded. He had become the subject of an international sting orchestrated by a secretive unit of the American Drug Enforcement Administration. Carlos and Luis worked for the United States.

• • •

One day in November, I drove to the headquarters of the DEA's Special Operations Division, in a generic office park outside Washington, D.C. I was there to meet Jim Soiles, a counter-narcotics agent who had spent two decades pursuing Kassar. Tall and imposing, Soiles wore a three-piece suit, a tie with a clip, and a gold chain around his wrist. His hair was pulled back in a ponytail, and he had a neatly trimmed salt-and-pepper beard. Soiles grew up in Massachusetts, in a community that was "ravaged by drugs," he told me. After graduating from Northeastern University and working for several years as a police officer, he joined the DEA and was sent to New York City in 1982. With eighty-four offices in sixty-three countries, the DEA has an unusually expansive network of agents and informants. Because there is often a nexus between narcotics and arms dealing, terrorism, and other international crimes, the agency's elite Special Operations Division sometimes undertakes multi-jurisdictional investigations that end up having nothing to do with drugs. "We start with the counter-narcotics," Soiles explained. "As the story unfolds, it takes us into other areas."

In the early 1980s, New York was what Soiles calls a "gateway city." Heroin and hashish were smuggled from the Middle East to Western Europe and then New York, where they were distributed across the United States. As a young agent, Soiles interrogated smugglers who had been arrested, and many alluded to a Syrian named Monzer al-Kassar. "Everybody we snatched would mention his name," Soiles recalled. Kassar was the biggest drug trafficker in Europe, they said. There were numerous spellings of the name—Manzer, Mansour, Kazar, Alkassar—but it came up again and again, eventually featuring in more than seventy-five DEA investigations. One of Soiles's colleagues likened Kassar to Keyser Söze, the mysterious, semi-mythical villain in the 1995 film *The Usual Suspects.*

Kassar was born in 1945 and grew up in the town of Nebek, outside Damascus. He has described himself as "a peasant, the son of a peasant," but his father was a diplomat who served as Syria's ambassador to Canada and India. Monzer studied law, but never practiced, and by 1970 his Interpol record had begun, with an arrest, for theft, in Trieste. "After the '67 war, there were a lot of very wealthy, very capable, usually well-educated Lebanese, Jordanians, and Syrians who went out to earn a lot of money any way they could," Sam Wyman told me. "The weapons industry and the drug industry were very lucrative. There was terrorism going on. There was almost a subculture."

According to the authorities, Monzer's mentor was his older brother Ghassan, who had entered the drug trade in the 1960s. Ghassan was more serious-minded than Monzer. "Most of our sources said Ghassan was the better trafficker," Soiles told me. "Ghassan was a righteous criminal." In the 1970s, Lebanon's Bekaa Valley became a major source of hashish and heroin, and by the middle of the decade Kassar was in London, where he lived on Sloane Square and took part in a complex scheme. Drugs were smuggled out of Lebanon in refrigerated meat trucks, then sold to buy weapons, which were smuggled from Europe back into Lebanon. The racket was uncovered by British authorities, and Kassar served a sentence of less than two years in a U.K. prison. (Years later, he amused friends with the Cockney rhyming slang that he learned there.) During the 1980s, Kassar began to focus on the arms trade. Ghassan had established connections in the Bulgarian armaments industry, and Monzer spent time in Sofia. He quickly picked up Bulgarian, and entertained his local friends in a manner that was decadent by the standards of Communism, sneaking them into the only casino in town, which locals were not permitted to enter. He always brought along a large supply of pistachios, a favorite snack that was unavailable in Sofia at the time.

"He liked to spend money," a longtime friend who met him there recalled, adding, "He liked to take risks." He and Ghassan occasionally argued about his spending. Before long, Kassar had found another source of weapons in Poland, where he forged a relationship with a national arms manufacturer, Cenzin. He established himself as a commercial representative of the People's Democratic Republic of Yemen and traveled to Warsaw on a Yemeni diplomatic passport. According to a former associate, he sometimes purchased a year's production in advance, becoming the de facto exclusive agent for Cenzin. In obtaining arms from Eastern-bloc manufacturers, and channeling them to small states and armed groups, Kassar prefigured the strategy of the notorious Tajik arms broker Viktor Bout, who in the 1990s began selling surplus weaponry from the Cold War.

Arms trafficking is a particularly elusive crime. International law is generally weak, and Interpol, which has no arresting power, is little more than a clearinghouse for warrants that individual nations may elect not to enforce. Moreover, a weapons shipment can represent a violation of international law but still be perfectly legal in many nations. "People like Kassar are not stupid," E. J. Hogendoorn, an International Crisis Group researcher who wrote a report on Kassar for the United Nations, told me. "They structure their deals so that they're not violating national law." In setting up transactions, Kassar often acted as what is known as a third-party broker. From his home in Spain, he could negotiate between a supplier in a second country and a buyer in a third. The weapons could then be shipped directly from the second country to the third, while his commission was wired to a bank in a fourth. Kassar never set foot in the countries where the crime transpired—and in Spain he had committed no crime.

By the early 1980s, when Kassar settled in Marbella, the town had become a Riviera for the Arab elite. Wealthy Arabs from Lebanon and the Gulf States were constructing extravagant villas there; many of King Ibn al-Saud's children built houses in the area. Prince Salman erected a mosque in Marbella and arrived for Friday prayers in a Rolls-Royce with a gold grille and door handles. Adnan Khashoggi, the wealthy Saudi arms dealer, docked his massive yacht, *Nabila,* in the harbor and was known for his elaborate parties and his private DC-8—a lifestyle that he claimed cost him a quarter of a million dollars a day. Marbella had also begun to attract a criminal element. "There were Arabs, there were Dutch, there were Brits," Soiles told me. Loosely policed, and a short boat ride from Africa, the town became a smuggler's haven. In Soiles's view, the Spanish authorities simply "weren't ready for that type of criminality."

Khashoggi, who was an occasional rival of Kassar's, once defended lavish living as an imperative of the arms trade, observing, "Flowers and light attract nightingales and butterflies." From the moment that Kassar moved to Marbella, he cultivated a flamboyant image. He purchased the mansion and hired a staff of forty to maintain it. In 1981, he married Raghdaa Habbal, the beautiful seventeen-year-old daughter of a prominent Syrian family in Beirut. (He jokingly referred to his wife as "my oldest daughter.") They had three daughters and a son, and divided their time among Marbella, Syria, and Vienna, where Alkastronic, Kassar's import-export company, was based. Alkastronic specialized in arms from Eastern Europe and, ostensibly, observed international laws on the sale and procurement of such weapons. Devoted to his family and surrounded by friends and business associates, Kassar became known for his hospitality and seemed always to be presiding over a barbecue or a party; although there was a chef on staff, he liked to prepare the food himself. A 1985 profile in *Paris Match* featured a photo spread of Kassar posing with his young family by the clover-shaped swimming pool, flanked by an entourage of uniformed servants standing at attention. The article described the mansion as something "from 'A Thousand and One Nights,'" and noted that "in a few years, this Syrian merchant became one of the most powerful businessmen in the world." Kassar baptized the house Palacio de Mifadil, a conflation of Spanish and Arabic that translates, roughly, as the "Palace of My Virtue." Two rusty mortar shells decorated the front entrance.

• • •

"Monzer is a very dangerous man, much as I like him," a British mercenary and arms broker named David Tomkins told me recently. "I've met Colombian cartel bosses, and they would never put the caution in me that he did." Tomkins was a safecracker and a thief who, in the 1970s, became a soldier of fortune; he served a prison sentence in the United States for a failed plot in which the Cali drug cartel hired him to murder Pablo Escobar. He told me that he met Kassar in 1984, through a mutual acquaintance, an arms dealer from Northern Ireland named Frank Conlon. For the next decade, Tomkins did various jobs for Kassar—what he calls "bits and pieces." In 1989, Tomkins says, Kassar asked him to set up a phony arms company in an office in Amsterdam, and contact a potential buyer with a list of items for sale. The buyers worked for Israeli intelligence. Kassar predicted that they would be interested in only one of the products on the list: ammunition for a type of Russian tank that the Israeli-backed Lebanese Christians had recently captured from Syria. Kassar didn't tell Tomkins about the operation's ultimate purpose, relaying only the next step: rent an office, make this phone call. But it gradually emerged that Kassar planned to lure two Mossad agents to the Amsterdam office, where they would be ambushed by hit men from the Popular Front for the Liberation of Palestine. (Kassar had long-standing ties with several Palestinian terror groups; a U.S. congressional report once referred to him as "the Banker of the PLO.")

Before the Israelis arrived, Tomkins was approached, in Marbella, by his old friend Frank Conlon. "He turned out to be a snitch," Tomkins recalls. Conlon told Tomkins that he had been arrested, and then later interrogated in Belgium, and had informed the authorities about the Amsterdam plot. Conlon suggested that they allow the operation to proceed, so that Kassar and the assassins could be arrested. "I've eaten food off this guy's table," Tomkins says that he replied. "I've never put anyone in jail, and I'm not going to start now. I'll give you twenty-four hours to get out of Spain."

Without mentioning Conlon's betrayal, Tomkins told Kassar to abort the operation. Later, at Palacio de Mifadil, Kassar led Tomkins down to a windowless room beneath the palace, where the two men sat by an underground swimming pool. Tomkins noticed that the pool's tiled floor was decorated with the image of a shark. Kassar questioned Tomkins about why the operation had gone awry, and said that he would find out exactly what had transpired from his contacts in Spanish intelligence. Shortly thereafter, Kassar called Tomkins and told him to go to Budapest. Tomkins checked into the Hilton there, and waited. Soon, Kassar and one of his aides knocked on the door. "He came in and gave me a big hug," Tomkins says. "Then he looked at his mate and said, 'You see? He's not afraid of me.' I said, 'Why should I be? I've never done you any harm.' And he said, 'I know you haven't.'" Kassar paused, then said, "I want you to kill Frank Conlon."

Tomkins refused, explaining that, as a rule, he did not kill British people. He and Kassar continued to work together; Kassar supplied weapons that Tomkins air-dropped to Chechnyan rebels in the 1990s. But Frank Conlon eventually went into hiding. "He never came back," Tomkins said. When asked about this incident, Sara Martinez, one of Kassar's Spanish attorneys, said that she knew nothing about it. But Kassar has been accused of other, similar plots. Bob Baer, a former CIA officer who spent years working in the Middle East, says that during the 1980s Kassar attempted to have a Syrian dissident in Paris assassinated. According to the DEA, Kassar tried twice to kill Elias Awad, a Lebanese member of the Palestine Liberation Front. Awad was Kassar's "drug competitor," Soiles says. The first attempt left Awad paralyzed, and the second sent a rocket through his living room window. A Justice Department affidavit maintains that Kassar ordered the murder because "Awad was interfering with his relationship with Yasir Arafat."

While Kassar had close ties with radical groups, he bore little resemblance to the ascetic jihadis associated with terrorism today. He was primarily a mercenary figure—political, perhaps, but driven more by deal making and the desire to maintain his relationships than by any zealous ideology. He was Muslim, but hardly devout, and his tastes were both Western and secular. His family celebrated Christmas and Easter, and his children learned English before they learned Arabic; he sent them to Western-style schools abroad. Kassar was sufficiently flexible, in fact, that during the Iran-contra affair he supplied covert weapons to the United States. Tom Clines, a weapons specialist formerly with the CIA, visited Marbella and negotiated the deal. Between 1985 and 1986, Kassar was paid $1.5 million through a Swiss bank account controlled by Oliver North and his co-conspirators, and in return he obtained more than a hundred tons of assault rifles and ammunition from Cenzin, in Poland. Asked about Kassar in the 1988 congressional hearings, John Poindexter, the national security adviser for the Reagan administration, said, "When you're buying arms . . . you often have to deal with people you might not want to go to dinner with."

Clines was much more generous. "He was a very gracious host," he told me recently. "The next morning, he came and made me breakfast, which I liked."

Kassar has denied any role in Iran-contra, saying, "I've never met or heard of this man North in my life. I can't even pronounce his name. Anyway, I wouldn't do business with the Americans. I don't accept money from my enemies."

Rumors always trailed Kassar, not least because he had evaded charges for so many years while the authorities tried, and failed, to accumulate enough evidence to prosecute him. One persistent, though erroneous, claim was that in 1988 he helped plant the bomb that blew up Pan Am Flight 103. Kassar cited the accumulated allegations against him as a reason to doubt each new charge. "They have accused me of nearly everything besides the Hiroshima bombing," he told one interviewer. He blamed the conjectures on "envious people," and denied any involvement with terrorism. He rejected the word "trafficker," and insisted that his business was entirely legitimate. On one occasion, he claimed that his "sector" within the arms trade was "guns for hunting animals." When the London *Observer* sent a correspondent to Palacio de Mifadil in 1987, Kassar invited him in and, with a sweep of his hand, asked, "Would a drug dealer and terrorist live openly like this?"

Alexander Yearsley, an arms researcher who investigated Kassar for the watchdog group Global Witness, says, "Monzer was vain enough to want the limelight." In Yearsley's view, Kassar's willingness to talk with the press amounted to a winking acknowledgment of the global impact of his weapons shipments. "Can you imagine how boring it would be to be causing regime change and for no one to know about it?" Yearsley pointed out. Arms dealers are an indispensable, if unsavory, instrument of geopolitics, and Kassar went to great lengths to make himself useful. Many governments, including that of the United States, make clandestine purchases from international arms brokers, because using guns from their own country might betray their involvement in covert operations. "The Kassars' ability to provide governments with access to arms and equipment through irregular channels allows them to do business with high-level government officials who wish to deal 'off the record' with terrorists or other politically sensitive groups," a 1992 investigation by the U.S. House of Representatives concluded. "Governments who receive such services apparently 'look the other way' with respect to the brothers' trafficking activities." (Ghassan remained close to Monzer and active in the arms business until his death, in 2009, of natural causes.)

"Kassar kept walking in, sort of waving a flag, saying, 'I'm a secret agent. I can provide a lot of information to the U.S. government,'" Vincent Cannistraro, a former CIA official, told me. "He wasn't looking for money—he was looking for cover." The agency did not take him up on his offers, Cannistraro maintains, but other governments did occasionally enlist Kassar. It has been widely reported that in the 1980s he assisted the French in securing the release of several hostages held in Lebanon. Some also suggested that he aided in the 1994 capture, by French intelligence, of Ilich Ramírez Sánchez, the Venezuelan terrorist known as Carlos the Jackal. Kassar denied any role in that operation, telling a reporter, "I would not have sold him for all the money in the world."

• • •

In 1992, Kassar was arrested in Madrid. A Spanish magistrate announced that he had been implicated in the Palestine Liberation Front's 1985 hijacking of the ocean liner *Achille Lauro*, which led to the

murder of a wheelchair-bound American, Leon Klinghoffer. One of
the plot's conspirators, who was being held in an Italian prison, had
told investigators that the AK-47 assault rifles and hand grenades used
in the attack had been supplied by an elegantly dressed man named
"Kazer." The authorities showed him a photograph, and he identified Kassar. Jim Soiles had been transferred to Paris by the DEA in
1988. Through a confidential informant in Poland, he obtained a series
of documents indicating that Kassar had opened a bank account for
Abu Abbas, the mastermind of the hijacking. Soiles offered his evidence to the Spanish prosecutors and said that he could testify. Kassar was held in prison for more than a year while the government
assembled its case against him. (After posting a bond of $15.5 million,
he was released.) Meanwhile, several former employees and associates
of Kassar's agreed to testify that he had personally flown to Poland to
procure weapons for the attack.

The trial, which began in December 1994 in Madrid, was a debacle
for law enforcement. Witnesses in Austria and Italy refused to travel
to Spain to testify. Soiles took the stand for close to a week. But the
documentary evidence was thrown out after Kassar's attorneys convinced the court that the confidential informant who supplied the
papers had no legal right to remove them from Kassar's residence in
Warsaw. One of the lawyers objected that Soiles was attributing a fan-
tastical array of crimes to Kassar. Soiles shot back: "If he's guilty of
only *half* the things he's been accused of, then he's still the biggest
criminal in all of Europe."

Kassar mocked the prosecution, arguing, in effect, that someone
of his wealth and public profile would never stoop to an operational
role in such an attack. "I am not sick or dumb enough to risk my plane,
which is worth five million dollars, to go to Poland to pick up four
Kalashnikovs," he testified. He accused the Spanish magistrate who
had initiated the suit of trying to extort $100 million from him in
exchange for dropping the case. But the most remarkable feature of
the proceedings was the string of misfortunes that began to strike the
witnesses for the prosecution.

One of the chief witnesses against Kassar, a former household
employee named Ismail Jalid, was found dead shortly before the
trial, having fallen from a fifth-story window in Marbella. His death

was initially ruled a suicide, then reclassified as a homicide. Kassar denied any involvement in the murder, and no link to him has ever been proved. The two children of a second witness were kidnapped on their way home from school, in Madrid. The witness, a former associate named Mustafa Nasimi, accused Kassar of orchestrating the kidnapping, a charge that Kassar angrily denied. A third witness, a former aide named Abu Merced, claimed that Kassar had warned him not to testify. Merced changed his testimony so frequently that the judges deemed him unreliable. In March 1995, Kassar was acquitted on all counts. He called the proceedings "a blackmail and a farce," and said, "The most important thing is that I have proven my innocence."

Mustafa Nasimi's children were returned to him after several days, and the local police ultimately concluded that the kidnappers, who worked for a Colombian drug cartel, had no connection to Kassar. One morning three years later, in Madrid, Nasimi was leaving his house when a gunman approached and shot him in the head. No link between the murder and Kassar has been established.

•   •   •

After Kassar's trial, Jim Soiles was eventually posted to Athens, but he continued to collect files on the Prince of Marbella. As the years went by, however, he began to give up hope of catching him. Then, in the summer of 2003, he got a call from the Justice Department. The ringleader of the *Achille Lauro* operation, Abu Abbas, had been captured in a raid by American forces in Iraq, and officials were exploring what charges might be brought against him. Abbas died in U.S. custody some months later. (After conducting an autopsy, the military concluded that he had died of heart disease.) But, seizing on renewed interest in the *Achille Lauro* incident, the DEA argued that Kassar was an even worthier target for prosecution. Since the terrorist attacks of September 11, 2001, new statutes had enhanced the power of "extraterritorial jurisdiction," enabling American authorities to investigate and try suspects for crimes committed outside the United States. Soiles agreed to work with federal prosecutors and the DEA's Special Operations Division, known as SOD, to put together a case drawing on that extraterritorial law-enforcement authority. "This ain't for the weak of heart," Soiles warned his colleagues. "This is for the long haul. And it's going to cost."

For the next two years, Soiles and a team of agents from the SOD pored over old case files, studying Kassar's operation. But gathering sufficient evidence of his involvement in various crimes was difficult, and pursuing Kassar for the *Achille Lauro* charges might be barred, because it would amount to double jeopardy. By early 2006, Soiles and his colleagues had decided that they needed to attempt something radical. Rather than try Kassar for a crime he'd committed in the past, they would use the strong conspiracy laws in the United States to prosecute him for something that he intended to do in the future. They would infiltrate Kassar's organization and set him up in a sting. Many European countries have "agent provocateur" laws to guard against entrapment, but in an American court it would be difficult for a trafficker with Kassar's history to protest that he was in no way predisposed to clandestine weapons deals. In a nod to the three decades that the agency had spent investigating Kassar, Soiles's team called the plan Operation Legacy.

The DEA has confidential sources in countries around the world. Some are former criminals who were arrested at one time or another, then sent back into the underworld on the agency's payroll. "In terms of actual contacts and informants on the ground, there are many regions where DEA has a better network than CIA," Jonathan Winer, a former State Department official who was responsible for international law enforcement in the Clinton administration, told me. During the course of his career, Soiles had amassed dozens of trusted informants. In 2006, he turned to a portly sixty-nine-year-old Palestinian named Samir. (At the DEA's request, I am omitting the last names of confidential sources.) A former member of the militant group Black September, Samir was originally arrested by Soiles in 1984 for smuggling heroin into New York. He was held at the Metropolitan Correctional Center, in lower Manhattan, where he refused to cooperate. Soiles decided to pay him a visit. He brought his lunch, sat down in front of Samir, and ate it. Samir said nothing. When Soiles finished, he got up and left, but a few days later he came back, and again a few days after that, and every time he brought his lunch. "Being of Greek descent, I had some understanding of his culture," Soiles told me with a smile. "I knew the kinds of foods that he probably would like. So I go there and I bring the little shish kebab, and I'd have the nice warm bread, I'd have the cheese. And I always brought enough for two people." For a month, Samir said nothing, and each time, Soiles ceremoniously threw the extra food into the trash. Finally, one day, Samir said, "What do you want?" The two have been working together ever since.

•   •   •

The plan was for Samir to travel to southern Lebanon and meet an associate of Kassar's named Tareq al-Ghazi. Samir would pretend that he was representing an arms buyer and ingratiate himself with Ghazi before asking for an introduction to Kassar. It took Samir ten months, but in December 2006 he telephoned Soiles and said, "I'm going to meet him."

Before the meeting, Samir would need an end-user certificate. Arms manufacturers require these documents, which often consist of a single sheet of paper, to establish that a buyer is legally entitled to purchase weapons. In practice, corrupt officials in countries around the world issue certificates for a fee, and they are often not thoroughly inspected. According to the UN, when Kassar wanted to send arms into war-torn Croatia in 1992, he presented a Polish supplier with a certificate issued by the People's Democratic Republic of Yemen, even though, two years earlier, North and South Yemen had reunited and the People's Democratic Republic had ceased to exist. The supplier provided the weapons anyway.

Even when the documents are legitimate, arms manufacturers seldom try to ascertain whether their products end up in the country that issued the certificate. "Everything in the business is 99 percent straight, until the moment of delivery," David Tomkins told me. Soiles and his colleagues hoped to catch Kassar using an end-user certificate from one country to smuggle arms into another, a tactic known as diversion. A young SOD agent named John Archer approached the government of Nicaragua and, without divulging any details of the operation, asked if it could provide an end-user certificate listing rifles, rocket-propelled grenade launchers, and other weapons. Then, on December 28, 2006, Samir went to the Diplomat Suite Hotel, in

Beirut, where Ghazi introduced him to Kassar, saying, "Samir is one of the freedom fighters. He was with us in the Palestinian resistance."

Kassar greeted Samir warmly. Samir was wearing a microphone as he explained that he represented a buyer who was interested in purchasing weapons and had insisted on doing business with Kassar. "He told me *Monzer*," Samir said. "He wants *Monzer*."

Kassar was flattered but guarded about Samir's unnamed buyer. "How do you know him?" he asked. "And since when?"

"I know him very well," Samir reassured him.

Kassar suggested that they meet again, in Marbella. The SOD team decided that their fictitious buyers should represent the FARC, which finances its arms transactions through the sale of drugs and is engaged in a protracted war with the government of Colombia and with Special Forces teams from the United States. The challenge was to find a couple of informants who could convincingly play the part. "It's almost like being a casting director," one of the agents told me. "You're putting your movie together and you're thinking, 'This is what the ending has to be. How are we going to *get* there?'" The choice was especially tricky in this instance, because the SOD wanted the informants to secretly videotape the negotiations. They needed people who had the nerve to walk into the home of a dangerous criminal, the acting ability to play criminals themselves, the presence of mind to improvise should the situation go awry, and a sufficient grasp of the American legal system to ensure that the whole charade would be explicable to a jury. They turned to two Guatemalan informants whom the agency had used before, Carlos and Luis. The agency pays its informants handsomely for their work, a point that is particularly troubling to Kassar's supporters. Carlos would receive $170,000 for the operation against Kassar. ("In Spain, we call them *mercenarios*," Kassar's Spanish lawyer, Sara Martínez, told me.)

A gruff gallows humor can develop between agent and informant after years of working together. When Carlos agreed to the undercover sting against Kassar, his handler joked that he should practice jumping off a building, to see if he could survive the fall. In January 2007, the agents assembled Carlos, Luis, and Samir in an Athens hotel room. Because Samir had initiated the operation, he could veto the agents' choices. He approved Carlos and Luis but insisted that they buy new shoes, observing that "if they show up with a nice suit but old shoes," Kassar would see through them immediately.

The three men ran lines, plotting the elements of a prosecutable conspiracy, with the agents coaching them to remember key pieces of dialogue: they must say that the weapons were meant to kill Americans; they must indicate that they intended to pay for the arms with drug money. "We flow charted it," John Archer recalled. The following month, Kassar welcomed the three informants to Marbella.

The initial meeting was not recorded, since the agents were concerned that the men might be searched. As it happened, they weren't. According to subsequent testimony, Samir introduced Carlos and Luis, who said that they worked for the FARC. Their end-user certificate from Nicaragua was a ruse, they explained; the weapons would go to Colombia. Carlos drew a map, showing the route that the shipment should take, from Europe to Suriname, then overland to Colombia. Kassar planned to obtain the arms from manufacturers in Bulgaria and Romania. As long as he presented them with the certificate from Nicaragua, all the parties to the deal would have plausible deniability. Kassar asked if the FARC was receiving any financial help from the Americans. Carlos told him that, on the contrary, the weapons would be used against the United States. Kassar agreed to the transaction.

So far, the meeting had gone off perfectly. Then Kassar asked Carlos how much he had paid for the end-user certificate. Carlos paused. He did not know the going rate for this sort of bribe. When they flow charted the dialogue in this exchange, this was a scenario they had not prepped for. Kassar was waiting for an answer.

"Several million dollars," Carlos said, finally.

Kassar scoffed, saying that with that kind of money he "could have bought a whole country." It was a significant blunder, but Carlos recovered, explaining that this was the price he had paid for multiple certificates, not just one. After a moment, Kassar seemed to relax, and suggested that if in the future Carlos needed to buy more certificates, he could get them for "a much better price."

The men went to a bar to smoke hookahs. Kassar put his arm around Carlos. "He told me he liked me," Carlos later testified. "He said he could provide me with a thousand men to help fight against the United States."

• • •

At a second meeting, the following month, Carlos hid a small video camera inside his bag and captured Kassar extolling the merits of anti-aircraft weapons in the Palacio's grand salon. When Carlos mentioned that he wanted to buy C-4 explosives, Kassar told him that it would be cheaper and safer to follow the example of insurgents in Iraq, and manufacture the explosives locally in Colombia. "We can send experts to make it over there," he volunteered. Kassar had an aide drive Carlos and Luis to an internet café in Marbella, so that they could wire a down payment of €100,000 to an account that he maintained under someone else's name. (He didn't want them to use a computer in his house, to avoid having the transaction traced back to him.) The DEA authorized a money transfer from an undercover account.

On May 2, Carlos and Luis met Kassar at a café, where he introduced them to a Greek ship's captain, Christos Paissis. "We've been working together for twenty-five years," Kassar said. "He's completely trustworthy." While the men drank Perrier and discussed the clandestine logistics of sending the weapons to Suriname aboard a smuggling ship called the *Anastasia,* the camera in Carlos's bag recorded their conversation.

By that time, the agents had enough evidence to prosecute Kassar in the United States. But after the disastrous *Achille Lauro* trial, Soiles was reluctant to arrest him in Spain. "That was his power base," he said. It was decided that Carlos would attempt to lure Kassar to Greece or Romania, where the trafficker might enjoy less protection. In June, Carlos informed Kassar that one of the leaders of the FARC would be traveling to Bucharest, where the organization had $3.5 million in drug proceeds that could serve as a partial payment for the weapons. But Kassar became uneasy, and claimed that he couldn't obtain a visa for his Argentine passport. He suggested sending one of his employees instead. As the hours dragged on, he grew increasingly frustrated that Carlos and Luis had not provided the balance of the payment for the deal. "I can't do anything without the money," he told Carlos.

Eventually, Soiles's team decided that they would have no choice but to execute the "takedown"—the final phase of the operation—in

Spain. The DEA had no jurisdiction to make an arrest, however. Normally, if law-enforcement officers know in advance that a fugitive will be in a foreign country, they file a "provisional arrest warrant" with Interpol and hope that local authorities will honor the warrant and make the arrest. But Kassar's connections in the Spanish government ran so deep that the DEA chose to notify very few Spanish officials that it was conducting its months-long sting. The agency was reluctant even to file an arrest warrant with Interpol, fearing that one of Kassar's contacts might tip him off.

On June 4, Carlos proposed to Kassar that he meet the FARC leader in Madrid. Sensing that something was wrong, Kassar telephoned one of his intelligence contacts, a Spanish counterterrorism official named José Villarejo. Kassar had already informed Villarejo of the impending deal, though he said that the arms were bound for Nicaragua. He explained that the buyer urgently wanted to meet him in Madrid. "I don't want some trap or something," he said, according to a transcript of the call, which Villarejo recorded. "Is it dangerous to go to Madrid?"

Villarejo knew nothing of the American operation, but he cautioned his friend, "Whenever there's any urgency to do something, that always means there's a trap."

Nevertheless, in a momentary lapse of caution, Kassar drove to the Málaga airport and boarded a flight to Madrid. "We didn't do anything until the plane was wheels up," Archer, the SOD agent, told me. As soon as the agents had word that Kassar was in the air, they filed a provisional arrest warrant with Interpol and staked out the airport in Madrid. They had briefed a local fugitive-apprehension team that morning, telling them that a major suspect would be passing through the airport. With less than an hour before the plane landed, they informed the team that the target was Monzer al-Kassar, and Archer and other DEA agents, who were dressed in civilian clothes, took up positions in the arrivals area. As passengers filed off the plane, the agents caught sight of Kassar and two aides, and as he made his way to the baggage claim, the team conferred by cell phone with Spanish officers, who were monitoring his movements on the airport's surveillance system. When Kassar leaned down to retrieve his luggage, the Spanish police arrested him.

The following day, the DEA team went to Marbella to execute a search warrant on Palacio de Mifadil. Under Spanish law, a criminal suspect is entitled to be present while the authorities search his residence. Never one to stint on hospitality, Kassar offered everyone drinks.

• • •

In June 2008, Monzer al-Kassar was flown, in shackles, from Spain to Westchester County Airport in New York, on a chartered jet. Jim Soiles and John Archer were on the plane. Kassar had fought extradition for a year, staged a hunger strike, and claimed that his capture was an act of "political vengeance" by President George W. Bush. In a special hearing in Madrid, Villarejo testified that Kassar had assisted Spain in intelligence investigations. Villarejo would not say what, precisely, Kassar had done, but he acknowledged that Spanish intelligence had a code name for the Syrian—Luis—and that on several occasions he had traveled outside Spain with Kassar on intelligence business. A second official, Enrique Castaño, whose work was so sensitive that he testified from behind a screen, said that Kassar had supplied Spain with information "concerning the activities of terrorist organizations."

"Thanks to my contacts and influence, we have been able to resolve kidnappings in the Arab world and avoid terrorist attacks in and out of Spain," Kassar told *El Mundo* when the extradition was finalized. "I fear I have been sold very cheaply." (When asked about Kassar, a representative of the Spanish government had no comment.)

Kassar's trial, in a federal court in lower Manhattan, was an illustration of American national security law at its most far-reaching. Kassar had never set foot in the United States, and apart from wire transfers that the DEA sent from New York, no element of the crime had unfolded on U.S. soil. In addition, four of the five charges against Kassar were conspiracy charges: conspiracy to kill Americans, conspiracy to kill officers and employees of the United States, conspiracy to supply material support to terrorists, and conspiracy to acquire and use anti-aircraft missiles. (The fifth charge was money laundering.) It was the first case in which federal prosecutors employed a powerful 2004 statute holding that anyone who conspires to sell surface-to-air missiles must receive a twenty-five-year sentence.

When asked how he pleaded to the charges, Kassar shouted, "Not guilty!" He blew kisses to supporters watching the trial and referred to the judge, Jed Rakoff, as "My Lord." He hired Ira Sorkin, a well-known criminal-defense attorney, who went on to represent Bernard Madoff. "There is no case here," Sorkin protested. "This was a sting operation against an individual in Spain, created out of whole cloth by the DEA." The lawyers for the prosecution presented an extraordinary reconstruction of the operation. They showed video clips of Kassar in his living room, talking about shooting down helicopters. They played audio recordings of calls that Carlos made to the secure phone. They presented catalogs that Kassar had shown to the informants, with vivid graphics of the weapons that he intended to sell. "You will see and you will hear what happened in these meetings, and you will watch the weapons deal unfold, in real time," Brendan McGuire, an assistant U.S. attorney for the Southern District of New York, told the jury. "These recordings will take you into the heart of this weapons deal designed to kill Americans."

John Archer testified about searching Palacio de Mifadil after Kassar's arrest and finding the Nicaraguan end-user certificate and the map that Carlos had drawn showing the smuggling route. Each juror received a three-ring binder that contained nearly a thousand pages of transcripts and translations.

Sorkin countered this barrage by arguing that Kassar had been stringing Carlos and Luis along with the intention of reporting them to his law-enforcement contacts in Spain. According to Sorkin, the jurors were witnessing not a sting but a double sting. When Kassar had been fighting extradition in Spain, however, he maintained that he had believed all along that the shipment was legitimate, and bound for Nicaragua.

During the extradition hearing in Spain, Sorkin had intimated, in his questioning of the two Spanish intelligence officials, that Kassar had also assisted the CIA. In the trial, Sorkin wanted to introduce evidence that would demonstrate Kassar's cooperation with U.S. authorities, but the Department of Justice objected that the evidence contained classified material. The court ultimately ruled that the evidence was irrelevant. In conversations with me, several of Kassar's friends and associates suggested that he had indeed assisted the CIA over the years. (The agency will neither confirm nor deny such suggestions.) When I asked Soiles about the matter, he said, "Did he have a relationship? We don't know. And we couldn't comment on that."

Samir and Carlos both testified in the trial. Sorkin emphasized that the first visit to Marbella, when Kassar allegedly promised to supply Carlos with a thousand men, was also the one meeting during which no recording equipment was used. "Do you sometimes find it difficult, when you play these parts for the DEA, to determine when you are telling the truth and when you are telling a lie?" he asked Carlos. Luis had planned to appear as well. But, after Kassar's arrest in Spain, he had returned to Guatemala; one day, early in 2008, he was attending a rooster fight, when two men approached and shot him dead. No connection to Kassar has been established.

• • •

Because Kassar was charged with conspiracy to kill Americans, it was important to the prosecutors and to the DEA that he come across as an ideological enemy of the United States. "Monzer al-Kassar commands a global munitions empire, arming and funding insurgents and terrorists . . . particularly those who wish to harm Americans," Karen Tandy, then the DEA administrator, said after his capture. "He operates in the shadows, the silent partner behind the business of death and terror." To combat the image of his client as a terrorist bent on hurting America, Sorkin called Kassar's twenty-four-year-old daughter, Haiffa, to the stand. "All my teachers were American," she said. "All my friends are American." When she was asked whether she had ever heard her father discuss the FARC, she responded, "I don't even know what FARC is."

"Do you even know what business he is in?" McGuire asked.

"No," she said. "No, I didn't know anything."

The jury deliberated for six hours over two days. According to an account published by one of the jurors, they chose to exclude the testimony of Carlos and Luis and to focus, instead, entirely on the recordings. When they filed back into the courtroom, Kassar's lips were moving, as he mouthed a silent prayer. Judge Rakoff asked for the verdict, and the foreman said that the jury had found Kassar guilty on all counts. Haiffa let out a sob.

In February 2009, Judge Rakoff sentenced Kassar to thirty years in prison. "Mr. al-Kassar is a very sophisticated person," Rakoff said. "A man of many faces." He cited the "overwhelming nature of the proof in this case, vast amounts of which were videotaped," and suggested that it would have been "totally irrational" for the jury to arrive at anything other than a guilty verdict.

Kassar was permitted to make a few remarks. "In all religions . . . God demands justice," he said. He suggested, once again, that he had been an intelligence asset. The classified material that the jury was not allowed to see would have shown that he had "saved lots of human lives," he said, demonstrating that he harbored no "animosity against America." After proclaiming his innocence one final time, Kassar concluded on a defiant note, saying, "Justice sometimes goes slow, but sure."

The prosecutors had agreed to bring their case against Kassar without mentioning the *Achille Lauro* incident, lest it prejudice the jury. But each day of the trial, two middle-aged women entered the courtroom and sat quietly, watching the proceedings. They were Ilsa and Lisa Klinghoffer, the daughters of Leon Klinghoffer. For years, they had followed the story of the ruthless Syrian who had been implicated in their father's death, and who still lived openly in Spain. "Even when he was caught, right up to the sentencing, he had this swagger," Lisa Klinghoffer told me. "Like he was untouchable."

Sara Martínez insisted recently that while Kassar had done things that "were not correct," he has been a legitimate businessman for the past fifteen years. She said that throughout the sting Kassar believed that the buyers represented Nicaragua. This appears to contradict the double-sting argument that Ira Sorkin raised at trial—an interpretation of events that Kassar's current lawyer, Roger Stavis, reiterated. Stavis maintains that Kassar traveled to Madrid not to complete the deal but to "see that the informants were arrested." He called Kassar's capture "a serious miscarriage of justice."

Everyone I spoke to who has worked with Kassar over the years expressed surprise that someone so cautious could be caught on tape agreeing to sell weapons to the FARC. One possible explanation is that compared with the last decades of the twentieth century—when conflicts in Africa, Europe, and the Middle East generated steady revenue—these are difficult times for weapons traffickers. When Samir first approached Tareq al-Ghazi in Lebanon, Ghazi told him that Kassar had been struggling to maintain his profit margins. A diminished demand for black-market weapons may be driving other arms traffickers to assume risks that they would never have taken in the past. A year after the capture of Kassar, the SOD team arrested Viktor Bout, the Tajik arms dealer, in Bangkok—using the exact same sort of sting. (He was extradited to New York and ultimately sentenced to twenty-five years in prison.) Tom Clines, the former CIA officer who negotiated the Iran-contra deal, believes that Kassar must have been in desperate need of cash to fall for such a trap. He expressed regret that U.S. authorities had imprisoned a man with such a wealth of underworld connections. "Don't cut the guy off at the fingers," he said. "Let him proceed, and work with him." Though the two men had met on only one occasion, Clines remembered Kassar fondly. "I hope the Syrians help him get back home," he said.

· · ·

Not long ago, I spoke with Haiffa al-Kassar, who remains fiercely loyal to her father. "It's a movie," she said of the videotaped evidence at the trial. "He hasn't done anything." She expressed skepticism at the idea of convicting someone for a crime before he has had an opportunity to carry it out. "It's only in America that they believe in conspiracy," she told me. "We don't believe in it here in Spain."

Haiffa described her father as warm and playful. She was allowed to visit him on only a few occasions when she was in New York for the trial, but at seven o'clock on some evenings she would stand outside the lower Manhattan jail where he was being held. Kassar's cell was on the ninth floor, and had a high window. He would switch the lights on and off, so that Haiffa knew which window to watch. Then he would jump up high enough to catch a glimpse of his daughter blowing him a kiss from the sidewalk below.

The palace in Marbella is empty now. The property is big and difficult to maintain, Haiffa explained, and it was too painful to remain there. The Kassar family has moved to a nearby villa. Haiffa's mother, Raghdaa, has been denied entry to the United States, so she could not attend the trial or visit Kassar in South Carolina, where he is serving his sentence at a medium-security federal prison. Kassar is healthy, friends say, and is appealing his conviction. He talks to his Mexican cellmate in Spanish, and has a job cleaning windows. He has been cooking for other inmates. Recently, he began teaching them languages as well. "I still believe in justice, and I will never stop legally fighting till the last breath," Kassar wrote to me recently. "No one can hide from the truth forever."

In the years between the *Achille Lauro* trial and the beginning of Operation Legacy, Jim Soiles kept an old safe in his coat closet at home, stuffed with files about Monzer al-Kassar. From time to time, he would open the safe, flip through the files, and think that perhaps it was time to shred them. But something always stopped him. "He was one of those guys who escaped," Soiles told me. "And there was a part of me that said maybe, someday, he'll come around again."

Monzer al-Kasser's appeals were unsuccessful. He is still serving his sentence, in Marion, Illinois, and is scheduled for release in 2033. He has a lively Facebook page, on which he staunchly maintains his innocence and argues that all of the evidence against him was fabricated by Jim Soiles and a cabal of "Zionists."

THE WORST OF THE WORST

Judy Clarke excelled at saving the lives of notorious killers. Then she took the case of Dzhokhar Tsarnaev. (2015)

"WE MEET IN THE most tragic of circumstances," Judy Clarke, the lead defense lawyer representing Dzhokhar Tsarnaev, began. She stood at a lectern, facing the jurors, in a dark suit accented by a blue-and-purple scarf that she wears so often it seems like a courtroom talisman. To her right, George O'Toole, the judge, looked at her over his spectacles. Behind her was Tsarnaev, the slim, soft-featured young man who was on trial for the bombing at the Boston Marathon on April 15, 2013—the worst domestic terrorist attack since September 11. Outside the courthouse, snow from successive blizzards had piled up in grubby dunes. Clarke, who lives in San Diego, despises cold weather, but she'd endured an entire New England winter. "Judy was in Boston for a year before the case went to trial, meeting with this kid," her friend Jonathan Shapiro, who has taught with Clarke at Washington and Lee University Law School, told me. It was early March, and nearly two years had passed since Tsarnaev, along with his older brother, Tamerlan, detonated two homemade bombs near the finish line of the marathon, killing three people and injuring 264; they then carjacked a Mercedes, murdered an MIT police officer named Sean Collier, and engaged in a shoot-out with the cops. Dzhokhar, nineteen at the time, accidentally killed Tamerlan, who was twenty-six, by running over him in the getaway car. Dzhokhar was discovered, wounded and expecting to die, inside a dry-docked boat in the suburb of Watertown. While he was recovering in the hospital, Miriam Conrad, the chief federal public defender in Massachusetts, contacted Clarke, and Clarke decided to take the case.

Clarke may be the best death-penalty lawyer in America. Her efforts helped spare the lives of Ted Kaczynski (the Unabomber), Zacarias Moussaoui (the so-called twentieth hijacker in the 9/11 plot), and

Jared Loughner (who killed six people and wounded thirteen others, including Representative Gabrielle Giffords, at a Tucson mall in 2011). "Every time Judy takes a new case, it's a soul-searching process for her," Clarke's old friend Elisabeth Semel told me. "Because it's an enormous responsibility." On rare occasions when Clarke withdrew or was removed from a defense team, a defendant received the death penalty. But in cases that she tried through the sentencing phase, she had never lost a client to death row.

The administration of capital punishment is notoriously prone to error. According to the Death Penalty Information Center, 155 death-row inmates have been exonerated, and it stands to reason that innocent people still face execution. Clarke does not represent such individuals. Her specialty is what the Supreme Court has called "the worst of the worst": child rapists, torturers, terrorists, mass murderers, and others who have committed crimes so appalling that even death-penalty opponents might be tempted to make an exception.

Tsarnaev was indisputably guilty; the lead prosecutor, William Weinreb, described in his opening statement a video in which Tsarnaev is seen depositing a backpack directly behind an eight-year-old boy on Boylston Street and walking away before it explodes. In January 2014, Attorney General Eric Holder, who had publicly expressed his personal opposition to the death penalty, announced that the government would seek to execute Tsarnaev, explaining that the scale of the horror had compelled the decision. The prosecution referred to Tsarnaev as Dzhokhar, his given name, which is Chechen and means "jewel." But as Clarke addressed the jury, she used the nickname that he had adopted as a high school student in Cambridge, Massachusetts: Jahar. In a capital case, a defense attorney seeks to humanize the client to the point that jurors might hesitate to condemn him to death. Clarke has said that her job is to transform the defendant from an unfathomable monster into "one of us." Her use of the nickname also signaled genuine familiarity. Clarke spends hundreds of hours getting to know reviled criminals. Her friend Tina Hunt, a federal public defender in Georgia who has known Clarke for thirty years, said, "Judy is fascinated by what makes people tick—what drives people to commit these kinds of crimes. People aren't *born* evil. She has a very deep and abiding faith in that idea."

Most of Clarke's success in death-penalty cases has come from negotiating plea deals. She often cites a legal adage: the first step in losing a death-penalty case is picking a jury. To avoid a trial, Clarke does not shy away from the muscular exertion of leverage. In 2005, she secured a plea deal for Eric Rudolph, who detonated bombs at abortion clinics and at the Atlanta Summer Olympics, after Rudolph promised to disclose the location of an explosive device that he had buried near a residential neighborhood in North Carolina. Soon after joining Tsarnaev's team, Clarke indicated that her client was prepared to plead guilty in exchange for a sentence of life without parole. Federal officials declined this offer. Clarke then pushed to move the trial out of Boston, arguing that local jurors would have an "overwhelming prejudice" against Tsarnaev. Judge O'Toole disagreed.

Clarke looked at the jurors one by one. "For the next several weeks, we're all going to come face to face with unbearable grief, loss, and pain caused by a series of senseless, horribly misguided acts carried out by two brothers," she said. She is tall, with straight brown hair and long arms that dangle, a little comically, like the boughs of a weeping willow. Clarke's style with a jury is warm, conversational, devoid of bombast. Whenever she paused for emphasis, the muted clatter of typing would fill the room as journalists with laptops live-tweeted the proceedings. "There's little that occurred the week of April the 15th— the bombings, the murder of Officer Collier, the carjacking, the shootout in Watertown—that we dispute," she said. Clarke was acknowledging her client's guilt. So why bother with a trial? Each juror had a digital monitor for viewing evidence, and Clarke flashed a photograph of Jahar as a young boy, dark-eyed and floppy-haired, sitting next to a much larger Tamerlan. Clarke said, "What took Jahar Tsarnaev from *this*—to Jahar Tsarnaev and his brother with backpacks walking down Boylston?"

Before-and-after photographs are standard exhibits in Clarke's repertoire. The effect is deliberately jarring, like seeing the yearbook photograph of a movie star before he became famous. Clarke promised the jury that she would not try to minimize or excuse Tsarnaev's conduct. Instead—in a vanishingly fine distinction—she hoped to present his life in a way that might mitigate his moral culpability. The jurors stared past her at Tsarnaev. He sat at the defense table, fiddling with his unruly dark hair, in a blazer and a shirt that was unbuttoned a little rakishly for a murder trial. "It's going to be a lot to ask of you to hold your minds and hearts open," Clarke said. "But that is what we ask."

•   •   •

Among death-penalty lawyers, Clarke is known, without irony, as Saint Judy, on the basis of her humility, her generosity, and her devotion to her clients. She has not given an interview to the mainstream press in twenty years. But in a 2013 commencement speech at Gonzaga University School of Law, Clarke said that her clients have obliged her to "redefine what a win means." Victory usually means a life sentence. Even so, Clarke said, she owes a debt of gratitude to her clients, for "the lessons they've taught me—about human behavior and human frailty—and the constant reminder that there but for the grace of God go I."

In some ways, Clarke's public persona resembles that of Sister Helen Prejean, the Catholic nun from New Orleans who runs the Ministry Against the Death Penalty. In her 1993 book, *Dead Man Walking*, Prejean describes the bond that she formed with a killer who had been condemned to death. The "weight of his loneliness, his abandonment, draws me," she writes. She abhors his crimes, yet senses a "sheer and essential humanness" in him. But Clarke is no nun. Her convictions are rooted in constitutional law, not the Bible, and in the courtroom she is unabashedly gladiatorial. In 1990, she told the *Los Angeles Times,* "I love the fight." Though she lacks the flamboyant manner often associated with trial lawyers, she is not above courtroom theater. In 2003, when she represented Jay Lentz—a former navy intelligence officer accused of murdering his wife—Clarke summoned to the stand Lentz's twelve-year-old daughter, Julia, who was four years old at the time of the killing. Julia told the jury that her father meant everything to her. The judge had warned Clarke that Julia was not to address her father, but Clarke defied this directive, asking her if she had anything to tell him. "I love you, Daddy," she said. The jury spared his life.

Clarke is driven by an intense philosophical opposition to the death penalty. She once observed that "legalized homicide is not a good idea for a civilized nation." Her friend David Ruhnke, who has tried more than a dozen capital cases, said, "It's not often you get to occupy the moral high ground as a criminal-defense lawyer, but I think in death-penalty law we do." According to friends, Clarke is also drawn to the intellectual problem posed by unconscionable crime. When Eric Rudolph went on the run from authorities in the mountains of North Carolina, Clarke told Tina Hunt, "If they ever catch him, I want to represent him." Hunt recalls saying, "Are you fucking nuts? He's a fanatic! He blows up abortion clinics! Judy, we need to make you some flash cards that just say 'NO.'"

According to Hunt, Clarke is perpetually seeking "the key that turns the lock that opens the door that would let a person do something like this." In this regard, Clarke evokes the French attorney Jacques Vergès, who represented Klaus Barbie (the Butcher of Lyon), Carlos the Jackal, and the Khmer Rouge leader Khieu Samphan. Vergès, who died in 2013, took a certain glee in upending the comforting pieties of criminal justice, by insisting that his clients were more human than others might be prepared to admit. "What was so shocking about Hitler 'the monster' was that he loved his dog so much and kissed the hands of his secretaries," Vergès once remarked. "The interesting thing about my clients is discovering what brings them to do these horrific things." As the Tsarnaev trial began, Clarke told the jury that she would not contest the "who" or the "what" of the case. She would focus on the "why."

• • •

Clarke, who is sixty-three, grew up in Asheville, North Carolina. From an early age, she told the *San Antonio Express-News,* she "thought it would be neat to be Perry Mason and win all the time." At Furman College in Greenville, South Carolina, she studied psychology and led a successful campaign to change the name of the student government to the Association of Furman Students, on the ground that the group had no actual governing authority. She married her college boyfriend, Thomas "Speedy" Rice—a jovial round-faced man who also became an attorney. After she completed law school, at the University of South Carolina, they moved to San Diego, where, in 1977, she joined a small office of federal public defenders. "At that time, you could count the number of women criminal-defense lawyers practicing in San Diego County on one hand," Elisabeth Semel, who met Clarke during this period and now runs the death-penalty clinic at the University of California Berkeley School of Law, recalls. Semel and Clarke went for ten-mile jogs on weekends. "We needed the camaraderie, because it was a hostile environment," Semel said, adding that the judicial establishment in San Diego was notably conservative.

Clarke worked tirelessly on behalf of undocumented immigrants, drug dealers, and others charged with federal crimes who could not afford a private attorney. She was soon running the office, doubling the number of lawyers, and tripling the budget. She asked new hires to sign a so-called blood letter, committing to work at least sixty hours a week. Clarke routinely put in eighty. In 1991, Clarke joined a large law firm, McKenna Long & Aldridge, where she could apply her formidable skills to defending white-collar clients. But, according to Bob Brewer, the partner who recruited Clarke, "she had a real problem charging people for her time." They devised a system in which Clarke would meet a new client, hear about the case, then politely excuse herself, allowing Brewer to swoop in and negotiate a fee. Clarke lasted a little more than a year. These days, when discussing her career, she has been known to deadpan, "I was sentenced to fifteen months of private practice at McKenna Long & Aldridge."

In 1992, Clarke moved to Spokane and took over the federal defenders' office for eastern Washington and Idaho. At the time, one of her law school friends, David Bruck, remarked that this was like Mozart arriving in town to direct the Spokane Symphony Orchestra. Bruck is a soft-spoken Montreal native with thick white hair. He moved to South Carolina in 1972 to attend law school and became one of the state's most prominent capital-defense attorneys. In 1994, he took on the case of Susan Smith, a twenty-three-year-old woman from the small city of Union, who was charged with murdering her two sons—both toddlers—by letting her car slide into a lake while they were strapped into the backseat. Initially, Smith claimed that a black man had carjacked her and kidnapped the children, but after a frantic, racially divisive manhunt she confessed that her boys could be found in the lake. The state sought the death penalty, which meant that Smith was entitled to a second attorney; Bruck turned to his old friend Judy Clarke. When she protested that she had never tried a death-penalty case, Bruck said, "That's not what I need. I need you."

In the Smith trial, Clarke developed many of the techniques that have become hallmarks of her work. She promised jurors that she wouldn't trivialize what Smith had done or present an "abuse excuse." Even so, she argued that the jury had an obligation to understand not just Smith's awful act but her whole life leading up to that moment. Smith's father, a mill worker, had killed himself when she was little. Her mother remarried, and her stepfather molested her. She had twice attempted suicide, and at the lake, Clarke argued, Smith had intended to die with her children; at the last second, a survival instinct propelled her out of the car, at which point it was too late to save the kids.

The prosecutors presented a devastating case. An ex-boyfriend of Smith's, the son of a wealthy mill owner, testified that a week before the killing he had sent Smith a breakup letter in which he wrote, "There are some things about you that aren't suited for me, and yes I mean your children." A diver testified about finding the car, overturned, at the bottom of the lake and spotting "a small hand pressed against the glass."

The defense summoned one of Smith's prison guards, who attested to her remorse. "Everyone has a breaking point," Clarke told the jury. "Susan broke where many of us might bend." Her star witness was Smith's stepfather. He tearfully confessed to molesting Smith and, addressing her directly, said, "You do not have all the guilt in this tragedy." Smith received a life sentence. In a subsequent interview, Clarke suggested that while it is sometimes prudent to move a trial away from where the alleged crime took place, in this instance it helped that Smith was tried by South Carolinians. "She was one of them," Clarke said.

After the case concluded, Clarke paid a Christmas visit to Smith in jail. Mindful of her clients' isolation, she remembers birthdays and holidays. South Carolina later passed a law barring courts from appointing out-of-state lawyers in capital cases.

• • •

A death-penalty trial consists of two parts: the "guilt phase," in which the jury determines whether the defendant committed the crime, and the "penalty phase," in which the jurors vote on a sentence. Although Clarke had effectively conceded Tsarnaev's guilt in her opening statement, this did not stop prosecutors from summoning people who had lost limbs, or family members, in the bombing. Some entered the courtroom in wheelchairs, others on prosthetic legs. With astonishing composure, they described how their bodies had been damaged by shrapnel from the blast. Before-and-after photographs are potent exhibits for prosecutors as well, and as William Campbell testified about how his twenty-nine-year-old daughter, Krystle, was killed, jurors saw a photograph of her at her First Communion, wearing a fluffy white dress.

After every witness, Clarke murmured, "We have no questions." Sometimes she thanked witnesses for their testimony. To cross-examine them would have been pointless, even offensive. "Defense attorneys have a fraught relationship with victims—not just in an individual case, but almost as a metaphysical concept," Reuben Camper Cahn, who runs the federal defenders' office in San Diego, told me. "You've got to be respectful and aware of them, but at the same time you've got to focus on your client." Cahn worked with Clarke on the defense of Jared Loughner, and says that she is "especially good at remaining open to the suffering of the victims, and thinking about how each move that she and her colleagues make will be perceived not just by jurors but by victims."

In the Tsarnaev case, Clarke was joined by Miriam Conrad, the federal defender in Boston, and David Bruck. They maintained a quiet intimacy with their client. Some nights when court was in session, Tsarnaev slept in a holding cell in the bowels of the courthouse, allowing him to be closer to Clarke and her team, who stayed at a nearby hotel. But Tsarnaev wasn't easy to manage. Each day, he sauntered to the defense table and slouched in his chair, his rangy limbs arrayed in a posture of insouciance, like a kid behind the wheel of a lowrider. Some commentators felt that Tsarnaev was smirking, though his lawyers noted in court that his features had been slightly twisted by nerve damage sustained when he was shot in the face by the police. One witness, a broad-shouldered man in his thirties named Marc Fucarile, had lost a leg in the blast; he revealed that he might yet lose the other. Prosecutors projected X-rays of his skeleton, and the dark spaces between his bones were perforated by bright-blue dots: BBs and other shrapnel that remained inside him. Fucarile, who had undergone nearly seventy operations, was in a wheelchair, but he glared at Tsarnaev as though he might launch out of the witness box and throttle him. Tsarnaev refused to look at him.

Clarke sat on Tsarnaev's left, and Conrad, an animated woman in her fifties, sat on his right, so that the jurors always saw him flanked by women. They whispered and exchanged little jokes with him, and they touched him—a pat on the back, a squeeze of the arm. This was deliberate: like the pope stooping to embrace a disfigured pilgrim at St. Peter's, the women were indicating that Tsarnaev was not a leper. Such gestures weren't aimed only at jurors. A training guide that Clarke helped prepare for defense attorneys in 2006 notes, "In capital cases, appropriate physical contact is frequently the one gesture that can maintain a defendant's trust." Under the terms of his confinement, Tsarnaev was not permitted to touch any visitors, even relatives, so the casual contact of his attorneys likely represented his only remaining form of tangible human connection.

The centerpiece of the government's case was a montage of photographs and videos taken on the day of the bombing. One image, captured shortly before the first blast, shows a family of five from Dorchester watching runners cross the finish line. Just behind them, semi-obscured by a tree, stands Tsarnaev, in a backward baseball cap. On March 5, the family's father, Bill Richard, a slim, haunted-looking man, took the stand. After the bomb blast threw him across the street, he recalled, he scrambled to find his children. He located his eleven-year-old, Henry, who was unharmed, and then saw his seven-year-old, Jane, lying by the tree. He picked her up, but her leg did not come with her. "It was blown off," he said. Bill saw his wife, Denise, hunched over their eight-year-old son, Martin, who had been closest to the blast. Bill wanted to help care for Martin, but his daughter was losing blood so rapidly that she was not likely to survive unless he got her to an ambulance. He took one final look at Martin. "I knew he wasn't going to make it," Bill said. "From what I saw, there was no chance."

He ran to an ambulance, and Jane survived. Denise was blinded in one eye. While jurors and spectators wept, a medical examiner described the blast's impact on Martin's body. Wearing rubber gloves, he held up the shorts that Martin had been wearing. They could have been long pants, he said—it was hard to tell. The fabric had melted.

This was an act of terrorism, surely, and prosecutors characterized the Tsarnaevs as jihadists who set out to kill American civilians in the name of radical Islam. Investigators had retrieved from Jahar's laptop a downloaded copy of *Inspire,* a publication associated with al-Qaeda, which featured an article titled "Make a Bomb in the Kitchen of Your Mom." In the Tsarnaevs' family apartment in Cambridge, the FBI had discovered the residue of explosives.

Prosecutors also had what amounted to a confession from Jahar. Believing that he was dying in the dry-docked boat, he had written a message in pencil on the fiberglass interior. Initially, the government wanted to remove the section of the boat bearing the confession and display it in court. The defense objected that the jury needed to see Jahar's message in its full context. This was vintage Clarke. When she represented Ted Kaczynski, she felt that the jury should see the cramped shack in the Montana wilderness where the Unabomber had built his letter bombs and composed his manifesto. The shack was hauled to Sacramento on a flatbed truck. One day in March, Judge O'Toole accompanied the lawyers, the jury, and Tsarnaev to a ware-house where the boat sat, raised, on a trailer. The boat was streaked with Tsarnaev's blood and riddled with more than a hundred bullet holes. "God has a plan for each person," Tsarnaev wrote. "Mine was to hide in this boat and shed some light on our actions." He was "jealous" of Tamerlan for having achieved martyrdom. "The U.S. Government is killing our innocent civilians," he added, noting that "Muslims are one body, you hurt one you hurt us all." The note was difficult to read, because bullets had ripped through it. But near the end Tsarnaev wrote, "I don't like killing innocent people it is forbidden in Islam but due to said [bullet hole] it is allowed. All credit goes to [bullet hole]."

For all the putative radicalism of these sentiments, there was an inescapable sense, even as the government presented its case, that Jahar Tsarnaev was less a soldier of God than a wayward child, curi-ously detached from his terrorist acts. He was hardly ascetic: at the University of Massachusetts Dartmouth, where he was a sophomore, Jahar was known as a pot dealer. Less than an hour after the bombs

exploded, surveillance cameras at a Whole Foods in Cambridge captured him selecting half a gallon of milk, paying for it, leaving, then
returning to exchange it for another half a gallon. Hours after the
bombing, he tweeted, "Ain't no love in the heart of the city. Stay safe
people," and, "I'm a stress free kind of guy." He went with a friend to
the gym. It was precisely this eerie remove that had led authorities to
identify him as a suspect. FBI officials, examining surveillance footage of the marathon, noticed a man in a baseball cap who did not react
when the first blast sent everyone else scrambling.

• • •

Clarke isn't a notably original legal theorist. The course that she has
taught at Washington and Lee is a practicum focused on the rules and
tactics of lawyering. She appeared twice before the Supreme Court
before she was forty, in cases involving technical matters of criminal
procedure—and lost both, unanimously. Still, in one of the cases, she
paused to explain the subtleties of an obscure point of criminal law,
and she clearly knew more about it than the justices did. In a guide
that Clarke prepared for federal defense lawyers, she invoked Thomas
Edison's formula for genius: "99 percent perspiration and 1 percent
inspiration." In a capital case, much of the exertion involves detective
work. Collaborating with investigators and mental-health experts,
Clarke assembles a "social history"—a comprehensive biography of
the client, often drawing on decades of family records. She tracks
down relatives, teachers, neighbors, and co-workers, looking for signs
of mental illness or instability in the client's past. Such interviews,
Clarke wrote in a court filing in 2013, can be "invaluable in building
the case for a life verdict by documenting the nature, extent, and consequences of trauma."

By searching for what Tina Hunt called "the key that turns the lock,"
a capital-defense attorney operates on the broad assumption that the
perpetrators of terrible crimes are also victims themselves—indeed,
that only victims of mental illness or awful circumstances could commit such crimes. "Nobody starts out as a killer," Jonathan Shapiro said.
"These folks are damaged goods when they come to us. They're like a
tangled-up piece of cloth. And our job is to try to untangle it, to figure
out what made them the way that they are." Clarke has said that most

of her death-penalty clients have endured "unbelievable trauma," and that "many suffer from severe cognitive-development issues that affect the core of their being." She often invokes a mantra of capital-defense work: "None of us, not any one of us, wants to be defined by the worst day or the worst hour or the worst moment of our lives."

You can oppose the death penalty on any number of grounds and still find this assertion curious. If we mustn't judge someone who kills a child for his willingness to kill a child, isn't that essentially saying that we should never judge anyone at all? I wondered if this line of reasoning was truly an article of faith for Clarke. Indeed, you might think that spending time with killers would disabuse a lawyer of any illusions about the virtues of humanity. But a dozen of Clarke's friends and colleagues assured me that she ardently believes in the essential goodness of each client. "She has a well of compassion that just runs a little deeper," Elisabeth Semel said.

Clarke goes to unusual lengths to establish bonds with her clients. "Many lawyers will go in to meet with the client, and if the client doesn't want to talk, they'll give up and leave," Laurie Levenson, a professor at Loyola Law School, said. "If Judy goes and they don't want to talk, she'll come back the next day and the day after that." David Bruck once told *The New York Times* that Clarke is a preternatural listener: "Even people who are quite mentally ill can identify someone who is real and who wants to protect them." When Clarke met with Jared Loughner, who suffers from paranoid schizophrenia, he threw chairs at her, lunged at her, and spat on her. (In court, Clarke and her colleagues downplayed these outbursts, arguing, in effect, that this was just Jared being Jared.) Before the Boston trial, Clarke went to the Caucasus, along with a Russian-speaking colleague, in order to meet Tsarnaev's parents. This labor of empathy can be consuming. In Bruck's words, "The client becomes her world."

Clarke's husband, Speedy Rice, is also a death-penalty opponent. In 2009, he helped defend a Khmer Rouge torturer, Kaing Guek Eav, in a war-crimes trial in Cambodia. (Kaing received life imprisonment.) Clarke and Rice have always had dogs—including a blind-and-deaf pug—but they have no children. Several of Clarke's friends suggested to me that it would have been impossible for her to raise kids and maintain the pace of her work. Because Clarke's cases unfold in federal courts across the country, the decision to take on a new client can mean months away from home. With the exception of the Susan Smith case, all Clarke's capital cases have been federal. Most death-penalty prosecutions occur at the state level, where innocent people have often been condemned to death. In such states as Alabama and Texas, there are not enough capable death-penalty lawyers, and even strong ones cannot secure adequate funds to prepare a case properly. In state cases, a defense counsel is sometimes given an investigation budget of only $1,000; attorneys' fees can be capped at as little as $30,000, even when a case demands more than a thousand hours of lawyering. "People who are well represented at trial do not get the death penalty," Justice Ruth Bader Ginsburg once said.

Federal death-penalty prosecutions are far rarer, and tend to be reserved for cases, like Tsarnaev's, in which the government has strong evidence of guilt. Often in these cases, defense attorneys are paid more and have latitude to hire experts, investigators, and additional attorneys. Though no figure has yet been released, Tsarnaev's defense could cost millions of dollars in public funds. To one way of thinking, a talented attorney who fiercely opposes the death penalty should concentrate on saving defendants who may be innocent. Reuben Camper Cahn said, "For a utilitarian, is there an overconcentration of talent and resources in the federal system? Yes." People who know Clarke explained her focus on federal cases by citing the severe financial constraints on capital-defense attorneys in the states where most executions take place.

In Boston, Clarke had ample resources, but she was hamstrung by another restriction: official secrecy. The government, citing the ongoing security threat that Tsarnaev might pose by communicating with co-conspirators—or by inspiring impressionable people to follow his example—invoked a protocol, known as "special administrative measures," that forbade the defendant to communicate with anyone outside his legal team and his immediate family. Secrecy also enveloped the legal process: many of the voluminous motions and filings made by both the government and the defense were sealed from the public record. Judge O'Toole granted the secrecy and explained his rationale in a series of rulings. But they, too, are secret. Matthew Segal, an attorney with the ACLU of Massachusetts, told me that the scale of official secrecy in the case was "extremely high" and hard to justify, given that Tsarnaev was "the lone surviving member of a two-person cell."

On April 8, 2015, the jury convicted Tsarnaev of all thirty counts in the indictment. During the guilt phase, the defense had called only four witnesses, all technical experts, who demonstrated that the fingerprints on the bomb-making tools were Tamerlan's and that, according to cell-phone records, while Tamerlan was purchasing pressure cookers and BBs, Jahar was far away, at college. On cross-examination, Clarke and her colleagues showed that radical-Islamist material constituted only a fraction of Jahar's internet diet. (He most often visited Facebook.) Tweets by Jahar that the government had presented as indications of extremism were shown to be rap lyrics or references to Comedy Central shows. The man who was carjacked by the brothers, Dung Meng, recalled Tamerlan boasting about bombing the marathon and shooting the MIT police officer; Jahar was quiet, asking only if the car stereo could play music from his iPhone.

• • •

For the penalty phase, Clarke and her colleagues summoned more than forty witnesses to tell Jahar's life story. He and his parents had come to America in 2002 and were later joined by his two sisters and Tamerlan. The family had applied for political asylum, citing Russia's wars in Chechnya. The parents, Anzor and Zubeidat, were attractive and ambitious but volatile: Anzor, who found work as a mechanic, suffered from night terrors; Zubeidat was by turns smothering and neglectful. The Tsarnaevs lived in a cramped apartment in Cambridge, and their immigrant hopes gradually eroded. Jahar's sisters married young; each had a child, got divorced, and returned home. Tamerlan failed in his efforts at a professional boxing career, and at everything else he tried. He married an American, Katherine Russell, and they soon had a child. She and the baby joined the others in the apartment. By 2010, Zubeidat and Tamerlan had become immersed in Islam—not the largely moderate form that is practiced in the Caucasus, but a strain of Salafism that had taken root on the internet. Tamerlan, who was unemployed, stayed at home with his child while his wife worked, and he spent hours watching inflammatory videos of atrocities suffered by Muslims abroad. In 2012, he traveled to Dagestan for six months, hoping to participate in jihad, though he apparently whiled away most of his time in cafés, talking politics. (According to *The Boston Globe,* Tamerlan heard voices and might have suffered from undiagnosed schizophrenia.)

Clarke's portrait of Jahar Tsarnaev was reminiscent, in some ways, of the one she helped construct for Zacarias Moussaoui. In that trial, defense testimony focused on the dislocation that Moussaoui had faced as a Moroccan in France, and on his tumultuous upbringing; his father, a boxer, was abusive, and ended up in a psychiatric institution. Moussaoui's sister, Jamilla, testified that he was the "sweetheart of the family." Jahar Tsarnaev was the sweetheart of his family—a doe-eyed, easygoing child who adored his older brother, made friends easily, and seemed to acculturate to American life more quickly than his relatives did. He did well in school, skipping the fourth grade and becoming captain of his high school wrestling team. Several tearful teachers took the stand and described him as bright and gentle. By the time he started college, however, his family was falling apart. His parents separated, and both eventually left the country. Tamerlan, meanwhile, was becoming more radical, walking around Cambridge in the kind of flowing white robe one sees in Saudi Arabia.

Neither the government nor the defense claimed that the brothers were part of a larger conspiracy; rather, in Clarke's awkward phrasing, Tamerlan "self-radicalized" through the internet. The question at the heart of the defense was whether Jahar did, too. In college, he spent evenings getting high and playing video games with friends. Photographs from that period exhibit a painfully American banality: cinder-block dorm rooms, big-screen TVs, mammoth boxes of Cheez-Its. Several of Jahar's friends testified about his kindness. Whereas Tamerlan lectured anyone who would listen about U.S. imperialism and the plight of Muslims abroad, Jahar rarely discussed politics. Some of his close friends didn't even know that he was Muslim. The prosecution said that he was living a "double life." But it was hard to imagine, looking at a photograph of him lounging on a top bunk, how he hid a life of religious devotion from his dorm mates.

The defense argued that Jahar didn't engineer the terrorist plot. Tamerlan bought the bomb materials, made the bombs, and shot Officer Collier. In Chechen culture, one defense expert testified, an older brother is a dominant personality whom the younger brother must obey. A cognitive scientist testified that teenage brains are impulsive, like cars with powerful engines but faulty brakes. This line of argument echoed the successful defense in a 2002 case that Clarke was not involved in: the prosecution of Lee Malvo, who, at seventeen, had accompanied a deranged father figure, John Allen Muhammad, on a shooting spree around Washington, D.C., that left ten people dead. Muhammad was put to death, but Malvo got a life sentence. Like Malvo, Tsarnaev was young, had no history of violent conduct, and fell under the spell of a charismatic mentor. Malvo, his lawyer maintained, could "no more separate himself from John Muhammad than you could separate from your shadow." It was a Pied Piper defense, and now Clarke was mounting a similar argument. One of Tsarnaev's teachers, whose husband had been his soccer coach, testified, "He's very coachable. He would do what the coach said."

Zacarias Moussaoui, a genuine zealot, was given to outbursts during his court proceedings, in which he condemned America and the case against him. Jahar Tsarnaev sat silently at the defense table, occasionally reaching for a carafe of water to refill his attorneys' cups. There was such dissonance between the grotesque crime and the mild-mannered perpetrator that outside the courtroom an avid group of supporters, many of them young women, maintained that he must be the victim of a frame-up. "It's a defense you don't often have recourse to in these types of cases: 'He was a good kid, one of ours,'" Carol Steiker, a death-penalty specialist at Harvard Law School, told me. "He also reads as white, which is very helpful in these kinds of cases."

Spectators in the courtroom could see mainly the back of Tsarnaev's head, but in overflow rooms for the press, closed-circuit monitors afforded a better view. One of the cameras in the courtroom was positioned to approximate the judge's view from the bench. David Bruck objected that the camera violated the defense team's "zone of privacy," but the camera stayed, offering an intimate perspective of Tsarnaev's detachment. He whispered and sometimes smiled with his attorneys, but he avoided looking at the witnesses, instead examining his fingernails or doodling. "I really miss the person that I knew," one of his college friends, Alexa Guevara, said, through tears, on the stand. She tried mightily to catch his eye, but he would not meet her gaze.

Tsarnaev broke this mask of indifference only once. His aunt Patimat Suleimanova came from Dagestan to testify. But when she took the stand, she was immediately convulsed by sobs. Tsarnaev dabbed tears from his eyes as she was escorted from the stand. This marked, in some ways, a promising development for the defense—a signal that the defendant had feelings, after all, and that his death would devastate his family. At the same time, it underscored Tsarnaev's implacability during weeks of harrowing testimony about the devastation he had caused.

Clarke, in her opening statement, said that Jahar's terrorist path was "created" and "paved by his brother." If he had fallen under the sway of a violent older sibling, it seemed logical that Tsarnaev, after two lonely years in prison, might feel remorse. Of course, a defendant's posture in the courtroom is an imperfect proxy for his state of mind. But Tsarnaev's demeanor betrayed no contrition. This was critical because, according to studies, capital juries are heavily influenced by whether the defendant shows remorse.

To prove that Tsarnaev was untroubled by his crime, the prosecution presented a still image taken by a surveillance camera in a holding cell in the courthouse. The image was captured on the day of his arraignment, several months after the attacks. Tsarnaev wears orange scrubs and scowls at the camera, his middle finger raised. "*This* is Dzhokhar Tsarnaev—unconcerned, unrepentant, unchanged," one of the prosecutors said. The defense immediately moved to show the jury the video from which the still was taken, and it emerged that Tsarnaev had aimed other gestures at the camera, including a two-fingered gang sign, in the casual pose of a teenager on Instagram. The camera had a mirrored surface, and he carefully tousled his hair.

To rebut the idea that Tsarnaev was remorseless, Clarke played one final card. She summoned Sister Helen Prejean, who explained that before the trial, the defense had brought her to Boston to meet Tsarnaev. Her first thought upon seeing him was "My God, he's so young." They met five times over the course of the trial, Prejean explained, and in one conversation they talked about the victims. According to Prejean, Tsarnaev said, "No one deserves to suffer like they did." She added, "I just had every reason to think that . . . he was genuinely sorry."

• • •

When Clarke first considered representing Susan Smith, she called Rick Kammen, a death-penalty lawyer she knew, for advice. "Every time you take one of these cases, you have to be prepared to see your client executed," Kammen said. Many lawyers try one capital case, then never do another. Those who persist often burn out, or turn to alcohol or drugs. Clarke's colleagues say that to maintain her sanity, she relies on her husband, devoted friends, and wry humor. She still runs to clear her head. The process of preparing a social history for a client is prone to artificial determinism: decades-old tragedies are portrayed as harbingers of recent behavior. When I asked Clarke's friends and colleagues to explain why she is so devoted to what she does, there was a uniform flatness to their answers: Clarke is deeply compassionate, and has always been that way. But if Clarke were preparing her own social history, she might underline one particular episode from her past.

Her father, Harry Clarke, was a conservative Republican who wanted to impeach the Supreme Court justice Earl Warren and was an early supporter of Senator Jesse Helms. The Clarke children were encouraged to debate ideas at the kitchen table, but there were limits. In 1972, Judy and her younger sister, Candy, told their mother, Patsy, that they intended to vote for George McGovern. Patsy was so shocked that she didn't tell their father. In 1987, when Judy was living in San Diego, Harry died, after the single-engine plane he was flying home from a business trip crashed near Asheville. Clarke had been close to her father and never felt that being a defense attorney was incompatible with his principles. Three years after his death, she told the *Los Angeles Times* that she was an absolutist when it came to the rights guaranteed in the Constitution. "Yes, I'm a defense lawyer," she said. "But I think I have very conservative values."

Judy's older brother, Bruce, also became a lawyer, and Candy became a high school teacher. Her younger brother, Mark, moved to Florida after college and became a lifeguard. In 1992, he told his mother that he was gay and dying of AIDS. Patsy, who considered herself a proper southern conservative, was shocked, but she devoted herself to caring for him. Judy went to Florida to support Mark, and he died in the spring of 1994. Upon Mark's death, Patsy grew frustrated that the family's old friend Jesse Helms had been blocking funding for research, claiming that gay men had brought the scourge upon themselves. Patsy later wrote a memoir in which she recalls Judy telling her, "You ought to write to Senator Helms about Mark." Patsy did so, asking that he not "pass judgment on other human beings as 'deserving what they get.'"

Two weeks later, Helms replied. "I wish he had not played Russian roulette in his sexual activity," he wrote of Mark. "I have sympathy for him—and for you. But there is no escaping the reality of what happened."

Patsy was so incensed that she launched a grassroots campaign, along with other mothers of victims, to oust Helms from the Senate. Judy also seems to have been galvanized. Several months after Mark's death, she joined her first capital case, defending Susan Smith.

"Judy was Judy before Mark died," Tina Hunt said. "But it may have intensified her drive for justice and for accepting people for who they are." Then she chuckled and added, "If anything could make Judy more intense."

• • •

Watching Tsarnaev in court, I sometimes wondered if Clarke was trying to save someone who didn't want to be saved. Perhaps he still envied Tamerlan's martyrdom. In death-penalty work, clients often come to desire a swift end. They may be suicidal, or hopeless, or insane; they might have made a considered decision that death by lethal injection would be preferable to a lifetime of solitary confinement. Such clients, known as "volunteers," present death-penalty lawyers with a dilemma. An attorney's job is to advocate vigorously for a client's interests. But there may come a point at which that duty diverges from the imperative to save the client's life. In 2007, Clarke took the case of Joseph Duncan, a drifter who had kidnapped two children—Dylan and Shasta Groene—in Idaho, after using a hammer to murder their older brother, their mother, and her boyfriend. Clarke joined the defense late, after another attorney had left the case.

According to Tina Hunt, who was in the Spokane office at the time, "The crime was so devastating that he could not emotionally handle it." He was a "phenomenal trial lawyer," Hunt said. "But he wasn't Judy."

After taking the two children to a remote campsite, Duncan had videotaped himself raping and torturing Dylan. He then forced Shasta to watch the video, before killing her brother in front of her, with a shotgun. Duncan was on a mountainside, about to bludgeon Shasta's head with a rock, when it occurred to him, in what he later called "an epiphany," that killing is wrong. He drove down the mountain with Shasta, and not long afterward a waitress at a local Denny's recognized them and summoned the police. Clarke spent hours talking with Duncan. She later characterized his ramblings as "head-spinning" and "crazy"—he seemed to have dissociative-identity disorder—but she remained patient. "Are you frustrated with me because I don't understand?" she would ask.

Clarke planned to center her defense on the fact that Duncan had been locked up, at the age of sixteen, in a facility for adult sexual offenders. But Duncan refused to introduce any mitigating evidence about his childhood. Instead, he wanted to take full responsibility for his actions. He was eager to make sure that Shasta would not have to undergo the trauma of appearing on the stand. He wanted to plead guilty and waive his right to appeal. "Tell me you're not on a suicide mission," Clarke said to him, according to a subsequent deposition. She suggested to Duncan that if killing was wrong, he should not allow the state to kill him. But it was no use. Clarke moved to withdraw from the case. "We are not gunslingers who do the bidding of someone who does not have a rational understanding," she told the judge. Duncan was subsequently sentenced to death. He is currently on death row in Indiana.

• • •

Since 1984, capital punishment has been illegal in Massachusetts. Nevertheless, under our federalist system, the Department of Justice can pursue a criminal sanction even if a state has judged it to be unconstitutional. Eighteen other states have banned or suspended the death penalty, and the Supreme Court has gradually narrowed the scope of who can receive the punishment, ruling out juvenile perpetrators and people with intellectual disabilities. You might think that in a liberal city like Boston, Tsarnaev's lawyers would not have to address his moral culpability in order to save his life; it would be enough to attack capital punishment itself. In 1999, when Clarke defended the white supremacist Buford Furrow, she argued that the death penalty was unconstitutional. In the Kaczynski case, the defense wrote, "Evolving standards of decency will eventually convince the American public that it is simply wrong and immoral to kill people, regardless of whether the killing is done by an individual or the government." In Boston, as the penalty phase began, David Bruck made a dramatic case against the death penalty. He has worked as an attorney or an adviser on scores of capital cases. He showed the jurors a photograph of ADX, the federal maximum-security prison in Florence, Colorado, where several of Clarke's former clients are held: a series of stark buildings nestled into barren, snow-covered terrain. It called to mind Siberia. If Tsarnaev was spared the death penalty, Bruck explained, he would live a life of near-total isolation at ADX. Because of the special administrative measures, he would have no contact with other inmates or the outside world. If the jury delivered a death sentence, Bruck continued, its decision would surely be followed by more than a decade of appeals, each one accompanied by a new wave of publicity for Tsarnaev and pain for the victims. Only then—maybe—would he be executed.

Supporters of the death penalty often argue that it brings "closure" to the victims, but Bruck's logic seemed unassailable: if you want a sense of finality, send him away. "No martyrdom," he said. "Just years and years of punishment, day after day, while he grows up to face the lonely struggle of dealing with what he did." On April 17, under the headline "To End the Anguish, Drop the Death Penalty," the *Globe* carried an open letter from Bill and Denise Richard. "The defendant murdered our 8-year-old son, maimed our 7-year-old daughter, and stole part of our soul," they wrote. "We know that the government has its reasons for seeking the death penalty, but the continued pursuit of that punishment could bring years of appeals and prolong reliving the most painful day of our lives." They urged prosecutors to accept a plea deal for a sentence of life without parole. Some victims strenu-

ously disagreed with this position. But the prosecution's most compelling witness was now begging to spare Tsarnaev's life. Hours after the
letter was published, Carmen Ortiz, the U.S. Attorney in Massachusetts, reaffirmed her desire to pursue the death penalty. She was doing
so, she claimed, on behalf of the victims.

Had the jury been selected from a representative sampling of Bostonians, there would have been little possibility of a death sentence.
But jury selection in death-penalty cases involves a procedure known
as "death qualification," in which prospective jurors are questioned
about their views on capital punishment, and anyone who opposes the
practice on principle is disqualified. This makes a certain amount of
sense, because a death sentence must be unanimous; if a single juror
objects from the outset, the whole proceeding might be a waste of
time. In Alabama or Oklahoma, where there is broad support for capital punishment, it is easy to death qualify a panel of jurors. But in Boston a jury that is death qualified is also demographically anomalous:
according to polls taken during the trial, 60 percent of Americans
favored executing Tsarnaev, but only 15 percent of Bostonians did.
During jury selection, a middle-aged restaurant manager was asked
if she could deliver a death sentence. "I don't really feel that *I'm* sentencing someone," she said. "It's like at work—I fire people, and I'm
asked, 'How can you do that?' I'm not the one doing that. *They* did it.
By their actions. Not coming to work, stealing, whatever." Elisabeth
Semel, the Berkeley professor, notes that with a death-qualified jury
"you are starting out with a jury that is conviction prone and death
prone, because if they weren't, they wouldn't be sitting there." The
restaurant manager became the forewoman of the jury.

• • •

On a May morning, as gulls hung on the breeze in Boston Harbor,
Clarke addressed the jury a final time. She dismissed the idea of Jahar
as a radical, arguing that he had been in his brother's thrall. "If not
for Tamerlan," she said, the attack "would not have happened." She
played video of Jahar putting his backpack behind the Richard family.
"He stops at the tree, not at the children," she insisted, a little lamely.
"It does not make it better, but let's not make his intent worse than it
was." Clarke called Tsarnaev a "kid" and "an adolescent drawn into

a passion and belief of his older brother." In his confession inside the boat, she argued, he was merely parroting the rhetoric of others. "He wrote words that had been introduced to him by his brother."

At one point, Clarke nearly conceded the logic of capital punishment. "Dzhokhar Tsarnaev is not the worst of the worst," she said. "That's what the death penalty is reserved for." Then again, you could argue that if Tsarnaev wasn't among the worst of the worst, Clarke would never have taken the case. And Clarke—who once defended someone who slashed a pregnant woman's belly and strangled her to death in order to steal the baby from her womb—has devoted her career to the notion that even the very worst among us should be spared. But she knew that these jurors didn't oppose the death penalty, so she appealed to their sympathy, repeating the words "us" and "we," reminding them that they were standing in judgment of one of their own. As her closing neared its crescendo, her normally casual demeanor assumed a frantic urgency, and she gesticulated—pounding her fist, slicing the air—as if she were conducting an orchestra. "Mercy is never earned," Clarke said. "It's bestowed."

Then William Weinreb approached the lectern for a rebuttal. "His brother made him do it," he said. "That's the idea they've been trying to sell you." Weinreb observed that Clarke, in her closing statement, had referred to Tamerlan "well over one hundred times." But Tamerlan was not on trial, and the defense's evidence had actually revealed that Jahar Tsarnaev was a fortunate child whose family had loved him and given him opportunity. "He moved with his parents from one of the poorest parts of the world to the wealthiest," Weinreb said. "They were looking for a better life, and they found it." Weinreb calmly dismantled the social history that Clarke and her colleagues had constructed. "The murders on Boylston Street were not a youthful indiscretion," Weinreb said. Clarke had called the killings senseless, "but they made perfect sense to the defendant." Even Prejean, Weinreb noted, was unpersuasive about Tsarnaev's sense of remorse. The sentiment he expressed to her was not so different from what he wrote in the boat: it was a pity when innocent people died, even if it was necessary. "That's a core terrorist belief," Weinreb said.

Miriam Conrad and David Bruck both fumed and raised objections. Clarke just stared at Weinreb, her chin propped on her left fist, her thumb digging deeper and deeper into her cheek. Earlier, one of Weinreb's colleagues had cited Emerson: "The only person you are destined to become is the person you decide to be." Now Weinreb assaulted the belief system upon which Clarke had staked her career. All of us, Weinreb said, should be judged on the basis of our actions. Tsarnaev should be put to death "not because he's inhuman but because he's inhumane."

• • •

Before the murderer Gary Gilmore was executed at Utah State Prison in 1977, bullets were distributed to the five-member firing squad; one of them was a blank. This dispersal of moral responsibility is a curious feature of our system of capital punishment: the message is that the state is doing the killing, and therefore no individual is culpable for the death. In lectures, Sister Helen Prejean rebuts this notion by saying, "If you really believe in the death penalty, ask yourself if you're willing to inject the fatal poison." In other words, we are all implicated when the state kills.

One common rationale for capital punishment is that it will deter others from committing awful crimes. But there is no evidence that this is the case. Arthur Koestler once pointed out that when thieves were hanged in the village square, other thieves flocked to the execution to pick the pockets of the spectators. A second justification is that the most violent criminals, even if they are jailed for life, could still endanger others. The government labored to suggest that Tsarnaev might someday be transferred out of seclusion and into the general population at ADX. One defense witness, a former prison warden, observed that in such an unlikely event his greatest safety concern would be for Tsarnaev. The remaining ground for capital punishment is retribution. In a 1957 essay, "Reflections on the Guillotine," Albert Camus described retaliation as a "pure impulse" that is ingrained in human nature, passed down to us "from the primitive forests." This does not mean, he argued, that it should be legal. "Law, by definition, cannot obey the same rules as nature. If murder is in the nature of man, the law is not intended to imitate or reproduce that nature. It is intended to correct it." As Oliver Wendell Holmes put it, retribution is simply "vengeance in disguise."

Before the jurors began to deliberate, they were issued a questionnaire that asked them to decide whether various "aggravating" and "mitigating" factors had been proved by the government and the defense. Though Judge O'Toole cautioned jurors not to simply tally the checkmarks and arrive at an answer, the exercise retained an air of sterile arithmetic. Clarke reminded the jury that, however they completed their forms, each of them was making a moral judgment. "This is an individual decision for each of you," she said. She could not let them think of the jury form the way the restaurant manager thought about errant employees, or the way the firing squad thought about that blank. As Clarke spoke, she looked straight at the forewoman, who glared back at her, arms folded across her chest.

After fourteen hours of deliberation, the jury returned with a death sentence. According to the jury forms, all but three of the jurors believed that even without the influence of Tamerlan, Jahar would have carried out the attacks on his own. Only two believed that the defendant was remorseful.

"Judy would probably say, if the public saw everything she sees, it would look at the client or the case differently," David Bruck once remarked. But in this instance Clarke had failed to paint a picture of her young client that was moving enough to save him. It may be that she simply never found the key. During her closing, she said, with frank bewilderment, "If you expect me to have an answer, a simple, clean answer as to how this could happen, I don't."

Judge O'Toole had warned the jurors not to read anything into the defendant's manner in court, but Tsarnaev's inscrutability appears to have hurt him. Most jurors declined to speak with the press, but one of them told *The Daily Beast,* "My conscience is clear . . . And I don't know that he has one."

Unbeknownst to that juror, and to the public in Boston, Tsarnaev had already expressed remorse for his actions. On June 24, six weeks after the jury dispersed, Judge O'Toole presided over the formal sentencing of Tsarnaev, and Clarke made a fascinating remark. "There have been comments over time with regard to Mr. Tsarnaev lacking remorse," she said. "It's incumbent upon us to let the court know that Mr. Tsarnaev offered to resolve this case without a trial." Tsarnaev had not simply agreed to plead guilty before the trial, Clarke revealed; he had written a letter of apology. But it was never shared with the jury—because the government, under the terms of the special administrative measures, had it sealed. I spoke recently with Nancy Gertner, a former federal judge in Massachusetts who now teaches at Harvard. "This could have been an immediate plea," she said. "He was prepared to cooperate with the government. Why go through with it all?" In Gertner's view, there is "no legal justification" for the secrecy surrounding the proceedings, given that Tsarnaev did not appear to pose an ongoing threat. "The classification was based on a premise that this was an international security issue, which is a little dishonest," she said. It seemed absurd that prosecutors had suppressed Tsarnaev's letter of apology on the ground that releasing it could be unsafe. (A spokesperson for the prosecutors declined to comment on why the letter was suppressed.)

Gertner offered a hypothesis for why the Justice Department was intent on a death sentence: it might relate to the politics of Guantánamo. Supporters of the U.S. detention facility have long argued that American federal courts are not equipped to try terrorists. But here was a case in which a civilian federal court could deliver not just a guilty verdict but the death penalty. Numerous people have been convicted of terrorism in civilian courts since September 11, but Tsarnaev is the first to receive a death sentence. Gertner said that the trial should not have been held in Massachusetts. If relocating was not appropriate in this case, she observed, when would it be? "They've essentially eliminated change of venue for anyone in the country," she said. The whole trial, she concluded, "was theater, as far as I was concerned."

A second juror, a twenty-three-year-old named Kevan Fagan, subsequently spoke to the press. Asked by the radio station WBUR about the Richard family's letter opposing the death penalty, he said, "If I had known that, I probably—I probably would change my vote."

Before Judge O'Toole could deliver the death sentence, Clarke said, "Mr. Tsarnaev is prepared to address the court." He rose, next to her, wearing a dark jacket and a gray button-down shirt. "I would like to begin in the name of Allah, the exalted and glorious, the most gracious, the most merciful," he said. He spoke in a thick accent that sounded vaguely Middle Eastern. (Before the bombing, he had sounded more conventionally American.) "This is the blessed month of Ramadan, and it is the month of mercy from Allah to his creation, a month to ask forgiveness of Allah," he continued. Turning to Clarke and her colleagues, Tsarnaev said that he wanted to thank his attorneys. "I cherish their company," he said. "They're lovely companions." Then he thanked the jury that had sentenced him to death. The Prophet Muhammad, he noted, had said that "if you are not merciful to Allah's creation, Allah will not be merciful to you." Tsarnaev went on, "I'd like to now apologize to the victims." He recalled that after the bombings he began to learn about the injured and the dead. "Throughout this trial, more of those victims were given names." When the witnesses testified, they conveyed "how horrendous it was, this thing I put you through."

Tsarnaev did not look at the many victims who had gathered in the courtroom. He stared straight ahead, his hands clasped around his belt buckle. Clarke sat motionless, watching him. "I am sorry for the lives that I've taken, for the suffering that I've caused," he said. He prayed that the victims might find "healing," and he asked Allah "to have mercy upon me and my brother and my family." Allah, he said, "knows best those deserving of his mercy." Tsarnaev spoke in precisely the language of religious devotion that the prosecutors might have predicted. But people often change considerably between the ages of nineteen and twenty-one. He had spent those two years in solitary confinement, with plenty of time to ponder his actions—and to read the Koran. Throughout the trial, Tsarnaev had been a cipher, and observers wanted him to demonstrate that he understood the gravity of his misdeeds. But I wondered, as he addressed the court, if Tsarnaev was mature enough—or distant enough in time from the bombing and from the death of his brother—to have arrived at a firm evaluation of what he'd done. The Koran, like other holy books, can be read to condemn such acts of violence or to condone them. On a given night, Tsarnaev might fall asleep believing that he would be rewarded in the afterlife, and the next night believing that he would be punished.

Tsarnaev will not be executed anytime soon. Since 1988, seventy-five defendants have been given the federal death penalty, but only three have been put to death. Appeals drag out for decades. Until a California judge ruled capital punishment unconstitutional in 2014, death-row prisoners there were seven times more likely to die of natural causes than of execution. (A death sentence, the judge observed, should really be called "life in prison with the remote possibility of death.")

The very scenario that Bill and Denise Richard hoped to avoid—the appeals, the publicity, the endless replay of the city's trauma in the interests of retributive justice—seemed as if it would now come to pass. Clarke has been known to say, of a death sentence that has not yet led to execution, "This case has a few miles to go."

Clarke's friends say that the loss has been devastating to her. In death-penalty work, Elisabeth Semel told me, you talk not about losing a case but about losing a client. When it happens, she said, "you suffer, and you have to figure out how to pick yourself up." Clarke, she pointed out, "has never experienced this before." Tina Hunt, noting that Clarke and her husband don't have kids, said, "To some degree, these clients are her children."

Clarke's friend Rick Kammen told me a story about Millard Farmer, who has represented scores of capital defendants in the South: "Millard would say, 'Everyone has a certain number of cases in them. You need to quit one trial early.' And it does take its toll on you, this work." But without exception the people who know Clarke agree that this will not be her last case: she will pick herself up and keep fighting. Recently, Clarke and her colleagues filed a motion for a retrial, maintaining, once again, that the case should not have been tried in Boston.

Tsarnaev concluded his courtroom remarks with a few final encomiums to Allah. Then he sat stiffly and waited for Judge O'Toole to deliver the death sentence. Clarke reached out and placed her hand on his back.

Tsarnaev was transferred to ADX (the same prison that would eventually house Chapo Guzmán). After one appeal of his death sentence went as far as the Supreme Court but did not succeed, he launched another appeal, on different legal grounds. No date has been set for his execution. Judy Clarke continues to take on notorious clients. In 2019 she joined the defense of Robert Bowers, who stands accused of murdering eleven people at the Tree of Life synagogue in Pittsburgh.

BURIED SECRETS

How an Israeli billionaire wrested control of
one of Africa's biggest prizes. (2013)

ONE OF THE WORLD'S largest known deposits of untapped iron ore is buried inside a great, forested mountain range in the tiny West African republic of Guinea. In the country's southeast highlands, far from any city or major roads, the Simandou Mountains stretch for seventy miles, looming over the jungle floor like a giant dinosaur spine. Some of the peaks have nicknames that were bestowed by geologists and miners who have worked in the area; one is Iron Maiden, another Metallica. Iron ore is the raw material that, once smelted, becomes steel, and the ore at Simandou is unusually rich, meaning that it can be fed into blast furnaces with minimal processing. During the past decade, as glittering mega-cities rose across China, the global price of iron soared, and investors began seeking new sources of ore. The red earth that dusts the lush vegetation around Simandou and marbles the mountain rock is worth a fortune.

Mining iron ore is complicated and requires a huge amount of capital. Simandou lies four hundred miles from the coast, in jungle so impassable that the first drill rigs had to be transported to the mountaintops with helicopters. The site has barely been developed; no ore has been excavated. Shipping it to China and other markets will require not only the construction of a mine but the building of a railroad line sturdy enough to support freight cars laden with ore. It will also be necessary to have access to a deepwater port, which Guinea lacks. Guinea is one of the poorest countries on the planet. There is little industry and scarce electricity, and there are few navigable roads. Public institutions hardly function. More than half the population can't read. "The level of development is equivalent to Liberia or Sierra Leone," a government adviser in Conakry, Guinea's ramshackle seaside capital, told me recently. "But in Guinea we haven't had a civil war."

This dire state of affairs was not inevitable, for the country has a bounty of natural resources. In addition to the iron ore in the Simandou range, Guinea has one of the world's largest reserves of bauxite—the ore that, twice refined, makes aluminum—and significant quantities of diamonds, gold, uranium, and, off the coast, oil. As wealthy countries confront the prospect of rapidly depleting natural resources, they are turning, increasingly, to Africa, where oil and minerals worth trillions of dollars remain trapped in the ground. By one estimate, the continent holds 30 percent of the world's mineral reserves. Paul Collier, who runs the Centre for the Study of African Economies, at Oxford, has suggested that "a new scramble for Africa" is under way. Bilateral trade between China and Africa, which in 2000 stood at $10 billion, is projected to top $200 billion in 2013. The United States now imports more oil from Africa than from the Persian Gulf.

The Western world has always thought of Africa as a continent to take things from, whether it was diamonds, rubber, or slaves. This outlook was inscribed into the very names of Guinea's neighbor Côte d'Ivoire and of Ghana, which was known to its British masters as the Gold Coast. During the Victorian period, the exploitation of resources was especially brutal; King Leopold II of Belgium was so rapacious in his pursuit of rubber that ten million people in the Congo Free State died as a result. The new international stampede for African resources could become another grim story, or it could present an unprecedented opportunity for economic development. Collier, who several years ago wrote a best seller about global poverty, *The Bottom Billion,* believes that for countries like Guinea the extraction of natural resources, rather than foreign aid, offers the greatest chance of economic progress. Simandou alone could potentially generate $140 billion in revenue over the next quarter century, more than doubling Guinea's gross domestic product. "The money involved will dwarf everything else," Collier told me. Like the silver mine in Joseph Conrad's novel *Nostromo,* the Simandou deposit holds the promise of supplying what Guinea needs most: "law, good faith, order, security."

As with deepwater oil drilling or with missions to the moon, the export of iron ore requires so much investment and expertise that the business is limited to a few major players. In 1997, the exclusive rights to explore and develop Simandou were given to the Anglo-Australian mining giant Rio Tinto, which is one of the world's biggest iron-ore producers. In early 2008, Tom Albanese, the company's chief executive, boasted to shareholders that Simandou was, "without doubt, the top undeveloped tier-one iron-ore asset in the world." But shortly afterward the government of Guinea declared that Rio Tinto was developing the mine too slowly, citing progress benchmarks that had been missed, and implying that the company was simply hoarding the Simandou deposit—keeping it from competitors while focusing on mines elsewhere. In July 2008, Rio Tinto was stripped of its license. Guinean officials then granted exploration permits for half of the deposit to a much smaller company: Beny Steinmetz Group Resources, or BSGR.

Beny Steinmetz is, by some estimates, the richest man in Israel; according to Bloomberg, his personal fortune amounts to some $9 billion. Steinmetz, who made his name in the diamond trade, hardly ever speaks to the press, and the corporate structures of his various enterprises are so convoluted that it is difficult to assess the extent of his holdings. The Simandou contract was a surprising addition to Steinmetz's portfolio, because BSGR had no experience exporting iron ore. A mining executive in Guinea told me, "Diamonds you can carry away from the mine in your pocket. With iron ore, you need infrastructure that can last decades."

Rio Tinto angrily protested the decision. "We are surprised that a company that has never built an iron-ore-mining operation would have been awarded an area of our concession," a spokesman said at the time. Company officials complained to the U.S. embassy in Conakry; one of them suggested that Steinmetz had no intention of developing the mine himself and planned instead to flip it—"to obtain the concession and then sell it for a big profit." Rio Tinto viewed Steinmetz, who was rumored to have extensive contacts in Israeli intelligence, as a suspicious interloper. According to a diplomatic cable released by WikiLeaks, the general manager of Rio Tinto told the U.S. embassy that he did not feel comfortable discussing the Simandou matter on an "unsecured" cell phone. Alan Davies, a senior executive at Rio Tinto, told me that the company had invested hundreds of millions of dollars at the site and had been moving as expeditiously as possible on a project that would have required decades to complete. "This was quite a shocking event for the company," he said.

In April 2009, the Ministry of Mines in Conakry ratified the agreement with Steinmetz. A year later, he made a deal with the Brazilian mining company Vale—one of Rio Tinto's chief competitors. Vale agreed to pay $2.5 billion in exchange for a 51 percent stake in BSGR's Simandou operations. This was an extraordinary windfall: BSGR had paid nothing up front, as is customary with exploration licenses, and at that point had invested only $160 million. In less than five years, BSGR's investment in Simandou had become a $5 billion asset. At that time, the annual budget of the government of Guinea amounted to just $1.2 billion. Mo Ibrahim, the Sudanese telecom billionaire, captured the reaction of many observers when he asked, at a forum in Dakar, "Are the Guineans who did that deal idiots, or criminals, or both?"

Steinmetz was proud of the transaction. "People don't like success," he told the *Financial Times,* in a rare interview, in 2012. "It's disturbing to people that the small David can disturb the big Goliath." He said that it was BSGR's strategy to pursue "opportunities in an aggressive way," adding, "You have to get your hands dirty."

In Conakry, there were rumors that Steinmetz had acquired the concession through bribes. According to Transparency International, Guinea is one of the most corrupt countries on earth. A Human Rights Watch report suggested that when Steinmetz acquired his parcel of Simandou, Guinea was effectively a kleptocracy, with its leaders presiding over "an increasing criminalization of the state." A recent report by the Africa Progress Panel, which is chaired by Kofi Annan, suggests that well-connected foreigners often purchase lucrative assets in Africa at prices far below market value, by offering inducements to predatory local elites. "Africa's resource wealth has bypassed the vast majority of African people and built vast fortunes for a privileged few," it says. The report highlights the billions of dollars that Vale agreed to pay Steinmetz for Simandou, noting that "the people of Guinea, who appear to have lost out as a result of the undervaluation of the concession, will not share in that gain."

In 2010, several months after the Vale deal was announced, Guinea held its first fully democratic elections since independence, ending half a century of authoritarian rule. The new president, Alpha Condé, had run on a platform of good governance and greater transparency in the mining sector. But as he took office, he faced the possibility that Guinea's most prized mineral asset might have been traded out from under the country. He could not simply void the contract. "There is continuity of the state," he told me recently. "I couldn't put things back where they had been—unless I had right on my side." BSGR denied any wrongdoing. "These allegations are false and are a smear campaign against BSGR," a company spokesman told me. If the Simandou license had been secured through bribery, then the deal could potentially be undone. But Condé and his advisers would have to prove it.

• • •

"I inherited a country but not a state," Condé told me when I first met him, in January 2013. He had come to the Swiss Alps to attend the World Economic Forum in Davos, and we met in a hotel suite that was bathed in sunlight reflecting off the snowbanks outside. Condé is a tall man with a high forehead, and he has small eyes that light up with wry amusement when he listens. He wore a brown suit and a red tie. Lowering himself into a wingback chair, he listed slightly to the right while we talked, in a posture of heavy-lies-the-crown fatigue. At times, his elbow appeared to be propping up his whole body, like a tent pole. When he was elected president, Condé was seventy-two years old, and he had spent much of his life in exile. He left Guinea as a boy, when it was still ruled by France, and eventually settled in Paris, where he became a leader of the Pan-African student movements of the 1960s. He studied law, lectured at the University of Paris, and emerged as perhaps the most famous member of the Guinean opposition.

For this distinction, he was sentenced to death, in absentia, by the first despot to rule an independent Guinea, and jailed for more than two years by the second, after he returned, in 1991, to run, unsuccessfully, for president. The 2010 election was bitter—his challenger, Cellou Dalein Diallo, had been a government minister when Condé was thrown in jail. After Condé was finally inaugurated as president, he pledged to be the Nelson Mandela of Guinea. First, he told me, he had to confront the legacy of a decades-long "state of anarchy." The government in Conakry had a Potemkin quality: a profusion of bureaucrats showed up for work at crumbling administrative buildings, but there was little genuine institutional capacity. "The central bank, they were printing *counterfeit money*," Condé marveled. Yet he couldn't fire every official; he'd have to make do with a civil service that had never known anything but graft. "Almost everybody who had any expertise was compromised," one person who has advised Condé told me. "So he had to balance between people who were competent but compromised and people who were upstanding but inexperienced." Condé was defensive about the fact that he had spent so much of his life abroad; when I raised the subject, he snapped, "I know Guinea better than those who have never left." But his outsider status meant that he was not implicated in the scandals of past administrations. And, having spent much of his life in France, he was strikingly at ease in places like Davos. The U.S. ambassador in Conakry, Alex Laskaris, told me, "Condé has a much broader circle of contacts and advisers globally than any other African head of state I've dealt with." Bernard Kouchner, the former foreign minister of France, went to high school with Condé, and is a good friend. Kouchner introduced him to George Soros, the billionaire financier, who became an informal adviser, and connected him with Paul Collier, the Oxford economist. Collier, in turn, introduced Condé to Tony Blair, who offered him assistance through an organization that he runs, the Africa Governance Initiative.

These Westerners saw in Condé an opportunity to save Guinea. Collier told me that what the country needed above all was "integrity at the top." Condé could be ornery; he had a tendency to lecture his interlocutors as though they were students. And, after a life spent in perpetual opposition, it was not clear how well he would govern. From the start, he had difficulties. He came into office with a commitment to complete Guinea's democratic transition by holding parliamentary elections, but he delayed them, ostensibly on procedural grounds, then delayed them again. Opposition riots broke out in Conakry, leading to a series of violent confrontations between demonstrators and government security forces. For all the tumult, Condé's foreign friends and advisers maintain faith in his ethics. "He is absolutely incorruptible,"

Kouchner told me. "He's not luxurious. He's not traveling. He is having a cold potato at night!"

Corinne Dufka, a senior researcher at Human Rights Watch, has not lost hope that Condé can succeed as a reformer. "There's a lot of work to be done for Guinea to overcome its legacy of abusive rule," she said. "Power remains too heavily concentrated in the executive, and without a robust judiciary or a democratically elected parliament there is next to no oversight, which they desperately need. But Condé has made real progress in confronting the disastrous governance and rights problems he inherited." It is no easy task to transform a country that is corrupt from top to bottom. During Condé's first months in office, he performed a kind of triage. With the assistance of Revenue Watch—an organization, backed by Soros, that encourages transparency in extractive industries—Condé established a committee to inspect existing mining contracts and determine if any of them were problematic. He didn't know Steinmetz—"I didn't know *any* miners," he said, with pride—but there were elements of the Simandou deal that appeared to warrant an investigation. "I found it a bit strange that they had invested $160 million and were going to earn billions," Condé said. "It's a little . . ." He smiled and gave a theatrical shrug.

• • •

Beny Steinmetz, who is fifty-seven, does not seem to live anywhere in particular. He shuttles, on his private jet, between Tel Aviv (where his family lives, in one of the most expensive houses in Israel), Geneva (where he technically resides, for tax purposes), London (where the main management office of BSGR is situated), and far-flung locations connected to his diamond and mineral interests, from Macedonia to Sierra Leone. He is technically not an executive of the conglomerate that bears his name, but merely the chief beneficiary of a foundation into which the profits flow. This is a legal fig leaf. Ehud Olmert, the former prime minister of Israel and a friend of his, described Steinmetz as "a one-man show." Olmert continued, "I don't quite understand the legal aspects—just know that he can work ceaselessly and will move from one side of the globe to the other if he identifies a promising deal."

Steinmetz is very fit and exercises every day, no matter where he is. With blue eyes, tousled sandy hair, a preference for casual dress, and a deep tan, he looks more like a movie producer than like a magnate. "I grew up in a home where diamonds were the subject," Steinmetz has said. His father, Rubin, was a Polish diamond cutter who learned the business in Antwerp before settling in Palestine, in 1936. A family photograph from 1977 captures Beny as a young man, sitting at a cluttered table with his two older brothers and his father, who looks sternly at the camera while Beny inspects a precious stone. That year, Beny finished his military service and struck out for Antwerp, with instructions to expand the company's international business in polished stones. According to a privately published history of the family business, *The Steinmetz Diamond Story,* Beny branched into Africa, in search of new sources of rough stones. The plan wasn't to establish mines but, rather, to make deals with the people doing the digging.

Approximately half the diamonds in the world originate in sub-Saharan Africa, and many ambitious Westerners have followed the lead of Cecil Rhodes—the founder of De Beers—and sought fortunes on the continent. "Unfortunately, there aren't any diamond mines in Piccadilly," Dag Cramer, who oversees Steinmetz's business interests, told me. "That's not where God put the assets." Instead, diamonds tend to be found in countries that are plagued by underdevelopment and corruption and, often, by war. This is enough to scare off many investors, but not all; some entrepreneurs are drawn to the heady combination of political uncertainty, physical danger, and potentially astronomical rewards. Ambassador Laskaris, who has done tours in Liberia and Angola, likened the diamond trade in much of Africa to the seedy cantina in *Star Wars.* "It attracts all the rejects of the galaxy," he said. "Low barriers to entry. It rewards corruption. It also rewards a little bit of brutality."

Steinmetz plunged into Africa's treacherous political waters. In the 1990s, he was the largest purchaser of diamonds from Angola; later, he became the biggest private investor in Sierra Leone. Today, Steinmetz is the largest buyer of rough diamonds from De Beers and one of the major suppliers of Tiffany & Company. And he has diversified his holdings into real estate, minerals, oil and gas, and other fields, with interests in more than twenty countries. A website that Steinmetz recently set up describes him as a "visionary" who used a "network of contacts on the African continent" to build "a multi-faced empire."

Paul Collier, however, takes a dim view of businessmen like Steinmetz, who have secured the rights to natural resources that they may not actually have the expertise to develop. "Their technical competence is a social-network map," Collier said. "'Who has the power to make the decision? Who can I reach?' They know how to get a contract—*that* is their skill." (Cramer rejected this characterization, insisting that Steinmetz makes sustainable investments wherever he operates. "BSGR is not a company that has ever been in the business of obtaining rights and flipping them," he told me.)

Despite his great wealth, Steinmetz has maintained an exceptionally low profile. In 2012, after *Hamakor,* a news program on Israeli television, devoted an episode to a battle that he was having with tax authorities in Tel Aviv, he threatened legal action and succeeded in blocking the program from being posted on the internet. "He's a very private guy," Alon Pinkas, a friend of Steinmetz's who once served as Israel's consul general in New York, told me. "His family is all he cares about—and his business." Steinmetz's diamond business, however, has occasionally engaged in some creative publicity. The company sponsors Formula 1 events, sometimes furnishing drivers with diamond-encrusted helmets and steering wheels. At a 2004 race in Monaco, a large Steinmetz diamond was affixed to the nose of a Jaguar race car. As the vehicle tore around a hairpin curve, the driver lost control and the Jaguar slammed into a guardrail. The diamond, which was reportedly 108 carats and worth $200,000, was never recovered.

• • •

General Lansana Conté, the dictator who ruled Guinea before Alpha Condé became president, was famously corrupt: he referred to his ministers, not without affection, as "thieves," and once remarked, "If we had to shoot every Guinean who had stolen from Guinea there would be no one left to kill." By 2008, after more than two decades in power, he had become ill and had largely stopped appearing in public; when he did, he was propped up by bodyguards and orbited by adjutants who often made a show of stooping to whisper in his ear, even when it was obvious, to a close observer, that the general was asleep. During this period, Steinmetz flew to Conakry and met with Conté. At the general's compound, they sat and talked beneath a mango tree. Conté was aware of BSGR because it had acquired the rights to explore two small parcels of land abutting the Simandou range—places where others in the mining industry had not thought to look. In 2006, one of Steinmetz's employees called him from the top of a mountain, using a satellite phone, and said, "Beny, you cannot believe. I'm standing on so much iron here, you have no idea." After this success, General Conté began to entertain the idea of reapportioning the Simandou deposit. It was not long after he met Steinmetz that he stripped Rio Tinto of its claim and gave BSGR a license to explore half the Simandou range.

Two weeks after General Conté signed the deal, he died. Hours later, a military coup installed an erratic young army captain, Moussa Dadis Camara. The junta was a nightmarish period for Guinea. In September 2009, during an opposition rally at a stadium in Conakry, government soldiers massacred more than 150 demonstrators. The United States evacuated most of its staff from the embassy, and the International Criminal Court described the violence as a crime against humanity. But BSGR stayed put. On one occasion, Steinmetz flew in with two of his sons to meet Captain Dadis. They invited him to Israel to attend the wedding of Steinmetz's daughter—a celebration with more than a thousand guests. (Dadis sent his regrets.)

To Steinmetz, this cultivation of the junta only proved his company's unshakable commitment to Guinea. "We put money in the ground at a time when people thought we were crazy," he told the *Financial Times*. BSGR and the junta eventually came to terms over how the company would export iron ore. It did not have to build a deepwater port or a railroad capable of carrying iron ore to Guinea's coast. Instead, BSGR could pursue a cheaper option: exporting the ore through Liberia, which already had the necessary infrastructure. For years, the government of Guinea had resisted such a scenario when Rio Tinto had proposed it. As a concession, BSGR agreed to spend $1 billion developing a passenger railway for Guinea. In December 2009, an aide shot Captain Dadis in the head. He survived and fled the country; another interim government took over. Once again, Steinmetz weathered the chaos, and in April 2010 he flew to Rio de Janeiro to finalize the $2.5 billion deal with Vale. Afterward, he stopped at a shipyard in Chile to check on the progress of a mega-yacht that he had commissioned to be built there.

• • •

When President Condé set out to clean up Guinea's mining industry, he discovered a generous ally in George Soros. "I was aware of the magnitude of the problem in Guinea," Soros told me. "I was eager to help." He enlisted Revenue Watch to provide technical support in revising the mining code. He also suggested that Guinea hire Scott Horton, an attorney at the U.S. law firm DLA Piper; Horton has conducted dozens of corruption investigations around the world. "There was no way, going up against a guy like Steinmetz, that the Condé government could compete effectively without outside help," Horton told me.

Another difficulty was that so many government officials had held prominent roles in prior regimes. "I can't task my gendarmerie to do the investigation," Condé observed to his advisers. "They'll come up with members of their own families." In the spring of 2011, Horton began to investigate the Simandou deal. For assistance, he turned to a man named Steven Fox, who runs a risk-assessment company in New York called Veracity Worldwide. When corporations want to do business in countries that suffer from political instability and corruption, Veracity can help them assess if such an investment would be prudent—and viable without breaking the law. Fox is in his forties, with the bearing of a man who feels most comfortable in a suit. He speaks softly, enunciating each syllable. At a recent meeting at his office in midtown Manhattan, he told me that until 2005 he had worked for the State Department and had spent time as a foreign-service officer in Africa. According to *Broker, Trader, Lawyer, Spy,* a 2010 book by Eamon Javers about the private-intelligence industry, Fox actually worked for the CIA. As we sat down to talk, I noted a bookshelf that was heavy on le Carré and Furst.

When Guinean government officials began looking into the Simandou contract, Fox told me, they had no evidence of malfeasance. "They only heard the rumors on the street," he said. Fox had met Steinmetz once, in London, and had found him quiet and unassuming, but his understanding was that Steinmetz enlisted employees to pave the way for him—"pointy-end-of-the-spear forward-reconnaissance people." Fox decided that his first essential task was to identify Steinmetz's man in Guinea. He soon pinpointed a candidate: Frédéric Cilins, a tanned, gregarious Frenchman, with thinning hair, who lived on the Riviera, near Cannes, but spent a lot of time in Africa. He had served as a scout for BSGR in Guinea. When I asked Fox how he had learned of Cilins, his response was enigmatic: "We knew a circle of people who knew a circle of people."

Cilins was "an operator—that's the best way to describe him," Fox said. His role at BSGR was to accumulate relationships and identify relevant power structures. In that respect, Fox realized, Cilins was not so different from him: they both excelled at parachuting into foreign countries and figuring out what "makes them tick." (Cilins declined to comment for this article.) One day in the fall of 2011, Fox flew to Paris and met with Cilins. They had been introduced by a mutual acquaintance; as Cilins understood it, Fox was working on behalf of a client who wanted to know how BSGR had secured the Simandou deal. Fox told me that, unlike some corporate-espionage outfits (and actual government spies), Veracity does not "pretext"—employ ruses to approach a potential source. Even so, he did not acknowledge that his client was the new government of Guinea.

Fox and Cilins went to a restaurant for lunch. Cilins was affable and surprisingly candid. While Fox took notes, Cilins explained that he first visited Guinea in 2005, after a BSGR executive in Johannesburg had informed him that the company wanted to "shoot for the moon"—a phrase that Cilins took to indicate Simandou. Cilins told Fox that he spent the next six months in Conakry, staying at the Novotel, a seaside property that is popular with mining executives. He became friendly with the staff in the business center and persuaded them to hand him copies of all incoming and outgoing faxes. In this manner, he learned details about the Conté regime's frustration with Rio Tinto. Each time that Cilins flew from France to Guinea, he brought gifts—MP3 players, cell phones, perfumes—which he disbursed among his contacts. They came to think of him as "Father Christmas," he told Fox. One minister informed him that the only person who mattered in the country was General Conté—and that

the way to Conté was through his four wives. (Plural marriage is tolerated in Guinea, a predominantly Muslim country.)

After further inquiries, Cilins focused on the fourth and youngest
wife, Mamadie Touré—a stout, almond-eyed woman who was still in
her twenties. "She was young, and she was considered very beautiful,"
Fox told me. "She's not a rocket scientist, but she had a certain dyna-
mism. Most important, she had the ear of the president." Cilins hired
Touré's brother to help promote the company's interests in Guinea,
then secured an introduction to her. Not long afterward, Cilins and
several associates from the company obtained an audience with the
president. At this meeting, Cilins told Fox, they gave General Conté
a watch that was inlaid with Steinmetz diamonds. At another meeting, they presented the minister of mines with a model of a Formula 1
race car that was similarly encrusted with Steinmetz bling. Soon
afterward, Touré's brother was named the head of public relations for
BSGR-Guinea.

When I asked Fox why Cilins would confide all of this to him, he
shrugged. "There's an element of arrogance," he said. "Or of complete
naïveté. Of believing they did what they did and there was no big
deal." Cilins seemed proud of his work in Conakry. He told Fox that
in his view the history of Guinea would henceforth be thought of as
dividing into two periods—"before and after BSGR."

It might have seemed to Cilins that giving gifts was simply the
cost of doing business in a place like Guinea. Many countries aggressively prosecute domestic corruption but are much more permissive
when it comes to bribes paid abroad. Until fairly recently, French
firms that gave bribes in order to secure business in foreign countries could declare them as deductible business expenses in France. In
recent years, however, international norms have begun changing. The
U.S. Justice Department has dramatically increased its enforcement of
the Foreign Corrupt Practices Act; the U.K. has passed its own strin-
gent Bribery Act; the Organisation for Economic Co-operation and
Development has instituted a convention against bribery, and several
dozen countries—including Israel—have signed it. Major companies,
like Siemens and KBR, have settled corruption investigations by paying hundreds of millions of dollars in fines. (Rio Tinto, too, has contended with corruption; in 2010, four representatives of the company

were convicted of accepting bribes in China.) Many multinational corporations have responded to the increased vigilance about graft by establishing robust internal-compliance departments that monitor employee behavior. BSGR says that it conducts itself ethically wherever it operates, and a company representative pointed out to me that neither Steinmetz nor his organization has ever been implicated in bribery. But BSGR does not have a compliance department, and it does not have a single employee whose chief responsibility is to monitor company behavior abroad.

Shortly after General Conté died, Mamadie Touré fled Guinea. Fox and his colleagues discovered that she was living in Jacksonville, Florida. The World Bank estimates that 40 percent of the private wealth in Africa is held outside the continent. In a recent civil-forfeiture proceeding against the son of the dictator of Equatorial Guinea, the Justice Department documented some of his possessions: a twelve-acre estate in Malibu, a Gulfstream jet, seven Rolls-Royces, eight Ferraris, and a white glove once worn by Michael Jackson. Jacksonville isn't Malibu. But when Fox and his team investigated, they discovered that Touré had purchased a McMansion on a canal there, along with a series of smaller properties in the vicinity.

• • •

When you disembark from a plane in Conakry, the corruption hits you almost as quickly as the heat. At the airport, a uniformed officer will stop you, raising no specific objections but making it clear, with his body, that your exit from the situation will be transactional. Out on the rubble-strewn streets, which are perfumed by the garbage that clogs the city's open sewers, the military presence is less conspicuous than in the past—security-sector reform has been a priority for Condé—but at night insouciant young soldiers position themselves at intersections, holding submachine guns; they lean into passing cars and come away with cash. In 1961, Frantz Fanon wrote of postcolonial West Africa, "Concessions are snatched up by foreigners; scandals are numerous, ministers grow rich, their wives doll themselves up, the members of parliament feather their nests and there is not a soul down to the simple policeman or the customs officer who does not join in the great procession of corruption." This description no longer applies to the region as a whole—Ghana, for example, is a prospering democracy—but in Guinea little has changed.

One afternoon, I went to a whitewashed building in Conakry's administrative quarter to meet Nava Touré, a former professor of engineering whom Condé had entrusted with running the technical committee on mines. Touré (no relation to Mamadie Touré, the general's fourth wife) has a round face, a melodious voice, and a decorous, almost ethereal, manner. During the months that I spent reporting this story, Nava Touré was one of the few officials in the government about whom I never heard even a rumor of corruption. He had been charged with establishing a new mining code that would create a more equitable balance between the interests of the mining companies and the people of Guinea. In addition, he had been asked to review all existing mining contracts and recommend whether any of them should be renegotiated or rescinded. But when he turned his focus on Simandou, he had no staff of trained inspectors, so he relied on DLA Piper, the law firm, and Steven Fox, the investigator. "It was outsourced," Touré told me.

Last October, he sent an incendiary letter to representatives of the joint venture between Vale and BSGR, identifying "possible irregularities" in the Simandou concession. It called Frédéric Cilins "a secret proxy" for Steinmetz, raised suspicions about Cilins's alliance with Mamadie Touré, and itemized gifts such as the diamond watch and the bejeweled model race car. The letter accused BSGR of planning all along to flip the rights to Simandou, in order "to extract immediate and substantial profits."

Nava Touré's accusations also implicated a man he knew: Mahmoud Thiam, who had served as the minister of mines under the junta that ruled Guinea after General Conté's death. Touré had been one of Thiam's advisers at the time. Thiam came to the job, in early 2009, with stellar credentials. After obtaining an economics degree from Cornell, he had worked as a banker at Merrill Lynch and UBS. Thiam was handsome, very polished, and a champion of Beny Steinmetz. In 2010, in an interview on *Closing Bell with Maria Bartiromo* on CNBC, Thiam praised the "very aggressive junior company, BSGR, that came and developed that permit to the point where it made it attractive to a big player like Vale." Simandou, Thiam said, would "catapult the country into the No. 3 iron-ore exporter in the world." He had attended the lavish wedding of Steinmetz's daughter in Israel, as a representative of the junta. According to Nava Touré's letter, Thiam not only took payoffs from BSGR; he effectively worked as the company's paymaster, meeting a corporate jet at Conakry airport, unloading suitcases full of cash, and then distributing bribes to the junta's leaders. Steven Fox, the American investigator, had discovered that while Thiam was minister, he took to driving around Conakry in a Lamborghini. Before he left office in 2011, he bought an apartment on the Upper East Side of Manhattan for $1.5 million and an estate in Dutchess County for $3.75 million. He paid for both properties with cash.

Thiam currently lives in the United States, running an investment-advisory firm. This spring, I visited him at his elegant office on Madison Avenue. He denied any wrongdoing. The Manhattan apartment, he explained, was paid for with money that he had made in banking. And he had bought the country estate on behalf of a Mozambican friend who was looking to invest in the United States. (Thiam refused to name the friend.) The Lamborghini was not a sports car but a four-wheel-drive vehicle, he pointed out. "You can't serve as mining minister without being accused of corruption," he said. He regards the review of the BSGR contract as little more than a witch hunt, but added that he still maintains the highest respect for Nava Touré.

During our meeting in the whitewashed building, I asked Touré how it made him feel to learn of such allegations about former colleagues. He paused. "The feeling of shame," he said at last. "Because, finally, what they have got personally—let's say ten million U.S. dollars, twelve million U.S. dollars—what does that amount to? Compared with the lives of the whole country?" The lights in the room suddenly shut off, and the air conditioner powered down. He didn't seem to notice. "I don't think that it is tolerable or acceptable from the investors," he continued. "But I'm more shocked by the attitude and the behavior of the national decision makers."

When BSGR received Touré's letter, it responded aggressively, dismissing the investigation as an effort by President Condé to expropriate its asset. The company insisted that it had never given a watch to General Conté; though the story about the miniature Formula 1 car was true, the model had a value of only $1,000, and BSGR routinely gave such "gifts to companies around the world." Frédéric Cilins had worked for the company, but "BSGR never told Mr. Cilins that it 'asked for the moon.'" Cilins might have distributed gifts among his contacts in Conakry, but the company denied any knowledge of them. Oddly, BSGR's written response insisted, more than once, that Mamadie Touré had not actually been the wife of General Conté.

BSGR faulted the Condé administration for failing to name the sources of its allegations, and noted that any payments made to public officials "would be easily identified by bank transfers, payment orders, copies of checks, etc." Again and again, BSGR returned to "the absence of the smallest amount of supporting proof." But how do you prove corruption? By its nature, corruption is covert; payoffs are designed to be difficult to detect. The international financial system has evolved to accommodate a wide array of illicit activities, and shell companies and banking havens make it easy to camouflage transfers, payment orders, and copies of checks. Paul Collier argues that there are often three parties to a corrupt deal: the briber, the bribed, and the lawyers and financial facilitators who enable the secret transaction. The result, he says, is "a web of corporate opacity" that is spun largely by wealthy professionals in financial capitals like London and New York. A recent study found that the easiest country in which to establish an untraceable shell company is not some tropical banking haven but the United States.

• • •

In the spring of 2012, one of President Condé's ministers took a trip to Paris. At the Hilton Arc de Triomphe, he was approached by a Gabonese businessman. According to an affidavit by the minister, the Gabonese man said that he had been in contact with Mamadie Touré, and that she had provided him with documents that would be interesting to President Condé. "Madame Touré was angry with Mr. Beny Steinmetz," the Gabonese man said. She believed that "she had been taken advantage of." The minister was astonished by the documents. They appeared to be a series of legal contracts, complete with signatures and official seals, between officers of BSGR and Mamadie Touré. The documents contained the signature of Asher Avidan, the head of the company's Guinea operations. Avidan was a former member of Israel's internal security service, Shin Bet. The contracts had been signed in Conakry in February 2008—five months before General Conté took the Simandou concession away from Rio Tinto and ten months before the northern half of that concession was given to Beny Steinmetz. The agreements stipulated that Touré would be granted a 5 percent stake in the northern "blocks" of Simandou, in addition to "two (2) million" dollars, which would be paid through a shell company. In exchange, she committed "to do all that is necessary" to help BSGR "obtain from the authorities the signature for the obtaining of said blocks."

An American lawyer involved in the case told me, "I've been involved in corporate corruption work for thirty years, and I've never seen anything like this. A *contract* for bribery that's actually signed by a senior executive? Corporate seals?" The Gabonese man intimated that the documents were potentially worth millions of dollars. He was not going to part with such a valuable commodity for free. He was associated with an investment company, Palladino, that had lent the Condé government $25 million to set up a mining project. Now, in return for the documents, the Gabonese man wanted his *own* stake in Simandou. (Palladino acknowledges that the Paris meeting took place, but denies that the Gabonese businessman made any such demands.) President Condé refused to make a quid pro quo deal for the documents, but at least the Guinean government knew of their existence. If they were genuine, they could be that rare thing: proof of corruption.

When I asked Steven Fox, the investigator, why any company would sign such a contract, he suggested that Touré might have insisted upon it. "There's a whole Francophone-African culture of these very legalistic documents that formalize certain arrangements," he explained. And Touré would have been concerned about securing her position. "Her sole value was that she was the wife of the president," he said. When the contract was signed, the general's health was in rapid decline, and "she knew that the minute he closed his eyes, she would have absolutely nothing." At first glance, it seemed odd that she had entrusted copies of the documents to the Gabonese man. But several people who have spoken to Touré suggested to me that she had grown to fear Steinmetz. The contracts—which, if exposed, could potentially imperil his position in Guinea—amounted to a form of insurance policy.

By this time, President Condé had come to fear for his safety as well. In 2011, he had narrowly survived an assassination attempt in which soldiers bombarded his residence in Conakry with machine-gun fire and rockets. He pressed on with his efforts to reform Guinea, but his situation grew more precarious. His Treasury chief, whom Condé had charged with investigating embezzlement by government officials, was driving home from work one night when her car was cut off by another vehicle; she was shot and killed. Bernard Kouchner said of Condé, "He is really isolated." After the attack on his residence, Condé moved into the presidential palace, a cavernous fortress, con-structed by Chinese contractors, which one diplomat referred to as "the Dim Sum Palace." Condé is married, but at night he often ate alone, occasionally watching a soccer game to distract him from his worries. He did not discuss the matter with me, but several people who have spoken with Condé told me that he believes that Steinmetz is eavesdropping on his communications. (BSGR denies this.)

Condé was also contending with an unstable capital. The violence that erupted after he delayed parliamentary elections did not abate. Rival factions fought one another in the street, and protesters threw rocks at police. In several instances, Condé's security forces fired on protesters. More than two dozen people died. To some, it looked as if Condé might replicate the sad pattern of many postcolonial African leaders who have started as reformers and then drifted into tyranny. In September 2011, Amnesty International declared that "President Alpha Condé is resorting to exactly the same brutal methods as his predecessors." Ehud Olmert told me that Steinmetz "is the last guy you want as an enemy." BSGR—sensing, perhaps, that Condé was politically vulnerable—went on the attack, labeling his government a "discredited regime" that was trying to "illegally seize" the Simandou deposit. The company also pointed out that Rio Tinto had reacquired the rights to the southern half of Simandou, eventually paying the Condé government $700 million to secure the deal.

But was this corruption at work? Rio Tinto's payment was, in part, a reflection of a new mining code, which levied higher taxes on international companies exporting Guinean resources. The company also granted the government up to a 35 percent stake in the mine. In this respect, the Condé administration was trying to bring mining into line with the more equitable deals made by the oil-and-gas industry. (Dag Cramer, the executive who oversees Steinmetz's business interests, told me, "There's a reason Arab families own half of London today. The bulk of the profits from oil are being extracted by the host countries. This hasn't happened yet in mining.") The Rio Tinto deal was also transparent: the contract was published, in its entirety, on the internet. "This is something that no other Guinean government would have done, at any point in the country's history," Patrick Heller, who works at Revenue Watch, told me. "It's a huge sign of progress." Moreover, the funds went not into numbered bank accounts but directly into the Guinean treasury.

Nevertheless, several BSGR employees suggested to me that the $700 million amounted to a colossal bribe. They further speculated that Condé had "stolen" the election in 2010 by collaborating with wealthy South African backers to rig the results. In conversations with me, friends of Steinmetz's likened Condé to Robert Mugabe and to Mahmoud Ahmadinejad. (Both the Carter Center and the European Union, which monitored the election, found that despite some procedural irregularities Condé's victory was "credible" and "fair.")

In September 2011, Condé invited Steinmetz to Conakry, to clear the air. Steinmetz arrived at the palace, and they sat in Condé's office, speaking in French. (Steinmetz is fluent.) "Why are you against us?" Steinmetz asked. "What have we done wrong?"

"I have no personal problem with you," Condé replied. "But I have to defend the interests of Guinea."

Steinmetz was not placated. Cramer told me that the company had to counter the corruption allegations as forcefully as possible, because, for Steinmetz, "the perception of him being an honest person" was crucial. "In the diamond business, a handshake is more important than a contract," Cramer explained. BSGR expanded its campaign against Condé and turned to a company called FTI, which is based in Palm Beach but has operations throughout the world. FTI practices an aggressive form of public relations, seeking not only to suppress negative media coverage about a client but also to plant unfavorable stories about the client's adversaries. An FTI spokesman blasted the Guinean government's review process, calling it a "crude smear campaign." The firm encouraged journalists to run negative stories about Condé; the president soon began to receive bad press about the delay in setting parliamentary elections and about several ostensibly dubious transactions made by people close to him, including his son, Alpha Mohamed Condé. It is not hard to imagine that at least some of Condé's associates have made side deals. "I practice the watch theory of politics," a Western diplomat in Conakry told me. "When a minister is wearing a watch that costs more than my car, I start to worry." During my interviews with officials in Conakry, I spotted more than one conspicuously expensive watch; in the Guinean fashion, the watches hung loose on the wrist, like bracelets.

Inside FTI, the decision to work on behalf of Steinmetz caused discord. In 2012, the company hired a new executive to oversee some of its accounts in Africa, and when he discovered that the firm represented Steinmetz and Dan Gertler—another Israeli diamond mogul, who has been involved in controversial deals in the Democratic Republic of Congo—the executive protested, then resigned. Mark Malloch-Brown, the former deputy secretary-general of the United Nations, is now FTI's chairman for the Middle East and Europe. He grew concerned that the company's reputation might be damaged by its association with Steinmetz, and earlier this year he terminated the relationship. The leadership at BSGR was incensed. As the company's troubles accumulated, Steinmetz and his colleagues began to direct their feelings of grievance at George Soros, who had financed Condé's initial investigation and provided seed money to DLA Piper. Soros also bankrolled Revenue Watch, the organization that had been assisting Nava Touré in revising Guinea's mining code, and supported Global Witness, an anticorruption watchdog group that had been looking into Steinmetz's activities in Guinea. BSGR executives became convinced that Malloch-Brown had terminated the FTI contract at the behest of an old friend of his: Soros. Cramer showed me an internal document, titled "The Spider," that depicted Soros and Condé at the center of a web of influence and identified Soros as "a hater of Israel." The firm sent Soros an angry letter, saying, "We can no longer remain silent letting you ceaselessly maul our company and maliciously attempt wrecking the investment."

Earlier this year, lawyers for Steinmetz sent a letter to Malloch-Brown, demanding that he acknowledge his "personal vendetta" against Steinmetz, sign a formal apology that they had scripted for him, and "clear" BSGR of any wrongdoing in Africa. When Malloch-Brown refused, BSGR sued him, along with FTI. The lawsuit claimed that Soros nurtured a "personal obsession" with Steinmetz; it also alleged that Soros had perpetuated a shocking rumor—that Steinmetz tried to have President Condé killed, by backing the mortar attack on his residence in 2011. (BSGR maintains that this rumor is entirely unfounded; the lawsuit was recently settled out of court, with no admission of wrongdoing by Malloch-Brown or FTI.)

When I asked Soros about Steinmetz, he insisted that he holds no grudge against him. A major philanthropist, Soros has long been committed to promoting transparency and curtailing corruption, and he funds numerous organizations in these fields. It is true that some of these groups have converged, lately, on the activities of Steinmetz. This may mean that Soros is obsessed with Steinmetz, but it might also simply be an indication that Steinmetz is corrupt. Soros told me that he had never met Steinmetz. When I asked Cramer about this, he said, "That's a lie." In 2005, the two men had attended a dinner at Davos and spoke to each other. Presented with this account, Soros said that he has gone to many dinners at Davos over the years. If he did meet Steinmetz, he had no memory of it.

• • •

One day in April 2013, Frédéric Cilins—the Frenchman who allegedly orchestrated the bribes in Guinea—flew to Jacksonville for an urgent rendezvous. Mamadie Touré met him at the airport. They sat in a bar and grill in the departures area, and she ordered a chicken-salad sandwich. Cilins suffers from high blood pressure, and as they spoke, in hushed tones, he was extremely anxious. He had come to Florida on a mission. He told Mamadie Touré that she must destroy the documents—and that he was willing to pay her to do it. She informed him that it might already be too late: she had recently been approached by the FBI. "They're going to give me a subpoena," she said. A grand jury had been convened, and the authorities would expect her to testify and turn over "all the documents."

"Everything must be destroyed!" Cilins said. It was "very, very urgent."

Cilins did not realize that he had fallen into a trap. Touré was wearing a wire. She had indeed been approached by the authorities and, aware of her own legal predicament, had agreed to cooperate with the FBI. As she subsequently explained in an interview with Guinean authorities, Cilins and his colleagues had "one single concern," which was "to get these documents back at any price." As federal agents observed from around the restaurant and the wire recorded every word, she asked Cilins what she should do if she was summoned before the grand jury. He responded, "Of course, you have to lie!" Cilins then suggested that she deny that she had ever been married to General Conté.

Touré and Cilins had spoken on the phone before meeting in Jacksonville, and at one point she had asked him if the plan to buy her silence had been authorized by an individual who is identified in court documents only as "CC-1," for "co-conspirator." Two sources close to the investigation told me that CC-1 is Beny Steinmetz. "Of course," Cilins replied. That call, too, was recorded by the FBI.

At the airport, Cilins said that he had seen Steinmetz the previous week. "I went specially to see him," he explained. He lowered his voice to a whisper and said he had assured Steinmetz that Touré would "never betray" him and would "never give away any documents whatsoever." Steinmetz's response, according to Cilins, was, "That's good . . . But I want you to destroy these documents."

Touré told Cilins that the documents were in a vault and assured him that she would destroy them. But he wasn't satisfied, explaining that he had been instructed to watch the papers burn. If she agreed to this plan, Cilins told her, she would be paid $1 million. He had brought along an attestation—a legal document, in French—for her to sign. (Cilins's comfort with formal legal agreements appears to have extended even into the realm of the cover-up.) "I have never signed a single contract with BSGR," the attestation read. "I have never received any money from BSGR." The arrangement included a possi-

ble bonus, Cilins said. If she signed the attestation, destroyed the documents, and lied to the grand jury, and if BSGR succeeded in holding
on to its asset at Simandou—"if they're still part of the project"—she
would receive $5 million. Before Cilins could leave Jacksonville, he
was arrested.

This put BSGR in an awkward position. The transcript of the
airport conversation looked very much like confirmation of bribery. Mamadie Touré's documents were now in the possession of the
Department of Justice. The government of Guinea had also obtained
a videotape, shot during the opening of BSGR's office in Conakry
in 2006, that seemed to further illustrate Touré's close relationship
with the company. It shows Cilins sitting next to Asher Avidan, who
is addressing a crowd of Guineans. Touré then makes an entrance,
resplendent in a white headdress and flowing robes and flanked by
members of the presidential guard—implicitly conferring, by virtue
of her presence, the approval of her dying husband.

When news of the arrest in Jacksonville broke, Vale released a
statement saying that it was "deeply concerned about these allegations" and committed to working with the relevant authorities. By
this time, it seems safe to assume, the Brazilian company might have
developed some buyer's remorse over its iron-ore project in Guinea.
When I visited the Conakry office of VBG—the joint venture of Vale
and the Beny Steinmetz Group—it was operating with a skeleton
staff, and the project was clearly on hold, though the executives there
would say nothing for the record. "The question for Vale is, what were
you thinking?" a diplomat in Conakry told me. "Did you really think
you would be able to start a fifty-year project exporting iron ore in the
remotest part of Guinea on the basis of a clearly dubious deal?" Having paid only half a billion dollars to BSGR so far, Vale has refused,
for the moment, to make any further payments on the $2 billion it still
owes.

• • •

In mid-June, I flew to Nice, on the French Riviera, and proceeded in a
taxi to Cap d'Antibes, a resort town favored by billionaires. I had spent
several months trying to meet with Steinmetz, without success. I had
visited the BSGR offices in London, and been told when I arrived that

Steinmetz would meet me in Paris. By the time I reached Paris, he had left on his private plane for Israel. I volunteered to fly to Israel, but was told that he wouldn't necessarily meet with me when I got there. After weeks of negotiation, I finally managed to speak to him by telephone, and after a brief conversation—in which he announced, flatly, "I don't give interviews"—he agreed to see me.

We met at a hotel that was perched above the Mediterranean. Steinmetz was staying on one of his yachts—an Italian model. A sleek white multistory vessel, it floated regally in the distance. As I entered the lobby, I brushed past a slim, deeply tanned man wearing a blue linen shirt that was unbuttoned halfway to his navel. It was Steinmetz. "Thank you for making the trip," he said when I introduced myself. He seized my hand with the formidable grip of someone who puts a lot of stock in a handshake. We left the hotel and made our way up a steep hill, toward a suite of offices. Steinmetz moved almost at a trot; I had to scramble to keep up.

"I'm totally open—totally transparent," Steinmetz told me when we sat down. "I never lie, as a principle." He resents the idea that he is secretive, and believes that he simply protects his right to privacy. "I don't consider myself a public person," he said. We talked for nearly three hours, until Steinmetz grew hoarse. He said that he felt blindsided by the controversy over Simandou. People who think that it is inherently outlandish to make billions of dollars on an investment of $160 million simply don't understand that the natural-resources business is a game of chance. "It's roulette," Steinmetz said; if you work hard, and take risks, you sometimes "get lucky." As a small company that was comfortable with risk, BSGR made investments that the major mining companies wouldn't. His company lost money in Tanzania. It lost money in Zambia. But in Guinea it won.

Steinmetz argued that the deal with Vale was not an effort by BSGR to sell off its asset but, rather, a partnership of the sort that is often necessary with ambitious, resource-intensive mining projects. "How did we flip?" he asked. "Why is bringing a partner in a flip?" In our telephone call, Steinmetz had described the saga of Simandou as "a very African story," and when we met, I asked him how his company has dealt with the pervasiveness of corruption in Africa. "Very strict instructions and guidelines to people on the ground," he said, insisting that even in jurisdictions that are notorious for graft, the company does not pay bribes. "We manage our business like the most transparent public company," he said. To hear Steinmetz tell it, the former leaders of Guinea were undeserving of the widespread censure they had received. General Conté was "more honest" than President Condé. Captain Dadis, the junta leader who presided over the stadium massacre, was "an honest guy" who simply "wanted the best for his country." President Condé was the real villain in this story, Steinmetz said. His loathing for Condé was so palpable that whenever Steinmetz mentioned the president, the tendons in his neck stood out. Steinmetz claimed that the accusations against him were the product of a concerted smear campaign, initiated by Condé and financed by George Soros. "According to the Jewish religion, if you say somebody is guilty of something without proof, this is a very bad thing to do," Steinmetz said. And the documents that were discussed in Jacksonville did not prove anything, he said—they were forgeries.

After failing to meet Steinmetz in Paris, I had met Asher Avidan, the head of BSGR's Guinea operations, for a drink. When I presented him with a photograph of a signature that appeared on one of the contracts, he had acknowledged that it was identical to his own but dismissed it as "a simple Photoshop." In Cap d'Antibes, Steinmetz elaborated on this theme, claiming that Mamadie Touré's documents were fake and that long before the FBI investigation began, she had tried to blackmail BSGR, using the fraudulent contracts as leverage. "We never paid her," Steinmetz insisted. "We never promised her anything." He pulled out color photocopies of the documents and pointed at sequential notations that had supposedly been made on each contract by the notary public in Conakry. These notations, he said, ran in descending rather than ascending order—proof that they were inauthentic. I told him that I could imagine a scenario in which the documents were forgeries, and conceded that Touré was not exactly an unimpeachable witness. But the transcript of the Jacksonville conversation did not look good for Steinmetz, and I told him that there was another factor that inclined me to consider the documents real: If they were fake, why would Frédéric Cilins fly across the Atlantic and offer Touré $5 million to destroy them? I posed the question to Steinmetz multiple times, in multiple ways, but he replied only that he would not "speculate" about Cilins while his case was before the courts. I pressed the matter. "Cilins told Mamadie Touré, 'I've spoken to Beny. He told me to do this.' Did you?"

"I didn't ask him to destroy these fake documents or any other documents," Steinmetz said.

Was Cilins lying about Steinmetz's directive, then? Or was he somehow mistaken? Steinmetz, growing impatient, reiterated that he did not want to speculate about Cilins. He did want to talk, however, about Condé's responsibility for the deaths of protesters in Guinea. "The guy has blood on his hands," Steinmetz said.

"Captain Dadis had blood on his hands, too," I observed. "And you invited him to your daughter's wedding."

Steinmetz stared at me for a second, then said, "I'm not going to argue or go into depth about the politics of Guinea."

Even as we were meeting in France, the leaders of the Group of Eight had assembled in Northern Ireland. A major goal was to assess the rules governing how executives from wealthy nations conduct themselves when they venture into the developing world. Before the summit, Prime Minister David Cameron of the U.K. published an op-ed in *The Wall Street Journal*: "We must lift the veil of secrecy that too often lets corrupt corporations and officials in some countries run rings around the law. The G-8 must move toward a global common standard for resource-extracting companies to report all payments to governments, and in turn for governments to report those revenues." In developing this ambitious agenda, Cameron had been closely advised by Paul Collier. "This is Africa's big opportunity," Collier told me. "But it's a nonrenewable opportunity." If companies are allowed to acquire natural resources without full transparency, the result will be plunder—or, as Collier puts it, "a tragedy of awesome proportions." At Cameron's invitation, President Condé traveled to London before the meeting. "If we are to fight against exploitation and bring about transparency, we are going to need the help of the G-8," Condé said in a speech at Chatham House, the foreign-policy think tank. He pointed out that "Mining companies are mostly in the West."

Steinmetz was appalled by the lionization of Guinea's leader. The current government, he said, is a "sophisticated" version of a corrupt regime, because "they are pretending to be honest." He repeated a claim that some of his colleagues had made—that Condé had stolen the 2010 election by promising to strip BSGR of its Simandou license and transfer the rights to his backers. "He sold our assets to South African interests who provided him with financial support to manipulate the election," he said. Even before Condé entered office, he had decided "that he was going to take Simandou from us." In Steinmetz's telling, Condé is like the title character in *Nostromo*—the "perfectly incorruptible" man who, through his own vanity and the spell of the mine, finally succumbs to corruption. "*We* are the victims," Steinmetz said. "We have done only good things for Guinea, and what we're getting is spit in the face."

With that, he wished me well. Dusk was falling, and I descended the hill while Steinmetz headed back to his yacht for dinner.

• • •

Shortly after Frédéric Cilins was arrested in Florida, I went to Conakry and visited President Condé at the Dim Sum Palace. He wore a white suit with short sleeves—a common style in Guinea—and looked tired. The violent opposition rallies showed no sign of stopping, and it was not entirely clear that Condé would hold on to power long enough to fulfill his reform agenda. Having failed to hold parliamentary elections, he was also at risk of losing his credibility as a genuinely democratic leader. Alexis Arieff, a Guinea expert at the Congressional Research Service, told me, "He came in with a real sense of having fought for the presidency and deserving a free hand in how he runs the country—'This is mine, I went to prison for this, I suffered for this.'" A European Union report recently blamed "Condé's governing style" for the escalating tension in the country.

Condé, for his part, felt that Steinmetz had played a role in the unrest; at Chatham House, he intimated that BSGR is funding the opposition movement. (Steinmetz told me that this was false.) When I asked Condé if he felt vindicated when the U.S. Justice Department began investigating the Simandou deal, he refused to take the bait. It is ultimately up to him to decide—on the basis of counsel from the Ministry of Mines—whether to strip BSGR and Vale of the Simandou license, and he did not want to say anything that might prejudice this process. Instead, he smiled and said, "The actions of the United States can help me advance in the struggle against corruption in Guinea."

Cilins's bail was set at $15 million, because of the danger that he might flee the United States. In May, he pleaded not guilty to obstruction-of-justice charges, and it's possible that he will decide to cooperate with authorities; in his court filings, he has not denied offering Mamadie Touré money to destroy the documents, or doing so at the behest of Steinmetz. BSGR continues to maintain that it never paid any money to Touré or signed any contracts with her. But Asher Avidan said something interesting in our conversation at the Paris bar. He repeated BSGR's claim that Touré had not been married to General Conté when he signed over the rights to Simandou. "She was not his wife," Avidan said. "Not even sleeping with him." Then he added, "She is a lobbyist. Like a thousand others."

It suddenly occurred to me why BSGR officials might be so committed to the notion that Touré had not been married to the old general. If she was not related to him, then she was merely another local influence peddler—a lobbyist. And it might be argued that as a legal matter paying a lobbyist is different from paying a bribe. If BSGR was ever forced to admit that it *had* paid Mamadie Touré, then here, in embryo, was a defense. Although the U.S. Justice Department will not comment on the case, Cilins is likely not the ultimate target of its investigation. When the grand jury in Manhattan began issuing subpoenas, earlier this year, it requested information not just on "the Simandou concession" but on Steinmetz himself. The FBI recently dispatched two teams of investigators to Conakry. According to *The Wall Street Journal,* the Serious Fraud Office in London has also opened an investigation into BSGR's activities. Because both Israel and France have been reluctant to extradite their citizens in the past, Steinmetz might never see trial in the United States, even in the event that he was indicted. Still, Scott Horton told me, "Steinmetz's future travel options may be limited."

When we spoke in Cap d'Antibes, Steinmetz did not seem worried. "We have zero to hide," he said. Steven Fox, the investigator, told me that Steinmetz and his colleagues were "very improvisational," adding, "They can think creatively and move fast in an uncertain situation. That's what accounted for their success, in a lot of ways. But it will probably also account for their downfall."

For the moment, the iron ore remains locked inside the Simandou Mountains, and the site is still cut off from the rest of Guinea. "Everyone wants Simandou," Condé told me as we sat in the palace. "It became the obsession, literally, of everybody." He continued to talk, in his professorial way, but a note of bewilderment crept into his voice. "Looking at the iron ore, the grade is world-class. The quality is world-class. Yet, in so many years, we haven't been able to benefit from any of these tremendous resources." President Condé paused. Then he murmured, almost to himself, "How can we be so rich and yet so poor?"

In January 2021, Steinmetz was convicted in a Geneva court for his role in the Simandou affair and sentenced to five years in prison. He was released, pending an appeal, and continues to deny the charges against him. Alpha Condé won a controversial third term as Guinea's president in 2020, after a constitutional referendum that allowed him to set aside the traditional two-term limit. He continued to face—and deny—allegations of corruption. In September 2021, he was deposed in a military coup. The iron ore at Simandou remains locked in the ground.

JOURNEYMAN

Anthony Bourdain's movable feast. (2017)

WHEN THE PRESIDENT OF the United States travels outside the country, he brings his own car with him. Moments after Air Force One landed at the Hanoi airport in May 2016, President Barack Obama ducked into an eighteen-foot, armor-plated limousine—a bomb shelter masquerading as a Cadillac—that was equipped with a secure link to the Pentagon and with emergency supplies of blood, and was known as the Beast. Hanoi's broad avenues are crowded with honking cars, storefront vendors, street peddlers, and some five million scooters and motorbikes, which rush in and out of the intersections like floodwaters. It was Obama's first trip to Vietnam, but he encountered this pageant mostly through a five-inch pane of bulletproof glass. He might as well have watched it on TV. Obama was scheduled to meet with President Trần Đại Quang and with the new head of Vietnam's National Assembly. On his second night in Hanoi, however, he kept an unusual appointment: dinner with Anthony Bourdain, the peripatetic chef turned writer who hosts the Emmy-winning travel show *Parts Unknown* on CNN.

Over the past fifteen years, Bourdain has hosted increasingly sophisticated iterations of the same program. Initially, it was called *A Cook's Tour* and aired on the Food Network. After shifting to the Travel Channel, it was renamed *Anthony Bourdain: No Reservations,* and it ran for nine seasons before moving to CNN in 2013. All told, Bourdain has traveled to nearly a hundred countries and has filmed 248 episodes, each a distinct exploration of the food and culture of a place. The secret ingredient of the show is the when-in-Rome avidity with which he partakes of indigenous custom and cuisine, whether he is pounding vodka before plunging into a frozen river outside St. Petersburg or spearing a fatted swine as the guest of honor at a jungle longhouse in Borneo. Like a great white shark, Bourdain tends to be photographed with his jaws wide open, on the verge of sinking his teeth into some tremulous delicacy.

In Bourdain's recollection, his original pitch for the series was, roughly, "I travel around the world, eat a lot of shit, and basically do whatever the fuck I want." The formula has proved improbably successful. People often ask Bourdain's producers if they can tag along on an escapade. On a recent visit to Madagascar, he was accompanied by the film director Darren Aronofsky. (A fan of the show, Aronofsky proposed to Bourdain that they go somewhere together. "I kind of jokingly said Madagascar, just because it's the farthest possible place," he told me. "And Tony said, 'How's November?'") A ride-along with Bourdain promises the sidekick an experience that, in this era of homogenized tourism, is all too rare: communion with a foreign culture so unmitigated that it feels practically intravenous. Parachuted into any far-flung corner of the planet, Bourdain ferrets out the restaurant, known only to discerning locals, where the grilled sardines or the pisco sours are divine. Often, he insinuates himself into a private home where the meal is even better. He is a lively dining companion: a lusty eater and a quicksilver conversationalist. "He's got that incredibly beautiful style when he talks that ranges from erudite to brilliantly slangy," his friend Nigella Lawson observed. Bourdain is a font of unvarnished opinion, but he also listens intently, and the word he uses perhaps more than any other is "interesting," which he pronounces with four syllables and only one *t:* "in-ner-ess-ting."

Before becoming famous, Bourdain spent more than two decades as a professional cook. In 2000, while working as the executive chef at Les Halles, a boisterous brasserie on Park Avenue South, he published a ribald memoir, *Kitchen Confidential.* It became a best seller, heralding a new national fascination with the grubby secrets and *Upstairs Downstairs* drama of the hospitality industry. Having established himself as a brash truth teller, Bourdain got into public spats with more famous figures; he once laid into Alice Waters for her pious hatred of junk food, saying that she reminded him of the Khmer Rouge. People who do not watch Bourdain's show still tend to think of him as a loudmouthed New York chef. But over the years he has transformed himself into a well-heeled nomad who wanders the planet meeting fascinating people and eating delicious food. He freely admits that his career is, for many people, a fantasy profession. A few years ago, in the voice-over to a sun-dappled episode in Sardinia, he asked, "What do you do after your dreams come true?" Bourdain would be easy to hate, in other words, if he weren't so easy to like. "For a long time, Tony thought he was going to have nothing," his publisher, Dan Halpern, told me. "He can't believe his luck. He always seems happy that he actually *is* Anthony Bourdain."

The White House had suggested the meeting in Vietnam. Of all the countries Bourdain has explored, it is perhaps his favorite; he has been there half a dozen times. He fell for the country long before he actually traveled there, when he read Graham Greene's 1955 novel, *The Quiet American,* and Hanoi has retained a thick atmosphere of colonial decay—dingy villas, lugubrious banyan trees, monsoon clouds, and afternoon cocktails—that Bourdain savors without apology. Several years ago, he seriously considered moving there. Bourdain believes that the age of the fifteen-course tasting menu "is over." He is an evangelist for street food, and Hanoi excels at open-air cooking. It can sometimes seem as if half the population were sitting around sidewalk cook fires, hunched over steaming bowls of *phở*. As a White House advance team planned the logistics for Obama's visit, an advance team from Zero Point Zero, the company that produces the show, scoured the city for the perfect place to eat. They selected Bún chả Hương Liên, a narrow establishment across from a karaoke joint on a busy street in the Old Quarter. The restaurant's specialty is *bún chả:* springy white noodles, smoky sausage, and charred pork belly served in a sweet and pungent broth.

At the appointed hour, Obama exited the Beast and walked into the restaurant behind a pair of Secret Service agents, who cleared a path for him, like linemen blocking for a running back. In a rear dining room on the second floor, Bourdain was waiting at a stainless-steel table, surrounded by other diners, who had been coached to ignore the cameras and Obama, and to focus on their *bún chả*. Like many restaurants in Vietnam, the facility was casual in the extreme: diners and servers alike swept discarded refuse onto the floor, and the tiles had acquired a grimy sheen that squeaked beneath your feet. Obama was wearing a white button-down, open at the collar, and he greeted

Bourdain, took a seat on a plastic stool, and happily accepted a bottle of Vietnamese beer. "How often do you get to sneak out for a beer?" Bourdain asked.

"I don't get to sneak out, period," Obama replied. He occasionally took the First Lady to a restaurant, he said, but "part of enjoying a restaurant is sitting with other patrons and enjoying the atmosphere, and too often we end up getting shunted into one of those private rooms." As a young waitress in a gray polo shirt set down bowls of broth, a plate of greens, and a platter of shuddering noodles, Bourdain fished chopsticks from a plastic container on the table. Obama, surveying the constituent parts of the meal, evinced trepidation. He said, "All right, you're gonna have to—"

"I'll walk you through it," Bourdain assured him, advising him to grab a clump of noodles with chopsticks and dunk them into the broth.

"I'm just gonna do what you do," Obama said.

"Dip and stir," Bourdain counseled. "And get ready for the awesomeness."

Eyeing a large sausage floating in the broth, Obama asked, "Is it generally appropriate to just pop one of these whole suckers in your mouth, or do you think you should be a little more—"

"Slurping is totally acceptable in this part of the world," Bourdain declared.

Obama took a bite and let out a low murmur. "That's good stuff," he said, and the two of them—lanky, conspicuously cool guys in late middle age—slurped away as three cameras, which Bourdain had once likened to "drunken hummingbirds," hovered around them.

Noting the unaffected rusticity of the scene, Obama was reminded of a memorable meal that he had eaten as a child, in the mountains outside Jakarta. "You'd have these roadside restaurants overlooking the tea fields," he recalled. "There'd be a river running through the restaurant itself, and there'd be these fish, these carp, that would be running through. You'd pick the fish. They'd grab it for you and fry it up, and the skin would be real crispy. They just served it with a bed of rice." Obama was singing Bourdain's song: earthy, fresh, free from pretense. "It was the simplest meal possible, and nothing tasted so good."

But the world is getting smaller, Obama noted. "The surprises, the serendipity of travel, where you see something and it's off the beaten track, there aren't that many places like that left." He added, wistfully, "I don't know if that place will still be there when my daughters are ready to travel. But I hope it is."

The next day, Bourdain posted a photograph of the meeting online. "Total cost of Bun cha dinner with the President: $6.00," he tweeted. "I picked up the check."

• • •

"Three years I haven't had a cigarette, and I just started again," Bourdain said when I met him shortly afterward at the bar of the Metropole Hotel, where he was staying. He cocked an eyebrow: "Obama made me do it." Bourdain, who is sixty, is imposingly tall—six feet four—and impossibly lean, with a monumental head, a caramel tan, and carefully groomed gray hair. He once described his body as "gristly, tendony," as if it were an inferior cut of beef, and a recent devotion to Brazilian jujitsu has left his limbs and his torso laced with ropy muscles. With his Sex Pistols T-shirt and his sensualist credo, there is something of the aging rocker about him. But if you spend any time with Bourdain, you realize that he is controlled to the point of neurosis: clean, organized, disciplined, courteous, systematic. He is Apollo in drag as Dionysus.

"He has his *mise en place*," his friend the chef Éric Ripert told me, noting that Bourdain's punctiliousness is a reflection not only of his personality and his culinary training but also of necessity: if he weren't so structured, he could never stay on top of his proliferating commitments. In addition to producing and starring in *Parts Unknown*, he selects the locations, writes the voice-overs, and works closely with the cinematographers and the music supervisors. When he is not on camera, he is writing: essays, cookbooks, graphic novels about a homicidal sushi chef, screenplays. (David Simon recruited him to write the restaurant scenes in *Treme*.) Or he is hosting other TV shows, such as *The Taste*, a reality competition that ran for two years on ABC. Last fall, during a hiatus from filming, he launched a fifteen-city stand-up tour. Ripert suggested to me that Bourdain may be driven, in part, by a fear of what he might get up to if he ever stopped working. "I'm a guy who needs a lot of projects," Bourdain acknowledged. "I would probably have been happy as an air-traffic controller."

As he sipped a beer and picked at a platter of delicate spring rolls, he was still fidgeting with exhilaration from the encounter with Obama. "I believe what's important to him is this notion that otherness is not bad, that Americans should aspire to walk in other people's shoes," he reflected. This idea resonates strongly with Bourdain, and although he insists his show is a selfish epicurean enterprise, Obama's ethic could be the governing thesis of *Parts Unknown*. In the opening moments of an episode set in Myanmar, Bourdain observes, "Chances are you haven't been to this place. Chances are this is a place you've never seen." From the moment Bourdain conceives of an episode, he obsesses over the soundtrack, and for the sequence with Obama he wanted to include the James Brown song "The Boss." When the producers cannot afford to license a song, they often commission music that evokes the original. For a *Big Lebowski* homage in a Tehran episode, they arranged the recording of a facsimile, in Farsi, of Dylan's "The Man in Me." But Bourdain wanted the original James Brown track, no matter how much it cost. "I don't know who's paying for it," he said. "But somebody's fucking paying for it." He sang the chorus to himself—"I paid the cost to be the boss"—and remarked that one price of leadership, for Obama, had been a severe constraint on the very wanderlust that Bourdain personifies. "Even drinking a *beer* for him is a big thing," he marveled. "He's got to clear it."

Before he said goodbye to Obama, Bourdain told me, he had underlined this contrast. "I said, 'Right after this, Mr. President, I'm getting on a scooter and I'm going to disappear into the flow of thousands of people.' He got this look on his face and said, 'That must be nice.'"

Tom Vitale, the episode's director, who is in his mid-thirties and has an air of harried intensity, stopped by to check with Bourdain about a shoot that was planned for later that evening. It generally takes Bourdain about a week of frantic work on location to film each episode. He has a small crew—two producers and a few cameramen—who recruit local fixers and grips. His team often shoots between sixty and eighty hours of footage in order to make an hour-long episode. Vitale, like others on the crew, has worked with Bourdain for years.

When I asked him what his interactions with the White House had been like, he said, with bewilderment, "I'm shocked we all passed the background check."

Bourdain was eager to shoot at a *bia-hoi* joint, a popular Hanoi establishment specializing in chilled draft beer. "We're hoping for beer?" he asked. "We're hoping for beer," Vitale confirmed. They had already scouted a place. "But if the energy there is only 50 percent, maybe not." Bourdain agreed. "We don't want to manufacture a scene," he said. He makes a fetish of authenticity and disdains many conventions of food and travel programming. "We don't do retakes," he said. "We don't do 'hello' scenes or 'goodbye, thank you very much' scenes. I'd rather miss the shot than have a bogus shot." When he meets someone at a roadside café, he wears a lavalier microphone, which picks up the sort of ambient noise—blaring car horns, shrieking cicadas—that sound designers normally filter out. "We want you to know what a place sounds like, not just what it looks like," Jared Andrukanis, one of Bourdain's producers, told me. "The guys who mix the show hate it. They hate it, but I think they love it."

Bourdain is exceptionally close to his crew members, in part because they are steady companions in a life that is otherwise transient. "I change location every two weeks," he told me. "I'm not a cook, nor am I a journalist. The kind of care and feeding required of friends, I'm frankly incapable of. I'm not *there*. I'm not going to remember your birthday. I'm not going to be there for the important moments in your life. We are not going to reliably hang out, no matter how I feel about you. For fifteen years, more or less, I've been traveling two hundred days a year. I make very good friends a week at a time."

Until he was forty-four, Bourdain saw very little of the world. He grew up in Leonia, New Jersey, not far from the George Washington Bridge. His father, Pierre, an executive at Columbia Records, was reserved, and given to reading silently on the couch for long stretches, but he had adventurous taste in food and movies. Tony recalls traveling into New York City with his father during the 1970s to try sushi, which at the time seemed impossibly exotic. The only experience of real travel that Bourdain had as a child was two trips to France. When he was ten, his parents took him and his younger brother, Chris, there on summer vacation, to visit relatives of his father's who had a home in a chilly seaside village. Tony had what he has since described as a Proustian encounter with a huge oyster, eating it freshly plucked from the sea. ("Tony likes to play up the oyster episode," Chris, who is now a banker, told me. "I have no idea if that's fact or fiction.") The brothers played in old Nazi blockhouses on the beach and spent hours reading Tintin books—savoring tales of the roving boy reporter and poring over Hergé's minutely rendered illustrations of Shanghai, Cairo, the Andes. The stories, Bourdain recalls, "took me places I was quite sure I would never go."

His mother, Gladys, was a copy editor at *The New York Times.* She was formidable and judgmental and often clashed with her son. In high school, Bourdain fell in love with an older girl, Nancy Putkoski, who ran with a druggy crowd, and he started dabbling in illicit substances himself. At one point, Gladys told her son, "I love you dearly, but, you know, I don't like you very much at present." In 1973, Bourdain finished high school a year early and followed Putkoski to Vassar. But he dropped out after two years and enrolled at the Culinary Institute of America in Hyde Park, New York. It was not his first experience in the kitchen: the summer after finishing high school, he had been a dishwasher at the Flagship, a flounder-and-fried-clams restaurant in Provincetown. In *Kitchen Confidential,* he recounts a defining moment, during a wedding party at the Flagship, when he witnessed the bride sneak outside for an impromptu assignation with the chef. The punch line: "I knew then, dear reader, for the first time: I wanted to be a chef."

The story captures Bourdain's conception of the cook's vocation as both seductively carnal and swaggeringly transgressive. One of his favorite movies is *The Warriors,* the cult 1979 film about street gangs in New York, and it was the outlaw machismo of the kitchen that attracted him. For a time, he walked around with a set of nunchucks in a holster strapped to his leg, like a six-shooter; he often posed for photographs wearing chef's whites and clutching the kind of long, curved knife you might use to disembowel a Gorgon. (The cover of *Kitchen Confidential* showed Bourdain with two ornamental swords tucked into his apron strings.) Long before he was the kind of international celebrity who gets chased by fans through the airport in Singapore, Bourdain knew how to arrange his grasshopper limbs into a good pose, and from the beginning he had a talent for badassery.

After graduating from the Culinary Institute in 1978, he moved with Putkoski into a rent-stabilized apartment on Riverside Drive. They married in 1985. She had various jobs, and Bourdain found work at the Rainbow Room in Rockefeller Center. When I asked about the marriage, which ended in 2005, he likened it to the Gus Van Sant film *Drugstore Cowboy,* in which Matt Dillon and Kelly Lynch play drug addicts who rob pharmacies in order to support their habit. "That kind of love and codependency and sense of adventure—we were criminals together," he said. "A lot of our life was built around that, and happily so." When Bourdain tells stories about the "seriously knuckleheaded shit" he did while using narcotics—being pulled over by the cops with two hundred hits of blotter acid in the car, being stalked by the Drug Enforcement Administration while trying to retrieve a "letter from Panama" at the post office—he vaguely alludes to "another person" who was by his side. He is careful not to mention Putkoski by name. Aside from the drugs, they lived a relatively quiet domestic life. In the evenings, they ordered takeout and watched *The Simpsons.* Every few years, after they saved up some money, Tony and Nancy went on vacation to the Caribbean. Otherwise, they did not travel.

But Bourdain did travel around New York, as a journeyman chef. At the Rainbow Room, he worked the buffet table, and he was a sous-chef at WPA, in SoHo. He worked at Chuck Howard's, in the theater district; at Nikki and Kelly, on the Upper West Side; at Gianni's, a tourist trap at the South Street Seaport; at the Supper Club, a night-spot in midtown where the emphasis was not the food. Eventually, he acquired a crew of associates who migrated with him from one restaurant to the next. His friend Joel Rose, a writer who has known Bourdain since the 1980s, told me, "He was a fixer. Anytime a restaurant was in trouble, he came in and saved the day. He wasn't a great chef, but he was organized. He would stop the bleeding." In 1998, he answered an ad in the *Times* and got the executive-chef job at Les Halles. It was an ideal fit for Bourdain: an unpretentious brasserie with its own butcher, who worked next to the bar, behind a counter stacked with steak, veal, and sausages.

Kitchen Confidential was inspired by *Down and Out in Paris and London,* in which George Orwell describes chefs as "the most work-manlike class, and the least servile." Karen Rinaldi, the editor who acquired the book for Bloomsbury, told me that she underestimated the impact it would have. "It was a flier," she said—the profane musings of a guy who broiled steaks for a living. "But a lot of the books that end up shifting the culture are fliers." *Kitchen Confidential* was filled with admonitions: Bourdain assailed Sunday brunch ("a dumping ground for the odd bits left over from Friday and Saturday") and advised against ordering fish on Mondays, because it is typically "four to five days old." The book was marketed as a dispatch from the scullery, the type of tell-all that might be more interesting to the naive restaurant goer than to the battle-seasoned cook. ("I won't eat in a restaurant with filthy bathrooms," Bourdain warned. "They let you *see* the bathrooms. If the restaurant can't be bothered to replace the puck in the urinal or keep the toilets and floors clean, then just imagine what their refrigeration and work spaces look like.")

But, for Bourdain, the most important audience was his peers. The final line of the acknowledgments page was "Cooks rule," and he hoped, desperately, that other professionals would see the book in the spirit he had intended, and pass gravy-stained copies around the kitchen. Bourdain did not quit his job at Les Halles when the book became a success. "I was careful to modulate my hopes, because I lived in a business where everybody was a writer or an actor," he recalls. For decades, he'd seen colleagues come into work crowing about their latest callback, only to see their grand designs amount to nothing. "So at no point was it 'So long, suckers.'" His confederates at Les Halles were amused, if mystified, by his blossoming career as a writer, and the owners were accommodating about the book tour.

When Bourdain started traveling to promote the book, something curious happened. He would amble into a restaurant alone and order a drink at the bar. Out of nowhere, a plate of *amuse-bouches* would appear, compliments of the house. It marked an affirmation for Bourdain: chefs were reading the book, and they liked it. But it also signified a profound inversion. He had spent the first half of his life preparing food to feed others. He would spend the second half getting fed.

• • •

Kang Ho Dong Baekjeong is a bright, cacophonous restaurant on Thirty-Second Street, a hipster riff on a Korean steak house. One frigid evening last February, I arrived, on time, to discover Bourdain waiting for me, already halfway through a beer. He is more than punctual: he arrives precisely fifteen minutes early to every appointment. "It comes from his kitchen days," Tom Vitale, the director, told me. "If he doesn't show, we know something's wrong." Bourdain used the word "pathological" to describe his fixation with being on time. "I judge other people on it," he admitted. "Today, you're just late, but eventually you will betray me."

I had dined at Baekjeong once before, but I was about to discover that eating at a restaurant with Bourdain is a markedly different experience. Throughout the meal, the head chef—Deuki Hong, an amiable, floppy-haired twenty-seven-year-old—personally presented each dish. One conspicuous hazard of being Anthony Bourdain is that everywhere he goes, from a Michelin-starred temple to a peasant hut on the tundra, he is mercilessly inundated with food. Because he is loath to spurn courtesy of any kind, he often ends up eating much more than he might like to. Bourdain calls this getting "food fucked." Now that he trains nearly every day in jujitsu, he tries to eat and drink more selectively. "Off camera, I don't go around getting drunk at night," he said; during the meals we shared when he wasn't shooting, Bourdain didn't so much gorge himself as graze. A big bowl of pasta is hard to enjoy if you know it will render you sluggish the next morning, when a crazy-eyed mixed martial artist is trying to ease you into a choke hold. Since he started doing jujitsu, three years ago, Bourdain has lost 35 pounds. (He now weighs 175 pounds.) But he adores the food at Baekjeong and was ready to indulge himself. After Hong arranged silky thin slivers of marinated beef tongue on a circular grill embedded in the table between us, Bourdain waited until they had just browned, then reached for one with chopsticks and encouraged me to do the same. We savored the rich, woodsy taste of the meat. Then Bourdain poured two shots of soju, the Korean rice liquor, and said, "That is good, huh?"

It is somewhat ironic that Bourdain has emerged as an ambassador for the culinary profession, given that, by his own admission, he was never an inspired chef. Alan Richman, the restaurant critic at *GQ*, who is a champion of white-tablecloth haute cuisine, told me that Les Halles "was not a particularly good restaurant when he was cooking there, and it got worse when he stopped." This seemed a little unfair: I frequented Les Halles before it closed, in 2016, and until the end it was rowdy and reliable, with a good frisée salad and a sturdy cassoulet. But it was never a standout restaurant. Bourdain used to genuflect like a fanboy before innovative chefs such as Éric Ripert of Le Bernardin. On page 5 of *Kitchen Confidential,* he joked that Ripert, whom he had never met, "won't be calling me for ideas on today's fish special." After the book came out, Bourdain was in the kitchen at Les Halles one day, when he got a phone call. It was Ripert, inviting him to lunch. Today, they are best friends, and Ripert often plays the straight man to Bourdain on *Parts Unknown.* A recent episode in Chengdu, China, consisted largely of shots of a flushed and sweaty Ripert being subjected to one lethally spicy dish after another while Bourdain discoursed on the "mouth-numbing" properties of Sichuan pepper and took jocular satisfaction in his friend's discomfort. Ripert said of Bourdain, "I have cooked side by side with him. He has the speed. He has the precision. He has the skill. He has the flavor. The food tastes good." He hesitated. "Creativity-wise . . . I don't know." Over the years, Bourdain has regularly been approached about opening his own restaurant, and these offers might have yielded him a fortune. But he has always declined, mindful, perhaps, that his renown as a bard of the kitchen might be difficult to equal in the kitchen itself.

Even so, everywhere Bourdain goes, young cooks greet him as "Chef." When I asked him if that felt strange, he bristled slightly. "Look, I put in my time, so I'm not uncomfortable with it," he said. "What makes me uncomfortable is when an actual working chef who cooks better than I've ever cooked in my life calls me Chef." As if on cue, Deuki Hong—who, before opening Baekjeong, worked under Jean-Georges Vongerichten and David Chang—appeared with a platter of steamed sweet potatoes, and addressed Bourdain as Chef.

Halfway through the meal, we were joined by Stephen Werther, a bespectacled entrepreneur who is Bourdain's partner in a new venture: a Manhattan market modeled on Singapore's hawker centers, or open-air food courts. It is scheduled to open, sometime in the next few years, at Pier 57, a cavernous former shipping terminal on the West Side. If Bourdain's show offers a vicarious taste of an intrepid culinary expedition, the market will provide an ersatz consumer experience of his show. The best street-food vendors will be recruited from around the world and awarded visas—assuming that the United States is still issuing them—allowing New Yorkers to sample their octopus tostadas and their yakitori chicken hearts. Bourdain Market, as it will be known, is a preposterously ambitious venture; it will be three times the size of the original Eataly—Mario Batali's super-emporium of Italian food in the Flatiron district. Werther was accompanied by Robin Standefer and Stephen Alesch, a married couple who run Roman and Williams, a design firm that creates seductive contemporary spaces, such as the Ace Hotel in New York. They had agreed to work on the market. Their background is in Hollywood set design, an ideal match for Bourdain's sensibility. "Imagine a postapocalyptic Grand Central Terminal, if it had been invaded by China," Bourdain said.

"But underwater," Standefer joked.

Bourdain elaborated that the market should bring to mind *Blade Runner*—high-end retail as grungy, polyglot dystopia. When Bourdain was growing up, his father used to rent a 16 mm projector and show movies by Stanley Kubrick and Mel Brooks. "I've never met anyone who has this catalog of films in his head," one of his longtime cameramen, Zach Zamboni, told me. A Rome episode of *No Reservations* made black-and-white allusion to Fellini. The Buenos Aires episode on *Parts Unknown* was a nod to *Happy Together*, by Wong Kar-wai. Most viewers are unlikely to catch such references, but for Bourdain that is not the point. "When other cinematographers like it, that feels good," he said. "It's just like cooking—when the other cooks say, 'Nice plate.' It's kind of not about the customers."

The producer Lydia Tenaglia, who, along with her husband, Chris Collins, recruited Bourdain to television for *A Cook's Tour* and now runs Zero Point Zero, told me that part of the reason Bourdain's experience is so often refracted through films is that until middle age he had seen so little of the world. "Books and films, that was what he knew— what he had read in Graham Greene, what he had seen in *Apocalypse Now*."

Singapore's orderly hawker markets combine the delights of roadside gastronomy with an approach to public-health regulation that could pass muster in post-Bloomberg New York. "They cracked the code without losing this amazing culture," Bourdain said. Some of his partners in the market will be established restaurateurs, like April Bloomfield, the Michelin-starred chef of the Spotted Pig and the Breslin. But Bourdain also wants the market to have an old-fashioned butcher shop, with "guys in bloody aprons breaking down sections of meat," and Asian street food that will attract not just the *Eater*-reading cognoscenti but also displaced Asians in New York who yearn for a genuine taste of home. "If the younger Korean hipsters *and* their grandparents like us, we're gonna be okay," he said. I wondered aloud if grilled heart could turn a profit in New York. Wouldn't the adventurous offerings be loss leaders, while more conventional attractions, like an oyster bar, paid the rent? "I'm an optimist," Bourdain replied. Tastes evolve, he insisted. Exposure to foreign cultures makes inhibitions fall away. "I grew up watching *Barney Miller,* and it was Asian jokes all day long. They made fun of Asian food. It smelled like garbage. That's not funny anymore." With his chopsticks, he gestured toward a bowl of kimchi between us. "Americans want kimchi. They want it on their *hamburgers*. It's like when Americans started eating sushi—a huge tectonic shift."

The new frontier for American tastes is fermentation, Bourdain continued. "That *funk*. That corruption of the flesh. That's exactly the flavor zone that we're all moving toward."

"This is the secret of the food world," Stephen Werther said. "Rot is delicious. No one will ever say that to your face. Aged steaks. 'Age' is code for 'rot.'"

"Cured," Bourdain said, warming to the riff.

"Alcohol is the by-product of yeast," Stephen Alesch chimed in. "It's the piss of yeast."

"Basically, what we're saying is that filth is good," Bourdain concluded.

Deuki Hong reappeared with a plate of marbled rib eye. "Korean restaurants don't usually dry age," he said. "But we're trying dry aged. This is, like, thirty-eight days."

"You see? The rot!" Werther exclaimed. "What happens after thirty-eight days?"

"Good things," Bourdain said.

"For Valentine's Day once, we made a stew by cooking this big beef heart," Alesch said.

"That's very romantic," Werther observed.

"It was," Alesch said. "We ate it for, like, four days."

We left the restaurant, with Hong in tow, and had a round of soju bombs at an unmarked bar on the third floor of a nearby office building. Our little party then proceeded to a Korean nightclub on Forty-First Street. A vast warren of karaoke rooms surrounded a central dance floor, where flickering lasers illuminated a crowd that was young, prosperous looking, and entirely Asian. In a VIP room overlooking the dance floor, Bourdain quizzed one of the owners, Bobby Kwak, a young Korean American man in a black T-shirt, about the clientele.

"If they go to a downtown club like Marquee, they stick out like a sore thumb," Kwak explained, shouting over thudding techno. He pointed at Bourdain. "*You're* the minority here."

Bourdain said that this was exactly the kind of crowd he wanted to attract to the market. He had no interest in catering to "the gringos." Instead, he wanted to teach the gringos that they could love a place that was legitimate enough to be popular with a crowd like this.

"It's going to be hard," Kwak said. "You'll get the Asian Americans . . ."

Bourdain insisted that he also wanted the young Koreans who had grown up in Seoul, not Fort Lee. It was nearly 2:00 a.m. "So, after they get out of here, where do they go?" Bourdain asked.

Kwak laughed, and shouted, "They go right to where you just ate."

● ● ●

In the summer of 2006, Bourdain flew to Lebanon to make a *No Reservations* episode about Beirut. He planned to focus on the city's cosmopolitan nightlife, nibbling kibbe, drinking arrack, and taking in the vibe at beachside nightclubs. In the episode, he explains in a voice-over, "Everyone's been through here—the Greeks, the Romans, the Phoenicians. So I knew this was going to be a great place to eat." But while Bourdain was strolling down the street one day, a convoy of vehicles rolled by, flying the yellow flags of Hezbollah. They were celebrating an ambush in which Hezbollah forces had crossed into Israel, killing three Israeli soldiers and capturing two others. The next day, Israel launched missiles at Beirut, killing dozens of civilians. Bourdain and his crew ended up at the Royal Hotel, on a hilltop not far from the U.S. embassy, playing cards while they waited to be evacuated. In a surreal accident of geography, they could watch the war unfold from the relative safety of the hotel pool.

All travel requires a degree of improvisation, and Bourdain and his cameramen are well versed in reconceiving a show on the fly. Once, when he was snorkeling off the coast of Sicily in search of seafood, Bourdain was startled to see a half-frozen octopus splash into the water beside him. His host, a deeply tanned, eager-to-please Sicilian, was dropping fish onto the seabed for him to "discover" on camera. Naturally, this violated Bourdain's dogma of vérité. He was outraged, but decided to incorporate the moment into the episode, to hilarious effect. ("I'm no marine biologist, but I know a dead octopus when I see one.")

In Beirut, there was no way to edit around the war. But Bourdain and his producers felt that they had a story to tell, and they put together a show about being stranded by the conflict. In the episode, viewers see Bourdain's cameramen worrying about getting home, and the local fixers and producers worrying about the safety of loved ones. At one point in the narration, Bourdain says, "This is not the show we went to Lebanon to get." Until he traveled to Beirut, wherever he had ventured, no matter how bleak, he had always ended the episode with a voice-over that was, if not upbeat, at least hopeful. At the conclusion of the Beirut episode, he said, "Look at us in these scenes . . . We're sitting around in bathing suits, getting tanned, watching a war. If there's a single metaphor in this entire experience, you know, that's probably it."

Darren Aronofsky describes Bourdain's show as a form of "personal journalism," in the tradition of Ross McElwee's 1985 documentary, *Sherman's March,* in which a story is pointedly filtered through the individual experience of the filmmaker. In Beirut, at a beach where a line of people stood clutching their belongings, Bourdain and his crew were ushered by U.S. marines onto a crowded American warship. At the time, Bourdain was in a new relationship. Éric Ripert had recently set him up with a young Italian woman named Ottavia Busia, who was a hostess at one of Ripert's restaurants. She and Bourdain both worked incessantly, but Ripert figured that they might find time to enjoy a one-night stand. On their second date, Busia and Bourdain got matching tattoos of a chef's knife. Eight months later, Bourdain returned, shaken, from Beirut, and they talked about having children.

"Let's spin the wheel," Busia told him, adding, dubiously, "Your sperm is old, anyway."

Their daughter, Ariane, was born in April 2007, and they were married eleven days later. Busia is also a jujitsu fanatic, and when I contacted her, she suggested that we meet at the school where she and Bourdain train, not far from Penn Station. "I'm here every day," she said. Busia is thirty-eight, with big brown eyes, a warm, toothy grin, and the dense, bunched-up shoulders of a gym rat. She sat cross-legged on a mat, wearing a black T-shirt that said, "In Jujitsu We Trust," and leggings that were decorated with cat faces. Busia first tried martial arts after giving birth, hoping to lose some weight, but she soon became consumed by jujitsu, and induced Bourdain to take a private lesson. (She bribed him, she maintains, with a Vicodin.) "I knew he was going to like the problem-solving aspect of it," she told me. "It's a very intellectual sport."

Years ago, while filming an episode in Rajasthan, Bourdain met a fortune-teller who told him that one day he would become a father. "That guy's full of fucking shit," Bourdain told one of the producers afterward. "I would be a horrible father." But Ariane is, by her parents' accounts, a well-adjusted kid. For a time, Busia brought her along on some of Bourdain's journeys, but when Ariane started elementary school, that became impractical. Once, Busia was startled awake in the middle of the night with the horrifying realization that a strange man was in her bed. Then she rolled over and remembered that it was just Tony; she had forgotten that he was home. (Last year, Bourdain spent only about twenty weeks in New York.)

Now that Busia is in peak physical condition, she is hoping to climb Mount Everest. Last summer, Bourdain told me that she was sleeping in a hypoxia chamber—a device that mimics the oxygen depletion of high altitudes. "It basically re-creates thirty-two thousand feet," he said, then shrugged. "Anyway, nobody's sitting at home waiting for me to *define* them."

When I asked about fatherhood, Bourdain grew reflective. "I'm shocked by how happy my daughter is," he said. "I don't think I'm deluding myself. I know I'm a loving father." He paused. "Do I wish sometimes that in an alternative universe I could be the patriarch, always there? Tons of kids? Grandkids running around? Yes. And it looks good to me. But I'm pretty sure I'm incapable of it."

• • •

Perhaps the most beautiful thing that Bourdain has written is a 2010 essay called "My Aim Is True," which is a profile of Justo Thomas, a fastidious middle-aged man from the Dominican Republic, who descends early each morning to the basement beneath Le Bernardin, where he prepares a series of sharp knives, and then, with the precision of a heart surgeon, disassembles seven hundred pounds of fresh fish. The fish come to the restaurant, Thomas says, "the way they catch," which, Bourdain explains, means whole, straight from the ocean—"shiny, clear-eyed, pink-gilled, still stiff with rigor, and smelling of nothing but seawater." It is Thomas's job to break each carcass down into delicate cuts that will be served upstairs, and the essay is a warm tribute to him and to the details of his largely invisible craft. ("The walls, curiously, have been carefully covered with fresh plastic cling wrap—like a serial killer would prepare his basement—to catch flying fish scales and for faster, easier cleanup.") By the time Thomas completes his shift, it is noon, and Bourdain invites him to have lunch in the dining room. In six years of working at Le Bernardin, Thomas has never eaten there as a guest. Bourdain gestures toward the patrons around them and notes that some of them will spend on a bottle of wine what Thomas might make in a couple of months.

"I think in life they give too much to some people and nothing to everybody else," Thomas tells him. But, he adds, "without work, we are nothing."

In Bourdain's estimation, writing is a less grueling art than cooking. "I think I've always looked at everybody I met through the prism of the kitchen," he told me at one point. "'Okay, you wrote a good book, but can you handle a brunch shift?'" Writing is ephemeral, he said.

More ephemeral than brunch? I asked.

"Three hundred brunches, nothing came back," he said, his voice hardening with the steely conviction of a combat veteran. "Three hundred eggs Benedict. Not one returned. It's mechanical precision. Endurance. Character. That's *real*."

When Bourdain tells his own story, he often makes it sound as if literary success were something that he stumbled into; in fact, he spent years trying to write his way out of the kitchen. In 1985, he began sending unsolicited manuscripts to Joel Rose, who was then editing a downtown literary journal, *Between C & D*. "To put it to you quite simply, my lust for print knows no bounds," Bourdain wrote, in the cover letter for a submission of cartoons and short stories, noting, "Though I do not reside on the Lower East, I have in the recent past enjoyed an intimate though debilitating familiarity with its points of interest." Rose eventually published a story by Bourdain, about a young chef who tries to score heroin but is turned away, because he has no fresh track marks. ("There's tracks there! They just old is all cause I been on the program!")

Bourdain bought his first bag of heroin on Rivington Street in 1980, and plunged into addiction with his usual gusto. "When I started getting symptoms of withdrawal, I was *proud* of myself," he told me. Addiction, like the kitchen, was a marginal subculture with its own rules and aesthetics. For Bourdain, an admirer of William S. Burroughs, heroin held a special allure. In 1980, he says, he copped every day. But eventually he grew disenchanted with the addict's life, because he hated being at the mercy of others. "Getting ripped off, running from the cops," he recalled. "I'm a vain person. I didn't like what I saw in the mirror." Bourdain ended up on methadone, but he resented the indignities of the regimen: being unable to leave town without permission, waiting in line to pee in a cup. He quit cold turkey, around 1987, but spent several more years addicted to cocaine. "I just bottomed out on crack," he recalled. Occasionally, between fixes, he would find himself digging paint chips out of the carpet in his apartment and smoking them, on the off chance that they were pebbles of crack. Things grew so bad that Bourdain recalls once sitting on a blanket on Broadway at Christmastime, with his beloved record collection laid out for sale.

Given Bourdain's braggadocio, there were times when I wondered if the bad years were quite as grim as he makes them sound. "There are romantics, and then there are the hard-core addicts," Karen Rinaldi said. "I think Tony was more of a romantic." Nancy Putkoski told me in an email that Tony is "pretty dramatic." She wrote, "It does look pretty bleak in the rearview mirror. But, when you're living it, it's just your life. You struggle through." Once, Bourdain was riding in a taxi with three friends, having just scored heroin on the Lower East Side. He announced that he had recently read an article about the statistical likelihood of getting off drugs. "Only one in four has a chance at making it," he said. An awkward silence ensued. Years later, in *Kitchen Confidential,* Bourdain pointed out that he had made it and his friends had not: "I was the guy."

In 1985, Bourdain signed up for a writing workshop led by the editor Gordon Lish. "He took it very seriously," Putkoski told me. In letters to Joel Rose, Bourdain referred to the workshop as a transformative experience, and talked about "life after Lish." (When I reached Lish by phone, he recalled Bourdain as "an altogether charming fellow, very tall," but he had no recollection of Bourdain's writing.) After getting sober, around 1990, Bourdain met an editor at Random House who gave him a small advance to write a crime novel set in the restaurant world. Writing had always come easily to Bourdain; at Vassar, he wrote term papers for classmates in exchange for drugs. He didn't agonize over the novel, he said: "I didn't have time." Every day, he rose before dawn and banged out a new passage at his computer, chain-smoking, then worked a twelve-hour restaurant shift. The novel, *Bone in the Throat,* was published in 1995. ("Two-hundred-and-eighty-pound Salvatore Pitera, in a powder-blue jogging suit and tinted aviator glasses, stepped out of Frank's Original Pizza onto Spring Street. He had a slice of pizza in one hand, too hot to eat.") Bourdain paid for his own book tour, and recalls sitting behind a table at a Barnes & Noble in Northridge, California, with a stack of his books, as people walked by, avoiding eye contact. That novel and a follow-up, *Gone Bamboo,* quickly went out of print. (They have since been reissued.)

In 1998, Les Halles opened a Tokyo branch, and one of the owners, Philippe Lajaunie, asked Bourdain to spend a week there, mentoring the staff. Bourdain fretted over how he'd survive the thirteen-hour flight without a cigarette, but once he landed in Tokyo, he was exhilarated. "This place is like 'Blade Runner,'" he wrote to Joel Rose in an email. "I'm speaking French, hearing Japanese, and thinking English all while still horribly jet-lagged, crazed on iced sushi, jacked up on fugu, and just fucking dazzled by it all." He described the thrill of walking into the most uninviting, foreign-seeming, crowded restaurant he could find, pointing at a diner who appears to have ordered something good, and saying, "Gimme that!"

Rose had recently had a child with Rinaldi, the book editor. He showed her the emails, and Rinaldi was impressed by Bourdain's bawdy vernacular. "Do you think he has a book in him?" she asked.

"You have no idea," Rose said.

Writing might have long been part of Bourdain's plan, but TV, according to Putkoski, "was never really in the picture until it was offered." Shortly after *Kitchen Confidential* was published, Lydia Tenaglia and Chris Collins started talking with Bourdain about making a show. He told them that he was planning a follow-up book in which he traveled around the world, eating. If they wanted to pay to follow him with cameras, why not? Putkoski was less enthused. "She identified television early on as an existential threat to the marriage," Bourdain said. "I felt like the whole world was opening up to me. I'd seen things. I'd smelled things. I desperately wanted more. And she saw the whole thing as a cancer." If you watch episodes of *A Cook's Tour*, you can sometimes spot Putkoski hovering at the edge of the frame. She had no desire to be on camera. She told me recently that her ideal degree of fame would be that of a Supreme Court justice: "Almost nobody knows what you look like, but you always get the reservation you want."

For a time, Bourdain tried to save the marriage. He remodeled their apartment with the extra money he was making. But it didn't work. "I was ambitious; she was not," he said. "I have a rampaging curiosity about things, and she was content, I think, to be with me. To go to the Caribbean once a year. There were things that I wanted, and I was willing to really hurt somebody to have them." Bourdain describes his separation from Putkoski as "the great betrayal" of his life. In an email, Putkoski wrote to me, "I'm big on shared experiences, which I'd thought had bulletproofed our partnership . . . We'd been through an awful lot of stuff together, a lot of it not so great, a lot of it wonderful fun." She concluded, "I just didn't anticipate how tricky success would be."

• • •

Outside the beer hall in Hanoi, under a tree festooned with Christmas lights, a stout elderly woman in billowy striped pants presided, with a cleaver, over a little stand that served roasted dog. Bourdain was relaxing nearby with Dinh Hoang Linh, a sweet-tempered Vietnamese bureaucrat who has been a close friend of his since 2000, when Linh was Bourdain's government minder on his first trip to Hanoi. Over the years, the recipe for Bourdain's show has subtly changed. When he first went to Asia, he joked that he was going to eat "monkey brains and poisonous blowfish gizzards." At a restaurant in Vietnam called Flavors of the Forest, he was treated to a delicacy in which the proprietor grabs a writhing cobra, unzips its belly with a pair of scissors, yanks out its still-beating heart, and drops it into a small ceramic bowl. "Cheers," Bourdain said, before knocking it back like an oyster. If, in subsequent seasons, Bourdain has eaten some other appalling things—bear bile in Vietnam, bull's-penis soup in Malaysia, the unwashed rectum of a warthog in Namibia—he is careful to distance himself from any suggestion that he trucks in gag-reflex entertainment. When he was getting started, a degree of sensationalism was "exactly the cost of doing business," he told me, adding, "I'm not going to sneer at it. Whatever gets you across the river." (He noted, diplomatically, that the Travel Channel currently has a show, *Bizarre Foods*, devoted to that kind of thing.)

He has never eaten dog. When I pointed out the dog hawker in our midst, he said, "I'm not doing it just because it's there anymore." Now, when he's presented with such offerings, his first question is whether it is a regular feature of the culture. "Had I found myself as the unwitting guest of honor in a farmhouse on the Mekong Delta where a family, unbeknownst to me, has prepared their very best, and I'm the guest of honor, and all of the neighbors are watching . . . I'm going to eat the fucking dog," he said. "On the hierarchy of offenses, offending my host—often a very poor one, who is giving me the very best and for whom face is very important in the community—for me to refuse would be embarrassing. So I will eat the dog."

Bourdain has softened in other ways. Although he still baits the food press with a steady stream of headline-ready provocations—

"Anthony Bourdain: Airplane Food and Room Service Are Crimes"; "Anthony Bourdain Wishes Death upon the Pumpkin Spice Craze"; "Anthony Bourdain Says No to Dining with Donald Trump: 'Absolutely F——ing Not'"—he often makes peace with people to whom he has taken a blowtorch in the past. In *Kitchen Confidential,* he relentlessly pilloried the TV chef Emeril Lagasse, noting several times his resemblance to an Ewok. Then they met, Bourdain ate Lagasse's food, and eventually he took it all back and apologized. Lajaunie, the former Les Halles owner, said of Bourdain, "He's extremely kind, but it's the genuine kindness that comes from deep cynicism." Lajaunie went on, "He has accepted that everyone has broken springs here and there. That's what most of us lack—the acceptance that others are as broken as we are." After Bourdain read *How to Live,* Sarah Bakewell's 2010 book about Michel de Montaigne, he got a tattoo on his forearm of Montaigne's motto, in ancient Greek: "I suspend judgment." Even Alan Richman, the *GQ* critic, whose snobbery Bourdain once savaged in an essay titled "Alan Richman Is a Douchebag," has become a sort of friend. When Bourdain was writing for *Treme,* he concocted a scene in which a character named Alan Richman visits a restaurant in New Orleans and has a Sazerac thrown in his face. He invited Richman to play himself, and Richman did.

In an era of fast-casual dining, Richman pointed out, the "rough-neck" cuisine that Bourdain celebrates has enormous appeal. Bourdain has helped create the circumstances in which one of the most widely praised restaurants in New York City is the Spotted Pig, April Bloomfield's West Village gastropub, which is known for its unfussy cheeseburgers. To the degree that one can extrapolate from the personal quarrel between Richman and Bourdain a larger philosophical debate about the proper future of American tastes, Richman readily concedes defeat. "I don't know anybody who is more a man of the twenty-first century," Richman told me. "The way he acts. The way he speaks. His insanity. His vulgarity."

As *Parts Unknown* has evolved, it has become less preoccupied with food and more concerned with the sociology and geopolitics of the places Bourdain visits. Lydia Tenaglia calls the show an "anthropological enterprise." Increasingly, Chris Collins told me, the mandate is "Don't tell me what you ate. Tell me who you ate with." Bourdain, in turn, has pushed for less footage of him eating and more "B roll" of daily life in the countries he visits. It has become a mantra for him, Collins said: "More 'B,' less me." Since visiting Beirut, Bourdain has gone on to Libya, Gaza, and the Democratic Republic of the Congo, seeking to capture how people go about their daily lives amid violent conflict. To viewers who complain that the show has become too focused on politics, Bourdain responds that food *is* politics: most cuisines reflect an amalgamation of influences and tell a story of migration and conquest, each flavor representing a sedimentary layer of history. He also points out that most shows about food are premised on a level of abundance that is unfamiliar in many parts of the world.

The program's shift in tone coincided, fortuitously, with the move to CNN. In 2012, the network was struggling with a dilemma that is common to cable news. "Big events happen in the world and viewers flock to you in droves, and as soon as the event is over, they disappear," Amy Entelis, an executive vice president at CNN, told me. The network wanted to create "appointment viewing": original shows that audiences would seek out week after week. "Tony's name came up right away," Entelis said. It has been a happy arrangement: the network gives Bourdain ample resources and near-total creative freedom. "I've never gotten the stupid phone call," he said. The show has been a ratings success, and it has won five Emmys and a Peabody Award. Eerily, one of the highest-rated episodes of *Parts Unknown* aired soon after the 2013 Boston Marathon bombing. It was an episode about Los Angeles, which Bourdain had shot exclusively in Koreatown, and it's great, but nobody believes that this accounts for the ratings. Millions of people had followed the manhunt, and the devastating aftermath of the attack, on CNN. By Sunday, they needed a break.

Bourdain is comfortable being seen as a purveyor of escapism; he is less comfortable with the responsibility that attends the show's more serious material. In an episode set in Laos, he ate freshwater fish and bamboo shoots with a man who had lost an arm and a leg when a U.S. explosive, left over from the war, detonated. In Hanoi, one of Obama's staffers told him that until the episode aired, some people in the White House had been unaware of the extent of the unexploded-ordnance problem in Laos. "Very casually, he said, 'So I guess you do some good after all,'" Bourdain recalled. "I'm a little embarrassed. I feel like Bono. I don't want to be that guy. The show is always about me. I would be bullshitting you if I said I was on some mission. I'm not." Nevertheless, Bourdain knows that most viewers who caught his Congo episode had read little about the conflicts there. I was reminded of how Jon Stewart, whenever someone observed that many young people got their news from *The Daily Show,* protested, unpersuasively, that he was just a comedian cracking jokes. Bourdain's publisher, Dan Halpern, said, "Whether he likes it or not, he's become a statesman."

Bourdain insists that this is not the case. "I'm not going to the White House Correspondents' Dinner," he said. "I don't need to be laughing it up with Henry Kissinger." He then launched into a tirade about how it sickens him, having traveled in Southeast Asia, to see Kissinger embraced by the power-lunch crowd. "Any journalist who has ever been polite to Henry Kissinger, you know, fuck that person," he said, his indignation rising. "I'm a big believer in moral gray areas, but when it comes to that guy, in my view he should not be able to eat at a restaurant in New York." I pointed out that Bourdain had made similarly categorical denunciations of many people, only to bury the hatchet and join them for dinner. "Emeril didn't bomb Cambodia!" he said.

● ● ●

One morning in August 2016, I got an email from Bourdain letting me know that he and Busia were separating. "It's not much of a change of life style, as we have lived separate lives for many years," he wrote. "More of a change of address." Bourdain felt some relief, he told me: he and Busia no longer needed to "pretend." In our conversations up to that point, he had celebrated the fact that Busia pursued jujitsu and her other interests in the same headlong manner in which he pursued his. But in the email he wrote, "She's an interesting woman. I admire her choices. But I married Sophia Loren. She turned into Jean-Claude Van Damme." (I learned subsequently that this was a standing joke between Bourdain and Busia, and not intended harshly.) Bourdain added that he was about to promote a new "family cookbook," called *Appetites,* which would "lead to some awkward interviews."

Chris Bourdain told me that when Anthony first became famous, his attitude was, "I have no idea how long this is going to go on, so I want to max it out while I can." Whenever a new opportunity presented itself, he said yes. By the time Bourdain met Busia, he had achieved a level of recognition and wealth that might have enabled him to slow down. But he didn't stop moving. *Parts Unknown* films two seasons a year. Even first-class travel can be punishing after a while, and Bourdain acknowledges that although he may still behave like a young man, he isn't one. "I think you're officially old at sixty, right?" he told me, soon after his birthday. "The car starts falling apart." However, TV stars forge bonds with their audience through habitual exposure, and it can feel risky to take a break. "It's a bit like *Poltergeist*," Nigella Lawson, who was Bourdain's co-host on *The Taste*, told me. "You get sucked into the TV and you can never get out."

At this point, Éric Ripert observed, Bourdain's show has "done the entire planet already!" Now, Bourdain says, the pleasure of making *Parts Unknown* lies in revisiting places to see how they've changed— Cuba five years ago is a different country from Cuba today—or in returning to a place with a fresh perspective. For a recent episode on Houston, Bourdain decided that he wanted "no white people," and provided instead a look at the city "as a Vietnamese and Central American and African and Indian place." Chris Collins suggested to me that the perpetual discontinuity of Bourdain's life might have assumed a continuity of its own, as if jet lag were his natural condition. "I've often thought, how would he ever go on without the show?" Lydia Tenaglia said. "It is such an inextricable part of him—who is Tony, apart from this?"

For years, Bourdain has had a recurring dream in which he finds himself in a Victorian-era hotel, wandering through well-appointed hallways, unable to find the front desk. A year ago, when I asked him how long he would stick with the show, he said, "Until it's not fun." In September, I posed the same question at a sushi restaurant in Manhattan, and this time he was more contemplative. "I have the best job in the world," he said. "If I'm unhappy, it's a failure of imagination." He was delighted with the Vietnam episode, which was about to air. CNN had wanted to lead with the Obama meeting, but Bourdain, ever one to play it casual, waited until nearly forty minutes into the episode to introduce the president. He got the James Brown song he wanted. ("I may have fibbed and told the network that I promised the president personally that we would get that for his walk-on music.") After the Vietnam trip, Bourdain had competed in a jujitsu tournament, in Manhattan, and had been defeated by a strong man who wrenched his head with such ferocity that he thought his fillings might pop. As an added indignity, Bourdain came away from the tournament with a skin infection that left him looking, he says, "like Quasimodo." (Ripert is puzzled by jujitsu: "It's supposed to be good for the body, but he seems to be in pain all the time.")

In a fit of self-exile, Bourdain flew to France and made his way, alone, to the oyster village that he had visited as a child. He had rented a big villa, with the intention of doing some writing. Bourdain cherishes the trope of the misanthropic émigré. "To me, *The Quiet American* was a *happy* book, because Fowler ends up in Vietnam, smoking opium with a beautiful Vietnamese girl who may not have loved him," he told me. But in France he found that he couldn't write. His body was itchy and swollen from the rash, and he had a throbbing pain in his head. Because he looked hideous, he left the villa only after dark, like a vampire. Finally, Bourdain sought out a French doctor, who gave him a battery of painkillers and anti-inflammatories. After impulsively swallowing a week's supply, Bourdain realized that he had not eaten in thirty-six hours. He drove to a café in a nearby town, Arcachon, and ordered spaghetti and a bottle of Chianti. He was halfway through the wine when he realized that he was sweating through his clothes. Then he blacked out.

When he woke up, Bourdain was lying with his feet in the café and his head in the street. A waiter was rifling through his pockets, in search of a driver's license, as if to identify a corpse. Bourdain's father had died suddenly, at fifty-seven, from a stroke, and Bourdain often thinks about dying; more than once, he told me that if he got "a bad chest X-ray," he would happily renew his acquaintance with heroin. Taking meds and booze on an empty stomach was just a foolish mistake, but it left him shaken. He stood up, reassured the startled onlookers, drove back to the villa, and immediately wrote a long email to Nancy Putkoski.

When I asked him what he wrote, Bourdain paused and said, "The sort of thing you write if you, you know, thought you were going to die. 'I'm fucking sorry. I'm sure I've acted like I wasn't.' We've had very little contact—you know, civil, but very, very little. 'I'm sorry. I know that doesn't help. It won't fix it; there's no making amends. But it's not like I don't remember. It's not like I don't know what I've done.'"

• • •

Anthropologists like to say that to observe a culture is usually, in some small way, to change it. A similar dictum holds true for Bourdain's show. Whenever Bourdain discovers a hole-in-the-wall culinary gem, he places it on the tourist map, thereby leaching it of the authenticity that drew him to it in the first place. "It's a gloriously doomed enterprise," he acknowledged. "I'm in the business of finding great places, and then we fuck them up." For the restaurant that welcomes Bourdain and his crew, there are conspicuous upsides to this phenomenon. Our food at the sushi place was middling; Bourdain avoided the fish and ordered chicken katsu, most of which he left uneaten. As we were leaving, Bourdain amiably obliged the owner's request for a selfie, and I witnessed a comically subtle tango as she maneuvered his body so that the photograph would capture the restaurant's sign (creating an implicit endorsement) and Bourdain gently swiveled her the other way so that the backdrop would be Third Avenue instead. In Hanoi, a few days after Bourdain's dinner with Obama, I mentioned that I was going to swing by the Bún-chả restaurant. As if recalling a bygone establishment, Bourdain murmured dreamily, "I wonder what it's like now."

I chuckled at this, but when I visited the next day, the restaurant had indeed changed. A sign outside said, in Vietnamese, "We Have No More Bún-chả!," and gawkers loitered around the entrance. In the kitchen, the woman who runs the restaurant, Nguyên Thi Liên, was smiling, perspiring, and clearly overwhelmed. Her family had owned the place for decades. She told me that Hanoi kids had been stopping by at night, long past closing, to have their picture taken.

One evening in Vietnam, Bourdain finished a shoot outside a noodle shop and loped over to the other side of the street, where I was sitting. "Want to go for a ride?" he asked. The crew had rented him a blue Vespa, and Bourdain told me that the only way to see Hanoi was on the back of a scooter: "To be anonymous, another helmeted figure in the middle of a million little dramas and comedies happening on a million bikes moving through this amazing city—every second is pure joy." I climbed on behind him. "I've only got one helmet," he said, handing it to me. I had scarcely strapped it on when he hit the gas and we were swept up in a surging river of vehicles. "I love this!" he shouted over his shoulder, picking up speed. "The smells! The traffic!" We shot through a perfumed cloud of smoke from a cook fire. Bourdain swerved to avoid an oncoming truck, and almost hit a woman on a scooter with a bale of green vegetables balanced precariously on the back. As we veered into a gutter, without breaking speed, it occurred to me that this would, at any rate, be a memorable way to die.

Bourdain slowed down to ask a pedestrian for directions, and the man indicated that to reach the Metropole Hotel, we should hang a left around Hoàn Kiếm Lake. But when we reached the lake—a tree-lined oasis with a tiny island in the center—Bourdain said, "Let's go this way," and turned right. Clutching my seat as we zoomed into another congested avenue, I realized that Bourdain had deliberately taken a wrong turn. He was courting uncertainty, trying to get lost.

The next morning, I met Bourdain in the lobby of the Metropole, and we drove to the outskirts of the city. He can hit the ground anywhere in the world, from Kathmandu to Kiev, and find a gym where people train in Brazilian jujitsu. "Everywhere you go, the etiquette is the same," he said. "We bump fists, then we try to kill each other for five minutes." On the second floor of a local athletic complex, we found a mirrored, padded room that served as a jujitsu gym. Bourdain changed into a white terry-cloth *gi*, strapped on his blue belt, and greeted several much younger Vietnamese guys.

He sparred with each man in a five-minute round. Bourdain had explained to me the complex protocols of jujitsu—describing how a blue belt can ask a white belt to spar, and a black belt can ask a blue belt, but a white belt can't ask a blue belt. He had always loved the kitchen because it was a tribe, and in jujitsu he had found another sweaty, grueling activity with its own hierarchy and lingo, a vocabulary of signs and symbols that would be impossible for an outsider to understand. I watched Bourdain, with his limbs tangled around the body of a Vietnamese blue belt who was roughly half his age, his toes splayed, his eyes bulging, his fingers grasping for purchase on the guy's lapel. In the heat of the clench, they whispered playful banter to each other; there was something intimate about it, like pillow talk. Then, abruptly, Bourdain flipped the guy's body over, pinning one of his arms and bending his elbow at an unnatural angle. The guy gently tapped Bourdain's shoulder, and Bourdain released the grip. They uncoupled and lolled on the floor for a second, like a pair of dead men. Then Bourdain looked up at the time clock. There was still nearly a minute left in the five-minute round. He rolled onto his knees, bumped fists with his opponent, and started again.

Anthony Bourdain took his own life on June 8, 2018.

ACKNOWLEDGMENTS

Another paradox of magazine writing: one author gets the byline, but it is a deeply communal enterprise. Each piece in this collection passed through many sets of careful hands: editors, fact-checkers, lawyers, copy editors. My first thanks go to the countless wonderful colleagues from *The New Yorker* who vetted ideas and facts and overwrought metaphors and dangling modifiers. A particular thanks to David Remnick, for his leadership, support, and example; to Dorothy Wickenden, Henry Finder, Pam McCarthy, Deirdre Foley-Mendelssohn, Mike Luo, David Rohde, Natalie Raabe, Alex Barasch, and Tyler Foggatt.

Peter Canby oversaw the fact-checking of all of these pieces. People often describe the *New Yorker* checking process as "notorious," like some intrusive medical procedure, but I love it. After months of working in solitude, I'm always grateful to welcome a smart colleague into the foxhole, and I've been saved by checkers—and learned valuable reporting lessons from them—on more occasions than I can count. Checkers rule.

The same goes for lawyers: given that I'm often writing about people who would prefer that I *not* be writing about them, I've enjoyed particularly close collaborations with attorneys. Lynn Oberlander and Fabio Bertoni are both incredibly capable and scrupulous—and very hard to rattle. At moments where I've had to summon a bit of courage, it helped that they possessed it in such abundant supply.

But it is Daniel Zalewski whose magic fingerprints are all over this collection. We've been working together since he first accepted a freelance pitch from me back in 2005. A number of these stories originated as his ideas, and I've never met anyone with such an intuitive grasp of what will and won't make a compelling narrative. From the broadest conceptual level to the neurotically minute, he has shaped these pieces and made them so much better than I ever could on my own.

I'm also indebted to Andrea Thompson Peed, who worked alongside Daniel on several of the earlier pieces.

Bill Thomas at Doubleday is my other longtime editorial partner. This is the fourth book we've worked on together, and I have learned so much from Bill and feel very fortunate to work with him. He is fearless and incisive, and he's got impeccable taste; it was thrilling to get to look back over a decade and a half of writing and collaborate with Bill to select the stories in this collection. Thanks also to all the incredible people at Doubleday, particularly Michael Goldsmith, Todd Doughty, Dan Novack, Khari Dawkins, Emily Mahon, John Fontana, Ingrid Sterner, and Maria Massey.

What more can I say about Tina Bennett? She's the best. I am blessed. Huge thanks also to Anna DeRoy and Andy Galker, and to Ravi Mirchandani, Kate Green, Grace Harrison, Roshani Moorjani, and everyone at Picador in London. Thanks to Molly Wright, and also to Karolina Sutton, Helen Manders, Jake Smith-Bosanquet, and the team at Curtis Brown.

Thanks to the many friends and colleagues who have consulted on ideas and read early drafts and introduced me to sources and let me crash with them on reporting trips. Thanks to the sources themselves, many of whom undertook some risk in talking with me. Thanks to the librarians and archivists, and the fixers and translators. Thanks to Michael Shtender-Auerbach, who says that all my best ideas come from him, and isn't altogether wrong. Thanks to Chopin, who was a puppy when the first of these pieces was written and died earlier this year.

I'm profoundly grateful, as always, to my parents, Jennifer Radden and Frank Keefe, and to my sons, Lucian and Felix. And to Justyna. In the summer of 2005, I had just passed the bar exam and accepted an offer to go and work at a law firm. Justyna told me to wait, that she would pay the bills for a few months and I should see whether, after years of trying, I could finally find work writing magazine articles. It was three months later that I got that first assignment from *The New Yorker.* Justyna has lived with the ups and downs of each of these pieces, parsed incoming legal threats, advised me not to accept that offer to ghostwrite Chapo Guzmán's memoir, and reorganized her own busy professional life to solo parent while I was on the road. *Rogues* is dedicated to her.

ABOUT THE AUTHOR

Patrick Radden Keefe is a staff writer at *The New Yorker* and author of *The New York Times* bestsellers *Empire of Pain,* which was awarded the Baillie Gifford Prize for Non-Fiction, and *Say Nothing,* which received the National Book Critics Circle Award and was named one of the ten best nonfiction books of the decade by *Entertainment Weekly,* as well as two previous books, *The Snakehead* and *Chatter.* The recipient of a National Magazine Award for Feature Writing and the Orwell Prize for Political Writing, he is also the creator and host of the eight-part podcast *Wind of Change.* Originally from Boston, he lives with his family in New York.